EARLY MEDIEVAL SURREY
Landholding, Church and Settlement
before 1300

JOHN BLAIR

D1555988

ALAN SUTTON PUBLISHING AND
SURREY ARCHAEOLOGICAL SOCIETY
1991

First published in the United Kingdom in 1991 by
Alan Sutton Publishing Ltd · Stroud · Gloucestershire and
Surrey Archaeological Society

Copyright © John Blair 1991

British Library Cataloguing in Publication Data
Blair, John
  Early medieval Surrey : landholding, Church and settlement before 1300.
  1. Surrey. Social conditions, history
  I. Title
  942.21

ISBN 0 86299 780 1

Library of Congress Cataloging in Publication Data applied for

Typesetting and origination by
Alan Sutton Publishing Limited
Printed in Great Britain

EAR

Landhol

Contents

List of Illustrations

Preface

This book was originally written as a doctoral thesis for the University of Oxford, begun in 1976 and submitted in 1982. Fourteen years have therefore passed between commencement and publication, and during this period scholarship has not stood still. Although I have done my best to assimilate new work, I have found, like many dilatory writers before me, that it is hard to re-formulate old concepts and re-think old thoughts. In particular, Alan Everitt's monumental study of Kent, *Continuity and colonisation*, appeared too late to have much influence on my work; readers of both books may, however, notice striking correspondences as well as obvious differences.

Among debts incurred during preparation of the thesis my greatest is to Barbara Harvey, for her unfailing guidance and for her kindness and patience with a wayward and disorganised research pupil. I also owe much to Elizabeth Gardner for her help; and to my parents, who encouraged my early interest in the history of Surrey and transported me to many of the sites and monuments mentioned in these pages. Brasenose College and The Queen's College have successively provided generous support for my research, and I would especially like to thank Philip Jones for the encouragement which he gave me in the early stages of my Oxford career. To Philip Riden, who helped to initiate several of the lines of thought pursued here, I owe a debt which is considerable if impossible to define. For access to unpublished sources I am grateful to Merton College (Dr J R L Highfield and Mr J Burgass), Westminster Abbey (the late Mr N Macmichael), Surrey County Record Office, Guildford Muniment Room, the College of Arms, the Bodleian Library, the British Library, the Public Record Office, the Greater London Record Office, Canterbury Cathedral Library, Lambeth Palace Library and the Minet Library.

Revision of the text for publication has been facilitated by the careful and constructive comments of my examiners (James Campbell and Eric Stone) and editors (Rosamond Hanworth and Elizabeth Stazicker). Among the many people who have given help and advice on specific points, I would especially like to thank Roger Bacon, Keith Bailey, Shirley Corke, Ralph Evans, Mark Gardiner, Jeremy Greenwood, Gerry Moss, Rob Poulton, David Robinson, Nigel Stanley, Lilian Thornhill, Dennis Turner, Heather Warne and Christopher Whittick. Last but not least, grateful thanks are due to Pat Lloyd, whose quick and accurate typing has made revision so much easier than it might have been; and to my wife Sarah, who has performed the miracle of making me finish this book.

JOHN BLAIR
The Queen's College, Oxford
August, 1989

KEY TO SHADING CONVENTIONS ON CHURCH PLANS

	Standing entire	Fragmentary
In the Anglo-Saxon tradition		
In the Norman tradition, before *c*1140		
*c*1140–80		
*c*1180–1220		

Plans generally omit all features later than the phase represented, and use the following conventions for reconstructions:

Shading as in left-hand column: Standing entire

Shading as in right-hand column: Excavated footings; walls pierced by later arcades but surviving above them; and the positions of doors and windows which are later in their present form but may reflect original positions.

Continuous outline: Later walls, arcades etc which seem likely to preserve the line of walls of the relevant period.

Broken outline: Conjectural reconstruction

Windows and doors shown in broken outline are purely conjectural

Introduction

The scope of this study

This is a study of institutions and the economy in one southern English county during the early and central Middle Ages. All its themes have long attracted historians, and all have seen much research in the last twenty years: the manorial structure, agrarian growth, field-systems, parish churches and the parochial system. But the more they are examined, the more hidden problems emerge and the less adequate the old generalisations seem. Only very detailed local studies will tell us what was really happening: such, inescapably, is the nature of the evidence. Unfortunately it is easy to become restricted thematically as well as geographically, and to view an institution not merely within a small region, but also without reference to other forces which moulded its development and the lives of those on whom it impinged. The present work tries to avoid this second weakness: its central aim is to show how systems of lordship, tenure, agriculture, ecclesiastical jurisdiction and pastoral care changed together and affected each other.

Historians used to favour a view of the manor which makes it secondary and incidental to the village, its late Anglo-Saxon lord 'gradually gaining the mastery over a rural community of ancient and independent growth'.[1] From its beginnings English rural society was based on townships, each with its nucleated settlement and common fields. The growth of the manor, which interposed private lordship between the king and these communities, failed to destroy them or obscure their organic nature. A dissenting note was sounded in 1958 by T H Aston, who argued that Anglo-Saxon settlement was always organised along seigneurial lines, and claimed of the peasantry that 'their tenements and tenure, their customs and even their status, have evolved from the beginning to meet the complex needs, private and public, of great lords from the king downwards'.[2] Yet a current textbook still unquestioningly assumes the antecedence of the village: 'the manorial framework was a landowning and land-management grid superimposed on the settlement pattern of villages and hamlets'.[3] This assumption is made more dubious than ever by recent work which sees medieval lordship influencing the formation and structure of the very institutions which have seemed to be immemorially stable. To re-interpret the origins of nucleated settlements, subdivided holdings and common agriculture has drastic implications indeed, for in the minds of earlier writers these were the very essence of the village community.

No view of social organisation can ignore the development of population and economy. A neat model of continuous growth, of a steady progress from the centre to the margins, will no longer do. It now seems likely that the population of Britain in the 4th century was as high as on the eve of the Black Death,[4] and the trend between these dates is a matter for debate. It is also becoming clear that the human geography of early medieval England was much more a matter of flux, of settlements moving, splitting and combining rather than simply growing. Sharply aware that the sources are selective and leave much unsaid, some historians now argue for high economic development in the mid-Saxon period, moving backwards the main 'age of expansion' by some centuries. It has become necessary to ask whether the evidence for changes in land exploitation and the pattern of lordship does, in fact, support this drastic shift of emphasis away from the late Anglo-Saxon and Norman centuries.

To think of the parish system as an institution which developed independently of its secular context is natural but anachronistic. The early minster parishes were based directly on the pattern of royal administration, and the great mass of rural churches were above all else a product of developing local lordship. It is the contention here that the real functions of churches can only be grasped by considering the landscapes which they served, while at the same time their creation is one of the most tangible signs of economic change.

To elucidate these problems further demands an intensive, integrated approach within confined areas. Anyone who attempts such work should know his region at first-hand: hence, in this case, the choice of Surrey. A poor and rather nondescript county, surrounded by areas with strongly-marked characteristics but with none of its own, it is scarcely appealing on other grounds. Yet in some ways this very character as a border zone makes it a good subject for local work directed towards general conclusions. The manorial structure and field-systems of medieval Surrey have tended to elude categorization. Most of their attributes can be matched in either Kent, Sussex, East Anglia or the Midlands, yet as a whole they will not square neatly with any of the familiar models. The more distinctive and self-consistent a region's customs are, the more it will seem peculiar to itself. But Surrey serves as a mirror, reflecting back the characteristics of better-known counties and highlighting common elements in institutions which have seemed only to contrast with each other.

No apology should now be needed for giving a due emphasis to topography; yet it must be admitted that local topographical data are hard to present clearly and simply. Sometimes points of substance cannot be made without detailed discussion of boundaries, settlement sites and field monuments, and these digressions into detail may be tiresome to a reader unfamiliar with the region. Constant reference should be made to the index maps of parishes and hundreds (figs 1 & 2) and the map of geographical zones (fig 3B), which will help to locate the main places and areas mentioned in the text.

The county of Surrey

Surrey, in P Brandon's words, 'recalls to mind not one landscape but a mosaic of four – the still densely wooded Weald; the wild, rough sweeps of heathland around Hindhead and Leith Hill; the Chalk upland of the North Downs; and the quiet, reposeful vales which interweave the other landscapes together'.[5] Though a small county, it has always been characterised by contrasting regions, based on geological strata which run in narrow bands from east to west (figs 3A and B). The North Downs, high and broad in the east and tapering westwards into a straight, narrow ridge called the Hog's Back, form the backbone of the county. On both sides the chalk dips below large overlying expanses of clay: northwards in the London Basin, continuing along the dip-slope of the Downs as a broad clay vale, and southwards in the Weald, extending across Sussex to the South Downs. Along the dip-slope, a narrow but fertile strip of Reading and Thanet Beds divides the chalk from the heavy London Clay. The scarp-slope, too, is separated from the Weald Clay by a broader band of lighter soil, the Lower Greensand Belt, which extends westwards from Kent through the Vale of Holmesdale and widens out to include most of south-western Surrey. This linear pattern is only broken in the north-west of the county, which lies on the barren, sandy soils of the Bagshot Series.

Surrey contains little good agricultural land. Both the Weald Clay and the London Clay are heavy to work, boggy and liable in their natural state to acquire a heavy oak cover. The broom-grown heaths of the Bagshot area are among the worst land in southern Britain, and even 18th- and 19th-century improvers tended to dismiss them as hopeless.[6] The chalk and Greensand are lighter, but relatively poor in their yield. The best soils lie in narrow ribbons along the dip-slope and the scarp-slope of the Downs: by the central Middle Ages the villages and field-systems strung out along these lines formed a strongly marked pattern. Geology has always dictated that the agrarian landscape of Surrey should be varied: a balance of different resources

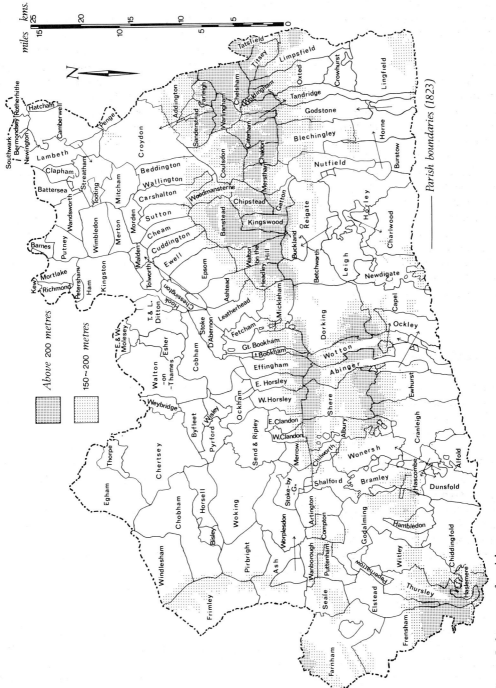

Fig 1 Index map of parishes

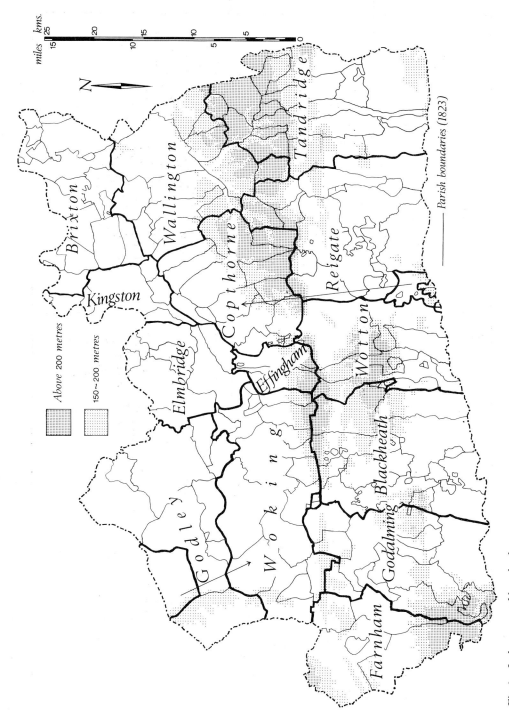

Fig 2   Index map of hundreds

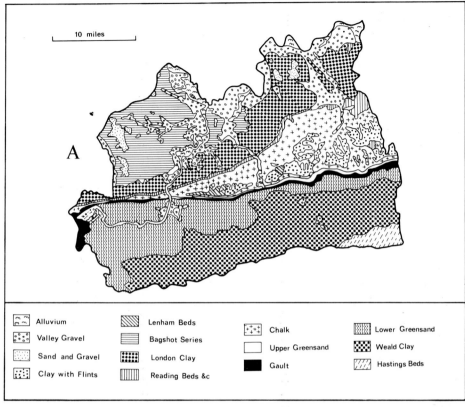

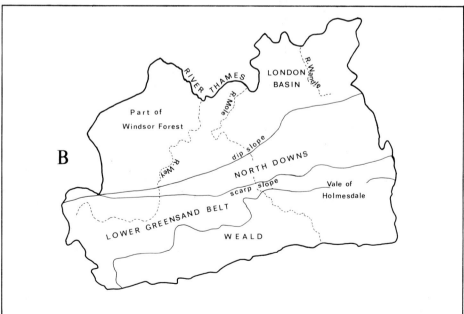

Fig 3   A Geology   B Geographical regions. (Based on Darby & Campbell, *Domesday geography of south-east England*, figs 106 and 118)

within short range of each other, rather than the great expanses of open field which characterised 'champion' England.

Naturally enough, the main lines of west-east communication have always been along the Thames and the chalk slopes. The existence of continuous North Downs trackways now seems dubious,[7] but both the main ridgeway and the line along the scarp-slope terrace may well approximate to ancient routes. Further north, an early trackway connected the villages dotted along the dip-slope (fig 15). The main arteries southwards from the Thames were the rivers Wey, Mole and Wandle, though all were too small to be of much use for large-scale navigation. Stane Street, the Roman road from Chichester to London, traversed the Wealden forest and linked the more settled areas of Sussex and Surrey. The whole of the Surrey Weald is broken up by long tracks running from north to south; some may be Roman trackways, but most are drove-roads produced by the complex transhumance grazing systems of the earlier Middle Ages.[8] They help to explain the persistent north-south linearity of boundaries which is so noticeable in the southern part of the county.

In the Roman period a crucial event for future Surrey was the foundation of London, towards which the road-pattern converged, and of a bridgehead settlement on the site of Southwark. The region contained several villas, presumably the centres of grain-producing estates; other significant products were pottery, tiles (notably from the Ashtead villa) and Wealden iron. London is the obvious destination for food-surpluses from the region. The absence of any significant town, combined with the concentration of sites along Stane Street and the road from Lewes, makes it hard not to suspect that Surrey was already what it was to be centuries later: a hinterland dominated by London.[9]

From the beginnings of written history, Surrey was neither a separate kingdom nor a stable element within a kingdom. Already in the annal ascribed to 568, when Ceawlin of Wessex 'fought against Æthelberht and drove him into Kent',[10] it appears as frontier territory buffeted between the southern English rulers, and this was to be its fate for nearly three centuries. Attempts to reconstruct political boundaries before the late 7th century have long taken account of the bewildering, sometimes contradictory evidence for cultural links derived from excavated grave-goods. But recent work has begun to disclose a new and crucial factor: the existence from a very early date of an orderly system of administrative districts and boundaries. To claim – as it no longer seems fantastic to claim – that the local government of early England was more organised and stable than the broad political structure, is to place the formation of the early kingdoms in a very different light.

It is widely accepted that there is a valid distinction between the 'Saxon' occupation of Wessex, Sussex and Surrey and the 'Jutish' occupation of Kent, the boundary between the cultures of Kent on the one hand, and of Surrey and Sussex on the other, lying roughly on the line of the river Medway.[11] But how did colonisation proceed? Did the first settlers of Surrey move northwards from Sussex as well as southwards from the Thames? Was Berkshire colonised from lands to the south, by penetration up the Thames Valley, or from some different direction?

Cemetery and place-name links between Sussex and Surrey are strong enough to imply at least a significant degree of early trans-Weald contact, presumably along Stane Street and the Roman trackways.[12] It has been argued that the *Paling-* names scattered along the line of Stane Street from Poling in Sussex to Pallinghurst and Pollingfold in Surrey 'strongly suggest that the coastal villages of Felpham and Poling had a group of dependent hamlets stretching right across the Weald beyond the borders of the South Saxon kingdom'.[13]

The evidence of early provincial boundaries, discussed below in ch 1, heightens the impression that Surrey had close links with Sussex and indeed with Kent: the whole area, with the notable exception of the westernmost third of Surrey, seems to resolve itself into one symmetrical series of territorial divisions radiating into the Weald (below, p22 and fig 8). Economically and topographically, the three south-eastern counties seem much of a piece.

Beside this must be set the obvious fact that a major line of Saxon advance was along the Thames. The earliest colonisation of northern Surrey seems to have followed the Wey, Mole and Wandle valleys, especially the Wandle with its group of large cemeteries in the Croydon/Mitcham area.[14] This is not, of course, incompatible with advance from the south, but it suggests a pattern in which the Thames acted less as a barrier between ethnic groups than as an artery from which one folk could infiltrate the land on either side. The name Surrey – *suðre ge*, 'the southern province' – has long drawn historians to a view summed up by Gover, Mawer & Stenton in 1934:[15]

> If the name Surrey is parallel to the names Suffolk and Eastry, it can hardly have meant anything else than the southern province of the original Middle Saxons. The early history of this people is extremely obscure. London and presumably the whole of Middlesex had come to form part of the East Saxon kingdom before the end of the sixth century, and there is no record of any Middle Saxon dynasty. On the other hand, it is hard to believe that a people bearing such a name as *Middel Seaxe*, strictly analogous in form to *Suth Seaxe* or *Middel Engle*, were originally confined within the narrow limits of the modern Middlesex . . . A territory comprising both Middlesex and Surrey would be large enough to support one of the smaller peoples of the sixth century, and its division into two parts by the Thames would be exactly parallel to the recorded division of the early Mercians into two provinces separated by the Trent.

M Gelling's survey of Berkshire has added another dimension to this hypothesis.[16] In her view the eastern arm of the county, separated from the rest by an under-developed tract rich in – *feld* names, has strong place-name links with Surrey.[17] She suggests that the Mid Saxon kingdom may also have included this part of Berkshire and the area of Buckinghamshire between the Thames and the Chilterns. In the lower Thames Valley she identifies a series of early territorial units, extending a pattern which used to be thought peculiar to Kent and Sussex (cf below, pp22–3). Hence boundary changes may not have been arbitrary fluctuations but the transference of coherent districts: this part of future Berkshire comprised one territory associated with the *Sunningas* and perhaps another associated with the *Rēadingas*, their names preserved today in those of Sonning and Reading.[18] Such provincial units, whether with or without tribal connotations, begin to seem more concrete entities than counties or even kingdoms.

Before pursuing this problem further, we may consider the one piece of solid evidence for the political origins of Surrey: the charter of 672 × 4 by which 'Frithuwold of the province of the men of Surrey, sub-king of Wulfhere king of Mercia', grants land by the Thames to Chertsey minster.[19] The north-west boundary of this estate was 'the next province which is called Sonning'; the east boundary was 'the ancient ditch, that is *Fullingadic*', identified here (below, p14) as an earthwork running southwards from the Thames at Weybridge. It appears that Frithuwold was not a native king of Surrey,[20] but a member of a great Mercian dynasty which also included Frithuric, founder of the Leicestershire minster of Breedon-on-the-Hill and first witness to the Chertsey charter.[21] An admittedly late and unreliable source, the Life of St Osyth of Aylesbury, makes Frithuwold a brother-in-law of King Wulfhere and mentions his palace at Quarrendon (Buckinghamshire);[22] it is arguable that he ruled a large sub-kingdom on the south-east fringes of Mercia, which extended down the Thames Valley between Mercia proper and the Middle Saxons and which thus included the Reading and Sonning *regiones*.[23] This hypothesis introduces another political entity of which Surrey could have been the *suðre ge*.

The difficulty of interpreting the name by reference either to the Middle Saxons or to Frithuwold's realm is that both seem to have been somewhat late and artificial creations: like the Middle Angles, they were amalgams of tribal territories only welded together under 7th-century

Mercian overlordship.[24] The Kentish -ge names, Eastry, Lyminge and Sturry, were all of earlier formation and all denote areas much smaller than Surrey; it is worth asking whether the original Surrey may have been equally small. For Bede it was not a 'provincia' but merely a 'regio';[25] the Chertsey charter, in a terminology different from Bede's, calls Frithuwold 'provinciae Surrianorum' and refers to the 'terminus alterius provinciae quae appellatur Sunninges' as though Surrey and the Sonning territory were of like kind. A neat solution to Surrey's conflicting affinities with the Weald and with the Thames Valley would be to suggest that suðre ge originally denoted merely that third of the later county which lies west of the *Fullingadic* line: in other words, which is economically and territorially of a piece with the Reading and Sonning units rather than with Kent and Sussex (below, p14). This could then be seen as the southern half of a lost 6th-century chiefdom, of which the remainder would be the Staines *regio* north of the Thames.[26]

Thus medieval Surrey was formed in a context of overlordship which was itself transient but which was based on much more stable entities, the organic tribal *regiones*. Orderly territorial division, perhaps older than the Anglo-Saxons themselves, was certainly older than the organised Anglo-Saxon states. Seventh-century kingdoms grew and shrank from one year to the next; it is hardly likely that they were more stable in the 6th. The political context in which land between Sussex and the Thames was appropriately called 'the southern province' probably lies in the lost years before the era of Mercian sub-kingdoms.

The eastwards enlargement of Surrey at the expense of Kent can apparently be dated closely. Chertsey minster had been founded *c*666 under King Egbert of Kent, as is explicitly stated in Frithuwold's charter of 672 × 4. By then the whole of later Surrey (or at any rate its boundary along the Thames) seems to have been in Frithuwold's hands, for the charter also mentions land opposite the port of London; Bermondsey minster was founded a few years later, evidently in the context of patronage by Frithuwold's family (below, pp103–4). Thus it seems not unlikely that Frithuwold had himself played a major part in the Mercian advance south of the Thames, and had been rewarded in kind. Possibly the events of this period explain the presence near the Surrey–Kent border of linear earthworks, facing Surrey as a defence against armies coming from the west.[27]

Surrey is not identifiable in the late 7th-century Tribal Hidage, unless we locate there the unintelligible 'Noxgaga' and 'Ohtgaga', or follow J C Russell's conjecture that 'Hendrica' and 'Unecungga' are scribal perversions of 'Sudrica' and 'Suningga'.[28] The latter suggestion, if correct, would give Surrey 3,500 hides, which may be compared with the 3,400 hides assessed to Eashing and Southwark in the Burghal Hidage, and with the 2,000 hides for which the county was assessed in 1086.[29]

By the late 680s Cædwalla had decisively turned the power-balance south of the Thames in favour of Wessex, and his Farnham charter of 685 × 8 shows him master of south-western Surrey.[30] It is certain that both Cædwalla and Ine after him exercised authority in Surrey, if perhaps uneasily and intermittently,[31] and a papal privilege of 708 × 15 locates the Surrey minsters of Bermondsey and Woking 'in provincia West Saxonum'.[32] We next hear of Surrey under the Mercian overlordship of Offa, whose confirmation of a grant to Woking church was issued from a royal vill 'in regione Suthregeona' (below, pp20, 95). From the victory of Ecgbert of Wessex in 825, when the men of Surrey, Kent, Sussex and Essex submitted to him 'because formerly they had been wrongly forced away from [allegiance to] his kinsmen',[33] Surrey was decisively part of Wessex. It was probably during the next few decades that it finally gained coherence as a West Saxon shire, with boundaries much as they remained until modern times.[34]

Yet Surrey was still something of a backwater. In the 10th century, indeed, it contained one place of ceremonial importance, for kings of the house of Wessex chose to be crowned at their vill of Kingston (below, p99). But Kingston, and still more the *burh* of Southwark, were on the

Thames and must have looked more towards London than towards Surrey. None of the other *villae regiae* were of much account in national events. Chertsey minster remained the only religious establishment of note; when Edward the Elder reorganised the West Saxon sees in 909 he left Surrey in Winchester diocese, of which it was the remoter archdeaconry until the present century.[35] Nor do the TRE data in Domesday Book reveal any great noble whose main power-base was in Surrey: the main lay landowners were Godwine and his sons, and the Kentish thegns Æthelnoth and Beorhtsige (below, pp115–19). In the 10th and 11th centuries as later, Surrey was not the focus of anything very important; the main influences to which it was subject came from London and Winchester.

The effects of the Conquest on the economy and society of Surrey were not notable. The trail of depreciated manors which some have ascribed to William's journey to London extends into north-east Surrey,[36] but there was no devastation on a scale to affect the basic pattern of rural life. Two important tenurial changes over the next three decades were the successive creation of the Clare and Warenne baronies. Richard fitz Gilbert was the biggest Surrey tenant in 1086, though even this estate was merely one element in a barony whose *caput* was in Suffolk.[37] In 1088 William de Warenne was created Earl of Surrey and endowed with extensive lands.[38] Despite his title the *caput* was again outside the county, at Lewes, but much of south-eastern Surrey passed into Warenne hands. Both baronies were strongly influenced by the pre-Conquest pattern: Richard fitz Gilbert inherited three substantial TRE estates *en bloc*,[39] while the Warenne manors were mainly those which had been Queen Edith's demesne.[40] Both lords, however, consolidated blocks of land around their respective local *capita*, which were in the south-east of the county. Richard fitz Gilbert united Blechingley and Chivington into one manor centred on Blechingley castle,[41] while Warenne added Betchworth with its outliers in Leigh, Newdigate and Horley to Queen Edith's great manors of Reigate and Dorking.[42] This regrouping, reminiscent of the far greater post-Conquest reorganisation of Sussex,[43] overlay and obscured the ancient linear pattern of boundaries (cf below, p17, and fig 11G).

With the royal castle at Guildford and Henry of Blois's episcopal palace at Farnham, Reigate and Blechingley castles were the main feudal and military centres of 12th-century Surrey.[44] On a humbler level are the simple mottes at Walton-on-the-Hill and Abinger (figs 41 & 40), the latter the *caput* of a small Surrey estate held under William fitz Ansculf.[45] By the 12th century the centre of county jurisdiction, which may once have been Leatherhead (below, p20), had settled in the late Saxon *burh* of Guildford. Several small market towns emerge into recorded history during the 12th and 13th centuries (below, pp56–8), but there was still nowhere of any real size: apart from Guildford and Southwark only Reigate and Blechingley were represented in Edward I's parliaments, and this because of their baronial rather than their urban importance.[46] Anglo-Norman monastic foundations – the Cluniac abbey of Bermondsey, the Cistercian abbey of Waverley and the Augustinian priories of Merton and Southwark – were important houses but scarcely among the greatest.[47]

Something which did significantly affect the economy of Surrey was the creation of Windsor Forest.[48] The only Domesday reference is in the Pyrford entry, which states that 'de hac terra habet rex 3 hidas in foresta sua'. Stoke-by-Guildford is said to be 'in parco regis', presumably Guildford Park which later appears as one of the walks within the forest.[49] Henry II afforested his manors of Woking, Brookwood and Stoke-by-Guildford,[50] and subsequently declared the whole county, or at least the royal demesne within it, to be forest. In 1191 Richard I disafforested everything except the north-west quarter of the county, the boundaries being fixed as the Wey eastwards, Guildford Downs southwards and the Berkshire border north-eastwards. These boundaries were reaffirmed in 1225, and (despite Henry III's wholesale disafforestation of 1226) again in 1280.[51] In fact it is clear from the Forest eyre rolls (below, pp40–3) that most of north-western Surrey was under the regarders' jurisdiction throughout Henry III's reign, and with Guildford Park the whole area appears on Norden's map of Windsor Forest surveyed in 1607.[52] It is highly likely that the Hog's Back and the Wey were for all practical purposes the boundaries from the Norman period onwards: the woods and sandy, gorse-grown heaths of Godley hundred and part of Woking hundred have a natural geographical affinity with the Berkshire and Hampshire parts of the Forest. Here the restrictions of forest law combined with the natural barrenness of the soil to make north-west Surrey a retarded area throughout the Middle Ages.

Sources from Domesday Book onwards give a rough measure of relative economic development. In 1086 Surrey was one of the more lightly settled parts of lowland England (cf fig 14). Only the manors in the immediate periphery of London were relatively well-populated, while the Windsor Forest area was among the few zones of conspicuously low density south of the Humber.[53] By 1334, when the Lay Subsidy returns indicate the relative distribution of moveable lay wealth, Surrey seems to have caught up a little with surrounding regions. The whole county except the Wealden hundreds and the Forest area has £10 to £19 assessed wealth per square mile, in common with about 60% of the lowland zone. Once again, it is the sandy area in the north-west which stands out as under-developed, with a lower incidence of wealth than virtually any other part of southern England.[54] Both in 1086 and 1334, pockets of very heavy settlement and exploitation such as existed in south Sussex and south-east Kent are conspicuous by their absence.

Medieval Surrey had the mixed economy appropriate to its varied soils. A major activity in the earlier Middle Ages was the seasonal droving of swine and cattle to summer pastures in the Weald; more localised grazing links also crossed the geological strata from one soil-type to another. Evidence from 13th- and 14th-century demesnes suggests 'a good mixed economy in Middlesex and Surrey, with plenty of emphasis upon wheat, barley and oats, many sheep, and a fair number of swine'.[55] But it was only for more specialised products that Surrey was at all notable. Fruit-growing flourished in a county which was to become famous for its market-gardens, and in the 14th century all the Merton College manors in Surrey had cider-presses.[56] Wealden timber went far afield; there is also evidence for medieval coppicing on the small Downland manor of Farleigh,[57] and in 1288/9 the monks of Westminster took building-timber from a demesne wood in Pyrford (below, p42). The Weald, of course, was a cradle for industries needing fuel: iron-working in Roman and medieval times, and glass-making in the Chiddingfold area from the 13th century.[58] A fulling-mill existed at Abinger by c1250, and in the later Middle Ages cloth-making flourished around Guildford.[59] These varied products were the more important in a county which lacked the natural resources to become a major grain-producer.

The two aspects of Surrey which most need emphasis here are its closeness to London and its abundance of woods and wastes. Fruit, iron, glass and cloth – not to mention grain and timber – were all products suitable for an urban market. Apart from Southwark, which to all intents and purposes was part of London, Surrey was essentially rural. Overwhelmingly, the commercial focus was London, and the stimulus which it gave to its hinterland is apparent even as early as Domesday Book (below, pp39–40). By the same token, citizens of London formed Surrey contacts and invested in Surrey land. The 12th century gives a few examples, such as the de Cornhills at Addington and Ralph the Vintner at Banstead,[60] while late 13th- and 14th-century deeds show Londoners taking an active part in the Surrey land-market (below, pp81–2). This factor should not be over-stressed, but in the absence of strong economic interests within the county it must have contributed to the general fluidity of land-tenure and society.

More fundamental here, though, is the fact that the population of post-Roman Surrey never rose to a level which drove the plough to the margins: it always remained, at least by Midland standards, a well-wooded county. The three Wealden counties share many agrarian peculiarities, and (though Surrey was always the poorest) all three supported the same kind of relatively free and prosperous peasantry. Even outside the Weald, the wastes and commons of Surrey never shrank to the point at which they became in really short supply. Surrey belonged to the 'wood-pasture' rather than the 'champion' zone of England: this fact lies behind many of the special characteristics which this study will describe.

The sources

Surrey is not rich in sources for its early history. It has nothing to set beside the charters which illuminate the early organisation of Kent, or those which provide so much topographical detail for the late Saxon see of Worcester. Even for the later Middle Ages there are relatively few large collections of estate documents: the fluidity of land-tenure, the lack of great local families and the constant pull of London were not conducive to the preservation of records. It is hardly surprising that most economic historians have passed Surrey by for richer pastures; yet its sources, scattered and fragmentary though they are, yield much of general interest.

The foundation charters of Chertsey and Farnham minsters[61] are among the earliest English diploma texts: although they only survive in later copies they seem to be basically genuine. Unfortunately the same cannot be said for the remainder of the long Chertsey series, which are essentially false though probably containing some genuine information (cf below, pp30, 52). Two Kentish wills, that of Ealdorman Alfred in 871 × 889 and that of Brihtric and Ælfswith in 973 × 987,[62] include several Surrey manors. Among other pre-Conquest texts the only notable item is the Merstham charter of 947,[63] which survives in the original and includes a useful boundary-clause.

The Surrey section of Domesday Book has had, of course, its commentators, though they have rarely extended their interpretation much beyond the limits of the survey itself.[64] It is, in Round's words, 'neither long nor of special interest',[65] and it has no marked abnormalities. Here it is mainly used as a guide to relative economic development (ch 2) and for its data on churches (ch 5).

The most useful series of court rolls and accounts are those for the manors of Merton College (Thorncroft, Farleigh and Malden) and Westminster Abbey (Pyrford and Horsell). These rarely provide direct information for periods before the late 13th century, but they throw a great deal of light on the development of smallholdings and are much used in ch 3. Various classes among the public records, notably the Feet of Fines, have provided incidental information about colonisation, field-systems and smallholdings.

Certainly the most useful written sources are the many hundreds of private deeds from the 12th, 13th and 14th centuries. These are scattered through many collections, the largest of which are in the British Library and the various Ancient Deeds classes in the Public Record Office. Monastic cartularies, especially those of Chertsey Abbey and Southwark Priory, provide much of the earlier material. Deeds give a different dimension to land-holding from that seen in manorial records, as well as containing a wealth of topographical detail for reconstructing the medieval agrarian landscape.

The landscape itself, of course, is in some ways the richest source of all. Except for its north-eastern third, now enveloped in suburbia, Surrey remains relatively rural, and early editions of the large-scale Ordnance Survey maps are reliable records of fields, roads and boundaries. Luckily these maps were compiled just before the parochial reorganisation of the 1870s, and hence preserve patterns of outliers which provide the key to territorial arrangements more than a thousand years old. Tithe maps, and intermittently surviving estate maps, take the picture back a little further. Several excavated medieval sites are used in ch 2 as evidence for settlement change. More important, architectural data are discussed in ch 5 for the light they throw on the origins of parish churches. Physical evidence alone, as is often observed, will rarely tell a clear story. A study such as this provides a good opportunity to test its value in filling out a relatively meagre written record.

1   The Administrative and Manorial Framework

It is appropriate to begin with the manor, for of all the institutions considered here it is the best recorded and most tangible. But manors themselves have an older context: the administrative, fiscal and juridical organisation of the early English kings.

Early territorial organisation

Anglo-Saxon landholding developed within a system which was in origin social and administrative rather than tenurial: the division of the countryside into *regiones* based on royal vills. The elucidation of this structure began in 1933–4 with the publication of two works by J E A Jolliffe. Jolliffe initially concentrated on Kent,[1] where written sources are particularly rich in traces of the primitive organisation. In its division into lathes he saw a system older than the hundred, the key to the 'free' character of Kentish gavelkind tenure. Before manorialisation, the lathe was the basic territorial and social unit. From a royal vill at its centre the king's authority permeated each lathe, and within it peasant obligations were assessed in round 80-sulung units. Hypothesising 'the settlement of the whole south-eastern area by a people who shared a common custom from the beginning',[2] he identified its social organisation as that of the continental Jutes.

Soon Jolliffe generalised this narrow, ethnic interpretation into a 'view of an England whose custom has an almost universal validity': the custom of folk-groups operating, from the time of the English settlements, within the framework of the *regio*-type unit in its various forms: lathes, rapes and small shires.[3] Subsequent work, indeed, suggests that the same essential pattern is widespread through both the English and the Celtic regions of Britain: far from being exclusively Jutish, it is not even exclusively Anglo-Saxon.[4] The message of an important new collection of essays is that *regiones* were the first Anglo-Saxon kingdoms, the foundations upon which political power was built up during the 6th and 7th centuries.[5] Characteristics which several historians have recognised in them are summarised thus by J Campbell.[6]

> The essence of the argument is that the system of lordship and local government over much, possibly all of early England resembled and, at least in wide areas, was connected with that of early Wales. The main unit in such a system was an area of varying but substantial size (say, not less than a hundred square miles) centred on a royal vill. To this vill the settlements within its area owed dues and services of some complexity . . . The area centred on the royal vill would often or always have common grazing. The subordinate settlements could vary in the nature of their obligations . . . Setting on one side questions of origin, it is reasonably certain that in much at least of early England the organisation of dues and services for the ruler was systematic, on schemes which methodically integrated settlements to their respective royal vills. The evidence of charters from the late 7th century on supports such a conclusion; for they strongly suggest that every settlement had an assessment in hides, and it looks as if these hidages related to round sum assessments for larger units centred on royal vills.

There are three main ingredients here: the *regiones*, the 'central places', and the round assessments. In Surrey, reconstruction of the first must depend largely on the antiquity of hundred boundaries and of territorial links between hundreds: they were the direct institutional successors of *regiones*, and were often formed through the subdivision of the larger, earlier units.[7] In 1086 Surrey already contained its full fourteen hundreds, differing only in trivial respects

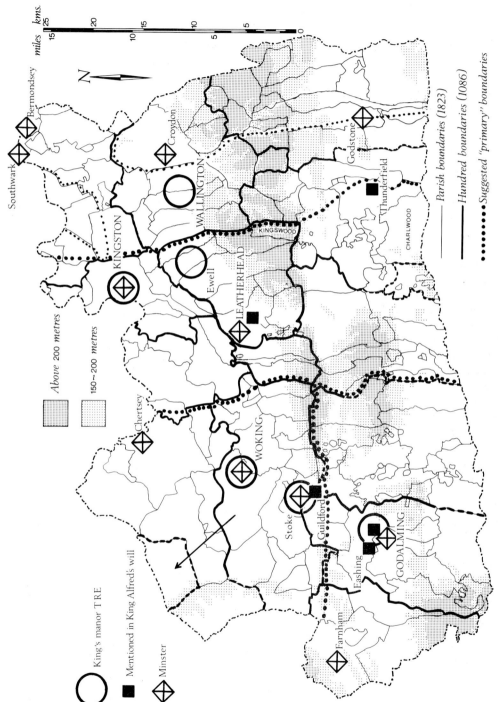

Fig 4 Hundreds, early territorial units and central places. (In a few cases, mainly in the Weald, where there is no Domesday evidence for hundred boundaries, 14th-century boundaries are shown in broken outline.)

from their 19th-century boundaries (fig 4). Five centred on royal hundredal manors (Godalming, Kingston, Wallington, Woking and Reigate), and a sixth on a hundredal manor in episcopal hands (Farnham).[8]

A key to reassembling hundreds into their 'primary' groups is provided by the relationship of manors and parishes to their outlying portions. The examples of Kent and Gloucestershire leave no doubt that these usually result from the division of land-units in a transhumance economy: as the territory was split up into manors, so too were its woods and commons fragmented into complex, interlocking archipelagos of individual pastures.[9] The outliers mapped on fig 5 are recorded as swine-denns in late Anglo-Saxon charters, as detached farms in medieval manorial records, as chapelries of mother churches, and as fragments of parishes on the earliest detailed maps.[10] This evidence is miscellaneous, and much of it rather late; not every link is necessarily ancient. Yet the overall pattern is remarkably consistent with the view that subdivision proceeded within defined territories approximating to groups of Domesday hundreds.

The Hog's Back and the Downs east of Guildford divide western Surrey into two halves: Woking and Chertsey hundreds to the north, and Farnham, Godalming and Blackheath hundreds to the south. Woking and Chertsey hundreds are clearly divisions of an earlier whole, for a wedge of Chertsey hundred cuts off Windlesham, a detached common pasture of Woking hundred and manor (below p95). As argued below (p25), Chertsey hundred is broadly identical with the estate granted to Chertsey minster in 672×4.[11] The charter states that the land lay between the Thames, the province 'quae appellatur Sunninges' (ie the territory of Sonning, Berkshire), and the boundary 'qui dicitur antiqua fossa, id est Fullingadic'. Presumably this ditch ran southwards from the Thames through Weybridge parish and on down the long, straight boundary between Byfleet and Walton-on-Thames (fig 6).[12] Its line is preserved by a road through Windlesham, ditches on St George's Hill, Walton, an intermittent bank across Wisley and Ockham commons, and the large bank which runs southwards into the Weald between Shere and Abinger parishes.[13] Already *antiquus* in the 670s, it must represent the eastern boundary of an earlier unit of which Woking hundred is surely the residue. It is a fair deduction that these two hundreds formed a district identified from an early date with the tribe of the Woccingas, comparable in size and shape to the adjoining Berkshire *regiones* of the Sunningas and Rēadingas (cf fig 8).

South of the Hog's Back were the hundreds of Farnham, Godalming and Blackheath. Territorial links are recorded within each of these hundreds (fig 5), but none between them. Their combined area was roughly equivalent to the 'Woking' unit, and they were self-contained to the extent that they contained no satellites of manors outside them. At the heart of this region, the large royal demesne of Godalming may be seen as the focus of a coherent territory from which Farnham hundred was detached in the 680s (below, p25). We may postulate, though only very tentatively, a *regio* of the Godhelmingas corresponding to that of the Woccingas.

The remaining two-thirds of the county, lying east of the *Fullingadic* line, show a quite different kind of territorial geography. Here Wealden outliers were attached to non-Wealden manors in a bewilderingly complex pattern of intersecting rights (fig 5). Clearly the primary units were not divided by the Downs, but stretched from north to south across the London clay, the chalk and the Weald clay. The pattern of outliers links the three hundreds along the dip-slope of the Downs with the three Wealden hundreds southwards. It can further be argued, if only tentatively, that the London Basin hundreds were components of the same overall pattern.

North of the Downs, there is a clear enough boundary separating Kingston, Elmbridge, Copthorne and Effingham hundreds to the west from Brixton and Wallington hundreds to the east. The line seems to have run south from the Thames, through Putney, Mortlake and Wimbledon parishes, to the north-eastern tip of Copthorne hundred.[14] From there it takes a straight course southwards as a hundred boundary between Cuddington and Cheam, and can

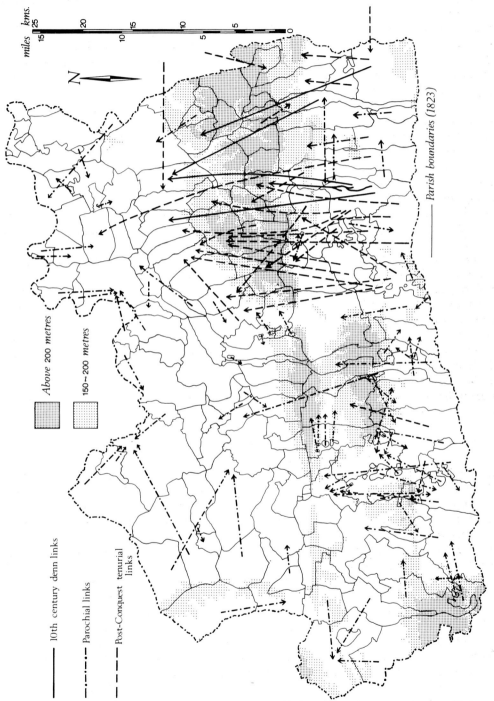

——— 10th century denn links

—·—·— Parochial links

— — — Post-Conquest tenurial
          links

Above 200 metres

150–200 metres

Parish boundaries (1823)

Fig 5   The evidence of territorial links

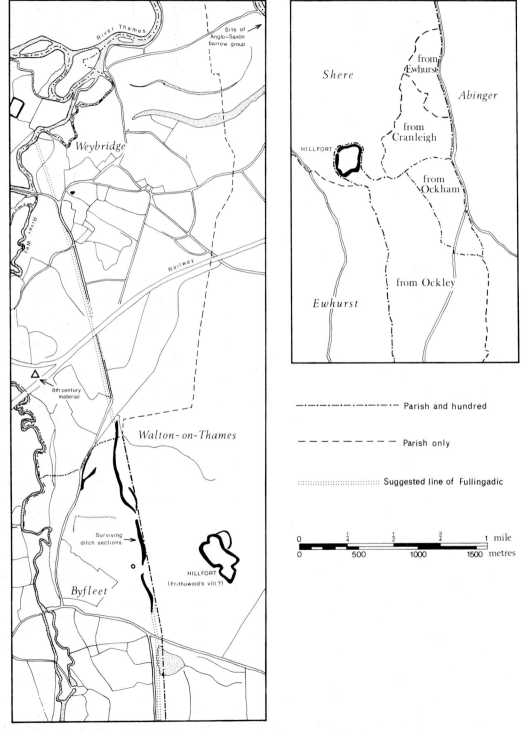

Fig 6   Two Surrey hillforts associated with territorial boundaries

then be traced as a track (Potter's Lane) which turns into a hollow-way south of Banstead Downs.[15] Continuing as a field-boundary along the east side of Kingswood, it runs down towards Reigate town. The two groups of hundreds on either side of this line show connections both within themselves and with Wealden land. Westwards, Copthorne and Effingham hundreds shared one meeting-place, and a large tract of downland which crossed the two hundreds but was known by the single name of Pollesdene suggests an early unity.[16] The links from hundred to hundred indicate a common origin for Copthorne, Effingham, Wotton and the western half of Reigate hundreds. The lie of the major boundaries, and the close correspondence with the pattern in Kent and Sussex (below, p22), would tend to place Kingston and Elmbridge hundreds in the same primary unit, though the absence of outliers to the south and the presence of a separate royal vill at Kingston suggests that they were split off at a relatively early date. Eastwards, tenurial and parochial links shown an equally clear relationship between Wallington, Tandridge and the eastern half of Reigate hundreds (fig 5). Topographical considerations, reinforced by the dependence of Burstow on Wimbledon from before 1100,[17] would seem to place Brixton hundred in the same group.

In the Wealden area from the Downs to the Sussex border, definition of the boundary between the two proposed primary territories is complex and difficult. Parishes in Reigate hundred, most notably Horley, originated as archipelagoes of manorial outliers which are far from easy to disentangle. The formation of the Warenne barony may have obscured the older pattern around Reigate as thoroughly as it did in Sussex, and the hundred boundaries make little sense in relation to early arrangements. Fortunately, detailed work on Horley by J Greenwood has gone far towards distinguishing early from not-so-early manorial links, while still supporting the view that the pattern of outliers reflects a major pre-existing territorial boundary. Greenwood's suggested line for this boundary runs 'from the top of Reigate hill southwards down Wray Lane and across Wray Common (TQ 267 509), and skirting Redhill and Earlswood commons to the west and Linkfield Street to the east (TQ 271 502). The boundary then follows the pre-turnpike path (TQ 275 499 – 279 485 – 280 470), passing to the east of Petridge common and then along the present main road (A23) to a point south of Bourners Brook (TQ 288 440). From here it passes south-west and along the boundary with Burstow (TQ 289 437 – 290 420).'[18]

Thus the central and eastern areas of Surrey resolve themselves with surprising clarity into two distinct, early territories extending from the Thames to the Sussex boundary. Where the easternmost territory is concerned, however, there are two complicating factors. First, Wallington, Titsey, Limpsfield and Lingfield had outliers on the Kent side of the county boundary, supporting Jolliffe's conjecture that the Kentish border lathe, which was abnormally small and lacked a *villa regia*, had included a strip of eastern Surrey.[19] Secondly, 9th- and 10th-century sources show that several manors near the county boundary were in Kentish hands. Paramount in size and importance was Croydon, the scene of a synod held in 809 and a possession of the archbishops of Canterbury from before the 9th century (below, pp25, 103). In about 871 Croydon was leased to Ealdorman Alfred for his life, with an option of permanent acquisition by his heir.[20] Alfred's will, made soon afterwards, bequeaths land at Sanderstead, Selsdon, Lingfield and Farleigh.[21] A century later, the mainly Kentish will of Brihtric and Ælfswith mentions land at Walkingstead (Godstone), Stratton and Titsey.[22] All these manors lie south of Croydon in a north-south strip some five miles wide, broadly delimited by two Roman roads and with traces of linear earthworks on its western boundary.[23]

It may be that the whole block should be interpreted as a lost archiepiscopal estate centred on Croydon, formed out of the border lathe in the mid-Saxon period in accordance with the prevailing pattern of north-south linear division.[24] The lease of c871 could have been the prelude to fragmentation which left only Croydon itself in the archbishop's hands. Perhaps the Surrey-Kent border vacillated from one side to the other of this conspicuously Kentish strip

Fig 7   Preston Downs, Banstead: boundary bank and Anglo-Saxon barrows as shown on a 17th-century
map. (After *SyAC* **34** (1921), opp 22)

between the 7th and 9th centuries, a possibility supported by the substantial linear earthworks
both on the present border and further east (above, p18). The primary territory bisected by the
present county boundary (fig 8) is so large that it probably represents two lathe-type units rather
than one, but if so the creation of the Croydon estate has obliterated the original line between
them.

At this point some cautious comments on the possible relationships between major boundaries
and 7th-century barrows seem appropriate. While the general thesis that single barrows
habitually marked boundaries must be regarded as unproven,[25] there does seem to be some
correlation between the larger Anglo-Saxon barrow groups and the suggested primary territorial
boundaries. The group at Walton Bridge, now destroyed, was just over a mile from where the
Fullingadic joined the Thames;[26] another on Wimbledon Common had a similar, though nearer,
relationship to the boundary between the 'Leatherhead' and 'Wallington' units.[27] Perhaps the
most striking case is further south on the same boundary, where the linear earthwork across
Banstead Downs ran between two groups of barrows (fig 7): westwards a cluster of twelve on
Preston Down, and eastwards a group of four called Gally Hills, one of which contained an
aristocratic male burial of *c*700.[28] Six barrows on Merrow Downs, probably 7th-century,
adjoined the boundary between the 'Woking' and 'Godalming' units.[29] The only other large
group is the long, very deliberately aligned series of fourteen late 6th- and 7th-century barrows
which crosses Farthing Down, Coulsdon, from north to south;[30] these are not near any known
frontier, but could be accommodated to the hypothesis of a lost lathe boundary destroyed by the
creation of the Croydon estate (above, p17). Archaeology suggests that such barrows are
generally of high status and often of late date, in the late 7th or even early 8th century:[31] some of

the people buried in them belonged to the generation who first recorded the boundaries of estates in charters. Overall, there seems good circumstantial evidence that the barrows were territorial markers; could these be the graveyards of a service nobility, men whom Latin writers would have termed *praefecti*,[32] buried on the frontiers of provinces which they had governed for the king?

The Surrey evidence, though inferior to that for Kent, reveals a similar pattern: the fourteen Domesday hundreds are divisions of four larger and older units. The second task is to identify the 'central places' within them, and here again it is necessary to work backwards from a pattern which can only be observed clearly in the post-Danish period. The main sources are King Alfred's will (872 × 888)[33] and the TRE data in Domesday Book (table 1). Both are late, and it cannot necessarily be assumed that the royal manors which they list (fig 4) were based on centuries-old sites. Minster churches on royal estates, closely linked though they were to administrative foci (below, ch 4), were often set at some distance from the secular centres and are not necessarily evidence for their exact early sites. It must also be remembered that continuity of site is not essential for continuity of administration: a centre could have moved from one place to another within its defined territory.

On general grounds, one group of sites which are highly likely to have been re-occupied by early Anglo-Saxon rulers are the Iron Age hillforts: there is no reason why south-western Britain should be peculiar in this respect.[34] Although there is no specific evidence for post-Roman use of any of the Surrey hillforts,[35] it is striking that three of the eleven (Holmbury, Felday, St George's Hill) lie on the primary territorial boundaries, and three more (Caesar's Camp, Dry Hill, Squerryes) on the county boundary: some defensive role within the Anglo-Saxon territorial system seems possible. It is worth noting in this context that the Holmbury hillfort, on the boundary between the proposed 'Leatherhead' and 'Godalming' units, was surrounded by a little cluster of outliers from four parishes in Blackheath, Wotton and Woking hundreds (fig 6).[36]

King Alfred's *hām* at *þunres felda*, presumably the *þunresfelda* where a royal council met in the 930s,[37] suggests another kind of survival from a more primitive age. It appears among Surrey property in the will, and there seems no reason to doubt the usual identification with Thunderfield Common in Horley, deep in the Surrey Weald.[38] It is hard to see the economic and administrative rationale for a 'central place' so far from early settlement; much of the area was still swine-pasture in the 10th century, when Merstham and Sutton had denns at Thunderfield (below, p52). It seems most likely that Thunderfield's importance was in origin religious. The name ('Thunor's open space') clearly refers to pagan worship, and in 1273 a nearby location was called Wedreshulle (probably 'Woden's hill').[39] The next parish has the significant name of

TABLE 1   Royal vills in Surrey: the late Anglo-Saxon evidence

	King Alfred's Will	Domesday Book (TRE)
Eashing	*hām* (to nephew Æthelhelm)	–
Ewell	–	manor (£20 p a)
Godalming	*hām* (to nephew Æthelwold)	manor (£32 p a including glebe)
Guildford	*hām* (to nephew Æthelwold)	75 *hagae* (£18 0s 3d p a)
Kingston	–	manor (£30 p a)
Leatherhead	land (to son Edward)	church (£1 p a)
Southwark	–	minster and waterway
Stoke-by-Guildford	–	manor (£12 p a)
Thunderfield	*hām* (to nephew Æthelhelm)	–
Wallington	–	manor (£15 p a)
Woking	–	manor (£15 p a)

Burstow (ie *burh stow*, 'meeting-place at a stronghold').[40] Together these names suggest a former pagan religious centre used for assemblies at some time in the Anglo-Saxon period.[41] Even in a Christian kingdom such a place may have retained some traditional importance, especially if associated with a royal residence. Possibly this helps to explain why nearby Godstone had a minster church by the 980s (below, p103).

The importance of Thunderfield, then, may have been largely ceremonial, and the silence of Domesday Book and later sources suggests that even this had lapsed by the Conquest. It evokes a lost class of central places in pagan Anglo-Saxon England: those which were religious rather than political. The pattern by which a mid-Saxon *regio* would have two centres, a royal vill and a minster church, may perpetuate pre-Christian arrangements. It is interesting here to note that Tuesley ('Tiwa's clearing'), another name denoting pagan worship, was the site of Godalming minster not far away (below, p99).[42]

The central division of the county contained two royal vills, and may have been split at a relatively early date into two administrative areas. Kingston upon Thames was important both as a secular and as an ecclesiastical centre. Its name ('king's *tūn*') belongs to what is now suspected to be a relatively late class of major place-names,[43] and may have replaced some older name. Perhaps the lost 'villa regali nomine Freoricburna . . . in regione Suthregeona' where Offa of Mercia and Ecgbert of Wessex issued charters[44] should be identified with Kingston upon Thames, which is first mentioned (as 'illa famosa loco quae appellatur Cyninges tun') in 838, the same year as the last reference to 'Freoricburna'.[45] The old settlement beside the church, on what was apparently once an island, was the heart of a considerable territory, as is suggested by the names of the satellite settlements Norbiton and Surbiton (ie the north and south *beretuns*).[46] Kingston can reasonably be interpreted as the primary centre of the *regio*; the creation of a second royal vill, at Leatherhead, by the late 9th century should perhaps be explained in the context of relatively early colonisation along the Downs dip-slope (below, pp43–5).

The royal estate at Leatherhead and Ewell had fragmented by 1086. The natural focus for this territory is the crossing of the Mole by the main west-east trackway, which presumably gave to Leatherhead one of the small group of surviving Celtic place-names in south-east England (*Letorito*, 'grey ford').[47] Leatherhead minster church appears in Domesday Book as an outlier appurtenant to Ewell manor but separated by a distance of five miles (below, p101). In view of the reference to Leatherhead in King Alfred's will, there is a strong suggestion here that a large demesne in Copthorne hundred had broken up, leaving the church in isolation. The area within which the minster probably stood was later held for sergeanty services associated with royal justice. These included finding a bench in the county court, which according to jurors in 1259 had 'always' been held at Leatherhead.[48]

It is *prima facie* likely that the early focus of the easternmost territory was the Domesday royal manor of Wallington, which gave its name to Wallington hundred and where evidence for 7th- or 8th-century occupation was excavated in 1976.[49] Wallington was assessed at only eleven hides in 1066, and the later township was tiny (fig 11F). It seems to have been left as a royal enclave by the creation of two episcopal estates: Croydon, for Canterbury, in perhaps the 8th century, and Beddington, for Winchester, in the late 9th (above, p17; below, p25). Wallington's importance may have been correspondingly diminished, its secular functions passing to Croydon which already had religious significance (below, p103). The service of guarding prisoners, which three Croydon cotmen owed in 1283–5 (below, p75), may preserve memories of such an arrangement.

Among the remaining places of known pre-Conquest importance, Woking and Godalming fit the normal pattern well enough. Both were large royal manors at the hearts of their respective territories; both had minster churches; and Godalming, like Croydon, had a hierarchical tenemental structure involving executive duties appropriate to a centre of royal justice (below, p75). King Frithuwold's Chertsey charter of 672 × 4, granting an estate carved out of the Woking *regio*, was issued 'iuxta villam Friðeuuoldi iuxta supradictam fossatum Fullingadic'.[50] It is perhaps most likely that this refers to the centre of the Woking *regio*, though since the medieval settlement of Woking (around the minster church) lies four miles west of the *Fullingadic* line, it would be necessary to postulate a lost palace site further to the east. A possible alternative is the large hillfort immediately east of the ditch where it crosses St George's Hill in Walton-on-Thames (fig 6), but this attractive hypothesis of a frontier fortress still occupied in the late 7th century will probably never be capable of proof.

The Burghal Hidage *burhs* of Southwark and Eashing, and the slightly later planned town of Guildford (below, pp56–8), are a case apart. Alfred's property at Guildford is perhaps identifiable with the Domesday manor of Stoke (ie *stoc*, 'stronghold'), and his property at Eashing with part of Domesday Godalming. These 'royal vills' may in fact represent nothing older than the defensive requirements of Alfredian Wessex, the latest layer superimposed on the early territorial framework.

Finally, mention should be made of an earthwork which may have served as an early assembly-point: the long north-south bank called Nutshambles on the boundary of four parishes at the centre of Copthorne hundred. The name appears in 1496 as *Motschameles*, and seems likely to mean *mot scaemol*, 'the seat of the moot'. The convergence of many roads at a high point on the line of the earthwork suggests an important meeting-place,[51] and it is possible that the name preserves memories of a folk-moot within the primitive provincial territory.

The third element in Jolliffe's model is cadastral symmetry: obligations assessed to the central vill in round units of 80 hides or sulungs.[52] Jolliffe's calculations were vitiated by poor mathematics, and although his figures have been re-worked in a rather more convincing fashion by K P Witney, the basic premise cannot really be regarded as proven.[53] Attempts to reconstruct the early cadastral system of Sussex have been no more successful: Jolliffe's identification of the post-Conquest rapes with earlier divisions is certainly invalid, and little more confidence can be placed in D K Clarke's subsequent attempt to work back from the rapes to earlier divisions.[54] Such arguments are especially prone to circularity and self-fulfilment; given the problems experienced with Kent, it would be rash to base much on the inferior Surrey evidence.

Whether hidations conformed to round-figure assessments, and whether they remained constant through the Christian Anglo-Saxon centuries, are still questions worth asking. Unfortunately the earliest Surrey evidence is unreliable. The Farnham foundation charter (60 hides) agrees with Domesday Book whereas the Chertsey foundation charter (300 hides) does not;[55] but these survive only in late and possibly corrupt texts. The fact that both hidages are multiples of twenty is, however, worth noting, since this assessment recurs in later charters. The (admittedly dubious) Battersea charter of 693 grants units of 28, twenty and twenty hides, which is not far off the 72 hides TRE.[56] Woking minster was endowed with twenty hides by Offa.[57] Four of the eight manors described in reliable charters between 947 and 1005 are stated to be of twenty hides, and three, possibly all four, of these had the same assessment TRE.[58] Taken in conjunction with the marked frequency of five-, ten- and twenty-hide manors in the Surrey Domesday as a whole, the evidence points to a stable 'basic' unit of twenty hides;[59] this would not, of course, be inconsistent with a still earlier 80-hide system which had undergone regular division. In a minority of cases there are discrepancies between charters and TRE hidations,[60] but these are scarcely evidence for late re-assessment since all could result from the splitting or combining of estates.

Another possibility, however, is that the TRE figures are distorted by the progressive addition of *new* hides. Jolliffe discounted this: 'the rape is an organic fiscal and jurisdictional entity . . . in no way reflecting contemporary reality. It is a state within the state, the hidated area only.' Thus newly-cleared land was distinguished by its lack of hidation: 'outside the sulungs' in Kent, 'outside the rape' or *forepeland* in Sussex.[61] The one indication of this arrangement in Surrey is the

947 Merstham charter, which appears to describe the denns at Petridge and Lake as *forraepe*, but a third at Thunderfield as a hide.[62] The implication seems to be that the old hidage assessment extended to territory near Thunderfield royal vill, but not to the surrounding commons as a whole.

Other references to hidated land in the Weald suggest that assessments were light in relation to the older-settled regions. Six hides at Lingfield mentioned in the late 9th century and again, in conjunction with the church, in the late 10th (below, p51) may have included the whole large parish. Domesday Chivington was assessed at twenty hides, of which nineteen and a half were the non-Wealden half of the manor: the Wealden common which was to become Horne parish and South Park was rated at only half a hide (fig 11G, below, p54). With the analogies of Kent and Sussex, the weight of the evidence is against 'new' hides. It would seem that the original hidages covered some but not all of the Surrey Weald, at much lower rates than those imposed elsewhere. Thus clearance sometimes proceeded within an existing framework of very large hides, sometimes in the non-assessed areas which became the forinsec land of the future.

While accepting the impossibility of aggregating TRE hidages within the central and eastern territories,[63] we can at least discount Jolliffe's view that fiscal symmetry existed in eastern but not in western Surrey.[64] The 'Godalming' and 'Woking' territories comprise well-defined groups of hundreds totalling respectively 248 and 241 hides, which might be interpreted in each case as three 80-hide units.[65] The most that can be said for the other territories is that a uniform structure of twenty-hide units is highly probable; one of 80-hide units not unlikely; and the regular apportionment of such units within the primary provincial territories possible though unproven.

The Surrey evidence must now be set in a wider context. Fig 8 shows the suggested provincial organisation of Surrey, in relation to that of Kent (as reconstructed by Witney)[66] and of Sussex (where at present it is impossible to do more than give an outline of the prevailing alignments). To these have been added the well-defined Berkshire *regiones* of Reading and Sonning,[67] and some Hampshire names of a tribal character which suggest similar territories. The result is a fuller political map of the early Anglo-Saxon south-east than any previously attempted, but further work could certainly extend the pattern northwards and westwards. Berkshire and, rather less clearly, Wessex, provide just the same kind of evidence for large early units.[68] With the evidence mounting in several parts of Britain, any idea that this type of organisation was peculiar to a circumscribed 'Jutish' region must be finally dismissed.

One thing is clear: the regularity of the south-eastern provincial boundaries results essentially from the presence of the Weald. The broad strips run inwards, north from the coast and south from the Thames, so that each includes enough woodland pasture to serve the settled non-Wealden areas. The pattern in east Kent leaves no doubt that access to the clay was the determining factor: the alignment of the lathes tilts round to radiate into the Weald, and in the extreme east of the county, where the Weald is outside convenient range, the linear pattern breaks down entirely. Neither does it appear west of the 'Leatherhead' and 'Steyning' units, where each territory had abundant common waste on the sandy heaths of the Windsor area and Hampshire. Thus the regularity which so struck Jolliffe reflects geographical rather than political factors.

This still leaves the most important and difficult question of all: when could such a system have come into being? That it represents organic development by similar social groups, moulded by the same geographical determinants, is not impossible;[69] yet in its regularity and its large scale it resembles the prehistoric systems of land-division which have lately been recognised.[70] Much recent work has emphasised ways in which early Anglo-Saxon communities adapted themselves to the territorial geography of Iron Age and Roman Britain;[71] this is no less likely in the south-east (especially in Kent where the debt to the Roman past is so evident in other ways) than

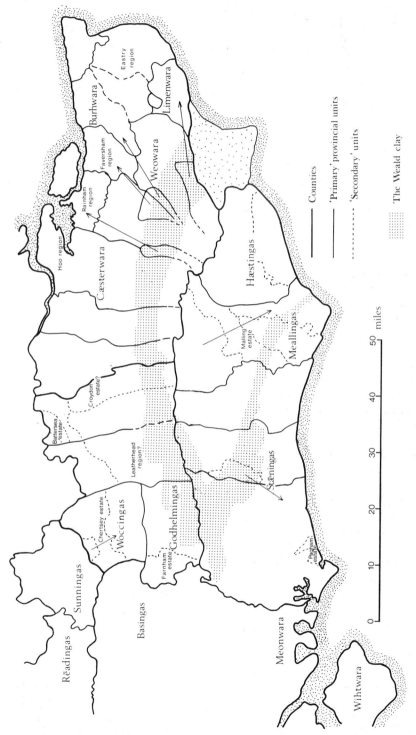

Fig 8   The early Anglo-Saxon territorial geography of south-east England

anywhere else.[72] In a recent discussion of cemetery evidence in relation to the territorial scheme proposed here, R Poulton has suggested that the Surrey *regiones* may have been taken over by the settlers in a more-or-less orderly fashion, the Godalming and Chertsey/Woking territories remaining British after the others had come under Anglo-Saxon control.[73]

Whether or not the framework is of pre-English origin, it is at least clear that it must have withstood all the political changes of the 7th and 8th centuries, an oddly stable sub-stratum in an unstable world. The territories were the building-bricks of the early kingdoms: the conquests by which Kent was reduced, and Mercia and Wessex successively enlarged (above, p8), must have involved the transference of *regiones* from one ruler to another as intact entities. Local organisation was sufficiently strong and stable to make capture of a royal vill almost synonymous with acquisition of its territory.[74] This institutional basis, still only dimly perceived, must have been a crucial factor behind the power of the early rulers and the gradual unification of England.

'Multiple estates' and the antiquity of small land-units

It has long been recognised that 'multiple' or 'federative' manors were a major element in the estate structure of pre-Conquest England. There is general agreement in defining them as large, complex groups of settlements or townships, sometimes discrete but more often in compact blocks, which were unified by dependence on single manorial centres; within each estate the specialised functions of the component vills provided broad economic diversity. In an important paper published in 1966, E Miller ascribed them to a form of social organisation which was alive and developing throughout England and during the whole Anglo-Saxon period.[75] He pointed out that while some 'federations' appear in the very earliest sources, others were being built up at various dates between the 8th and 11th centuries. Essentially they existed to further a type of seigneurial exploitation which was still mainly concerned with renders in kind: 'la groupe fédérale qui dépendait d'un centre était tout premièrement une groupe tributaire', and was 'le produit de l'accroissement et de la consolidation du pouvoir seigneurial dans la société primitive anglaise'. In the 11th and 12th centuries the model ceased to dominate, as demographic growth and changing means of exploitation caused the great estates to fragment into 'unicellular' manors. Thus the trend everywhere, though varying in proportion to the level of economic advancement, was towards the classic manorial regime of the 13th century.

A different approach, stressing administrative continuity rather than economic change, has attracted more notice. In a series of papers, G R J Jones has emphasised similarities between English 'multiple estates' and the formalised, multi-tier estate models of the Welsh law-codes. Just as the Book of Iorwerth describes land in a descending hierarchy of 'multiple estates', vills, holdings, sharelands and homesteads, so cases can be found throughout England of estates divided symmetrically into tithings, tithings into hamlets and hamlets into tenements. One of Jones's examples which, for its closeness to Surrey, is especially relevant here is the archiepiscopal estate of South Malling in Sussex. Just as several Surrey manors stretched southwards into the Weald from the scarp slope of the Downs, so this manor extended northwards into the Weald from the old-settled area around Lewes. It comprised two groups of six *borghs*, respectively 'within' and 'without the wood'; the *borghs* were themselves divided into smaller units, termed hamlets and virgates, which were bound to the archbishop's *curia* at South Malling by complex and well-differentiated services.[76]

We should not too readily adopt the multiple estate as a comprehensive model for British and early English land organisation.[77] To interpret every estate in accordance with Jones's scheme risks ignoring fundamental differences between different kinds of multi-vill territorial units, and different stages in their evolution. Most important, it risks an automatic equation of tribal, administrative, exploitative and tenurial entities, which may be related in structure yet functionally and chronologically distinct. Clearly, multi-vill estates must be seen in relation to the early territorial framework described above. Integral with the estates and the territorial framework is a third element, the antiquity of *very small* land-units, for an essential part of the Jones model is complex internal division. If a clear perspective on these primitive foundations of landholding can be attained, the decline of the multi-vill estate and the development of the classic manor will also become clearer.

In 1066 Chertsey Abbey held a large tract of land broadly identifiable with Godley hundred.[78] Frithuwold's endowment charter of 672 × 4 describes what was unmistakably the same area, with some detached portions.[79] The components of the main estate are named as Chertsey, Thorpe, Egham, Chobham, Woodham (in Chertsey) and *Huneuualdesham* (in Weybridge). The east boundary was the well-marked line of the *Fullingadic*; correlation of the other names in Frithuwold's charter with later sources gives a compact block, differing only in minor respects from the estate and hundred as they appear in Domesday Book (fig 9A).[80]

Chertsey's sister foundation at Barking also had land in Surrey. A corrupt but probably basically genuine charter text records Bishop Eorcenwold's transfer to Barking of an estate received from King Cædwalla during 685 × 7.[81] This comprised 28 hides in Battersea, twenty in the *villa* called Wassingham and twenty on the west side of *Hidaburna* (probably the Falcon Brook). Bounds attached to the charter, presumably reliable for the 10th or 11th century, enclose Battersea, Wandsworth and Putney.[82] Though much smaller than the Chertsey block and recorded in a dubious source, this may be a genuine 7th-century estate of three distinct components (fig 9B).

By a charter of 685 × 7 Cædwalla of Wessex endowed a new church with land called Farnham, comprising 60 hides of which ten were in Binton, two in Churt, and the rest in *Cusanweoh* and other places which the 12th-century copyist failed to transcribe.[83] By c800 the church and land had been annexed to the see of Winchester, which held them at the Conquest and after.[84] Charter-bounds of the 10th century correspond more or less exactly with the boundary of the medieval manor and hundred.[85] Farnham hundred can therefore be accepted with some confidence as the estate of the 680s, then already subdivided into at least three components and probably many more (fig 9C).

Only these three cases have early written evidence, but Surrey contained other multi-vill estates. Mortlake and Croydon seem to have been acquired by the Archbishops of Canterbury in the 8th or perhaps even 7th century.[86] Mortlake, assessed at 80 hides in Domesday Book, comprised the later parishes of Mortlake, Putney, Barnes and part of Wimbledon;[87] it seems to have been of much the same size and shape as Eorcenwold's Battersea estate, which it adjoined, though with the addition of a large Wealden common at Burstow (below, pp53–4). Croydon, also 80 hides TRE, may have been the remnant of a still greater manor, running the whole length of the Kent–Surrey border, which fragmented in the 870s (above, p17). In c900 the royal estate at Wallington was depleted by the creation of a 70-hide estate at Beddington for the see of Winchester:[88] this probably comprised the Domesday manors and later parishes of Beddington and Carshalton (25 + 25 + 27 hides), which shared a tract of Downland common and completely surrounded the residual royal land at Wallington (below, p33; fig 11F).

As late as the Domesday survey, much of southern Surrey still consisted of broad estates stretching into the Weald and reminiscent, on a rather smaller scale, of South Malling. One such was Bramley (fig 9D), a TRE manor of the Kentish nobleman Æthelnoth. Parochial and tenurial links prove that it covered the whole western half of Blackheath hundred, including West Shalford, Wonersh, Hascombe, Dunsfold, and numerous small sub-manors such as Utworth and Rydinghurst.[89] Others were Godalming, which included the Wealden parishes of Chiddingfold and Haslemere (fig 47), and Shere, which extended into Cranleigh and may once have

Fig 9   'Multiple estates' in Surrey. A: Chertsey estate (bounds from S1165 and S621, *PNSy* 105–6n, 114n, 119n, 132n). B: Battersea estate (bounds from S1248 and *PNSy* 12–13n, with amendments kindly suggested by Keith Bailey). C: Farnham estate (bounds from S382 and *PNSy* 165–7n). D: Bramley estate (TRE manorial boundaries reconstructed after Turner & Blair, Manors and churches in Blackheath hundred). The names and hidages of units granted in extant pre-Conquest charters are shown in italics. In a few places the plotting of the charter bounds is somewhat schematic

comprehended the eastern half of Blackheath hundred.[90] Such Wealden manors resemble South Malling in their tendency to contain multiple settlement units formalised as tithings. Godstone had four,[91] Bramley at least twelve,[92] while Dorking provides the best parallel with six *borghs* including a 'Walde Borough' or *borgh* in the Weald.[93] Perhaps most of the area south of the Downs was once divided into these large, regular blocks. Some element of overall design is suggested by the fact that Queen Edith's TRE demesne in Surrey comprised two such manors (Shere and Dorking), together with a third (Reigate) which although less regular was also large and partly in the Weald.[94] The late Saxon queens were dowered with a stable group of manors,[95] and it may be that the Surrey Weald displays some deliberate, systematic apportionment within the royal demesne.

Does Surrey, then, support claims for the multi-vill estate as the archetypal manorial structure? Such estates contained at least 30% of the county's acreage; if their survival in the Weald is due to its retarded development, there is an implication that others once existed in the more advanced areas. Nonetheless, to see them as the essential, immemorial framework, the cradle of all later manorial types, is for two reasons misleading. First, their origins are, at least in the south-east, essentially subsequent to the comprehensive structure of provincial territories within which they were created. Secondly, they can be defined simply as very large bundles of the same basic units which, in varying quantities, composed *all* manors, of all shapes and sizes.

Seventh-century kings gave bookland principally for one purpose: the establishment of the young English Church on a basis of firm prosperity. Multi-vill estates seem so prominent in early sources largely because the initial grants to sees and great minsters were especially liable to take this form. This was a general pattern in the West Midlands,[96] and it clearly applies to Chertsey, Farnham, Battersea and South Malling. Hence these very large estates, often comprising as much as a third or a half of the provincial territories from which they were carved, reflect the specific circumstances of the 7th and 8th centuries: the urgent and exceptional demand for large-scale endowments, at a time when the land of the territory was still reasonably free of entrenched rights. Often the primary territory was divided into two parts, only one of which would remain directly subject to the royal vill. Even at this stage, the need for each part to retain adequate common grazing might result in split land-units: thus the Malling estate separates the settled area around Wilmington from its woodland patures to the north-east, and the Chertsey estate drives a wedge between Woking manor and Windlesham (fig 8 for both). There is nothing about the topography or internal structure of secular multi-vill estates to mark them out as different in kind from their documented monastic counterparts, except that they tend on the whole to be smaller.

So far as our evidence goes, then, multi-vill estates were, as estates, essentially a product of early Christian England. Does this mean that the systematic internal divisions, so strikingly exemplified at South Malling, evolved within them and are later still? Not necessarily: it seems likely that the subdivisions often pre-date them and belong to the same stage of development as the primary territories. The language of the charters certainly suggests this: the Chertsey, Farnham and Battersea estates could be described *at their creation* as groups of named and hidated units. Insofar as the hypothesis of early, symmetrical hidation (above, pp21–2) can be accepted, it implies that the provincial territories could be broken down into twenty-hide sub-divisions, and these into individual hides.

Multi-vill manors may thus have been founded on an existing organisational structure. If the central royal vill of a territory was alienated as part of a new complex estate, it would simply continue, as the manorial centre, to control such of its former dependencies as had been alienated with it. At South Malling, for example, pre-existing links between the former territorial centre and what became the *borghs* of the manor may have provided a basis for the complex services which had evolved by *c*1273. More frequently the estate gained a new focus, often the minster community for whose benefit it was created; this left the *villa regia* at the head of a fragmented royal manor made ever more exiguous by later grants. Often, as at Woking and Godalming, the 'rump' was more or less compact, but another common result was a disjointed archipelago of fragments, such as Ewell with its outliers at Leatherhead, Kingswood and Shellwood.

If a structure of small, distinct hidated units was indeed antecedent to manorialisation, we would expect lesser manors to contain them too; and this is exactly what we seem to find. Many Surrey manors included components which were in some sense self-contained and were of the order of one or two hides apiece. In the West Midlands, D Hooke has shown that late Saxon boundaries often comprehended distinct 'township' entities of a hide or a little more, largely invisible in Domesday Book and later sources; thus 'the typical West Midland parish appears to have been a 'multi-township' one, with internal divisions in existence at a very early date'.[97] Although Surrey lacks this rich charter evidence, it is clear that the Domesday accounts of manors conceal the existence of innumerable subdivisions. Very many individual farms have habitative place-names of Anglo-Saxon origin, ignored by all the early sources; it is striking, for instance, that thirteen of the 31 reliable -hām names describe units recorded neither as Domesday estates nor as medieval parishes.[98]

Domesday Book and later sources are nonetheless revealing for the small minority of such entities which were tenurially separate. Here they provide grounds for thinking that individual hides as first defined retained some kind of long-standing territorial identity, however changed their economic potential. For the Domesday clerks a hide in terms of the TRE geld burden was also, sometimes at least, a hide in some other sense. A few one-hide or two-hide units appear as manors in their own right. In most such cases no hidation is given, as if the statement '*X* tenet *Y* hidas' implies automatically that 'TRE se defendebat pro *Y* hidis'.[99] Where a TRE hidage *is* stated, it invariably corresponds with the number of hides that the holding is stated to contain: thus, 'istae 2 hidae . . . TRE pro 2 hidis se defendebant, modo pro dimidia'.[100] Sometimes we are told the name of a manor, its TRE hidation, and then that a certain whole number 'of these hides' have since been alienated.[101] This kind of language would make no sense unless a tract which had gelded at one hide before the Conquest was normally a stable entity and likely to remain so. This is not to deny that by 1086 the hides of the old assessment were fiscal units which had long ceased to reflect productive acreage;[102] it is merely to suggest that they were not *purely* fiscal, but had retained by ancient custom some distinctness in the fabric of land-tenure or rural society.

Are these topographical entities, or simply distinct property rights within united townships? Some at least are of the former kind, for they can be identified with later medieval farms and hamlets. Generally they seem to have supported between one and half-a-dozen smallholders, often with a demesne plough and occasionally a serf. Typical examples are:

Littleton in Artington (2 hides): 1 demesne plough; 1 villan and 1 cottar with 1 plough.[103]
Anstie in Dorking (1 hide)
Litelfeld (½ hide)   } 1 demesne plough; 1 bordar.[104]
Tuesley in Godalming (1 hide): 1 [demesne] plough, 1 serf; 1 villan and 6 cottars.[105]
Tyting in Chilworth (1 hide): 1 demesne plough; 1 villan and 6 bordars with 1 plough.[106]
1 hide in Dorking (Hampstead?): 1 demesne plough, a mill at the hall; 1 bordar.[107]
2 hides in Elmbridge hundred (Norwood Farm, Cobham?): 6 villans with 2 ploughs.[108]

Others are revealed by stray references in deeds, and sometimes their physical compactness can be demonstrated. A Warenne charter of c1110 grants Betchworth and 'the hide of Wonham',[109] the latter referring to a small unitary estate called Wonham Manor which appears on the Betchworth tithe-map (fig 11H). Shoelands in Puttenham is revealed as another such by charter-bounds of c1210, and its name, which implies ownership by a monastic community, carries it back to an unrecorded past.[110] Such chance evidence suggests that many of the little compact 'manors' first seen in post-medieval sources may be just as old. In the one-hide units which remain topographically distinct, we may well have actual examples of the *terra unius familie* as conceived when the assessments were first imposed. Economically, it is interesting that many of these had come to support small communities of peasants by the 11th century, only to re-emerge as single farmsteads in the later Middle Ages; tenurially, they argue a high degree of traditional continuity in the fabric of local society which makes it easier to understand the stability of larger manors. Thus beneath the apparent comprehensiveness of manor, village and fields can be glimpsed an older, more cellular structure of compact units with defined boundaries.

In other regions it has been suggested that minor land-holdings of this kind, in what may be termed the order of magnitude ranging between 'hide-size' and 'parish-size', are pre-English. CC Taylor has argued that a network of sub-parochial divisions covers large continuous areas of Dorset, and concludes that 'the basic arrangement of settlements and their estates in Dorset is likely to be Romano-British or Celtic rather than Saxon in origin'.[111] The idea that stable 'sub-parish' units existed by relatively early in the Anglo-Saxon period is developed by Gelling in Berkshire, and by Hooke in the West Midlands.[112] Attempts to identify 'parish-type' territories as Roman villa estates by distribution analysis[113] are stimulating and well worth pursuing, even if by their very nature they are inconclusive. An area of inquiry which promises more solid results, and where knowledge is rapidly growing, concerns the survival of planned Roman and

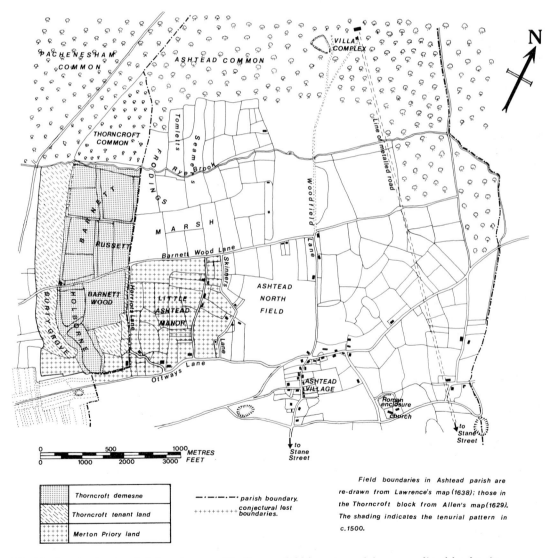

	Thorncroft demesne
	Thorncroft tenant land
	Merton Priory land

—·—·—·— parish boundary.

++++++++ conjectural lost boundaries.

Field boundaries in Ashtead parish are re-drawn from Lawrence's map (1638); those in the Thorncroft block from Allen's map (1629). The shading indicates the tenurial pattern in c.1500.

Fig 10   Leatherhead and Ashtead: a possible Roman field layout surviving as medieval land-units

pre-British boundaries. Here Surrey provides a possible example, on the London clay near the Roman villa at Ashtead (fig 10). A pattern of lanes divides an area of ancient enclosures into six or possibly nine irregular squares, aligned on a more-or-less straight trackway from the villa site to Stane Street. The squares are respected both by the parish boundary and by estate boundaries: two comprised a compact outlier of Thorncroft manor in Leatherhead,[114] a third was the manor of Little Ashtead, and Ashtead north common field largely occupied the fourth.[115] In the light of well-attested early divisions of this kind now identified in many parts of Britain,[116] it is arguable that boundaries connected with the Ashtead villa survived to delimit small land-units in the early Anglo-Saxon period. It is perhaps in such points of detail that we are most likely to trace landmarks from the thoroughly settled countryside which the Anglo-Saxons found.

The early social and economic character of the small units, and their relationship to their component households and their neighbours, is hard to glimpse. Some place-names seem to define townships by reference to their specialised function in the extensive economy of the *regio*: thus the eastern division of Surrey contains Gatton ('goat-farm'), Chaldon ('calf-down'), Merstham ('*hām* at the horse enclosure'), Banstead ('place where beans are cultivated') and Chipstead ('place with a market'),[117] while the central division has both a Kingswood ('wood attached to royal centre') and a Charlwood ('wood of the peasants').[118] Such 'defining' place-names may, however, refer to specialised tribute obligations rather than to an exclusively specialised economy: the township which owed renders of goats may still have produced other goods for local consumption. Nor was all grazing necessarily transhumant: local commons could have been shared from an early date by neighbouring cultivators.[119] There may, therefore, be some sense in which collections of small units are pre-manorial, representing groups of farmers sharing localised resources as well as the general resources of the *regio*. Wherever it existed, the early scheme of hidation influenced manorial developments, and the recurrence of twenty-hide manors as late as the 10th and 11th centuries suggests some basic continuity of early groupings. But the great social and economic changes of the 10th and 11th centuries worked on this material and transformed it, giving to rural communities a more strongly marked local identity and a higher level of economic self-sufficiency.

The development of the 'classic manor'

Not all early estates were of the 'federative' type. Aston has argued that unitary manors under lay proprietors are assumed by written sources from the late 7th century onwards, and may be still more ancient.[120] Units of a magnitude similar to normal medieval manors begin to appear in Surrey documents as early as do the multi-vill estates. The original Chertsey endowment of 672 × 4 included discrete holdings at Cobham, at Molesey and near London.[121] Mortlake seems likely to have belonged to Christ Church Canterbury as a single manor from the 8th or 9th century,[122] and scarcely any of the Surrey manors described in 10th-century charters exceeded twenty hides (cf fig 11).[123]

Thus the 'federative' system co-existed with small, self-contained manors over some centuries. But for much of this period it was a static rather than an evolving type, preserved largely by the inertia of property rights. Quite apart from whatever re-structuring of the countryside resulted from economic growth, units of land-lordship must have come under increasing pressure from the expanding thegnly class. England was coming to support an extensive country gentry, and the most active participants in the land-market were the multitudes of men seeking five or ten hides to support the status of a thegn.

The evidence noted elsewhere for the formation of new multi-vill estates during the mid to late Anglo-Saxon period has no parallels in Surrey.[124] The long list of manors attributed to Chertsey

Abbey in its forged charters probably has a genuine pre-Conquest basis,[125] and could be taken to suggest that a large group of manors on the Surrey Downs, the whole of Effingham hundred, and some smaller blocks each comprising two or three later parishes, had been assembled piecemeal. It seems equally likely, however, that these lists record old multi-vill estates in the process of fragmentation (cf above, p25), a process which was largely complete by Domesday Book. Otherwise the trend is wholly towards fission. As early as 871 × 888 Ealdorman Alfred's will lists a collection of manors in eastern Surrey ranging betwen two and 32 hides, possibly the *disjecta membra* of a recently-dismantled archiepiscopal estate (above, p17). This reflects not only an overall impoverishment of the Church but also an evolution towards estates composed of separate manors. The distribution of the Surrey property acquired by late Saxon archbishops reflects this tendency:[126] by the Conquest, none of the six archiepiscopal manors adjoined each other.[127] Outside the main estate, the TRE manors of Chertsey Abbey were equally scattered (fig 38). Of lay estates existing in 1066, none but Osweald's suggests even faintly a policy of grouping, and even this amounts to nothing more than a concentration of five holdings in near but non-contiguous parishes.[128] Whatever was happening elsewhere, the landlords of late Saxon Surrey had no disposition to amalgamate their manors into compact blocks. By the Conquest we have already reached the stage at which land was usually exploited in self-contained units of normal manor size, run from their own centres; correspondingly, the 'federative' structure was in decline.

Here tenurial and economic factors go hand in hand. By the very fact that they belonged to bishops and monasteries, the largest and earliest estates preserved a greater appearance of stability than those which were subject to all the vagaries of lay descent. But below the surface the creation of sub-tenancies was everywhere a strong if insidious solvent.[129] From the 1070s subinfeudation can be seen at work on estates of all sizes, causing small tenurial units to proliferate. Many knights were endowed with mere fractions of pre-Conquest manors: thus a *miles* held one-and-a-quarter of the eight hides of Malden in 1086, and a fee of the 1140s comprised a compact half-hide carved out of the demesne of Thorncroft.[130] The same process was affecting the great estates both before and after the Conquest. Out of the 73 hides on the main Chertsey estate, ten-and-a-half had passed out of demesne by 1066[131] and a further nine were subinfeudated during the next twenty years.[132] At Farnham seven-and-a-half of the 60 hides were in tenants' hands by 1086, as well as the church and glebe.[133] Notwithstanding the stability of these great manors at tenant-in-chief level, they were experiencing a process which was both alien and inimical to the integrated multi-vill economy. The breakup of lay estates is obvious even superficially: between 1086 and c1250 the great Bramley manor dissolved from apparent coherence into a collection of small independent holdings.[134] This should not be seen as a distinctively post-Conquest phenomenon, but rather as the continuation of a late Anglo-Saxon trend into an age in which we can perceive it.

A major cause of this fragmentation was economic growth. The multi-vill manors which proved resilient beyond the Conquest contained a high proportion of under-developed land; as will be shown in ch 2, it was above all the development of this land which heralded their breakup. The later the clearance, the longer the archaic pattern survived; the dissolution of Bramley probably reflects what had already happened to lay manors outside the Weald. But simply through stability of lordship, the Chertsey and Farnham estates continued to display the outward form of a dying economic system.

Thus later Saxon and Norman Surrey was increasingly dominated by 'normal' manors comparable to, or smaller than, the average medieval parish. A striking feature of the few available sets of charter bounds is the tendency of most to correspond more or less exactly with the boundaries of modern parishes (fig 9A–C, fig 11 A–D). The evidence, sparse as it is, suggests a pattern similar to the West Midlands where nearly half the charter units are

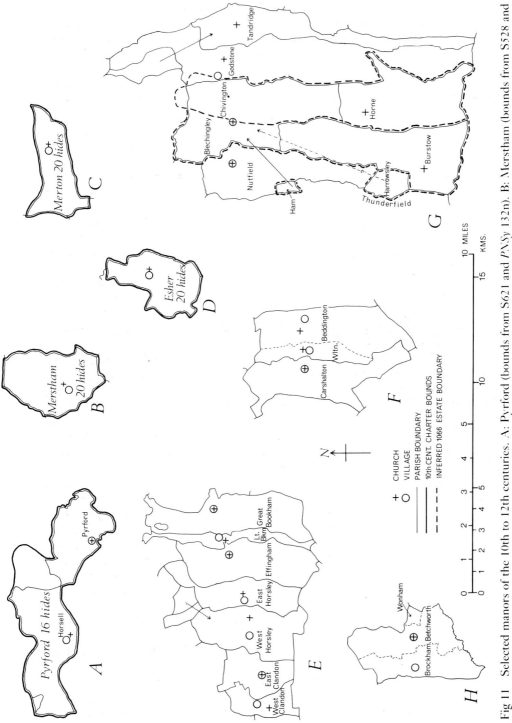

Fig 11   Selected manors of the 10th to 12th centuries. A: Pyrford (bounds from S621 and *PNSy* 132n). B: Merstham (bounds from S528 and Rumble, The Merstham (Surrey) Charter-Bounds). C: Merton (bounds from S747 and *PNSy* 25n). D: Esher (bounds from S911 and *PNSy* 92–3n). E: A group of parishes on the Downs dip-slope. F: Carshalton, Wallington and Beddington. G: A group of parishes in the eastern Surrey Weald (TRE manorial boundaries reconstructed after Blair, Surrey endowments of Lewes Priory, fig 7). H: Betchworth, Brockham and Wonham. The names and hidages of units granted in extant pre-Conquest charters are shown in italic. In a few places the plotting of the charter bounds is somewhat schematic

coterminous with parishes.[135] This is not evidence for the antiquity of parishes as such: parishes only crystallised in the 12th century, and in Surrey many contain two or more independent Domesday manors (below, ch 6). What the boundaries do suggest is a long-standing tenurial stability which was slightly, but only slightly, blurred by simple combination and division. Furthermore, the uniform and symmetrical hidations of the 10th-century charters imply that tenurial changes had respected not merely the ancient boundaries but also the primitive cadastral divisions, townships and sub-township units. The basic continuity of rural organisation is once again apparent.

The emphasis of the foregoing argument has been on manors as larger or smaller collections of distinct components. This is, of course, an inadequate definition. As conventionally understood the classic manor had centralised institutions: a demesne, a manorial curia, and a structure of tenant holdings bound together by like services, common agriculture and nucleation of settlement. Most medieval township communities were organised in units much larger than a hide or so, and in general such units were either coterminous with manors or bore some perceptible relationship to them. Aston suggests that Ine's laws of the late 7th century already assume 'that dichotomy between demesne and peasant land which is central to manorial history'.[136] To an extent this is true, yet it tells us nothing about how manors were organised internally. The antithesis of *inland* and *gestett land* need not in itself imply anything more advanced than that of 'king's vill', 'reeve's vill' and 'bond vill' in the multiple estates of primitive Wales.[137] Within a manor of any size, a new central place might inherit such authority as the royal vill had once exercised over its dependencies; but by the 13th century we find something more, a sense of internal coherence. Do manors already have this kind of integration when they come into view in the 8th, 9th and 10th centuries?

Confining ourselves for the moment to estate morphology, there is one particular development which suggests the influence of economic factors. This is the formation of manors on a north-south linear pattern to take in a variety of different soils. Such units are the basis of the long, narrow 'strip parishes' which are so marked a feature of the Downs dip-slope (fig 11E, F; fig 22) and the Weald (fig 11G); comparison with Domesday Book indicates that in many cases this tenurial geography had often, but not always, taken shape by 1066. In Surrey as in Kent,[138] fragmentation into small strip-shaped manors is a distinctive feature of the Downs and dip-slope regions, with their rapidly-developing class of manorial gentry.

Such recurrent linearity implies some internal coherence, depending on the balance of arable, open grazing and wooded commons. By dating its appearance we will pinpoint a significant stage in the evolution of the rural economy. Some units of this kind may be ancient: they reproduce in miniature the linearity of the provincial territories and Wealden multiple estates, doubtless enhanced by the presence of numerous north-south droveways. Yet none of the reliable pre-Conquest charters mentions them, while certainly some were formed in the late 10th, 11th or 12th centuries by the regular division of larger, more amorphous units. Thus Carshalton, Wallington and Beddington (fig 11F) are lineal fractions of an earlier whole, with a single tract of common pasture called Woodcote split between the manors (below, p49); part at least of this division occurred between 963 × 75, when Beddington appears as an intact 70-hide estate, and 1086, when Domesday Book shows it as two manors totalling only 50 hides.[139]

Nomenclature is revealing, for the strip parishes on the dip-slope include three 'pairs': West and East Clandon, West and East Horsley, and Great and Little Bookham (fig 11E). One of the Chertsey forgeries, which may include genuine late Saxon data, lists land-units 'apud Bocham cum Effingeham' and 'apud Clendone et in altera Clendone'.[140] It may be suspected that the Clandons on the one hand, and the Bookhams and Effingham on the other, had been whole units not long before the list was first complied, distinct enough now to be given separate names, yet with each group still lumped together under a single hidation. These cases are pre-Conquest, but a Warenne charter of *c*1210 records the partition of Betchworth and Brockham into separate manors by a line running from north to south along hedges and other landmarks (fig 11H).[141]

As R A Dodgshon has argued, 'the proprietary break-up of a township did not lead automatically to its physical splitting into separate sub-townships on the ground. There was a choice: landowners could divide their shares in the form of sub-divided fields or they could split them into discrete units or sub-townships'.[142] One of the main determining factors would have been the internal structure of the township: what degree of integration it had developed, and whether or not it had organised itself into linear blocks creating natural lines of fission. Some townships withstood tenurial splitting: the manor of Esher (fig 11D) became four separate holdings between 1005 and 1066,[143] yet it remained 'Esher' in some sense real enough for it to emerge intact as the medieval parish. In other cases, by contrast, township division sometimes preceded division of ownership. The need to describe one tract of land held by one lord as 'Clandon' and 'the other Clandon' suggests that the name 'Clandon' had come to mean a defined area which was now split into two parts for reasons unconnected with property rights. In the Betchworth case, the language implies that 'the land of Brockham' and 'the land of Betchworth' were already distinct, presumably linear townships co-existing within one manor before they were split tenurially. The needs of a divided lordship might then, in its turn, lead to major reorganisation of the evolving farming communities.[144]

Settlement, field-systems and peasant tenure are the themes of later chapters. But this evidence is largely post-Conquest; the tenurial framework is important because it suggests, if only indirectly, a broad chronology for the changes taking place within it. So far as it goes, the Surrey material agrees well with the conclusions of Maitland and Dodgshon.[145] Manorial fission was well-advanced in Surrey by 1066, and for some time it had tended to follow a linear pattern; sometimes, perhaps usually, this linearity was a result of divisions which had occurred during the previous eighty or hundred years. In so far as tenurial developments reflect social and economic change, attention rests on the two or three centuries for which Domesday Book is the half-way mark.

Conclusion

This chapter has described a process of fragmentation. Whatever institutions of kinship or lordship united the first English communities, they were soon overlain by a system of organisation, economic as well as jurisdictional, which aggregated regular blocks of hides into large provincial territories. Early manorialisation followed closely the sub-units of the territory, which might be granted either in groups – the multi-vill estates of the future – or as single entities. Thereafter, symmetrical hidations witness to a strong continuity: manors of the 10th and 11th centuries may often have been exact reflections of the pre-manorial scheme. The groups of farm units carried with them their rights of transhumance grazing, perpetuating in the denn system the old pattern of economic interconnections within a large territory.

Further division, into self-contained manors and along lines set by the evolving local pattern of farming and settlement, was notably a feature of the late Saxon and Norman centuries: not in itself universal, it was one sign of a more developed pattern which overlay and often subsumed the old, distinct hidated units. To this extent the 'manorial grid' remains a valid concept, but only as one part of an evolving whole. On the one hand, the estate structure changed in response to changes in settlement, agriculture and the farming community which were just as great. On the other, local conditions which moulded the structure of seigneurial organisation were also moulded by it.

2 Land Exploitation and the Form of Settlement

The chronology of growth and organisation in the Anglo-Saxon countryside has recently occasioned much debate. On the one hand, awareness of major gaps in the evidence has banished time-honoured blanks from the map of Domesday England, and has encouraged a train of thought the extreme expression of which is P H Sawyer's claim that 'the rural resources of England were almost as fully exploited in the seventh century as they were in the eleventh'.[1] On the other hand, recent work has revealed a mobility of settlement types and field-systems which suggests widespread reorganisation during the late Anglo-Saxon and Norman centuries.

This chapter will suggest a chronology for land exploitation in Surrey. The debatable ground lies between the two extremes of the 'Sawyer dictum' and the traditional view which emphasises the colonising achievements of the 12th and 13th centuries. How far later conditions existed by the time of Domesday Book, and from how long before, must therefore be the recurring themes. The various geographical regions will be discussed in turn, for Surrey is diverse and cannot sensibly be viewed as an undifferentiated whole. The development of villages, and their relationship to scattered settlements around them, will then be analysed within this broad context of land-use.

The evidence

In the absence of written sources, place-names are of major relevance for the early stages. Especially important in Surrey are the large group of minor elements which reflect the progress of woodland clearance. Six are sufficiently common to permit distribution analysis: the widespread - *leah* and - *hyrst*, and the more localised - *ersc*, - *falod*, - *ceart* and - *scēat*. The maps (figs 12 and 13) are based on analysis of forms collected in *The place-names of Surrey*.[2]

Domesday data for settlement and exploitation are especially difficult to use in a region where many of the resources listed were undoubtedly several miles distant from their parent manors. Mapping by hundred, as attempted in *The Domesday geography of south east England* (fig 14), is more valid than mapping by individual manor, though still risking serious distortion in the hundreds which traverse geological boundaries. Thus a third course has been adopted here. Surrey has been divided into five geographical regions, from each of which five Domesday manors or groups of manors have been selected (table 2), the criteria being their geographical stability and likely correspondence with post-medieval parish boundaries. All have a relatively straightforward tenurial history in the 13th century and after, and are represented by parishes either singly or in simple combination. This is especially important in the Weald, where none of the places chosen is known to have contained outliers of non-Wealden manors; on the other hand, a degree of distortion from the hidden Wealden dependencies of manors in other areas (for instance Mortlake and Ashtead) is unavoidable. The parish acreages have then been used (table 3) to calculate the average incidence of people and teams per 1000 acres over the five parishes in each group. The method is rough and ready, and open to objections: the classification of regions is only valid in broad terms, and few parishes fit neatly into one geographical zone. But this approach may come somewhere near to giving the Domesday data, with all their shortcomings, a localised geographical dimension.

Finally, the 1334 Lay Subsidy quotas for the same five groups of parishes have been totalled and then divided by the parish acreages (table 4). As an absolute measure of population and wealth

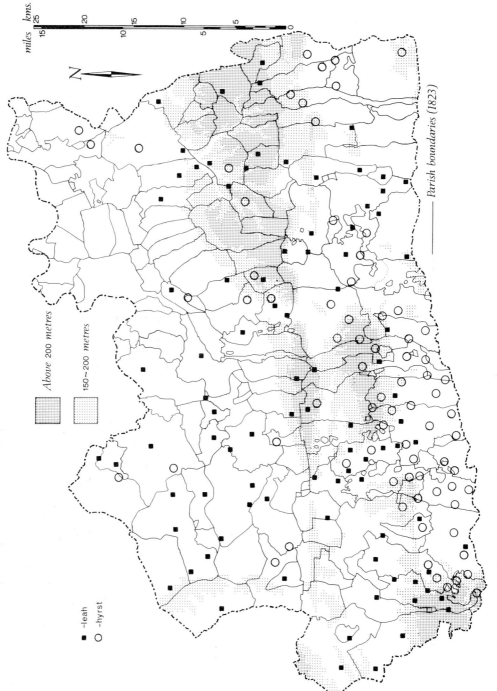

Fig 12   Clearance name elements: *-leah* and *-hyrst*

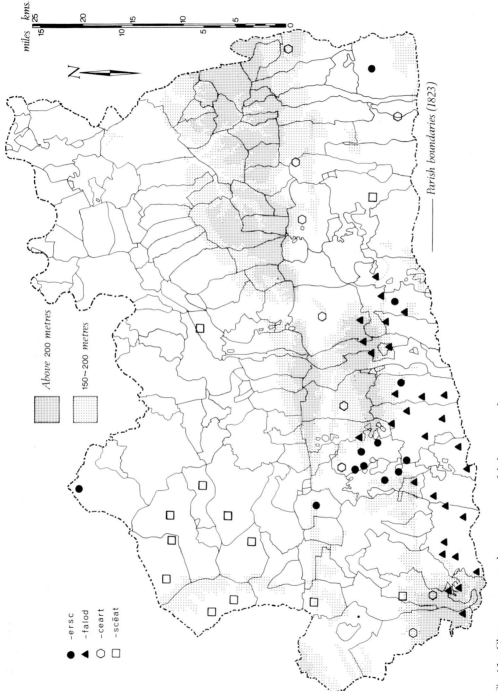

Fig 13   Clearance name elements: *-ersc*, *-falod*, *-ceart* and *-scēat*

TABLE 2   Domesday data for selected parishes in five regions of Surrey

	Population	Teams	Ploughlands	Acreage (Modern parish)
North-East Surrey (London Basin)				
Barnes	13	5	6	1027
Merton	69	20	21	1763
Mitcham/Whitford	28	8.5	–	2916
Morden	14	7	–	1475
Mortlake/Wimbledon/Putney	110	33	35	7037
Totals	234	73.5	–	14218
Dip-slope				
Ashtead	53	16	–	2645
Bookham, Great	39	19	19	3281
Clandon, West	9	2.5	3	1003
Epsom	44	18	17	4413
Horsley, West	35	10	8	2672
Totals	180	65.5	–	14014
Downs				
Chelsham	42	11	8	3357
Chipstead	18	7	7	2419
Farleigh	6	2	2.5	1051
Headley	22	6	–	2066
Tatsfield	26	2	–	1303
Totals	114	28	–	10196
Weald Clay and Greensand				
Abinger/Paddington	39	13	18	7560
Blechingley/Chivington/Horne	74	26.5	28	9972
Farnham hundred	89	43	–	26213
Hambledon	22	7	4	2721
Nutfield	45	16	12	3576
Totals	269	105.5	–	50042
North-West Surrey (Forest area)				
Byfleet	12	3	2	2045
Chobham	49	16	–	9057
Egham	57	12	40	7624
Pyrford/Horsell	54	7	13	4782
Woking/Sutton	58	24	9	8802
Totals	230	62	–	32310

TABLE 3   Analysis of Domesday data for the parishes listed in table 2

	Pop. per 1000 acres	Teams per 1000 acres	Teams per 10 of pop.
North-East Surrey	16.5	5.1	3.1
Dip-slope	12.8	4.7	3.6
Downs	11.2	2.7	2.5
Weald Clay and Greensand	5.4	2.1	3.9
North-West Surrey	7.1	1.9	2.7

Note: all figures are to nearest 0.1

TABLE 4   1334 Lay Subsidy quotas for the parishes listed in table 2

	Total quota of parishes in the group (£)	Total acreage (From table 1)	£ per 1000 acres
North-East Surrey	9.1	14218	0.6
Dip-slope	13.8	14014	1.0
Downs	9.5	10196	1.0
Weald Clay and Greensand	45.1	50042	0.9
North-West Surrey	23.0	32310	0.7

Source: R E Glasscock (ed), *The lay subsidy of 1334* (London, 1975)

Notes: (a)   all figures are to nearest 0.1
(b)   the totals include estimated figures for two parishes where the stated quotas are for combined townships
(c)   one quota (Byfleet), recorded as a tenth, has been converted to a fifteenth
(d)   the separate quota for the planted town of Blechingley is omitted

these data are virtually useless, but as a rough index to relative prosperity within a limited area, they may throw some light on rates of development over the previous 250 years. These tables provide a background for the more specific local evidence which will now be reviewed.

Colonisation of land: the London Basin and Windsor Forest areas

The north-eastern third of Surrey between the Thames, the Downs and the river Wey was extensively settled during the 5th and 6th centuries, as is clear above all from the large and numerous pagan cemeteries.[3] The rectilinear field layout in the north of Leatherhead and Ashtead parishes (above, pp29–30) implies, if indeed Roman, some continuity of land-use on the

London clay; while the numerous -*hām* names, indicators of early settlement (above, p28), tend to lie on or near Roman roads (for instance the group formed by Hatcham, Woldingham and Streatham). In 1086 the incidence here of population and teams was very markedly the highest in the county (table 3). North-east Surrey would clearly have attracted settlers from the time of the first Germanic incursions up the Thames Valley, and its development during succeeding centuries can only have been stimulated by the proximity of London. The contrast between this area and the rest of the county scarcely needs further explanation.

Throughout the Middle Ages most townships on the London clay retained heavy commons with a mixture of oak and brushwood cover, generally termed *bruera* in local deeds. On some manors the woodland pasture zones, whether contiguous or detached, were well-defined by the late Anglo-Saxon period. Thus the 983 charter-bounds of Thames Ditton perambulate the estate proper and then, separately, an area of wood hemmed in by enclosures and landmarks.[4] Another clear case is Penge, a member of Battersea lying near the Kent border some eight miles from its head manor. In the 957 Battersea charter it is firmly characterised as a pasture, *se wude þe hatte Pænge*,[5] but by the mid 13th century Penge had acquired compact arable holdings with houses and crofts.[6] The 'tenentes de bosco' in late 13th-century Lambeth (below, p79) are suggestive of another woodland tract opened in relatively recent times to the plough. These cases reflect a pattern which will recur: the deliberate preservation of wood-pastures in a well-exploited landscape, followed by their deliberate destruction when demographic pressure outweighed the interests of the transhumance economy to which they belonged.

On the heavy clay commons of the dip-slope and London Basin townships, a trickle of small assarts seems to have continued until *c*1300. Oxshott, in Stoke D'Abernon parish, is first mentioned in the mid 12th century and appears in deeds of *c*1200–20 as a mixture of woodland, enclosures and recent purprestures.[7] Such encroachments might make inroads into neighbours' common pasture, with consequent legal problems: a settlement of such a dispute in 1242 shows that many acres of waste in the north-east of West Horsley parish had recently been enclosed and cultivated.[8] A similar agreement of 1287/8 between the lords of Leatherhead and Stoke D'Abernon, concerning enclosure of *bruera* on the boundary between their lordships,[9] may be connected with the former's replanning of nearby Pachenesham as a 'satellite village' (below, pp61–2). In several townships, enclosures were advancing northwards from the heavily-farmed Reading and Thanet beds onto the London clay. These assarts, in the most densely settled part of the county, were on poor soil and their contribution to resources was probably slight. In this area common waste now remained in sufficiency rather than in abundance.

Godley and Woking hundreds, in the sandy north-west corner of the county, present a total contrast. Some -*hām* place-names are found along the Roman road towards Staines and beside the Thames and Bourne,[10] and this stretch of the Thames Valley is beginning to show a concentration of mid-Saxon settlements on the river-gravels; the presence of Chertsey minster and a royal vill nearby must have stimulated development in the river-valleys. Outside this narrow strip, however, settlement evidence is negligible, and in 1086 these hundreds as a whole were sparse in population and still sparser in ploughteams (fig 14; tables 2, 3). Some large areas, such as Frimley and the western half of Chobham (fig 9A), provide virtually no evidence for settlement before the 13th century. Windlesham began as a forest pasture of Woking, and a narrative source (below, p95) states that it only supported three householders before late 12th-century expansion.

Certainly the main reason for this late development was the wretched quality of the soil, graphically illustrated by the plight of a Send tenant at the beginning of the 13th century who migrated to Yorkshire because 'non potuit morari super terram illam pro parvitate terre'.[11] But another inhibiting factor was the inclusion of most of the area in Windsor Forest. However strict in theory, forest law was not in practice an absolute barrier to assarts and encroachments. From

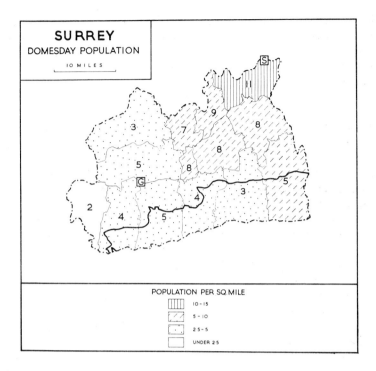

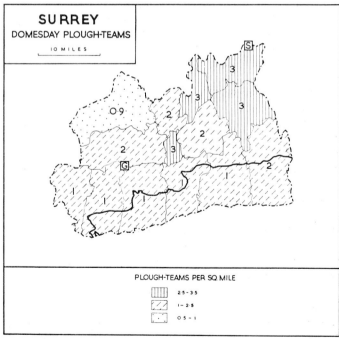

Fig 14 Population and plough-teams in 1086: densities mapped by hundreds. (From Darby & Campbell, *Domesday geography of south-east England*, figs 108, 110)

as early as the mid 12th century the need was tacitly recognised, and clearances allowed in return for fines and rents.[12] Nonetheless, a peasant wishing to colonise in the royal forest needed to overcome a whole additional set of petty hindrances and financial disincentives. In any case, it was not only the king who had an interest in restricting clearance. The concern of lords to maintain the ancient rhythm of seasonal grazing, and hence the pastures on which it depended, was a restrictive influence throughout Surrey. As late as 1234/5, litigation over pannage rights in Brookwood, Woking, shows that the grazing of large swine-herds was still important in the forest area.[13]

Thus the poverty of the soil and the restraints of crown and landlords combined to make this a landscape which developed late. From the deeds, court rolls and accounts of Chertsey and Westminster Abbeys the process can be traced from c1270 onwards; and since the region lay under forest law throughout the 13th century, detailed records of assarts and purprestures appear in forest eyre rolls for 1256 and 1269.[14]

The placename element -scēat (fig 13) supports the idea that cultivation of the woods and broom-grown heaths progressed south-westwards from the rivers, and gives a clue to the form which it probably took. This is the only clearance element with a restricted distribution which is not mainly Wealden: nine of the twelve -scēats lie in the western halves of Godley and Woking hundreds. The basic sense is 'a corner of land', often projecting into a different type of countryside; it could apparently describe both a neck of woodland between two fields and a strip of cultivated land surrounded by wood.[15] The frequency of this element evokes just such a landscape as 13th-century sources describe: a patchwork of small enclosures, crofts of moor and strips of alder coppice, enlarged by a steady stream of small purprestures. Thus in 1228/9 Alan Basset granted to William de la Rude a Woking virgate augmented by three acres of moor and a purpresture of thirteen perches next the road from Horsell to Sidewood, in return for a release of all purprestures made or to be made by Alan and his heirs in the manor of Woking.[16] Possibly the -scēat names reflect, in an earlier phase, this distinctive pattern of colonisation by means of innumerable tiny enclosures.

The forest eyre rolls of 1256 and 1269 include surveys of encroachments for which fines were imposed, listed individually with their acreages and classified as 'old and new assarts' and 'old and new purprestures'. Unfortunately these data (table 5) are not a complete record of colonisation in the period covered. Since 'old assarts' were evidently those surveyed in previous regards,[17] the lack of correspondence between the 'new assarts' of the earlier record and the 'old assarts' of the later suggests that at least one intervening roll is missing. But even a full set of returns would have been far from comprehensive: by now most large-scale assarters were working under royal exemptions which put them outside the jurisdiction of the regarders.[18] Thus the 747 acres of assarts and purprestures in north-west Surrey known to have been registered over some two or three decades can be only a fraction of the total.

The difference between assarts and purprestures in the eyre rolls was mainly one of size and use, purprestures being tiny and in general non-arable (below, p87). Even the assarts were very small, with a median plot size of 1.5 acres. A few large encroachments of 10–20 acres, the work of Chertsey Abbey and other important landlords, are very much the exception; as recorded by these surveys the process was overwhelmingly one of peasant initiative.

Three slightly later sources supplement this evidence: accounts for the Westminster Abbey manor of Pyrford from 1276; court rolls for the same manor from 1335; and abstracts of Chertsey Abbey court rolls from 1327.[19] At Pyrford we find the monks clearing a demesne wood at 'Petingle' in 1288/9, when many cartloads of great oaks (robura) and young rafter-standards (cheveron') were felled and shipped to Westminster; four years later the roots were grubbed out and the area sown with 36 quarters 7 bushels of oats.[20] But more regular and conspicuous are the tenants' assarts: scarcely a single year's account fails to show increments and 'new rent' from

TABLE 5   Assarts and purprestures surveyed in forest eyres of 1256 and 1269

	Median plot size (in acres)		Total acreage (in acres)		
	Assarts	Purprestures	Assarts	Purprestures	Both
Artingdon	–	1.0	–	6.0	6.0
Ash	2.0	1.0	49.5	23.0	72.5
Bisley	–	0.006	–	1.008	1.008
Byfleet	–	0.006	–	2.6	2.6
Chertsey	1.0	0.3	50.5	57.0	107.5
Chobham	1.0	0.5	9.5	22.6	32.1
Compton	–	0.75	–	54.6	54.6
Egham	–	0.006	–	1.5	1.5
Frimley	1.0	0.5	11.5	29.6	41.1
Horsell	5.0	0.006	10.0	15.1	25.1
Pirbright	–	0.5	–	21.6	21.6
Pyrford	–	0.5	–	15.6	15.6
Thorpe	–	0.006	–	0.013	0.013
Walton-on-Thames	1.75	2.0	38.0	45.0	83.0
Wanborough	–	1.0	–	76.5	76.5
Windlesham	–	0.006	–	7.1	7.1
Woking	2.0	0.5	7.0	30.1	37.1
Worplesdon	1.0	0.75	75.0	67.1	142.1
	1.5	0.5	251.0	476.0	727.0

Sources: PRO, E32/195; E32/194

Notes: (a)   Ash includes Henley and Wyke; Chertsey includes Anningley and Addlestone; Egham includes Trotsworth; Woking inclues Mayford and Sutton
   (b)   0.006 acre = 1 perch

encroachments on the waste. The court rolls not only confirm and amplify this evidence, but also show that the flood of tiny assarts continued unabated until the Black Death. At Ash in 1331 four men had licence to hold in common a purpresture called la Throte, enclosed by them, containing three acres; at Pyrford in 1334 Nicolas Pychard was allowed to hold in bondage half a rood of the lord's waste at le Swer'.[21] These are merely two of the innumerable cases involving freemen and villeins, groups and individuals, at least one or two of which were noted at the majority of courts on every manor covered.[22]

Colonisation of land: the Downs and dip-slope

Between the London Basin northwards and the Greensands below the scarp-slope southwards lie two distinct groups of parishes: the elongated ones of central and eastern Surrey, descending from the London clay, traversing the Thanet and Reading beds and rising up the dip-slope of the Downs; and the more compact parishes which lay wholly or largely on the chalk. The former group was more populous and its economic balance more highly ordered, but common problems of interpretation make it convenient to consider together the chalkland and the more fertile belt which followed its northern edge.

Studies of colonisation in the south-eastern counties have generally concentrated on the Weald at the expense of the Downland, but Everitt's recent work on Kent redresses this imbalance. In his view the Downs, like the Weald, were a pasture zone for the first Anglo-Saxons, but were colonised so early that their character as a region of 'secondary' rather than 'primary' settlement is

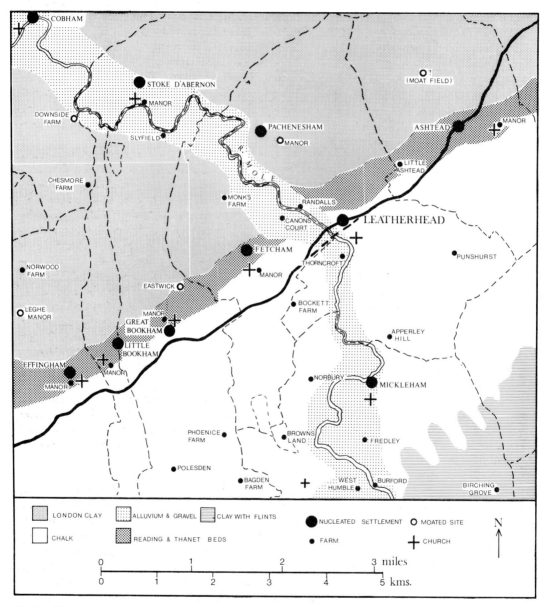

Fig 15   The settlement pattern in part of Copthorne and Effingham hundreds in c1300. (Mainly from data in PNSy, supplemented from other sources in the case of Leatherhead parish)

far less obvious.[23] While it might be objected in general terms that this is altogether too rigid a view of settlement history, the important and continuing role of woodland pasture in the economy of the Downs certainly needs emphasising. Furthermore, Everitt's model of the Downs as an area of small and proliferating manors, where the initiative was taken by the developing gentry class rather than by great landlords,[24] matches very well with the Surrey evidence.

The frequency of -hām place-names in or near the line of dip-slope villages – Bookham, Fetcham, Pachenesham, Mickleham, Epsom[25] – argues strongly for primary Anglo-Saxon settlement along the lines of Stane Street and of the west–east trackway on which the villages lie (fig 15); the large cemetery at Hawk's Hill has produced up to a hundred inhumations of late 6th- to early 7th-century date.[26] Whether the communities which it served were already nucleated on the sites which now bear their names is another matter. The royal tūn and minster site at Pachenesham, and the suggested Roman field-system nearby (above, p29; below, p101) were both on the London clay two or three miles north of the line of villages. By 1086, at all events, the townships were relatively well-developed, their density of population and teams surpassed only by the area near London (table 3). The recurring pattern of nucleated village, common subdivided field, arable enclosures and waste appears firmly established when topography first becomes visible in 13th-century deeds.

In the purely Downland parishes, by contrast, agrarian organisation was more haphazard and few settlements seem ever to have been more than hamlets. Common fields existed, but they were usually small and are less well documented than those on the fertile downwash of the dip-slope (fig 21). On the Downs medieval cultivation was less intensive, but not necessarily less ancient. Conventional interpretations of settlement history, which would unhesitatingly classify such land as marginal, must now reckon with mounting evidence that Downland in southern Britain was extensively farmed even by the Neolithic period;[27] and large areas of 'Celtic' fields at Leatherhead and Coulsdon are proof of Iron Age agriculture on the Surrey Downs.[28] It would be simplistic to assume that exploitation was continuous, but equally so to ascribe all medieval Downland cultivation to a progressive growth which only reached such terrain at times of land-hunger. One recent archaeological study concludes that 'the small agricultural settlement based on mixed farming', with a tendency to remain stable over long periods, was the main social and economic unit on the East Sussex Downs during the late Iron Age and Romano-British periods.[29] Another suggests that the economic basis for the Surrey hillforts of Anstiebury, Holmbury and Hascombe 'rested on scattered farmsteads to the north, sited in favourable positions on the chalk of the North Downs and on the dip slope beyond'.[30] So far as purely physical evidence goes, these small farm units seem much of a piece with those which existed on Leatherhead and Mickleham Downs some thirteen centuries later (fig 16). Since the remarkable discoveries at Chalton, Hampshire (below, p55), historians can no longer assume that Downland settlements and fields were abandoned between the departure of the Romans and the advent of 12th-century colonists.

Significant 5th- and 6th-century settlement on the higher reaches of the Surrey Downs is suggested by a cluster of cemeteries (at Banstead, Beddington, Carshalton and Coulsdon), and by four parish names in – hām (Chelsham, Sanderstead, Warlingham and Woldingham).[31] Cultivation during the mid Saxon period is implied by a will of 871 × 889 which bequeaths 32 hides in Sanderstead and shows that the little manor of Farleigh produced enough grain to owe a yearly corn-render of 30 ambers.[32] The Domesday data for the selected townships (table 3) suggest a population considerably higher than in the Weald and Windsor Forest areas, though perhaps rather lower than in the parishes crossing the dip-slope. Clearly the region supported established settlement and agriculture in 1086 and had done so for some centuries.

The ratio of teams to people, however, is the lowest in Surrey. Partly this may reflect the lightness of the chalky soil, requiring fewer ploughs to till it, but it also suggests communities in which cultivation was still less important than grazing. The Downs, like the Weald, had woodland for pannage, but the grazing of animals other than pigs in the open hillsides would also have had its place in the primitive Anglo-Saxon economy. Place-name evidence for the specialised grazing functions of some Downland townships is discussed above (p30); such nomenclature suggests that the main agrarian development of these places post-dated the great age of transhumance grazing.

At Merstham, charter bounds of 947[33] give a clearer picture of the late Anglo-Saxon landscape. The parish lies on the scarp-slope, its northern two-thirds rising steeply over the Downs and bisected by a dry valley. The most fertile ground traversed by the perambulation was to the south-west, on the greensand at the foot of the scarp slope. Here names suggesting habitation and farming concentrate on a short length of the Merstham-Gatton boundary: Becc's *hamm*, Beaduweald's enclosure (*hagan*), Toda's *camp* (an interesting archaism, derived from *campus*, which possibly denotes an untilled open tract)[34] and Scyn's curtilage (*weorþ*).[35] Such names also existed, however, on the summit of the Downs: the boundary passes clockwise around the north-east quarter of the parish from the bean-plot between the two *hamms* to Esne's *hamm*, and thence to Tunel's curtilage (*weorþ*).[36]

The elements compounded with personal names in the Merstham bounds mostly suggest enclosure: *hagan*, *weorþ* and *hamm* (the last to be distinguished, of course, from *hām*). The particular frequency of *hamm* is reinforced if a charter of 967 which grants land at a place called *Cealvadune* refers to Chaldon in Surrey, a parish adjoining Merstham.[37] Detailed analysis would be needed both to confirm this identification and to plot the bounds, but the presence of no less than four *hamms* among the eight boundary-points (*beonningham, stig ham, fern ham* and *blosham*) is striking. On the Downs as in the Weald, so many *hamms* must clearly be understood as 'enclosures' or 'curtilages' rather than 'river-meadows'.[38] As revealed in these boundaries, the man-made landscape was principally one of small enclosures, sometimes arable (the Merstham 'bean-plot' is a clear case) though not necessarily always. Interlying areas of woodland and scrub also find their place in the Merstham charter.

Were any of these names habitative? In the Merstham bounds one enclosure name, *tunles weorþ*, survives as Tollsworth Farm,[39] and a visible rectangular earthwork south of the farm would correspond closely with the boundary point.[40] The 'bean-plot between two hamms' (*bean stede betwih þam twam hammum*) is identifiable as a point halfway between two medieval settlement sites, Netherne Farm and Woodplace Farm, each about half a mile from the boundary.[41] These cases strongly suggest that *hamm* or *weorþ* described small compact farm units, homesteads surrounded by their own arable and pasture enclosures on the pattern visible in later sources. Such a view is supported by the occurrence of *weorþ* in other minor Surrey place-names (below, p62). If so, it was possible by the 10th century to find two contiguous farms on the summit of the Surrey Downs with tilled land extending to the boundary.

Many farmsteads of this kind are described in 12th- and 13th-century sources, the economic basis of a relatively substantial freeholding class. Two Downland farms in the south of Leatherhead parish were Aperdele and Punsherst, examples respectively of the *-leah* and *-hyrst* elements denoting clearance. Both occur in a deed of c1170,[42] and from then until the early 14th century the de Aperdeles and the de Puneshersts were among the leading families of Copthorne hundred. A group of long-established farms on Leatherhead and Mickleham Downs (fig 16) can be accurately mapped in their late 13th-century form (below, p73), and since one of these was a parochial outlier its boundaries were probably fixed before c1180. Such farms on open Downland were generally smaller than their Wealden counterparts, perhaps a consequence of the lighter soil and of a pastoral economy which relied more on common sheep-runs than on waste areas within tenement boundaries.

As usual, it is easier to illustrate individual farm and settlement types than to trace the general

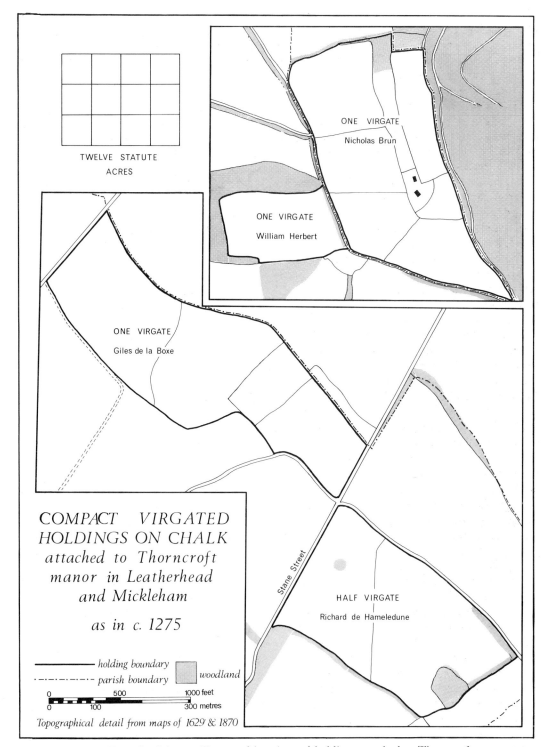

TWELVE STATUTE
ACRES

ONE VIRGATE
Nicholas Brun

ONE VIRGATE
William Herbert

ONE VIRGATE
Giles de la Boxe

COMPACT   VIRGATED
HOLDINGS ON CHALK
attached to Thorncroft
manor in Leatherhead
and Mickleham

as in c. 1275

Stane Street

HALF VIRGATE
Richard de Hameledune

———————— *holding boundary*
–·–·–·–·–·– *parish boundary*   *woodland*

0   500   1000 feet
0   100   300 metres

Topographical detail from maps of 1629 & 1870

Fig 16   Compact Downland farms, illustrated by virgated holdings attached to Thorncroft manor

chronology of growth. One approach, botanical dating of hedgerows, has recently been attempted for the Downland parish of Chelsham. This study[43] identifies two groups of enclosures with hedges 900–1300 years old, one around the church and the other around Ficklesole Farm. Both sites are on high ground in the north-east of the parish near a Roman roadline, and are surrounded by a thin scatter of 'early' hedges. From these, it is suggested, clearance spread during the 12th and 13th centuries, first along the central ridge and then onto lower ground. The reliability of this kind of evidence is still very uncertain,[44] and in any case it would obviously fail to show the presence of an unhedged common field, which Chelsham may well have possessed. The 11th-century arable must have extended some way at least beyond the small 'early' enclaves, for Domesday Book lists 42 inhabitants and 11 teams (table 2). The Chelsham hedge survey cannot adequately reflect land exploitation before 1100, though it may give a distorted reflection of an agrarian initiative belonging to the 11th and 12th centuries rather than earlier.[45]

Growth in these centuries is also suggested by the rapid appearance of churches on dip-slope and Downland manors (below, pp124–6). The proportion of churches in this area which first appear during the period 1086–1160 is the highest in Surrey; especially notable (fig 35) is the extent to which the close-spaced line of churches along the dip-slope seems to have been a product of the Norman period. It will be argued below that proprietary interest was the main motive for these foundations. It is nonetheless also true (below, p120) that the incidence of Domesday churches shows a distinct correlation with the population and resources of the manors which they served. It is unlikely that the Norman church foundations are wholly unrelated to economic growth.

The townships discussed above are all typical of the estate geography of this part of Surrey: self-contained and independent. However small, Merstham, Chaldon, Thorncroft (Leatherhead) and Chelsham were manors in their own right, not members of larger manors. By the 10th and 11th centuries, if not long before, such places supported settled communities which combined stock-rearing with some arable farming. To colonise and exploit was in landowners' interests; the absence of any charter evidence for large-scale clearances near the centre of a demesne economy on the Surrey Downs suggests that by c1150 the main work was done. The few references to assarting in such contexts suggests a leisurely nibbling at the numerous pockets of residual woodland.[46] Large areas of Downland wood and scrub were, indeed, colonised during the 12th century; but these, by contrast, were usually outlying and subordinate parts of larger manors which had preserved something of the old economic balance.

The clearest illustration is Kingswood, the large royal wood-pasture attached to Ewell manor (above, p30). In 1158 Henry II granted Ewell with its members to the canons of Merton,[47] who soon began a parcelling-out of Kingswood to potential assarters. In 1177 × 80 the prior and convent granted to Luke son of William de la Dene and his heirs 42 acres 'quas Godwinus Prat avus eius per nos in nemore nostro de Kingeswude assartavit',[48] while another charter of the same priorate records the formal definition of new holdings:[49]

> Sciant presentes et futuri quod ego Robertus dictus prior ecclesie Sancte Marie de Meriton, et humilis eiusdem loci conventus, concessimus Turberto servienti nostro pro servicio suo totam terram illam que iacet ex utraque parte vallis inter duas silvas de Kingeswude, a terra scilicet quam Willelmus et Wulfricus de nobis tenent usque ad viam eiusdem nemoris que vocatur Stonestret; terram dicimus in latitudine habentem ad superius capud tres quarentenas cum quadem mara, ad inferius vero capud quarentenam et dimidiam, sicut ego Robertus prior et quidam fratrum nostrorum eam perambulavimus et divisimus presente et vidente halimoto de Ewelle.

Later Kingswood deeds refer back to 12th-century assarts: re-grants of 24 acres and 25 acres in 1198 and 1218, of thirteen acres in 1238 × 49, and of seventeen acres in 1249 × 52.[50] In 1189

Richard I acquitted the Priory of forest dues on 101 acres of assart in Ewell and its appurtenances.[51] The work was done by the hands of tenants, but the canons' initiative made it possible: Kingswood had been deliberately preserved as woodland pasture, and then equally deliberately assigned for clearance. While stock from the main manor was still being grazed there in the late 12th century (the grant to Turbert allows him 'communem pasturam peccoribus suis in nemore cum nostris dominicis peccoribus'), such extensive controlled clearance must indicate that this function was in decline.

A second case is the fragmented Winchester manor represented by Beddington, Carshalton and Bandon (above, pp25, 33; fig 11F).[52] In c 900 (when it was 'fully stocked', though only recently 'stripped bare by heathen men') it had seven bondsmen, 90 acres under crop and some 300 full-grown livestock, of which something under half were pigs and the rest sheep.[53] For a 70-hide manor this is scarcely an impressive list: it suggests both a generally light exploitation and a pastoral bias. There must therefore have been large areas of common waste, which presumably included the tract of Downland at the south ends of Beddington and Carshalton townships which was known by c1200 as 'la Woodcote'. One Luke de la Woodcote and his prolific family were established here by John's reign on substantial arable holdings. Apparently la Woodcote was already being exploited by 1189,[54] and 13th-century deeds reveal a small community of substantial peasants farming land in large measured-out blocks (below, p84). This evidence, less explicit than that for Kingswood, points to a similar development.

Banstead was another manor which rose southwards up the dip-slope to a Downland pasture, the *Suthemeresfelda* ascribed to it in late Anglo-Saxon charters.[55] Two late 12th-century deeds reveal arable holdings here similar to those at Kingswood and Woodcote: a compact virgate which 'iacet ante portam de Sumeresfeld',[56] and another, recently assessed, which was two-thirds assart land and one-third wood (below, p84). A lease of two virgates at *Suthmerefeld* in 1181 lists five plough-beasts, twenty sheep, eight pigs, and sixteen acres under crop.[57] This rare glimpse of a small Downland farm in operation demonstrates the continued importance of both open and woodland grazing, alongside an arable area of recent growth and perhaps of relatively recent origin.

These cases illustrate the vitality of 12th-century assarting on the Surrey Downs. Yet it was a short-lived phenomenon, one aspect of a phase of exceptionally rapid developments in the manorial economy. The much fuller documentation from the 13th century reveals no clearances comparable to Kingswood, Woodcote and *Suthmerefeld*; all these areas had served pastoral functions within a broader system which must have prompted their 10th-, 11th- and early 12th-century lords to preserve them. From the rather sudden abandonment of this policy arose peasant opportunities which were never to recur.

Colonisation of land: the Weald clay and Greensand

For few parts of England is settlement history so controversial as that of the Weald. J H Round's statement of 1899 that the Weald 'was still, at the time of the Conquest, a belt some twenty miles in width, of forest, not yet opened up, except in a few scattered spots, for human settlement',[58] sums up the traditional view. Current work is still far from a consensus. In pointing out that the ostensible Domesday picture of an empty waste may be highly misleading, Sawyer argues for extensive, well-established settlement in the eleventh-century Weald.[59] Yet in 1973 A R H Baker could still write of the Low Weald that 'we should envisage it in 1086 as a wooded area, with woods and swine pastures attached to settlements outside the Weald, and with only occasional centres of cultivation'.[60] A reappraisal of the Surrey evidence is timely, especially after the important studies of Kent by Witney and Everitt.[61] For present purposes the whole of Surrey south of the Downs will be considered together, comprising both the main expanse of Weald clay and the Greensand bordering it to north and west.

It is now a commonplace that the absence from Domesday Book of place-names on the clay and Greensand is misleading, reflecting an undeveloped estate structure, not necessarily a lack of settlement.[62] Within a large estate the data for many settlements, pasture tracts and denns might be lumped together under one name, as Maitland realised long ago in relation to Farnham:[63]

> We certainly must not draw the inference that there was but one vill in this tract. If the bishop is tenant in chief of the whole hundred and has become responsible for all the geld that is levied therefrom, there is no great reason why the surveyors should trouble themselves about the vills. Thus the simple *Episcopus tenet Ferneham* may dispose of some 25,000 acres of land.

This makes interpretation of the economic data in Domesday Book peculiarly difficult, for a high proportion of the area's resources will, from an uncritical mapping of manorial centres, appear to lie outside it. In a transhumance economy Domesday pannage renders are, of course, useless as a guide to the distribution of woodland. An analysis of selected manors which were unitary, well-defined and lay wholly on the clay and Greensand (tables 2, 3) suggests that the Wealden population was far from negligible, though distinctly sparser than in other regions. The surprisingly high ratio of teams to people perhaps reflects the need for more intensive ploughing on the heavy Wealden soils. Discrepancies between the manors chosen suggest that settlement density within the Surrey Weald was very variable, though with a slight increase from west to east: Farnham hundred has the sparsest listed population with only 3.4 individuals per 1,000 acres, whereas Nutfield, with 12.6 per 1,000 acres, was as heavily settled as the dip-slope manors.

The broad conclusion must be that by 1086 some form of settlement and agriculture existed right across the clay and Greensand belt. Was this already ancient, or was it recent and still quickly expanding? Were the peasant communities concentrated on the Greensand, or were they widely scattered through the former forest? Such questions cannot be answered from Domesday data alone.

The Weald was largely forest when the first Germanic settlers arrived, and so their descendants long described it: 'the great forest which we call Andred' is the term used by the Anglo-Saxon Chronicle under the year 893.[64] Those who would argue for significant Wealden settlement in the pagan Anglo-Saxon period must explain the paucity there of the etymological and archaeological evidence which is elsewhere so plentiful. The Surrey Weald has produced not a single cemetery, and the only excavated settlement site in the area lies on the Greensand.[65] Place-names containing -*hām* and -*ingas* are rare on the Greensand and completely absent from the clay.[66] The likelihood of major early religious centres at Thunderfield and Farnham (above, pp19–20, 25) is not evidence for clearance and settlement: the tendency of Germanic pagans to worship in remote woodland places implies rather the opposite.

The Farnham charter of 685 × 7 (above, p25) has been used to support arguments for very early colonisation of the Weald and its periphery. It certainly shows that this large multiple estate was already divided up into named and hidated tracts, though there is no evidence that the marginal areas bore anything but the light assessments characteristic of Wealden land (above, p22). Sawyer suggests that since the charter and Domesday Book both assess Farnham at 60 hides, its arable resources failed to increase significantly between the 680s and 1066.[67] But if the TRE hidations are indeed as ancient and formalised as is claimed above (p21), this argument falls. Economic growth would not have changed the Farnham assessment; it would simply have made it less and less real. But even if it could indeed be shown that this estate was extensively settled by the 680s, there would be no grounds for extrapolating to the adjoining Weald clay. Farnham hundred lies mainly on the Greensand, and the absence of a heavy forest cover may have encouraged early clearance. Small, widely dispersed settlements may have been established early, but then prevented from expanding by the limitations of the soil; in 1086 Farnham was in fact one of the least densely settled parts of the county. There can be no analogy here to prejudice evidence for the later development of the Weald; and such evidence, etymological, documentary and physical, is certainly not lacking.

Place-name elements suggesting clearance in and around the Weald tend to be localised. The element -ceart (a rough common with undergrowth) is confined to the greensands along the northern fringe of the Weald (fig 13); continuing a pattern equally conspicuous across Kent, these names may reflect an early advance towards the forest margins from settlements on the edge of the Downs.[68] It remains likely that this strip was always exploited more heavily than either the chalk or the clay – a view which the Merstham charter bounds (above, p46) tend to support.

Other elements record the piecemeal destruction of the forest from within, but marked vagaries in their distribution imply differences either in chronology or in local usage.[69] In the Kentish Weald, -denn, 'clearing at the heart of a swine-pasture', is the most common and characteristic primary clearance name; yet it is less common in Sussex[70] and hardly occurs at all in Surrey. This must reflect localised terminology, combined perhaps with the later survival of the denn system in the eastern Weald (below, p54): it is unquestionable that numerous Wealden settlements in Surrey began as swine-pastures. The nearest Surrey equivalent may be -falod (a 'fold' or enclosure for animals, not necessarily sheep),[71] which is virtually confined to the south of Godalming, Blackheath and Wotton hundreds (fig 13), spreading into the adjoining area of Sussex. Two further elements, -hyrst ('a wood or wooded eminence') and -ersc ('stubble-land or plough-land'),[72] concentrate in the same area as -falod (figs 12,13), though the first is very common and is found throughout Surrey.

It is possible that differences in the incidence of clearance place-names are sometimes chronological. Thus -leah, that most characteristic such element throughout Anglo-Saxon England,[73] does not show marked concentrations within Surrey, though it is notably absent from the north-east (fig 12). On its own it suggests assarting which was no more dynamic in the Weald than outside it. Possibly the other elements reflect later phases: -hyrst the first serious attack on the woodland, and -falod and -ersc an intensive, localised colonisation of the western Surrey Weald and adjoining Greensands. The -falod communities such as Alfold, Chiddingfold and Dunsfold, agrarian by the 12th century, must have been pastoral in origin, while -ersc (in Wonersh, Rydinghurst, etc) carries connotations of newly-broken arable. Whatever the date of these names, they evoke the rapid exploitation of large, under-developed tracts.

Written evidence for pre-Domesday settlement in the Surrey Weald is confined to the two easternmost hundreds, Reigate and Tandridge. Ealdorman Alfred's will (871 × 889) bequeaths six hides in Lingfield and one at Linkfield, Reigate.[74] The first of these properties is very likely identical with the six hides at Lingfield which Queen Æthelflaed (dead by 964) reputedly gave to Hyde Abbey with two hides at Langhurst.[75] Another Anglo-Saxon will, that of Brihtric and Ælfswith (973 × 987), mentions the manors of Titsey and Godstone and ten hides at Stratton.[76] Despite the evidence for extensive later assarting (below, pp53–4), south-eastern Surrey evidently contained significant arable areas by the late 9th and 10th centuries. But the absence of such data from the other Weald and Greensand hundreds is striking, and it is no coincidence that Reigate and Tandridge hundreds appear more populous than the rest of the Surrey Weald in 1086 (fig 14). Further west the very localised -falod and -ersc names, as well as some of the -hyrst names, suggest a contrasting pattern: an intensive primary exploitation in the very late Anglo-Saxon period.[77]

Church buildings (ch 5) support the view that the Surrey Weald, and especially its western half, was expanding fast in this period. Despite major difficulties in interpreting the evidence, a strong impression emerges that this area, like the Downland, was acquiring new churches exceptionally rapidly through the 11th and early 12th centuries (figs 32, 35). Four late Saxon buildings in the Godalming area were identical in size and proportion, suggesting that little churches were springing up in the area with a speed which even encouraged stereotyped planning (fig 31; below, p122). Three of these are on the clay, and one (Alfold) retains an early Norman font – surely a clear sign of established settlement. Further east, the Chertsey Abbey denn at Horley had probably not long possessed a church in 1086, while the steady expansion of Wealden communities over the next fifty years is reflected in a succession of church foundations which are almost certainly post-Domesday (below, p126).

Some parts of the Surrey Weald evolved as unitary tracts, others as complex archipelagos of manorial outliers. The second pattern predominates in the area straddling the 'Leatherhead' and 'Wallington' territories (above, p17). Here parish boundaries do not neatly reflect older units but sprawl untidily across the complex of intersecting rights, with numerous outliers remaining into the 19th century.[78] There are clear traces here of multiple denn systems analogous to those which survived later and more conspicuously in the Weald of Kent.[79] Most of the evidence is late and describes Wealden farms and fields owing rents to distant head manors, but occasional pre-Conquest sources establish the sequence of development from denn to dependent arable holding.

Horley and Newdigate parishes illustrate the process. Most of Horley was divided between estates immediately northwards on the Downs dip-slope. Part was attached to the Chertsey Abbey manor of Sutton, to which its church belonged;[80] two Chertsey forgeries which probably include genuine pre-Conquest material list Sutton with appurtenant woods and 'cum cubilibus porcorum' in Thunderfield, Horley.[81] But this can only have been a fraction of the modern parish. In 947 Merstham had dependencies at Petridgewood, Lake and Thunderfield, all in Horley,[82] while in 963 × 75 the 70-hide estate at Beddington had 'rura . . . cum silvis sibi pertinentibus' at *Cysledun*, Tandridge and Lake.[83] The last of these, at a more developed stage, presumably explains the 20s 'de redd' de Horle et de Lake' in a late 14th-century Beddington rental.[84] The Wealden swine-pastures attached to twenty hides at Cheam[85] were perhaps identical with the holdings at Duxhurst, Horley dependent on the archiepiscopal manor of Cheam in 1283/5.[86] Later evidence links other tenements with the manors of Banstead,[87] Walton-on-the-Hill and Woodmansterne, and even post-medieval Horley remained a bewilderingly complex patchwork of outliers.[88]

The Newdigate evidence, entirely post-Conquest, is otherwise very similar. Part of Newdigate was held of the Warenne lordship, and its chapel seems to have been subject either to Reigate or to Leigh.[89] But much of the parish, which remained a detached part of Copthorne hundred into modern times,[90] comprised dependencies of Leatherhead, Ashtead and Ewell. Two virgates in Newdigate can be traced through the Thorncroft (Leatherhead) court rolls and rentals from c1270 onwards,[91] their last remnant, a house and small curtilage, appearing on a manorial survey of 1629.[92] Fourteenth-century deeds suggest that land in Leatherhead and Mickleham was often held with land in Newdigate.[93] Sixteenth-century Ashtead rentals list property in Newdigate comprising a freehold called Breles, fields of ten acres called Ockeleys, a dwelling and pasture called Rolfes, a farm called Marshlands, a tenement called Horseland, a tenement called Beameland, and 60 acres of land.[94] Property in Newdigate called Kingsland is identifiable with a messuage and 60 acres there held as ancient demesne in 1291 and owing rent at the court of Ewell.[95] The pattern resembles Horley and clearly reflects a similar origin in multiple swine-pastures.

All the later medieval sources describe tenements and settled homesteads; the 10th-century sources, with one or two exceptions, describe denns and nothing else. The listing of individual denns in pre-Conquest charters implies that enclaves had already been created and equipped with shepherds' huts: this may be the sense of *rura cum silvis* in the Beddington charter of 963 × 75. Clearance proceeded within this late Anglo-Saxon framework. Systematic assarting is indicated by the blocks of long, linear farm units in central Horley, which contrast with the less regular and perhaps older topography of the riverside enclosures near the parish church.[96] This, like Kingswood, suggests a large area parcelled out *en bloc*, though the work may have been carried out rather earlier. Even without deliberate clearance, the innate destructiveness of grazing animals would have caused a rapid decline in the woodland cover once denns were established. Whatever the precise chronology, the implication of the charters is unmistakable; settlements which were pastoral and perhaps merely seasonal in the 10th century had become agrarian communities by the 13th. Again our attention focusses on the 11th and 12th centuries.

Exploitation of unitary estates in southern Surrey was curiously uneven. The advanced development of Lingfield and Godstone has already been noted,[97] and other manors were populous and well-stocked by 1086. Thus Nutfield rivals the dip-slope townships with 12.6 people and 4.6 teams per 1,000 acres (table 2), and numerous long-established settlement sites distributed through the parish have recently been identified.[98] While the largest concentrations were probably on the Greensand strip, it cannot be doubted that many of the inhabitants of these manors were scattered widely in small settlement nuclei. On the royal manor of Godalming and its church glebe,[99] the high proportion of bordars/cottars to villans (41 to 55) possibly reflects the presence of a nucleated bond settlement at the manorial centre on the Greensand (below, p75). On the other hand the adjoining manor of Witley, which was almost wholly on the Greensand, had 37 villans but only three cottars.[100] Here the Domesday categories seem to reflect the social and topographical antitheses evident in later agrarian arrangements (below, pp74–7). The bordars/cottars probably lived in servile nucleated communities with some form of common agriculture, whereas the villans, like their descendants, mostly farmed isolated severalties.

The two groups of manors which comprised Blackheath hundred (above, pp25–7) show a demographic contrast. Domesday Book lists total populations of 105 for the 'Gomshall half' (Gomshall, Shere, Albury and Chilworth) and 209 for the 'Bramley half' (Bramley, East Shalford and their members). Thus the 'Bramley half' supported twice the population of the 'Gomshall half', notwithstanding that it was much the same size geographically,[101] and it is interesting that the incidence of *-falod* names in the 'Bramley half' is considerably greater. That 11th-century Bramley had a population which was both scattered and relatively numerous is also suggested by the presence there of three churches by 1086 at the latest (below, pp116–19). Does this mean that the 'Gomshall half', which was largely royal demesne, had been organised in a conservative fashion which still reserved large Wealden pastures, whereas assarting had been encouraged throughout Bramley by Æthelnoth of Canterbury and his successor Odo of Bayeux? Again agrarian expansion reflects its tenurial context; with active seigneurial encouragement and the removal of restrictions it was bound to proceed more quickly.[102]

This becomes still clearer after the Conquest. Subinfeudation, which created self-contained tenurial units (above, p31), significantly increased the pace of Wealden exploitation. A knight's direct and undiluted interest in his new, under-developed holding must have been a powerful stimulus in transforming it from a scatter of denns into an independent settled community. The granting of a former woodland common as a knight's fee must imply that its economic development was either accomplished, proceeding or envisaged; conversely, its previous lack of identity suggests that such development was still relatively recent in the late 11th century. Emergent Wealden communities must often lie concealed in unspecific Domesday entries such as 'A knight holds two hides of this manor'. Two examples which can be identified are the adjacent parishes of Burstow and Horne, in origin the southern, wood-pasture halves of two long, strip-like estates (fig 11G).

Burstow's primary association with Blechingley, likely on topographical grounds, is undocumented; it first appears as a member of Wimbledon twenty miles away. Domesday Book either ignores it or subsumes it in the entry for the main manor, but by c1090 its lord, the archbishop, had farmed it for £8 pa to a family which quickly adopted the surname of de Burstow. The church, dedicated to a saint with Canterbury associations, was built or rebuilt at about this time (below, pp126, 147). This cannot mark the beginning of Burstow's development: the rent was substantial, and there is a hint (above, p20) of a meeting-place here well before the Conquest. But subinfeudation firmly divorced it from a federative estate economy and established it as the main demesne manor of a knightly family.[103]

In 1086 half a hide was held of Chivington manor by Roger d'Abernon, here as elsewhere a tenant of Richard fitz Gilbert.[104] This is identifiable with land in Horne, probably the farm later known as Bysshe Court. The church and an adjoining ditched homestead (fig 43) existed by c1160–80, by which date Horne seems to have been subinfeudated by the d'Abernons or their successors to a local family taking its name from the Bysshe area.[105]

The evolution of these two parishes was similar but not contemporaneous. A local family had immediate control of Burstow by c1090, when its development was well advanced. On Roger's half-hide in Horne Domesday Book only lists one plough and five bordars, the latter perhaps indicative in this case of newly-cleared land.[106] It was evidently some decades before the manor acquired a resident lord, and charter evidence (below, p84) shows that significant assarts were still being made there in the later 12th century. This contrast between adjoining tracts of similar soil cannot have a purely economic cause. Burstow's transhumance grazing functions may have been sacrificed earlier because it lay so far from the parent manor, making separation convenient. Horne was physically attached to Chivington, and here the ancient pattern may not have started to decay until the 1070s. In each case, the advent of a substantial resident family and a church heralds the coming of age of the young manor.[107]

By the late 11th century, then, farming communities existed throughout the Weald and Greensand areas of Surrey. Significant colonisation continued well beyond 1100; thus a Nutfield deed of c1180 × 1200 grants to John de Heddresham 'totum nemus illud in villa de Nutfeld' quod vocatur Widihorn . . . ita quod predictus Johannes vel heredes sui predictus nemus essartare poterunt, si voluerint, et ad proprios usus convertere'.[108] The Cheam denn of Duxhurst in Horley is stated to have been assarted in the time of Archbishop Hubert Walter (1193–1205),[109] and a group of Oxted deeds shows active if relatively small-scale assarting around 1200.[110] On the Greensands of Farnham and its townships, piecemeal clearance by means of tiny assart plots can be traced through the 13th and early 14th centuries on a scale comparable to that of the Windsor Forest area.[111]

But overall the pace was slackening. Private deeds often mention small assarts but rarely very large ones; the earliest specific evidence, from c1180 onwards, suggests that most new intakes could be fitted into a topographical framework and described by the landmarks of a settled countryside (below, p84). In this Surrey differs from parts of the Sussex Weald, where the 12th and 13th centuries have long been recognised as the great age of assarting. It has been shown that Battle Abbey was founded in an almost totally unexploited terrain, while Brandon's study of the East Sussex Weald shows large-scale clearance continuing through the 13th and even into the early 14th century.[112] By the 13th century a similar divergence existed between the two halves of Wealden Kent, the western resembling Surrey, and the eastern retaining the whole elaborate system of denns and droving.[113]

The Surrey Weald nonetheless retained many wooded areas (as indeed it does today), and many less tangible traces of its past. The characteristically large Wealden virgates, a result of generous assessment for obligations, reflect the high proportion of woodland and unexploited areas within their bounds (below, p74). Mid 12th-century grants of pannage rights prove that transhumance grazing still retained a certain importance.[114] In 13th-century legal sources we occasionally glimpse the last stages of a conflict of interests which must have begun when the first Wealden land came under the plough. 'Leftsilver' (a payment in recognition of the right to cultivate) reminds us that regular cropping of the denns began under sufferance, while the yearly 'sumerhus' which Shellwood tenants were still obliged to build in 1226 had originally been for the lord's use when he came to inspect the pannage in late summer.[115] Geological and geographical limitations made it impossible for Wealden settlement and agriculture ever to reach the stage of intensity found elsewhere in Surrey (below, p85), and large areas of the Wealden land surface were permanently fossilized as chase, park or warren.[116] In agreeing with most recent work that the traditional chronology is incorrect, we must not ignore the many sharp differences between the Weald and surrounding areas. By c1100 the Surrey Weald was extensively settled and farmed; but this settlement and farming was based on a relatively recent woodland past whose traces were everywhere apparent.

The development of settlement types

Throughout Surrey, nucleated and dispersed settlements existed side-by-side. Within the county, the pattern varied somewhat: strongly-marked lines of villages amid a scatter of farms characterised both the dip-slope townships (fig 15, and above, p45) and the Greensands of the Vale of Holmesdale under the scarp-slope, whereas Wealden and Downland villages were more tenuous and diffuse and the farmsteads around them more numerous. Conventional settlement history once provided an easy interpretation: the nucleated villages are characteristically Anglo-Saxon, founded by the first settlers or their near descendants; on the poorer soils farms proliferated later in response to medieval population growth.

In 1961 a study of the scarp-foot villages between Guildford and Reigate by E M Yates gave a new slant to this well-worn theme.[117] He pointed out that the pattern of farms and hamlets seems well-established when it first becomes clearly visible in the early 14th century, and must have resembled parts of Kent where a primary pattern of dispersed settlement has long been accepted. Some homesteads of the original colonisers (such as Chilworth, Tyting, Abinger, Dorking and Betchworth) developed as hamlets or villages because of their geographically favourable sites along the Pippbrook, Tillingbourne and Mole. Thus the villages respresent primary settlements but were not in origin large clusters of dwellings, while an equally early origin for other farms which failed to grow is not, by implication, excluded. Unfortunately Yates failed to cite early evidence in support of this hypothesis; and his suggestion of a 'Jutish' origin for dispersed settlement in Kent and Surrey Holmesdale has perhaps, at a time when ethnic interpretations are unfashionable, caused him to be taken less seriously than he deserves.

Since Yates wrote, a new orthodoxy has replaced the old, static view of English settlement.[118] Excavation and fieldwork have destroyed all credibility in the assumption that villages as we know them were established early in the Anglo-Saxon period. While many 5th- and 6th-century settlements have now been excavated, they tend to be haphazard clusters without alignment, streets or plot-boundaries; to quote P Rahtz, 'in no case is anything like a nucleated or "green" village plan in the medieval sense discernible'.[119] So far as the very meagre evidence goes, mid- to late-Saxon 'villages' were equally formless. On the other hand, investigations at Chalton, Hampshire have proved that existing valley-bottom villages were merely the final stage in a long sequence of development. Irregular clusters of dwellings on the summit of the Downs, themselves at least one stage removed from the primary, discrete settlements, were abandoned during c900–1000 in a general population shift; thus, in Fowler's words, 'Domesday Book represents developments which took place mainly in the previous two centuries and not the previous five'.[120] C C Taylor's analysis of field evidence has revealed 'polyfocal' villages, complex nucleations fusing together earlier discrete elements, and emphasises the mutable rather than the static elements in village topography.[121] Fieldwork in East Anglia has suggested that existing 'green' villages originated in a post-Conquest shift from mid- or late-Saxon settlement sites identified by scatters of pottery.[122]

This barrage of new evidence emphasises the danger of preconceptions. It is, for instance, common but wholly fallacious to assert that any particular village, as such, is mentioned in Domesday Book; still more so to date its creation by the *-hām* or *-ingas* name which it now bears. However stable the nomenclature and boundaries of a geographical area, the precise form of settlement within it is more likely to have changed many times over than to have remained static. For Surrey, it must be made clear from the outset that there is no archaeological evidence to establish a pre-Conquest origin for any later medieval village. The physical record is confined to small groups of huts at Farnham and Ham for the early Saxon period, and fragmentary occupation evidence at Wallington, Battersea, Weybridge and Croydon for the mid- to late-Saxon period;[123] none of this bears any significant relationship to the perceptible medieval pattern.

The three pre-Conquest *burhs* are a case apart.[124] The late 9th-century Burghal Hidage mentions Southwark (*Suðringa geweorce*) and Eashing (*Escingum*).[125] Eashing is now visible only as a flat, lightly fortified promontory overlooking the Wey;[126] it was quickly abandoned, probably during Æthelstan's reign and presumably for strategic reasons, in favour of Guildford.[127] A mint existed at Guildford by the 970s, and the basic street-plan and encircling ditch are probably pre-Conquest.[128] Southwark's importance was considerable, for it guarded the southern approach to London bridge and the city.[129] A mint existed under Æthelred, and the *burh* figured prominently in the Danish raids of the late 10th and early 11th centuries.[130] By the Conquest the functioning *burhs* must both have been commercial as well as military centres. In 1086 twelve rural manors scattered widely through eastern Surrey maintained town houses in Southwark, while Guildford contained a recorded 77 *hagae* and four *domus*, three of these properties being attached to the nearby manors of Bramley and Shalford.[131] To these two major centres of population we can probably add at least one other: with its religious importance and links with the dignity of the West Saxon crown (below, p99), Kingston upon Thames must surely have attracted significant settlement by the 11th century.[132] How much this was true of the other *villae regiae* and minster church centres we cannot even guess.

By 1300 Surrey contained the usual sprinkling of market towns, none large and some hardly distinct from the surrounding villages. Little can be added here to M O'Connell's survey,[133] but it is important to note that several of the small towns were founded or replanned during this period on a new, regular layout. Sometimes this may have happened before 1100: it is hard otherwise to explain the abandonment of the isolated minster at Godalming in favour of a smaller church in the present town centre (below, p99).[134] Farnham and Reigate stand out as planned towns of the mid 12th century, the former probably the work of Bishop Henry de Blois and the latter of the Earls Warenne.[135] Chertsey (fig 18) adjoins the precinct of the great Abbey; a fair was granted in 1133[136] and excavation of one burgage has demonstrated continuous occupation beginning in the 12th century.[137] The very regular plan of Haslemere may plausibly be associated with a market grant of 1221, following a reorganisation by the Bishop of Salisbury in which it superseded an earlier settlement at Pepperhams.[138]

Smaller centres become visible during the 13th century: Dorking with a market by 1241,[139] and Croydon with a market grant in 1276 and slightly later references to urban property.[140] Two interesting cases, suggesting seigneurial replanning influenced by tenurial factors, are Leatherhead and Blechingley (fig 17): both on Clare manors, both with pre-existing churches as their foci and both based on road-systems at estate boundaries. At Leatherhead, a track dividing the separately-held manors of Thorncroft and Pachenesham seems to have been re-aligned to allow

Fig 17   Suggested interpretation of the origins of Leatherhead and Blechingley towns. (Built-up frontages are represented schematically)

tenement plots to be laid out entirely on Pachenesham territory; thus a new crossroads and central market were superimposed on the ancient lane and field pattern. This had happened by the 1280s, and is possibly to be associated with the grant of a market and fair in 1248.[141] Blechingley town lies on a boundary between the Domesday estates of Blechingley and Chivington, united in the hands of Richard fitz Gilbert shortly before 1086. The quasi-urban layout, which almost certainly existed by 1225, is based on an earlier crossing of the north-south boundary road with the road between Reigate and Godstone, its funnel-shaped market place occupying the site of an arable croft mentioned in 1138 × 52.[142] As well as creating new foci for local trade, both acts of re-planning suggest internal changes: an economic coalescence of Thorncroft and Pachenesham on the one hand, and of Blechingley and Chivington on the other, around new main settlements. These deliberately planned 'market villages' blur the dividing-line between towns and purely rural settlements.

The pioneer work of B Roberts has shown the value of village plan analysis. Contrasts in settlement forms, identified by systematic classification, throw light on the dates and original functions of the settlements.[143] Villages were neither static nor the product of one period only; a full analysis of their development in Surrey would go beyond the scope of this study. Some broad similarities and differences are, however, relevant to early medieval conditions, and certain types of settlement may be closely associated with tenurial and agrarian changes. This discussion (based largely on the Ordnance Survey maps of the 1860s and 1870s) will follow Roberts's classification, in which the main factors are the degree of regularity, the form of layout, and the presence or absence of a green.[144]

Except in the Windsor Forest area, most rural nucleations north of the Downs were based on rows, their house-plots closely grouped without interlying wastes or greens. Few villages had rows flanking all four arms of a crossroads. Most are of the simplest possible linear form: two blocks of strip-plots facing each other across a single road, sometimes with back lanes defining the far ends of the crofts. These dip-slope and Thames Basin villages are generally more regular than the agglomerations elsewhere, a regularity which is particularly evident on manors held by Chertsey Abbey (fig 18). Chobham, Egham and Great Bookham are excellent illustrations of regular two-row plans, while Sutton, Epsom and Effingham, more changed in recent centuries, show traces of the same arrangement. Putney seems to have begun as an equally formal two-row village, its tofts with equal ten-perch frontages.[145]

On the Weald clay, the scarp slope, the Downs and the Windsor Forest sands, linear plans are the exception rather than the rule. Wealden villages tend to sprawl irregularly over a larger area, though they usually contain fewer house-plots. Several, such as Hambledon, Thursley and Charlwood, are 'polyfocal', not true nucleations so much as groups of individual farms scattered around the same complex of road intersections. At Cranleigh, Elstead and Westcott (the latter proclaimed both by its name and by its location as a satellite settlement of Dorking), three roads with straggling plots converge on a village green. Downland and Greensand villages, some of which have probably suffered depopulation, are either formless and very small (as at Buckland, Gatton and Woldingham) or again of irregular 'green' type (as at Coulsdon and Warlingham). Much the same can be said of virtually all the old settlements in the sandy hinterland of Godley and Woking hundreds; typical examples are Windlesham, a diffuse scatter of farms around a circuitous road-system, and the small, shapeless clusters at Bisley and Horsell.

The essential contrast is between the compact, regular villages in areas of heavy Domesday settlement, and the haphazard clusters in area of light, individualistic agriculture and large assarts. Villages in a strict social sense – the nuclei of communities unified by custom and obligation (cf below, p75) – were villages in a strict topographical sense also. The agglomerations of severalty homesteads in the heavily wooded areas appear more the products of accident or convenience, their formation perhaps spread over many generations. Thus the gradual expansion

Fig 18 Regular row-plan villages on manors of Chertsey Abbey. (Great Bookham after map of 1618 reproduced *PLDLHS* **2**. 10 (1966), 281–3; the rest after OS Surrey 25″ 1 edn sheets. Built-up frontages are represented schematically.)

of Windlesham from three housholds, still remembered locally in the early 13th century (below, p95), has left a permanent record in the untidy sprawl of the village.

Rural settlements in Surrey are more easily classified than dated. For the 'irregular' plans, indeed, there is no evidence beyond occasional charter references which show that some villages in the Weald and below the scarp-slope existed in the 13th century: Cranleigh by c1270, Ewhurst by 1295, and Alfold by 1305/6.[146] For Puttenham, unusually specific evidence is provided by a charter of c1200 × 20 granting a virgate 'ubi masagia sedent in exitu de Puteham';[147] the modern village, a simple double-row with irregular house-plots, is indeed on the edge of the parish. For the Kentish Weald, Witney has noted that most later villages are first mentioned as *ville*, *villate* or *ville borge* between the 1190s and c1300.[148] This is not conclusive evidence either that the settlements were nucleated or that they had only recently become so. However, his general conclusion that Wealden villages began to develop during the 12th century, when the balance had tipped firmly from pannage to cultivation, may well be right; it was, at least, at this time that Wealden communities acquired sufficient stability and internal cohesion to justify the name of *villata*. The presence of a church may often have provided a focus for nucleation; on the available evidence it is impossible to say whether 12th-century Wealden churches were built in villages, or whether they caused villages to grow around them (below, p135).

The orgins of the 'regular' villages are scarcely less obscure. Detailed work has shown that the orderly layout of Ewell was established in essentials by the 14th century, and many others certainly existed by this date, including most of the Chertsey Abbey villages.[149] Expansion is suggested by late 12th-century deeds which imply the recent development of open-field arable for house-plots: at Mitcham, land variously described as the acre 'quam Galfridus inedificavit' and the acre 'ubi Galfridus ad Crucem manet',[150] and at Wandsworth, half an acre 'que iacet apud Cleiputte super quam Sigar sedit'.[151] None of this throws much light on village origins. But a notable feature of a few townships, discussed further in ch 3, is the correspondence between regularly-apportioned subdivided holdings and regular groups of tofts. At Godalming each cotland was attached to a house-plot in a specific and identifiable area of the town (below, p75). The pattern is reminiscent of County Durham, where regular double-row villages, in existence by the end of the 12th century, have been identified as a product of precise, regular apportionment of holdings together with their obligations.[152]

Such repetitious symmetry must have had a once-for-all cause. In County Durham Roberts attributed it to reconstruction after the Harrying of the North. Discovery of the same pattern in southern England weakens this interpretation, but the case for deliberate re-planning is unimpaired. With mounting evidence for the systematic rearrangement of subdivided field-systems in the 11th and 12th centuries (below, ch 3), it becomes easy to envisage the apportionment of dwelling-plots as part of the same process. Even outside this agrarian context, the concept should not now be hard to accept. Historians have long been familiar with seigneurially planned towns, and no clear line divides small market centres like Leatherhead and Blechingley from surrounding villages. Economic growth and major tenurial changes were powerful stimuli for reorganisation, and both characterised the 150 years following the Conquest. The regular Chertsey Abbey villages (fig 18) may reflect a systematic policy, perhaps linked with the building of new churches on Abbey estates around the mid 12th century (below, p129). Chertsey itself is typical of the settlements which were appearing before monastery gates through much of Northern Europe, prompting Peter Abelard's complaint that Benedictines had 'built great villages on monastic sites, and thus they have returned to the world, or rather have brought the world to them'.[153] Might not the monks have extended the same activities to their rural manors?

Some nucleated settlements were still developing in the 13th century. References in the forest eyre rolls of 1256 and 1269 to 'purprestures with houses built on them' (below, p88) suggest a

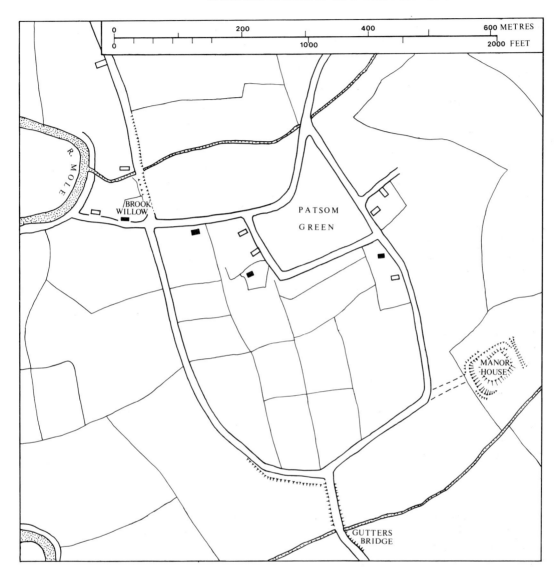

Fig 19   The remains of the deserted settlement at Pachenesham, Leatherhead. (After W J Blair, A small 14th-century cragloft house at Leatherhead, Surrey, *Antiq J* **61** (1981), 328–31, fig 2)

significant growth of housing in Godley and Woking hundreds. Even on the London clay, some landlords continued to augment their rents and services by answering the needs of a rising population. In 1252 × 92 Merton Priory granted to Simon de la Hoke an acre in Tolworth which his father had held in villeinage, 'ita quod idem Symon tenebit dictam acram et eam edificabit et inhabitabit'.[154] Patsom Green, nearly two miles north-west of Leatherhead on the sparsely settled clay, lies near the former site of Leatherhead minster church (above, p101). However, the settlement here may be associated with enclosures from the waste, realignment of roads and the rebuilding of the nearby manor-house, all carried out by Sir Eustace de Hacche in the 1280s and 1290.[155] In 1343 it supported ten villein households, and a survey of *c*1380 shows a series of regular ten-acre holdings in the process of amalgamation and engrossment.[156] These lay in compact blocks to the north of Gutter's Bridge, where a scatter of small houses around a green between the moated site and the river (fig 19) preserved traces of the former village into the post-medieval period. This typifies perfectly the 13th-century marginal settlement: established on poor soil with servile tenancies, it succumbed quickly and easily to post-plague depopulation.

When we turn to isolated farms, we find nothing which marks them out as secondary to the nucleated villages. The quantity of farm names collected in *The place-names of Surrey* leaves no doubt that they sprinkled the whole county by the 13th century, when the main sources appear. In this respect the area shown in fig 15 is typical.[157] In this chapter and the next, several examples are given of compact holdings which existed by the late 12th century and which probably contained their own homesteads. Where they can be equated with round units in the old hidage assessment (above, p28), they are likely to be very ancient indeed. Until field evidence of an entirely new kind is found, it may well be asked whether the Surrey villages are necessarily older than, or indeed as old as, the farms around them.

It has been argued (above, p46) that dispersed settlement existed on the Downs throughout the Anglo-Saxon period, and that 'Tunēl's *weorþ*' and 'the two *hamms*' mentioned in the 947 Merstham charter were homesteads identifiable with later farms. This approach can be extended to other areas by means of certain place-name elements compounded with personal names. One which provides an exceptional number of such compounds is -*weorþ*. Seven of these were near the Thames (Apers, Chadsworth, Ember, Lislesworth, Papercourt, Trottsworth, Wandsworth), two on the London clay (Batsworth, Tolworth), four on or near the Downs (Betchworth, Lollesworth, Tollsworth, Winkworth) and the remaining three in the Weald (Abinger, Edgeworth, Utworth).[158] The example of Tollsworth ('Tunēl's *weorþ*') and more general parallels would suggest that some at least of these widely scattered locations were actually the homesteads of the people whose names they bear.[159] Most names which reliably include -*hamm* are located in the Weald, including all cases compounded with personal names (Pepperhams, Prinkham, Sugham, Tedham);[160] here, as on the Downs (above, p46), the element must bear a broad meaning of 'field' or 'enclosure'. The elements -*hyrst* (fig 12), -*cumb* and -*denu* (valley) and -*dun* (hill)[161] all provide compounds with personal names distributed across the county. In 'Aylivehaw' and Edser,[162] respectively in dip-slope and Wealden parishes, -*hagan* recalls the 'Beaduweald's *hagan*' of the Merstham bounds.

There is no evidence that all these names are habitative rather than merely possessive. It seems highly likely, though, that some or many of them are; at least they suggest a pattern of severalty farming which would be most consistent with dispersed settlement. Furlong names in common fields (below, p77) sometimes tell the same tale, for they suggest that the field-systems in which they occur had evolved through the subdivision of compact holdings. There is a distinct suggestion here that dispersed farms were not merely as old as the nucleated villages, but may actually have preceded them.

Notwithstanding the evidence for compact holdings at this very early date, excavation has shown that many farm sites were first occupied in the late 12th and 13th centuries. This is true of the manor-houses at Pachenesham in Leatherhead, Alsted in Merstham and the king's manor-house in Guildford Park,[163] as well as the humbler moated sites at Hookwood in Charlwood and Lagham in Godstone,[164] and a fragmentary homestead near Tandridge.[165] It has become clear that most Surrey moats were dug after *c*1240, though at Pachenesham and Park Manor (following a pattern now familiar elsewhere) they surround sites already occupied for fifty years or more. This may also apply to the visible earthworks at Church Farm in Horne and Moat Farm in Tandridge, two Wealden homesteads mentioned in the mid 12th and early 13th centuries respectively (below, pp142, 157 and fig 43). The creation of the moat at Langshott Manor,

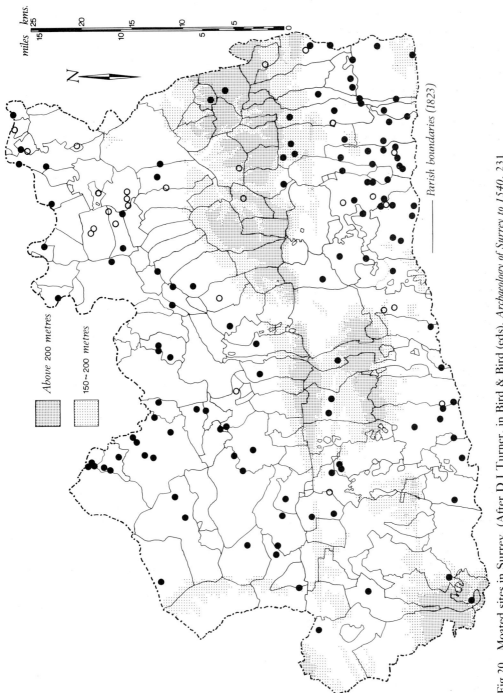

Fig 20 Moated sites in Surrey. (After D J Turner, in Bird & Bird (eds), *Archaeology of Surrey to 1540*, 231 Solid circle: certain. Open circle: doubtful)

Parish boundaries (1823)

Above 200 metres

150~200 metres

Horley is probably recorded in a deed of 1249 × 52 by which Merton Priory confirms to Robert de Horle 'quatuor acras terre extra nemus de Langset' in qua de novo edificavit'.[166]

High concentrations of moats are often interpreted as primary assart settlements reflecting late colonisation. This has been proved in the case of late 12th- and 13th-century peasant clearances in the Forest of Arden, and may be generally true over Midland and Eastern England.[167] The same explanation has recently been extended to the Surrey Weald,[168] implying more large assarts after c1180 than the present interpretation (above, pp53–5) admits. But this evidence must be treated cautiously. A distribution-map of known sites (fig 20) shows that, although there is indeed a distinct concentration in the eastern Weald, moats also occur widely scattered across Surrey, with the Downland forming the only notably blank area. The fact that so many exist in central and north-eastern Surrey, and on the old-settled strip of river-gravel beside the Thames near Chertsey, is sufficient evidence that numerous moats are compatible with a long-established human presence.

Moated sites were a fashion of the 13th and early 14th centuries: thus the presence of a moat suggests building activity during that period. But there need be no other difference between moated and unmoated homesteads beyond the fact that the former are easy to locate. Essentially, then, the sites known to us are those which their 13th-century owners chose to rebuild or refurbish. Frequently, or even normally, this may have involved a change of location. The desire for better conditions, or better drainage, may have caused the widespread abandonment of unmoated houses which are now lost, and the construction of new moated ones which are still conspicuous. The lack of known earlier sites is merely part of the general dearth of settlement evidence from Anglo-Saxon England as a whole: the earlier inhabitants of Surrey, both Wealden and non-Wealden, must have lived somewhere. The total number of farmsteads doubtless did increase, and the partition of large holdings in the Weald may have been an especially frequent cause. But the moated sites do not, on the whole, testify to the colonisation of marginal land; they are merely one element in a pattern of dispersed settlement which had been evolving over many centuries.

Conclusion

It is virtually impossible to prove *absence* of human activity in an undocumented period. This chapter has, however, described evidence for major expansion between the 10th and 13th centuries, and has argued that some important characteristics of medieval rural society appeared, or at any rate crystallised, during this period. Geographically, there are sharp contrasts in the time-scale: effective colonisation of the London Basin and dip-slope areas was achieved early in these centuries or before them, whereas clearance of the Windsor Forest area lagged far behind the rest of the county. The main general effect of the process was to reduce the heterogeneity of Surrey's geographical resources. It was far less a county of contrasting regions in 1334 than it had been in 1086: the Lay Subsidy quotas (table 4) suggest little local variation in the incidence of movable wealth. If we could look back another two centuries before Domesday Book, we would probably find the distinctions within Surrey as a whole between arable, grazing and pannage zones, between settled communities and their commons, drawn yet more strongly.

As such distinctions faded in the face of general growth, the structure of exploitation changed. The 'federative' system was decisively in decay when areas defined as pastures within its complex framework began to develop as independent communities. During the 11th and 12th centuries this was happening throughout Surrey: Penge in the London Basin, Windlesham in the Forest, Kingswood on the Downs and Horne in the Weald are essentially similar in their origins. Preserved intact for so long, they were colonised rapidly when their proprietors began to anticipate richer gains from the rents and services of settlers. The corollary of the larger 12th-century assarts is the decline of transhumance grazing. Diversity of functions within a large territory was the very essence of multi-vill organisation: the more the components developed their own internal economic balance, the more obsolete the old order became. But the importance of individual seigneurial policies makes it easier to understand why some manors grew so rapidly while their neighbours seem to have remained static.

A parallel consequence of growth was stronger organisation within the elements: these microcosms of the old federative systems required new foci. In this light the problems of village origins become less intractable, for a phase of rapid nucleation would be very consistent with the evolving estate structure and general context of agrarian growth. Changes in field layout, too, are now widely associated with the nucleation of previously scattered communities.[169] Thus the clear evidence for ancient dispersed settlement, combined with the presence of subdivided field-systems by at least the 12th century (below, pp74–7) might suggest that nucleated communities were developing in the later Anglo-Saxon period in a landscape of existing farms.

Surrey still lacks the field evidence available for other regions. Recent work in Northamptonshire places the dual process in the 8th century, when 'on the one hand the small early Saxon sites were deserted to form the present nucleated villages, and on the other the landscape was divided up on a massive scale into strips' (ie field furlongs).[170] In East Anglia, too, the post-Conquest villages seem to have replaced earlier nucleated settlements.[171] Whatever the chronology in Surrey of the evolutionary first stages (and they may well have been later than in either of these cases), the conditions existed by the Conquest for that rearrangement of settlements which we seem to detect in the 11th, 12th and 13th centuries. But this is only half the story: for further signs of organisation systematically imposed, we must turn from the villages to the fields which supported them.

3　Smallholdings in the Agrarian Landscape

Compared with Kent, East Anglia and the Midlands, Surrey field-systems have received little attention. H L Gray's account, published in 1915, remains the most substantial: Baker & Butlin, who devote only ten pages to Surrey and Sussex, comment that 'a detailed and comprehensive analysis of the field systems of Surrey has not yet been attempted'.[1] A stimulating paper by Bailey & Galbraith[2] which appeared in 1973 outlines some of the important issues, but no later work has pursued them further.

This gap will not be filled here. Field-systems are best analysed retrospectively, and a full discussion would involve extensive work on late- and post-medieval sources. The theme here is essentially the development of peasant smallholdings, though since these are inseparable from their agrarian context we must begin with an outline survey of medieval farming practice.

Agriculture in medieval Surrey

Much of Surrey was not ideally suited to arable farming. Southwards lay the heavy clay of the Low Weald; northwards the almost equally uninviting London Clay and the infertile sands of the Windsor Forest area. The land between was more promising: the Greensands of the Vale of Holmesdale, and the varied, often relatively fertile beds on the slopes of the Downs.[3] The major contrast in the organisation of farming was between Wealden and extra-Wealden Surrey, for only the latter provides evidence for common fields. The prevalence of pre-18th-century inclosure makes it much harder in Surrey than in the Midland counties to gain a clear picture of medieval open-field farming. The earliest evidence mainly takes the form of references in deeds and fines to land *in campo de X* or *in communi campo de X*, or merely to holdings dispersed in acre or half-acre strips. Fig 21 plots all available references to subdivided fields from these and later sources.[4]

The coverage is sufficiently thorough to show that subdivided fields occured in some form in virtually every non-Wealden parish. In the Surrey Weald, as in Kent, agriculture never evolved beyond the stage of severalty farms and inclosures.[5] Oxted, which contained Downland grazing in the north, inclosed demesne fields on the best land of the scarp slope, and a mixture of woodland, pasture and arable severalties occupying the southern two-thirds of the parish, typifies the farming landscape of Wealden Surrey.[6] Even in non-Wealden Surrey common fields were small, often occupying less than half the total parish arable and set amid compact holdings. By the 13th century at least, most demesnes lay apart in blocks rather than intermixed with tenants' strips.[7] Parishes north and south of the Downs display a recurring pattern in which the common subdivided field lay on the best ground (the Reading and Thanet beds in the former case and the Lower Greensand beds in the latter) between chalk downs with sheep-runs on one side and heavier inclosed arable on the other. Thus a continuous band of subdivided land followed the dip-slope through the central Surrey townships, stamping even such small sub-parochial units as Waddon in Croydon (fig 22) with the same topographical symmetry.[8] It was common here for a nucleated settlement on the fertile strip to lie between a small North Field, in which subdivided furlongs and inclosures lay intermixed, and a much larger subdivided South Field. Thirteenth-century deeds for Bandon in Beddington mention a handful of plots, some open and some inclosed, in the 'north part' or 'north field' of the vill,[9] and a far bigger number of strips in numerous named furlongs in the 'south field'.[10] This was therefore a mere topographical distinction between land on the north side of the village and land on the south, not a division of

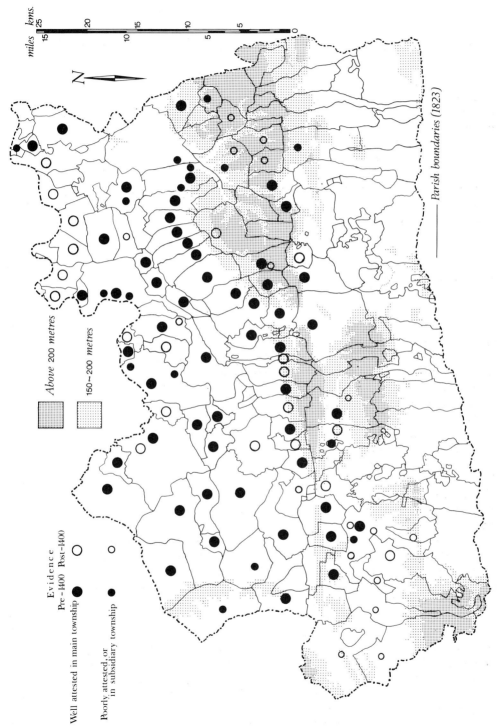

Fig 21 Evidence for subdivided fields in Surrey

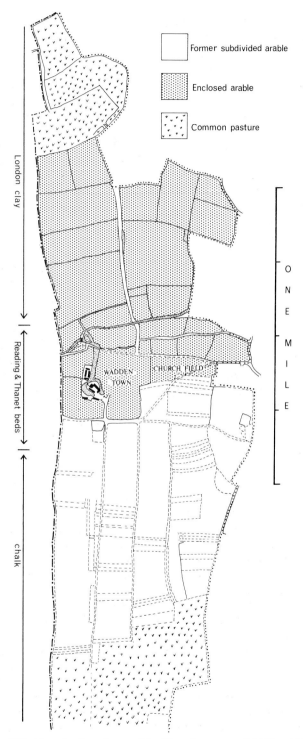

Fig 22   The township of Waddon, in Croydon parish. (Based on map of 1692 published to accompany L Thornhill, *A Croydon backcloth: some little-known estate maps in Lambeth Palace Library*.)

the subdivided arable into equal halves. Sometimes, as at Leatherhead and Waddon (fig 22) the 'north part' contained no subdivided land, in which case strips in the main 'south field' were located by the simple designation *in communi campo*.[11]

Elsewhere the pattern is more varied. In the early modern period Mickleham had subdivided land in East Field, West Field and Greenham Field, Wandsworth in Bridge Field, North Field and South Field, and Chobham in Burifield, Beanlonde, Gretestene and Lytilstene.[12] Subsidiary townships within a large parish sometimes had their own fields. Godalming contained the common fields of Godalming, Tuesley, Hurtmore, Farncombe and Shackleford;[13] Kingston its own common arable[14] together with the West Field of Surbiton[15] and the North and East Fields of Norbiton.[16] Numerous medieval deeds assign strips to named locations of uncertain status, and it is often hard to decide how many 'fields' a particular township contained.

Did these 'fields', like their Midland counterparts, represent organised cropping units? Struck by their heterogeneity and the lack of evidence for any orderly system, Gray concluded that they did not: 'the fields were numerous, were curiously named, sometimes being called furlongs, and the distribution of the acres of a holding among them was irregular'. He proposed a flexible 'multi-field' cropping system, based essentially on the furlong, in which the larger 'fields' containing the furlongs were ill-defined and unimportant.[17] This view was challenged in 1927 by H E Malden, who argued that inquisitions post mortem describing three-course rotations on demesnes at Paddington (Abinger) and Dorking in 1349/50, and the explicit statements of 18th-century agriculturalists, were conclusive evidence that the three-field system had once prevailed in Surrey.[18] But the detailed work of Bailey & Galbraith on Epsom, Ewell, Ashtead and Putney tends wholly to support Gray: cultivation was based on furlongs, among which holdings were distributed at random, and though township 'fields' existed 'the nomenclature appears vague, and descriptive rather than functional'.[19]

The weakness of Malden's case is his assumption, for a region where demesnes were generally compact, that their cropping patterns extended to whole townships. Numerous examples of regular demesne rotations could be given. The Christ Church demesnes of Cheam, Charlwood and Merstham had a two-course shift in 1211;[20] a century later the Bishop of Winchester practised a three-course rotation at Farnham on large inclosed fields called Westfield, Wynyerde and Langeham, and other Surrey landowners followed this pattern.[21] Free from interdependence with tenant holdings, demesnes could be cultivated by whatever method their proprietors favoured or circumstances allowed. Inquisitions post mortem for the Dorking area show that the intensity of demesne cultivation varied with the quality of the soil from 20% to 40% under crop at any one time.[22] The Southwark Priory demesne at Banstead is a clear case of an individually-created cropping system: by the 1280s ten blocks of land acquired from various grantors had been grouped as three 'seasons' of 58, 65 and 51 acres.[23] In a county of variable soils, lords selected rotations without reference to any wider scheme. There is certainly no hint in the deeds that tenants' strips were evenly divided between two or three fields: generally they were dispersed at random through a multiplicity of fields and furlongs. Most Surrey deeds locate open-field parcels by furlong names alone, and to the clerks who wrote them the furlong was clearly the dominant unit.

Absence of two or three distinct common fields is not, however, incompatible with two- or three-course rotations. H S A Fox has argued that it was not rotations but 'a desire to set aside each year a new compact half or third of the land for fallow grazing' which demanded a regular field layout. 'Many . . . examples could be cited . . . of three-course rotations which operated without the existence of three fields. . . . Townships with systems of this kind had assigned each of their many fields and furlongs to a particular season in order to facilitate cropping, but had not experienced the need to introduce comprehensive fallowing arrangements'.[24] It can only be said that Surrey has hitherto produced no evidence for 'seasons' organised by township custom. This is far from being proof that they never existed, but freedom of choice is suggested by private agreements which stipulate unconventional cropping patterns. Thus a Bandon deed of *c*1260 demises two acres, dispersed in three plots, which are to be sown yearly with 1 acre of barley, ½ acre of wheat and ½ acre of peas or vetch,[25] presumably a holding on which high fertility combined with intensive manuring had temporarily eliminated fallow. There are still no solid grounds for disputing that the cropping patterns of Surrey common fields were essentially flexible and free from customary control.

By contrast, there is good evidence for control of common fallow grazing. This was maintained and enforced into the post-medieval period even on manors, such as Ashtead,[26] which lacked all trace of common cropping. A Malden byelaw of 1281 declares 'quod campus A de Chelesham, sicut alie terre de villata, quolibet tertio anno debet jacere ad warectum et ad communam de antiquo consuetudine, nec debet herchiare in tertio anno nisi per licentiam domini'.[27] Since this rule applied to an individual tenant's field, it implies that compact as well as subdivided holdings were subject to triennial commoning; equally, there may be a suggestion here that A de Chelesham's *campus* had only recently been inclosed from the open fields. Nothing is said about predetermined cropping, which is positively unlikely on a compact holding, and it may be that the individual farmer was regulated in nothing more than the choice of his fallow year. On subdivided land such comprehensive pasture courses could be made compatible with flexible rotations by folding and tethering animals, as at Ashtead in 1575, 'in such sorte that they hurte not their neighbours corne'.[28] Nonetheless, the impression of controlled fallow without controlled cropping deserves further study.

Even if regulated fallow grazing on the lines of the Malden byelaw was common in medieval Surrey, it is doubtful if it often transcended estate boundaries. In some multi-manor townships, even at a much later date, such rights seem to have been apportioned at manor rather than at township level.[29] Even at Malden, grazing of the stubble did not extend to the whole township: in 1293 the lord of the main manor found it necessary to make a reciprocal agreement with a local freeholder, Adam le Cros, which gained for his customary tenants free common in Adam's field called Crosesdon in the open time after harvest.[30] Disputes between neighbours concerning pasture rights over arable[31] show that in Surrey, as in Kent, the commoning of inclosed land was often a purely private matter to be negotiated between individuals.[32]

The importance of fallow and stubble grazing was outweighed by that of the plentiful common wastes. There is little Surrey evidence for the intercommoning of large forest areas by the tenants of several manors, still widespread at this date in Kent and Sussex,[33] but this is a case where absence of evidence must be misleading. Although the fact could scarcely be deduced from medieval sources alone, the Weald certainly retained extensive tracts of waste:[34] where common grazing was so abundant, it was rarely contentious and so failed to enter the written record.

Outside the Weald, waste dwindled and boundaries and rights were defined with corresponding precision. Neighbouring lords quarrelled over interlying commons which their predecessors had shared in peace. For instance, the contiguous commons of Beddington and Mitcham were used by tenants of Beddington, Bandon, Wallington and Mitcham until Easter 1240, when armed men from the first three vills expelled the Mitcham men from Beddington common and impounded their beasts. The lords of Beddington defended their action by claiming that Mitcham could have no common there because it belonged to a different barony, the boundary being clearly marked by an ancient ditch.[35]

But if wastes were defined more closely during the 13th century, it was in terms of lordship rather than of community. However economically unified a township might appear, each manor within it tended to have its distinct common. This was the case at Leatherhead, a parish which extends northwards onto clay and southwards onto chalk. A memorandum of *c*1610 defines these areas respectively as 'a lower common for greate cattell in which every lord's soyle is bounded and knowen', and an 'upper common' for sheep called Leatherhead Downs where all the lords and their tenants could intercommon without stint.[36] The 'lower common' had been divided into blocks held by the lords of Thorncroft, Pachenesham Magna and Pachenesham Parva since at least the 14th century,[37] and if the Downs were free for all by c1610 they had not always been so; in c1300 the area called le Kingesdone was the exclusive right of three Leatherhead freeholders to whom their Mickleham neighbours paid a fine for its use.[38] Not far away, Fetcham Downs were divided up between the d'Abernons and their neighbours by a series of hedges and ditches.[39] These severally-owned commons emphasise the continued independence of small Surrey manors and the failure of township organisation to transcend it.

Rights in the manorial waste were often stinted, generally being apportioned by the virgate on a *pro rata* basis.[40] As early as c1140 a hide at Oxshott, a member of Stoke D'Abernon, carried with it the right to graze 120 sheep in the common forinsec pasture of Stoke, and a century later another Oxshott holding had grazing for six 'animals' and 60 sheep in the same pasture; possibly we see here a fixed allowance of one sheep per acre in the fiscal hide.[41] In the 13th century the tenants of Oxenford farm in Witley manor, like the other men of Witley, were allowed as many animals in the common pasture of Witley during summer as they wintered on their own holding.[42] Sometimes commoners' beasts were unstinted except for a prohibition of destructive breeds.[43] In a region where swine-rearing had been so important it is no surprise to find temporary restrictions during the pannage months; thus in the late 13th century the canons of Southwark had free common in the Earl of Warenne's wood at Reigate except in the swine-mast season, when they were allowed twelve pigs there free of pannage.[44] A final non-arable resource, meadow, often remained a tenemental appurtenance rather than property in its own right, being 'doled' out to virgated holdings by annual lot as late as the 13th and early 14th centuries.[45] Its character may, however, have been changing, for in other townships deeds of similar date grant individual pieces of meadow located by fixed boundary-points.[46]

The agriculture of 13th-century Surrey was not without its orderly features, but it lacked the integrated regulation of cropping, fallow and grazing, organised at township level, which marks the fully-developed common field system. To explain its idiosyncratic development involves further study of its landholding basis. The rest of this chapter will consider the evolution of individual holdings, and the influence of this evolution on the agrarian landscape and its institutions.

The nature of the Surrey virgate

Smallholdings throughout Surrey were assessed by the virgate (*virgata*). One exception is a late 13th-century Ewell customal listing thirteen-acre *iugera*, a Kentish term which has caused speculation.[47] In fact these holdings resembled the dispersed virgates of surrounding manors rather than the compact yokes of Kent, and there is probably nothing more significant here than the vagary of an individual clerk. Otherwise the virgate was universal except on the handful of manors which contained distinct groups of smaller service holdings (below, p75).

Manorial clerks often assumed an acreage-equivalence for virgates within one township. In the Ewell customal which lists a long series of *iugera* but only gives the acreage of the first, it is implicit that all the others are identical. An inquisition of 1344 listing various Headley virgates states confidently that 'continet quelibet virgata 16 acras', while at Petersham in 1266 the annual maintenance of a chaplain was distributed among the tenants at a rate of one bushel of rye per ten-acre virgate.[48] Table 6 summarises virgate sizes on a sample of manors where the evidence points to this regular correspondence between virgates and acres.

An interesting fact here is that some acreages tend both to recur and to be exactly half the size

TABLE 6   Virgate sizes on manors with a regular acreage-equivalence for the subdivided virgate

Manor	Virgate Size (acres)	Source
Lambeth	32?	Cant Cath Lib, MS E24, ff147ᵛ–8
Farleigh	32	See p80
Leatherhead (Thorncroft)	26	See pp73, 79–80
Cheam	21	Cant Cath Lib, MS E24, f155ᵛ
Claygate	20	Harvey, *Westminster Abbey*, 206n
Morden	20	Harvey, *Westminster Abbey*, 208
Pyrford	20	Harvey, *Westminster Abbey*, 208
Headley	16	See p71
Malden	16	MM, 4782
Merrow	16	See p80
Battersea	15	Harvey, *Westminster Abbey*, 434
Wandsworth	15	Harvey, *Westminster Abbey*, 434
Cobham	15	Chertsey Abstract, No 121
Putney	15	Bailey & Galbraith, Field systems, 80
Ewell	13	See p71
Leatherhead (Pachenesham Parva)	13	See p73, 79–80
Petersham	10	See p71

Notes: (a) Acreages underlined are deduced from sources which only describe virgates in fractions.

(b) Except at Putney (late- and post-medieval court rolls), all the acreages derive from 13th- and 14th-century manorial records.

of other recurring acreages. Thus two manors had virgates of 32 acres and three of sixteen; one had virgates of 26 acres and two of thirteen; and three had virgates of twenty acres and one of ten. The appearance of the same acreage units within the same limited area presumably reflects patterns of seigneurial practice or local custom pertaining when the holdings were first apportioned. But why are there so many cases of virgates exactly half the size of those on other manors? That we are not contrasting different basic units, but merely comparing the half with the whole or the whole with the double, is confirmed by comparing the virgates on two Leatherhead manors, for here we know that Pachenesham Parva had been formed out of Thorncroft in *c*1170.[49] Thus the 26-acre virgates of Thorncroft and the thirteen-acre virgates of Pachenesham Parva recorded in *c*1300 had originally formed one series of tenements; subsequently the unit of assessment was either doubled on one manor or halved on the other. At Thorncroft, thirteen-acre half-virgates predominated heavily when the tenemental structure first appears, and we should not automatically assume that a large unit had been halved rather than vice versa. At Petersham, where tenants had been quite explicitly assessed in 1266 on ten-acre virgates (above, p71), a court roll of 1328 describes such a holding as a half-virgate.[50] Perhaps these instances simply show that we should not take terminology too seriously: whether the scribe on a particular manor described the predominant assessed holdings as virgates, half-virgates or *iugera* may simply reflect his own training or an *ad hoc* administrative decision. Whatever we call these units of assessment, the important fact is their persistent regularity.

But are we entitled to assume that this regularity is real, not a fiscal convention? It has recently been claimed that 'if there is any sign of uniform acreage between separate holdings, either singly or in simple combination, the acres are almost certainly fiscal ones, for no village community was so egalitarian as to give its members precisely the same number of arable strips or area of land'.[51] For Surrey, this argument is effectively dismissed by the detailed descriptions of tenant holdings at Thorncroft and Pachenesham Parva. On these manors, every 'half-size' unit which can be itemised as common-field strips proves to have contained almost exactly 13 customary acres, and one 'full-size' holding proves to have contained 26 (table 7). The point can be sufficiently demonstrated by summarising three examples as recorded in c1300:

(a)   5 acres on Stangrene, 1 acre at Stretende, 1 acre called Longeker, $\frac{1}{4}$ acre called Verthe-halveker, 1 acre called la Putacre, 1 acre called le Stretaker, 2 acres at la Clayhelve, 1 acre at la Valtegh, 1 acre meadow in Southmed, a messuage at Cherlane between tenements of Gilbert le Glover and William Glover. [Total: messuage, $13\frac{1}{4}$ acres][52]

(b)   Capital messuage with curtilage and parcel of la Lynche, 1 acre at Longfforlonge, 2 acres at la Lymhost, 1 acre next land of Maud Gavelestre, 3 *particuli* at Jonescrouch, 1 acre at Lomlesheghe, 1 acre at Hardon, $\frac{1}{2}$ acre at Wellonde, 1 acre at Widegate next Brockhole, 1 acre at Tentes, $1\frac{1}{2}$ acres at Pinchunescrouch against Hardone, a meadow called Horsecroft, $\frac{1}{2}$ acre at Stoneshende. (Stated total: messuage, 13 acres, 1 rood.)[53]

(c)   Messuage, 2 acres at Lyndene, 3 acres at la Wydegate, 1 acre at Someslane, $\frac{1}{2}$ acre abutting on le Kenchescrofte, $\frac{1}{2}$ acre on Lombesheghene, $\frac{1}{2}$ acre 1 rood on Hardone, 1 acre at Plumlye, 1 acre on la Falteghe, 1 acre in la Grenedene, 1 acre on la Falteghe next la Mulleweye, 1 acre next la Dondene. [Total: messuage, $12\frac{1}{2}$ acres, 1 rood.][54]

It is obvious that these were not formalised fiscal units, but bundles of actual strips which their tenants could add up to a total of c13 acres. Thorncroft and Pachenesham Parva are exceptional in the quality of available evidence, but the pattern thus revealed can scarcely have been peculiar to these manors. Whenever Surrey deeds describe open-field virgates acre-by-acre they appear, though less clearly, to reflect a structure of equal units.

Yet not all Surrey virgates were of this regular kind, and even the townships which contained them also had others of a very different character. In areas of extensive post-Conquest clearance the range of virgate sizes is much wider, extending in the Weald as high as 80 acres (below, p74). Even in some non-Wealden manors the virgates were uneven, or only partly standardised.[55] Thus a Banstead customal of 1325 lists virgates of almost every possible size between ten and 48 acres, though the largest single group (some 35% of holdings) are half-virgates which, from the absence of any stated acreages, are perhaps to be regarded as uniform.[56] This contrast, between a conspicuous standardisation and a conspicuous lack of it, can only mean that *virgata* is a single word describing different things.

For further light we may return to Thorncroft, where virgated holdings were to be found not only in the subdivided common field but also on the rising dip-slope of the Downs to the south-east. Four of these, all identifiable with virgates and half-virgates in a rental of c1275, can be traced continuously through the manorial records and are plotted in fig 16.[57] The acreages of these holdings were disparate and unrelated to the notional assessment in virgates. Richard de Hameldune's half-virgate was roughly equal in size to Nicholas Brun's virgate; both were smaller than the virgate held by Giles de la Boxe and more than three times larger than that held by William Herbert. Clearly a virgate on this manor could be either an equal share in the common field, or a compact farm of indeterminate size but within the same system of assessment. In less detailed records the distinction would not necessarily be apparent, and it is almost certainly in this sense that the Banstead customal should be read: the hard core of unspecified virgates comprised common-field land, while those of variant acreages were unitary farms. In this very parish compact Downland virgates were still being formed in the late 12th century (below, p84).[58]

The nature of the sources encourages a definition of virgates as 'typical peasant farms'. It is perhaps more helpful to think of them, as contemporaries assuredly did, primarily as units of obligation, overlying and moulded around customary tenemental divisions rather than identical with them. Some individual compact virgates may genuinely have been quarter-shares of primary assessed hides: hence, perhaps, the startling disparity in their sizes. But the virgatal systems of the manorial records were still fluid and evolving in 1200. They included all holdings, compact and discrete, old and relatively new; while their main purpose was for defining rents and services which only crystallised in the 12th century.[59] At some point the structure must have been imposed comprehensively, and thereafter extended to new holdings on an *ad hoc* basis. What mattered to the lord was not the topography of his tenants' holdings but the fact that they owed him defined obligations which might be exacted at a rate of so much per virgate.[60]

Virgates in the Weald were compact or near-compact, often abnormally large, various in size and liable to fragment, as at Leigh and Charlwood in 1325 where customary holdings included 60-acre virgates and ferlings of twenty acres.[61] We should not deduce that Wealden peasants were necessarily more prosperous, but rather that, in an under-developed terrain, units of obligation were generously defined at the outset. Battle Abbey pursued a similar policy on its developing Sussex estate by establishing fiscal hides of eight virgates each, later rearranged as conventional four-virgate hides as more land came under the plough.[62] This explains the prevalance of ferlings in the 13th-century Surrey Weald: the larger and more primitive the original virgate, the greater the likelihood that a half or quarter fraction would quickly take its place as the normal assessed unit.

The assessment of new holdings eventually ceased. At the end of the 12th century in Surrey as a whole, and as late as *c*1220 in parts of the Surrey Weald, parcels of old and new land were still being grouped together as virgates and half-virgates (below, p84).[63] But the fossilization of the virgate, even in the Weald, soon becomes apparent in sources which contrast a core of assessed customary land with free assarts or purprestures. Thus an early 13th-century Alfold deed grants 'unam fernlingatam terre . . . quam Reginaldus Turtel aliquando tenuit in vilenagio exceptis purpresturis', while a Farnham man died in 1261 holding two virgates 'de antiqua tenura' for rents and services and 32 acres 'de nova terra' for rents only.[64] This echoes the type of firm chronological distinction between assessed and non-assessed land which seems to be a particular feature of Sussex Wealden manors.[65]

This discussion has made it clear that Surrey virgates will not conform to any simple definition. A neat model, contrasting assessed land held and farmed in one way with non-assessed land held and farmed in another, is inappropriate here. The virgate was a unit not of topography but of seigneurial assessment, representing the size and form of one man's holding at the moment when the individual assessment was imposed. The virgatal structure preserved the memory of various tenemental types which had existed between the late Saxon and Angevin periods; the historian can use this structure to go behind it, tracing the original form and purpose of institutions which had often already become archaic when manorial clerks first described them.

The early development of subdivided holdings

We have already seen that the virgatal structure of many, perhaps most open-field parishes had a core of uniform subdivided holdings. Established within a narrow range of predetermined sizes, they stand out as something separate and distinct from the irregular holdings, both virgated and non-virgated, which may often have outnumbered them. By c1300 they were no more than the vanishing relics of an older pattern; how are we to interpret these signs of an archaic order?

It has recently been argued that this kind of regularity is more to be associated with unfree communities than with free ones: bondsmen were more subject to seigneurial organisation and control, and the imposition of lordship created a greater need for tenants to act together as a common body.[66] This gives a new twist to the familiar contrast between unfree nucleated communities with their common fields, and free peasants farming their holdings in severalty from isolated farmsteads. In Surrey, where lordship was light and the pressures of an active land-market strong, such distinctions had often disappeared by the age of specific records. But on a few manors, notably components of large estates in stable ownership, change had been slower and explicit evidence has survived of a more orderly, hierarchical structure.

In 1283–5 surveys were made of Cheam, Croydon and Wimbledon, ancient manors of the see of Canterbury, which divide the customary holdings into categories.[67] At Cheam fourteen cotmen held 35 acres comprising seven 5-acre cotlands; they lived in a separate hamlet and were responsible for heavier services than the other customary tenants, who had regular 21-acre holdings. At Wimbledon the tenants were divided into three groups: 60 customers holding 25 hides, twenty rodlanders with twelve and a quarter hides, and $24\frac{1}{2}$ cotmen with two hides. Croydon had 38 'tenants', thirteen rodlanders and three cotmen; the last, who held five-acre cotlands like their counterparts at Cheam, included among their services the exceptional duty of guarding criminals in gaol. Another case is Godalming, at the opposite end of the county. Here Domesday Book lists twelve cottars on the church glebe, and from a customal of the rectory manor in c1340 a series of twelve equal holdings, each comprising a messuage and twelve acres in the common fields, may be reconstructed.[68] On the main royal manor fourteen cotland tenements seem to have comprised similar subdivided twelve-acre holdings, and the house-plots of these lay together along one street identifiable in the modern town of Godalming.[69] In addition to more normal services, these tenants were responsible for hanging criminals. In the context of an ancient royal head manor this is just such an office as we might expect to find particularly associated with demesne servants, and it is interesting that on the Sussex 'multiple estate' of South Malling ten *bovarii*, six of whose tenements were 'in the middle of the demesne', owed a similar service.[70]

These cases suggest a primary relationship between regular subdivided holdings, dwelling-sites in a nucleated settlement and specific seigneurial demands. The third factor only survived clearly where heavy or exceptional services had preserved to a special group of tenements their distinct identity, but there are hints here of a hierarchical structure in which all subdivided holdings of equal size had once carried equal obligations and status. Sometimes, as in the case of the Ewell *iugera*, the tenants of all standardised holdings remained unfree and shared a core of common services,[71] while at Reigate reeve service was obligatory on tenants of virgates and half-virgates, and beadle service on tenants of farthinglands and cotlands, as late as the 16th century.[72] The association of nucleated settlements with regular subdivided landholding survived more widely; whenever evidence is available, such tenants lived not in isolation but on village toft sites.[73] All open fields had their villages, and most villages, except the attenuated and late-formed Wealden hamlets, had their open fields.

A deliberate process of shareholding, by which each tenant was allotted an equal fraction of the resources of the township, has often been proposed as the basis of organised common fields in Britain.[74] In their earliest visible form, subdivided holdings in Surrey fit this model well: only the hypothesis that the strips had once been distributed among a group of tenants in predetermined shares can explain their regularity. It is also clear that each share had once been assigned a proportional interest in non-arable resources (above, p71). These Surrey holdings are dissimilar both from the compact *iugum* of Kent[75] and from the classic Midland virgate with its symmetrically-disposed strips. The East Anglian *eriung* comes closer. Like its Surrey counterpart it frequently contained twelve or 24 acres; generally it lay in discrete though not widely scattered parcels,[76] and this lack of wide dispersion is also apparent in Surrey.[77] In their size, form and tendency to occur in whole- and half-size units, the Surrey virgate and the East Anglian *eriung* have much in common.

In his recent study of a Norfolk manor B M S Campbell concludes that 'the creation of these standardized holdings was almost certainly the work of the manorial authorities and was probably associated with the general downgrading in status of the manorial population which took place some time after 1086'.[78] Yet numerous East Anglian tenements and glebes listed by Little Domesday were of standard *eriung* size,[79] while the glebes of many Surrey churches founded by the early 12th century often seem to have conformed to the local patterns of standardised holdings (below, p140). Like the cotmen of Cheam and Croydon, a high proportion of Middlesex bordars and cottars in 1086 had five acres each.[80] In Surrey it is at present only at Godalming (above, p75) that a numerical correspondence between Domesday tenants and later holdings can be suggested, but relatively few manors preserved so static a tenemental structure. Some regular groups of subdivided holdings existed, then, at least by the early Norman period. The grand original sharing-out may often have been integral with the creation and planning of the village which housed the shareholders, part of the same protracted development spanning the 10th to 12th centuries. Further work may reveal equal size-units on manors of one landlord; it is interesting that out of five Westminster Abbey manors in Surrey, three had virgates of twenty acres and two of fifteen acres (table 6).

Significantly, signs of further order and symmetry in subdivided fields seem to be confined to the earlier sources. While there is never any suggestion of strips distributed equally between two or three common fields, 12th- and 13th-century references hint at a residual though once widespread pattern of subdivided holdings associated with compact land, often in roughly equal proportion. In *c*1300 William le Maleville held at Leatherhead two thirteen-acre virgates, one subdivided (above, p73, example (c)), the other compact and lying at Catebardene.[81] A Malden tenement of 1212 comprised eight and a half acres in scattered plots and eleven and a half acres lying together in the North Field,[82] while at Carshalton in *c*1250 nine acres of a holding were dispersed and the remaining thirteen and a half acres grouped together in Hugestescroft and Thurkillescroft.[83] These are unlikely to be coincidental, for occasionally we can perceive a definite concept of holdings split between two parts of a township. A mid-13th-century Hooley tenement comprised all the land held there by Reynold de la Putte 'in duabus partibus', while one early source, a Carshalton deed of *c*1150, grants 'totam terram quam Wluardus filius Brictrig tenuit in sud et in nort'.[84] The topography of this last case is interesting, for Carshalton was one of those strip parishes which contained a south common field and a smaller 'north part' made up of small inclosures (above, pp66–9); it may be inferred that Wulfward's holding had comprised subdivided land to the south of the village and compact land to the north.

There is a strong suggestion here that on some manors inclosed land had been apportioned among the regular subdivided holdings. The entitlement of such holdings to equal shares in pasture and meadow might extend to newly-cultivated arable on the less fertile soils, associating outfield with infield along familiar lines.[85] But the 'possessive' enclosure names in the examples just cited – Catebardene, Hugestescroft, Thurkillescroft – suggest a former proprietorship in their own right, while the rough acreage-equivalence of the two elements implies a single allocation rather than the piecemeal addition of new land. Perhaps the most likely hypothesis is a general rearrangement in which each subdivided holding was assigned a less fertile outfield, roughly equal in size; this might have been either old demesne, assart land, or the remains of a former compact farm. This interpretation, which sets subdivided holdings in a context of existing severalty farms, is at least no less tenable than the conventional view of expansion outwards from a primary subdivided core.

We may also have here at least a partial explanation for the recurring pattern of 'half' and 'whole' units. Division between heirs does not explain this wholly convincingly, for a significant proportion of tenants must have had more than two sons. Furthermore, the evidence of glebes in Surrey, and of both Domesday Book and glebes in East Anglia, suggests that the pattern existed as early as c1100.[86] But to postulate small 'basic' units which might or might not be augmented in fixed proportion with land lying outside the subdivided system suits the evidence well. B Dodwell has shown for East Anglia how Norman rearrangements sometimes caused tenements to be enlarged or combined in fixed multiples; a mid 12th-century Brancaster holding comprised 24 acres which were half villein land and half old demesne.[87] Cases like this, and the 'big bovates' and 'little bovates' of some Lincolnshire townships,[88] suggest possible analogies for Surrey. At Leatherhead the 13-acre virgates would on this interpretation represent 'basic' units, sometimes doubled in size with compact land and sometimes (eg table 7) combined in pairs. The process need not have been universal, and in the 13th century the bonds linking the compact and subdivided halves usually succumbed to the solvent effects of the land-market. Yet despite the anarchism of agrarian arrangements in later medieval Surrey, there are suggestions here of an earlier and more orderly state.

It is hardly likely that common fields were themselves created at a stroke. Tenemental symmetry must result from the re-apportionment of holdings which were already subdivided, and the origins of which lie beyond the reach of records. Current work favours an evolutionary model: compact severalty holdings, or farms comprising 'a few large, wide, strip-shaped blocks stretching back from the habitation area of a hamlet', were progressively broken down by partible inheritance and added to by progressive clearance.[89] In Northamptonshire, the initial formation of open-field furlongs has been linked to settlement nucleation and placed in the 8th century (above, p65). This important problem can only be approached through topography and toponymy, and there would be scope for detailed studies of furlong layouts in Surrey. Certainly the field-names sometimes hint at a superseded structure of compact holdings. Thus Leatherhead common field was full of furlong and landmark names suggesting ancient proprietorship: Buntanlond,[90] Dondene,[91] Edolvesdone,[92] Godhivedene,[93] Katerbardene, Kenchescrofte, Lomleshegg', Lyndene,[94] Swyndolvestorne,[95] Tibeliesdene,[96] Tonnerscroft.[97] K Bailey's important recent study of Putney suggests a similar pattern, with the planned village succeeding scattered pre-Conquest farmsteads commemorated by names in the open fields.[98] Fragmentation of holdings and nucleation of settlement combined to produce the conditions for remodelling in the centuries on either side of the Conquest.

Holding sizes in the 13th century: the land-market and the dissolution of the virgate

By the late 13th century, when we have our first clear view of Surrey virgates, their breakup was already well advanced. No longer was the virgate or half-virgate the dominant unit of tenure: rentals and court rolls record a wide spectrum of smaller holdings, based on a formal structure which was becoming ever less real. A true picture of landholding in this period cannot be gained from these sources alone; the effects of the innumerable small transfers through the land-market are only made apparent by accumulations of private deeds. One man's transactions might cross many manorial boundaries and fail to appear completely in the records of any one manor.

To understand how tenure was evolving we need to use both kinds of evidence: rentals and court rolls, in which the breakup of assessed holdings is seen through the eyes of established landlords, and deeds, which show the recombination of the resultant fragments in the hands of

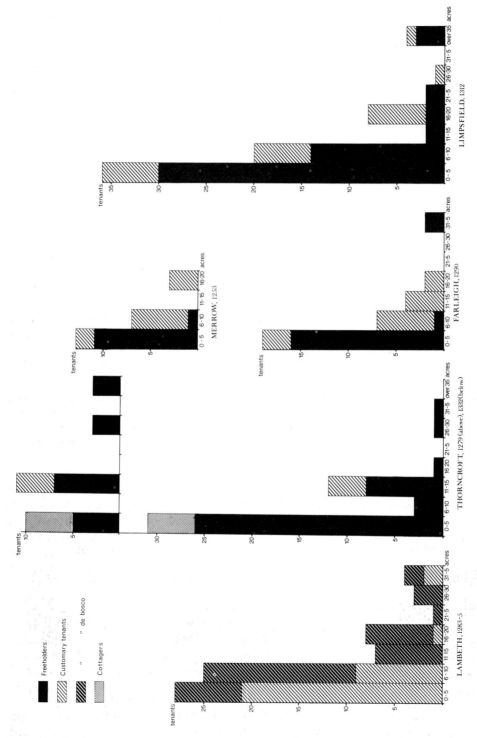

Fig 23   Sizes of smallholdings on five manors. (At Thorncroft, Merrow and Farleigh virgated holdings of otherwise unknown size have been translated into the acre-equivalents recorded for these manors, despite the fact that some compact virgates failed to conform to standard measure.)

TABLE 7   The tenure in 1332 of Henry the Shepherd's former virgate held of Thorncroft manor

Tenant	Holding	Rent
Mabel atte Slovene	Capital messuage, 4 acres	8¼d
John and Nicholas de Leddrede	3½ acres	8d
The king	3 acres	6d
William le Tannere	2½ acres	10d
Nicholas le Tannere	2 acres	8d
John Scot	1½ acres	4d
Maud Gavelestre	1½ acres	3d
William Ewelle	1½ acres	3d
John de Bradmere	1 acre	4d
Christine de Chinthurst	1 acre	4d
William atte Burgh	1 acre	2d
Thomas Jelyng	1 acre	2d
John Scot	1 acre	3d
William le Tannere	1 acre	1d
	Capital messuage, 25½ acres	5s 6¼d

Source: MM, 5779d

rising freeholders. To illustrate the spectrum of landholding on individual manors, five geographically different examples have been chosen: Lambeth, in the London Basin; Thorncroft and Merrow, crossing the dip-slope of the Downs; Farleigh on the Downland; and Limpsfield in the Weald. Fig 23 shows in graph form the patterns of holdings recorded in customals of these manors.

All the archiepiscopal manors in Surrey had an abnormally low proportion of freeholders, and at Lambeth in 1283–5 there were none at all (fig 23A). The customal of that year[99] preserves only the faintest suggestion of a 32-acre virgatal structure, though most of the smaller tenants owed services identical with those of the two intact virgates. An interesting feature is that whereas most customary tenements on the main manor were extremely small (only about a third contained more than five acres), the range of the group headed 'tenentes de bosco' was decidedly bigger. On this manor in a populous and advanced region subdivision had occurred early – probably before the final systematisation of services and the tightening of restraints on partitioning customary land; nonetheless, the larger and less broken-up holdings produced by woodland assarting still retained a distinct character at the end of the 13th century.

Thorncroft in Leatherhead illustrates with unusual clarity the dissolution of free virgates (fig 23B). A tenant list compiled for a scutage assessment of 1279 portrays a near-intact virgatal structure: of eighteen free tenants, thirteen hold whole, half or double virgates, in addition to which there were four villein half-virgates and five cottage holdings with one acre each.[100] Dramatically different was the position recorded in a rental of 1332.[101] The villein and cottage holdings were unchanged, but of the free virgates and half-virgates only those in compact blocks were still tenurial realities. The regular thirteen-acre and 26-acre freeholds in the common field were now redistributed between numerous tenants in tiny fractions (eg the example in table 7); more than half the freeholders held five acres or less, and the only large freeholds were a small group of old-established compact farms. Several new holdings amalgamated fragments of old ones: Gilbert le Glovere had supplemented his compact half-virgate with parcels from the former virgates of Chereburgh, Dru and Boxe, not to mention a messuage and one and a half acres held of another old virgate on the neighbouring manor of Pachenesham Parva.[102]

We should not attribute all this subdivision to the previous half-century; the symmetry of the 1279 list is an illusion, produced by an administrative policy which ignored sub-tenancies in exacting obligations.[103] A release of a Thorncroft half-virgate in c1250–60 shows that five sub-tenants were holding of it,[104] and late 13th-century court rolls note the sale or farming of individual components from virgated holdings.[105] Fragmentation of free virgates was well under way by c1300 and complete by 1332, at which date, by contrast, the four villein half-virgates in the common field remained intact.

At Merrow, where the virgate contained sixteen acres, the main source is a rental of 1253 (fig 23C).[106] Of the twelve freeholds all but one (a half-virgate) were very small and expressed in acres; the eleven customary holdings, which despite their disparity in size owed identical services, comprised three virgates, five half-virgates and three smaller unvirgated units. This pattern corroborates the evidence of earlier deeds that Merrow freeholds were already fragmenting during the first half of the century.[107]

At Farleigh, a small Downland manor, subdivision may have occurred rather later than in the more fertile dip-slope townships. Holdings were assessed on a 32-acre virgate;[108] in 1290[109] (fig 23D) there were two free virgates and seventeen very small freeholds, probably fragments of a third. About half of the fifteen villein tenements are described in terms of ferlings (quarter-virgates) and the rest in acres; six holdings can be reassembled as two-and-a-half former virgates (table 8) while the remaining nine total c48 acres, presumably representing another one-and-a-half virgates. As table 8 shows, rents and services had been imposed on the larger units and divided with them. In one case a one-and-a-half virgate tenement which owed services, 4s rent and an exceptional hospitality payment called 'guestingsilver' had first been divided into two uneven parts between which these obligations were split equally; the larger portion was then halved, and its half-share in the original payments and duties was divided accordingly. By the time these services were defined in detail the virgatal structure had already lost some of its symmetry; but the process of subdivision which made the ferling the dominant customary unit must have been later still, carefully controlled to safeguard obligations.

TABLE 8   Six Farleigh villein tenements in 1290

Tenant	Holding	Rent	Guesting-silver		Services
Crispin atte Hage	messuage, 1 ferling	1s	–	Specified in detail	Total 1 virgate (ie 32 acres)
Richard le Wyte	messuage, 1½ ferlings	2s	–	As C atte H	owing 4s rent and services
Gregory de Farle	messuage, 1½ ferlings	1s	–	As C atte H	
Walter atte Hage	messuage, 1½ ferlings	2s	1s 6d	Specified in detail	
John atte Hage	messuage, 15 acres land, 3 acres wood	1s	9d	Half W atte H	Total 1½ virgates (ie 48 acres) owing 4s rent, 3s
Richard le Yungge	messuage, 15 acres land, 3 acres wood	1s	9d	Half W atte H	guestingsilver and services

Source: MM, 4890; the payments totalling 3s are defined as guestingsilver in a rental of 1333 (MM, 4894)

Limpsfield, in the Weald, had no trace of a virgatal structure in 1312 (fig 23E).[110] Even on this heavy soil, and in the complete absence of subdivided fields, fragmentation had proceeded apace, with well over half the free tenants holding five acres or less. Once again, a markedly higher proportion of the customary than of the free holdings were in the range of c15–30 acres and may thus have represented intact virgates and half-virgates.

Conspicuous in all these cases is the advanced fragmentation of the free virgate. Like the contemporary Kentish *iugum*, it had lost most of its tenurial and topographical significance and was now largely a fiscal unit, fragments of which might be combined with other land to form new *tenementa*.[111] Notwithstanding such occasional amalgamation, the holdings of free tenants within individual manors were overwhelmingly very small. Over the five manors considered here an average of 75% of freeholders had less than six acres, and a further 12% had between six and twelve acres. A small minority of freeholds in the range of c25–40 acres were mainly compact farms still in the hands of old-established families. Excepting these hardy survivors, the landholding basis of the free farming community in early medieval Surrey had largely been destroyed by 1300.

This was the culmination of a process which spanned the 13th century, and indeed had begun before the virgatal structure finally crystallised. As early as the 1180s and 1190s, occasional grants itemising heterogeneous collections of open-field strips must have cut across any established tenemental structure,[112] while at Thorncroft and Merrow sub-tenancies were evidently well-established on the free land by c1250. The rapidly growing rate of small transactions is evident from Surrey feet of fines, in which the proportion concerned with individual strips or plots rather than hides or virgates rises steadily between 1195 and 1250.[113]

Predictably, customary holdings had fragmented less and preserved more of the old assessed structure. On the five manors studied the size-range was spread more evenly: 32% of holdings below six acres, 31% between six and ten acres and 32% between eleven and twenty acres. Cottage tenements of one acre are distinguished at Thorncroft and probably form a distinct element in the undifferentiated customary holdings elsewhere. Contrasts between manors reflect variations both in economic development and in administrative control. Just as the readiness or otherwise of individual landlords to capitalise by enfranchising small tenancies had determined the proportion between free and customary land,[114] so seigneurial policy affected the later development of unfree holdings. A structure of villein virgates survived almost intact on the Westminster manors of Battersea and Wandsworth,[115] but had disappeared by 1283/5 at nearby Lambeth. In the former cases the monks actively preserved 'the units of landholding that were the livelihood of their dependent villein families';[116] in the latter the archbishops seem to have permitted unchecked division, exacting nonetheless a full quota of services from each resulting fragment. At Farleigh, some distance from London and probably less susceptible to demographic pressure, we find a regular, controlled partition of rents and services, probably a more recent process and very different from piecemeal fragmentation. Generally speaking, those manors which retained an intact structure of customary virgates until c1250 retained it for at least a further century; obligations were the *raison d'être* of the virgate, and the more precisely its services were defined the hardier it was likely to prove.

The prevalence of sub-tenancies and temporary demises make it impossible to say how closely the evidence discussed above reflects the actual pattern of occupation.[117] At the level of formal tenure, however, it is temptingly easy to picture a society in which most customary holdings were reasonably adequate and most freeholds were minute. The fallacy of this view is made clear by examining, through the evidence of their own deeds, the kinds of people named in rentals as the tenants of such exiguous freeholds. Far from living on the verge of poverty, they were often substantial men whose prosperity is concealed by the very variety of their resources.

There was a thriving land-market in 13th-century Surrey for two main reasons: closeness to

TABLE 9   The early development of the Fitznells estate: acquisitions by Robert de Cuddington (1–5) and Gilbert de Ewell (6–14)

	Date	Parish	Land acquired	Cartulary No.
1	1218/19	Cuddington	2½ acres in 3 furlongs	107,47
2	1220 × 30	Ewell	10 acres in 6 furlongs	57,47
3	1220 × 30	Cuddington	8 acres 1 rood in 9 furlongs	34,47
4	1220 × 30	Cuddington	4 acres in 4 furlongs	45,47
5	1220 × 30	Cuddington	2 acres in 6 selions	110,47
6	c1230	Cuddington	2 acres in 2 furlongs	38
7	c1230	Ewell	1 acre in 2 furlongs	37
8	c1230	Ewell	curtilage, 1 acre headland	86
9	1230 × 8	Cuddington	10 acres in 4 furlongs	5
10	1230 × 8	Cuddington	6 acres in 7 furlongs	75
11	1230 × 8	Cuddington	6½ acres lying together	12
12	1230 × 8	Ewell	4½ acres in 3 furlongs	7
13	1230 × 8	Ewell	2 acres in 3 furlongs	109
14	1231 × 8	Ewell	messuage with buildings	74

Source: *Fitznells Cartulary.*

London, and the high proportion of free land. London provided an exceptional market for surpluses, the proceeds from which could be used to enlarge the producers' holdings; it also contained numerous merchants and craftsmen anxious to invest their own capital in the surrounding rural areas.[118] By c1300 the free land, especially in north-east Surrey, was held by a mixture of local men from both old and parvenu families, yeoman farmers from nearby villages, and Londoners. For example, the 13th-century deeds for Beddington, Bandon and Wallington record long series of small purchases by Robert Payn of Bandon,[119] John Mauncel of Croydon,[120] and Walter Rokesle, citizen of London.[121]

While the individual acquisitions were usually trivial, their sum total could be impressive. The Fitznells estate at Ewell originated in a long series of small purchases from c1220 onwards by Robert rector of Cuddington, his nephew Gilbert de Ewell, and Gilbert's son William.[122] Table 9, which summarises their earlier acquisitions, shows that some 60 acres in the open fields of Ewell and Cuddington were amassed during the first twenty years. A later but equally striking instance, showing a consistent policy of acquisition, is provided by the early 14th-century Headley freeholder Richard atte Leghe.[123] Starting with a small estate which his father John had built up in Headley, Walton-on-the-Hill and Epsom, Richard accumulated a long series of small acquisitions in the contiguous areas of Leatherhead, Ashtead and Headley parishes over some forty years from the early 1290s. In Leatherhead he concentrated his efforts on the inclosed land east of the common field, where the fields, mostly identifiable, called Sepehale, Little Colecrofte, Pinchonesfelde, Pinchonesgrove, Hameldonesfeld, Ponshurstefeld and part of Joyesfeld passed successively into his hands. In 1317 he began acquiring individual acres and half-acres in Ashtead south common field, and throughout his active life he was slowly building up strips and parcels in his native township of Headley. By 1335 he had amassed an estate of at least some 70 arable acres, not counting his father's holdings and perhaps acquisitions elsewhere which the extant deeds fail to record.[124] The impression is of a fair-sized Downland farm, much of it compact and the rest lying within a mile's radius, which could also have supported a sheep-flock on the fallow and the abundant common pasture of the surrounding chalk.[125] This estate had a clear economic logic which owed nothing to traditional agrarian arrangements.

By c1300 there were many freeholders of this substantial kind. Several names in the 1332 Thorncroft rental (as in table 7) recur in contexts suggesting a certain prosperity, sometimes as parties to other transactions in or near Leatherhead. Although freehold estates had been building up through the 13th century, it is the fifty years or so from c1280 which provide the most impressive examples and the greatest volume of deeds. These Surrey 'kulaks' remind us of John atte Grene in early 14th-century Cuxham, or the Peterborough tenants who were engrossing large amounts of free land during the same period.[126] Such figures seem most conspicuous during the half-century before the Black Death, though in Surrey, and probably wherever free tenure predominated, their presence can be traced some generations earlier.[127]

New families rose at the expense of old ones: many ancient Surrey names disappear between 1280 and 1350. Thus several of Richard atte Leghe's Leatherhead properties were acquired from the de Punesherts, established in the parish from at least the 1170s (above, p46), who vanish from local sources thereafter. Landholding was now dominated by new men on newly-assembled farms, which cut across not merely the old virgated holdings but also the very manors to which the virgates were attached. Rentals and surveys of the reigns of the three Edwards are more relevant to a superseded tenurial system than to that prevailing when they were actually compiled.

The development of compact holdings

It has already been suggested that compact farms were ubiquitous in Anglo-Saxon Surrey. When sources become numerous it is predictably in the Weald that such holdings remain most prominent, and retain most clearly the character of primary tracts. But in all areas where it survived, this simple pattern can be seen diversifying from the late 12th century onwards in response to population growth and massive subdivision. In the Weald at least, the boundaries as first laid out certainly encompassed a high proportion of under-exploited land. Twelfth-century deeds rarely describe such holdings more precisely than as *terra de X, terra que vocatur X,* or *terra quam Y tenuit,* the first two of these sometimes making clear, by reference to some topographical feature, that the land was compact.[128]

Such family farm units acquired a certain stable identity, the memory of which often lasted for many generations. A fair number may have remained tenurially intact, though it is hard to distinguish such early survivals from the results of post-plague engrossment in those Wealden parishes which were later dominated by large unitary holdings.[129] Church glebes, inherently the most stable kind of smallholdings, often best illustrate this once-dominant type (see ch 6). On the Downland small but evidently long-established farms survived into the 13th and 14th centuries (above, pp45–9).

This continuity was exceptional: in general early farms were subdivided or (less frequently) amalgamated, though the resultant new holdings were often described in terms of the primary units. A chronological summary of tenemental descriptions from one Wealden parish (table 10) illustrates this diversifying pattern. Sometimes a simple division into fractions necessitated new hedges and ditches; an early 13th-century holding near Abinger is described as 'tantum terre quantum tenui de terra Wlgari de Montibus sicut modo fossata est', and in 1219 a half-hide in Chipstead was divided in two along a new north-south boundary running through a marlpit in 'la middelfeld'.[130] Large farms of a hide or more might break down into component virgates, as at Newdigate in 1229 when John de Hale alienated two virgates of his holding but retained a third contiguous virgate.[131] The 13th century also saw much subdivision on a smaller scale: the

TABLE 10   Charter descriptions of smallholdings in Tandridge

Date	Description	Source
1121 × 45	Land of Felbridge	Blair, Surrey endowments of Lewes Priory, 103
c1130 × 50	Land of Nortun	Minet Library, Deed 3605
c1200 × 20	My land of Fosseslawe	Minet Library, Deed 3610
c1200 × 20	All land which Blakeman held and all land which Hodgar held in my vill of Tandridge	SRO, 60/11/1
c1270 × 90	All that land which I have in Tandridge of that land called Goldyvelond	Minet Library, Deed 3608

increasingly frequent formula *X acre in campo qui dicitur Y*,[132] implying fragmentation of an existing named field, proves that in some areas the average plot-size was getting steadily less.

This happened wherever large assart farms remained from an earlier phase of colonisation. In the Woodcote area of the Downs (cf above, p49) the disintegration of such holdings can be traced in detail. The core of William Baudri's land, a block of fields here including two of nine acres each and one of 30 acres, was dismembered piecemeal during the mid to late 13th century.[133] Other deeds, which state the precise dimensions of plots, record the partial breakup over the same period of Geoffrey de la Woodcote's assart tract, transforming it into a group of separately-owned closes (fig 24). In a third instance, members of the Colswein family progressively alienated parcels in and around a former unitary field called Colswayenesfeld.[134]

In addition to fragmentation of existing arable, a steady trickle of clearances contributed to the evolution of the inclosed landscape. Both on the chalk and in the Weald, assarting seems to have diminished in scale by the later 12th century, a matter now of filling-in waste areas between established fields. Thus a deed of c1180 for the Wealden parish of Horne[135] grants to Walter de Marini

> totum campum quem Rogerus de Frith tenuit inter terram Ricardi filii Ade et terram ipsius Rogeri Birstowe iuxta Alfladescroft; et omnia nova essarta que sunt inter essartum Ricardi filii Ade et terram Rogeri de Frith; et preter hos quoddam incrementum terre inter defensum meum et essartum quod idem Walterus tenuit de patre meo, ita ut fossum eius sit inter defensum meum et rotundam garam, et longitudo incrementi sit a bosco Sancti Pauli quantum terra eiusdem Walteri durat quam de patre meo tenuit.

In north-west Surrey compact holdings were acquiring 'increments' of new land in predetermined shares. In 1191–8 Newark Priory was given half a hide together with a little croft and 'ad incrementum, tantum terre ab austro collateraliter adiacentis quantum sufficit ad unam carucatam terre'.[136] Elsewhere heterogeneous collections of assarts and existing arable closes were still being grouped within the virgatal structure. A Sanderstead quarter-virgate of 1199 comprised 'unum campum terre iacentem ut novam terram et quinque acras in Hadfeld quas Ricardus filius Suein' essartavit', while a Banstead deed of c1180 grants 'totam terram quam Hugo clericus aliquando de me tenuit et 20 acras de essarto et 10 acras de bosco, scilicet unam bonam carucatam terre'.[137] Of two half-virgates in early 13th-century Hambledon, one is described as 'totam terram quam Saild de Prato de me tenuit, et totum assartum quod Galfridus de Bosco de me tenuit, et totum assartum quod Johannes le Clop tenuit, et totam terram in

Lafirþingland quod Reginaldus Nort' tenuit'; the other comprised a croft and messuage, fifteen acres of inclosed land in a wood next an assart, and six acres of inclosed land in the same wood.[138]

Thirteenth-century holdings on the Weald clay and Greensand could be extremely complex, sometimes running to a dozen contiguous or near-contiguous plots of land, meadow and wood.[139] But here again, this complexity was not confined to the Weald. Gray noted the 'curious and varied descriptions of the parcels of a virgate' which occur so often in northern Surrey; cases like the Wandsworth holding of 1247 which comprised nine acres in Nortfeld, ten and a half acres in Suetingedich, $21\frac{1}{2}$ acres in Suthfeld and three acres in Leye imply a mixed tenurial pattern hardly less remote from primary compact farm units than from the pristine regularity of subdivided shares.[140]

The inclosed landscape had thus tended towards a greater heterogeneity. Holdings had fragmented, and the process had left its mark in the proliferation of little irregular closes within the sweeping assart boundaries. Yet the basic nature of farming outside the common fields had probably changed much less. If many holdings were not strictly compact their components lay within close range, and farmers, especially in the Weald, still preferred to live on isolated homesteads amidst their land.[141] Agriculture never reached the intensity of even the simpler kinds of open-field system: as J L M Gulley has pointed out, the geographical shortcomings of the Weald hampered further progress. Soil was variable within small areas and rarely very good, transport was hard in winter along muddy clay roads, and a farmer needed to be near his fields to use them to best advantage when they were neither cracked nor boggy; 'these difficulties were allied with deficiencies in the soil . . . and their combined restrictions rarely allowed food production sufficient or sufficiently regular to support the greater populations of nucleated settlements'.[142]

In Surrey the same kind of compact farms, diversifying and fragmenting to the same limited extent, were to be found everywhere outside the immediate purlieu of nucleated settlements. Nowhere did common agriculture ever gain total supremacy; the older pattern, preserved by geographical constraints, continued to develop along its own separate course.

Fragmentation and assarting: the expansion of subdivided fields?

Even as late as the 13th century, the end-products of clearance and subdivision might potentially be absorbed into common fields in the strict sense. T A M Bishop's classic demonstration shows some Yorkshire assarts divided among groups of cultivators and integrated into existing common fields, while others of unitary origin had met the same fate within a few generations.[143] Recently, B M S Campbell has shown how 13th-century population growth and the demands of an active land-market were met on one Norfolk manor by subdivision of plots, greatly increasing the number of common-field parcels and breaking up existing inclosures.[144]

Can such expansion of the subdivided arable be found in the south-east? In Kent, gavelkind descent certainly led to the fragmentation and intermixture of compact holdings.[145] In Surrey the impartible inheritance custom of Borough English was evidently normal by the 13th century, as indeed it remained for long afterwards.[146] Nonetheless, descent to heiresses and transactions *inter vivos* might give rise to the regular parcellation (as distinct from haphazard fragmentation) of holdings. Discrete strips or closes sometimes underwent a systematic parcel-by-parcel division, so enduring was the ancient concept of aliquot shares.[147] Whether this was effected by sun-division (as with the half-share of a Mitcham holding in 1235 'que ubique iacet in campis de Inlond, Bery, Battesworth, Burforlang, Spirihey, Westebroc versus umbram'),[148] or expressed in terms of compass-points,[149] each topographical unit was physically split in two. This process must have tended both to reduce the size of inclosures and to divide open-field strips along the furrows between their component selions – surely the best explanation for those common and

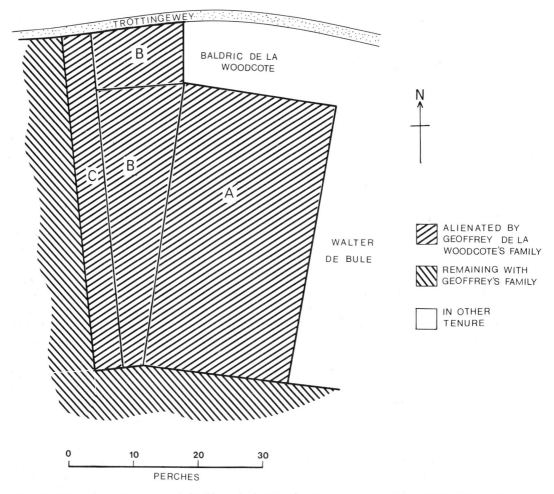

Fig 24   The dismemberment of Geoffrey de la Woodcote's compact holding, c1260–80: a schematic reconstruction. A: Granted by Geoffrey's widow to Ralph and Levinia de Dorset (Add Chs 22923, 22937). B–B: Granted by same to same (Add Chs 22938, 22998). C: Granted by Geoffrey's son to Simon de Epsile (Add Ch 22954). The rest of the land shown hatched represents the known residue of Geoffrey's holding. The land was at East Woodcote in the field called Heye

much-discussed cases of subdivided holdings where each plot adjoins the same neighbour's land.[150]

We have seen how unitary blocks might fragment into groups of separately-owned closes. Even in the 13th century this process could produce narrow, elongated plots resembling elements of a common-field system: one component of a Woodcote holding (fig 24, plot C) took the form of an 'acre' 50 by 4 perches, analogous in size and shape to an open strip and doubtless similarly reflecting the ploughman's needs. It is much less clear that the process resulted either in new common fields or in the enlargement of old ones. Small though the new plots were, deeds show that they generally lay in a miscellaneous patchwork lacking any regular alignment of strips or furlongs. More significant, it is clear that most were permanent inclosures, hedged or ditched: variants of the standard formula *sicut sepibus et fossatis undique includitur* are widely used in 13th-

and 14th-century Surrey deeds for plots of no more than one or two acres. A late 13th-century Hambledon grant by William de Anekecneppe of an acre in his croft called Eldeleme, conceding to the grantee 'quod possit dictam acram sibi includere fossato et haya prout melius voluerit', illustrates piecemeal fragmentation followed immediately by inclosure of the individual fragments.[151]

The effects of clearance were sometimes similar. Even in the Weald, the practice of sharing out co-operative assarts in small parcels survived into the 13th century, suggested for instance in a Horne deed of *c*1220 granting 'una acra terre cum gardino que est in novo assarto de la Bysse'.[152] But as a region of dynamic colonisation, the Weald was now being outstripped by the Bagshot sands of north-west Surrey, and here we have apparent evidence, at first sight both extensive and impressive, for a new landscape of subdivided fields. As shown above (p42), deeds and eyre rolls list numerous tiny assarts and purprestures colonised by individual smallholders; it would be easy to infer that large-scale co-operative efforts were extending the common fields of Chertsey and its neighbouring townships. But the nature of these encroachments needs closer examination.

In deeds the words *assartum* and *purprestura* seem virtually interchangeable, but the forest eyres make a general distinction, not always consistently observed, on the basis of size and use. Purprestures were on average much smaller: the total acreage of assarts recorded in the eyres is over half that of the purprestures (251 acres as against 476), but the proportion of individual plots is enormously less (98 assarts as against 589 purprestures). This reflects the large number of minute purpresture plots containing only one or two perches each, scarcely viable as individual ploughing units. Indeed, it is clear that these were generally non-arable; thus in the 1269 roll it is only assarts which are described as 'in bladata', while several small purprestures had houses built on them. More often these were probably no more than patches of waste inclosed for rough grazing or for cropping the timber and underwood: Chertsey Abbey deeds often refer to 'purprestures of moorland', sometimes apparently used as alder coppice.[153]

The assarts listed by the forest justices, with an average plot size of 2.6 acres and a median of 1.5 acres, were generally under cultivation, while other sources for the forest area provide abundant evidence of small, newly-won arable plots. But clearance in small units does not necessarily produce open fields. A large proportion of both assarts and purprestures, especially those of very small size, were probably encroachments on the margins of existing unitary holdings. Thus in 1272 Chertsey Abbey inclosed a parcel of common adjoining land of Gilbert de la Felde for the enlargement of Gilbert's tenement, while in 1341 a Westminster Abbey tenant at Pyrford received licence 'elargare . . . tenementum suum versus communiam etc. de vasto domini de una roda terre'.[154] Even when 13th-century assarts lay intermixed, it was normal both to inclose them with permanent boundaries and to regard them thereafter as something distinct from open-field land. A group of Chertsey deeds records the recent and current inclosure of moorland in parcels of between one and three acres, divided up by newly-established hedges and ditches.[155] Other Chertsey Abbey documents make a clear distinction between open land in cultures and furlongs on the one hand and series of small closes on the other.[156]

It is surely an essential characteristic of a common field that cropping and grazing are organised at least within individual furlongs, if not within larger units; and of an open field that permanent physical obstacles to these activities are absent. The products of fragmentation and assarting in 13th-century Surrey failed to meet either requirement: they lay apart, each parcel securely hedged or ditched against wandering animals, distinct from earlier open land if often lying near it. Arguments *ex silentio* are dangerous, but the absence of any explicit reference in innumerable deeds and estate records suggests very strongly that the formation of new open fields in Surrey was already rare, if not unknown, when our sources first mention such matters.

The consolidation of subdivided land

The 13th-century market for free land was bound to have topographical as well as tenurial consequences. Fragmentation and intermixture were not the only possible result: on the contrary, some buyers made distinct efforts to concentrate acquisitions within a small area, efforts which may have resulted both in new agrarian arrangements and in the inclosure of open-field land.

Surrey was a region of ancient inclosed demesnes, and in the 13th century some landowners were busily gathering piecemeal acquisitions into compact blocks where crop-rotations could be imposed at will (above, p69).[157] Such activity was not long confined to big estates: the amalgamation of existing inclosures was becoming increasingly common (above, p82). It seems a fair conclusion that as the land-market expanded, and as new families rose from the mass of the peasantry to re-fashion the fragments of earlier holdings, improvements which big landowners had been effecting since *c*1200 were now attempted more widely. It is less certain how often this led to the consolidation of open-field land: in the case of Fitznells at Ewell, for instance, scarcely any of the strips acquired can have been contiguous (above, table 9). It is obvious from the widespread survival of Surrey common fields beyond the Middle Ages that the process was never very comprehensive, and Brandon's recent study goes no further than to suggest that 'enclosure into small hedged fields had begun by the early 15th century'.[158] Yet its beginnings, if piecemeal in character and trivial in scale, were nearly two centuries earlier.

Grants of open-field strips adjoining land already in the hands of the grantee are very common among 13th- and 14th-century Surrey deeds. In a few collections, such as the early 13th-century Newington charters of Christ Church Canterbury,[159] this feature occurs with a frequency suggesting that groups of two, three or four contiguous acres, either within one furlong or in adjoining furlongs, must have been coming into single ownership. Sometimes this limited consolidation can be demonstrated (table 11), though no 13th-century case has been found which extends to the components of an entire furlong. Exchanges between tenants enabling each to hold adjacent plots become common in the early 14th-century court rolls of Chertsey Abbey manors,[160] and must reflect a growing feeling that land was more conveniently farmed in larger units.

Such groups did not always re-fragment with the next generation. There are occasional hints, increasingly common from the early 14th century onwards, of hedges and ditches around what had once been open land. A piece of land 'cum sepibus, fossis et fossatis' in Beddington south common field in 1336 is perhaps such a case; an earlier and more telling one, which plainly suggests recent inclosure, is a reference of 1274 to two acres in Bandon 'que fuerunt Radulfi le Serder' et nunc includuntur sepibus'.[161] The results of this process are still apparent on 17th-century estate maps, which often show odd patches of hedged and ditched common-field land beside the more extensive inclosures of later centuries. Lack of common control left much wider scope for the impact of private initiative on the farming landscape, with results that can be seen in, for example, the contrast between early inclosure in the 'wood-pasture' areas of Devon and much later inclosure in the 'champion' regions.[162] In 13th-and early 14th-century Surrey we have traced two near-contemporary but contrasting trends: the division and intermixture of plots on the one hand, and their consolidation and inclosure on the other. But the contrast is not a total one, for both developments tended to produce a landscape of small closes. The one type of land-unit which was indubitably proliferating throughout Surrey was the small field of some two to six acres enclosed by hedges and ditches. This development was only partial, and the distinctive contrasts of the Surrey landscape well survived the period considered here. Yet on the one hand inclosed holdings were losing their primitive unitary character, and on the other the area of subdivided arable under even a limited agrarian control was very gradually shrinking. In

TABLE 11   Eudes le Jop's acquisitions of contiguous plots in Bandon

Date	Grantor	Property	Bounds	BL Add Ch
1271	Sibil Maubon	1 acre in Bandon field in Buttininge	Between Thomas de Bandon S and Thomas Trigold N, abutting Schortefurlang W and Waddoningemarke E	22818
c1260 × 80	Thomas Trigold	1 acre in Bandon S field at Butininge	Between said Eudes Jop and the parson, abutting Wadduninge marke E and Sortefurlange W	22767
c1260 × 80	William le Duc	½ acre in Bandon field in Sortefurlang	Between William son of the parson and Thomas Trigold, abutting John Rubius W and formerly Eudes Moryn E	22996
c1260 × 80	Thomas Soaper	1 acre in Bandon S field at Sorteforlange	Between Sir Thomas Huscarle N and Walter de Rokesle S	22722
c1260 × 80	William Baudry	2 curtilages in Bandon	Between water called Nortbroc N, Peter Soaper S, Thomas Lemmer E and highway W	22713
1277	Thomas son of Peter le Soaper	messuage in Bandon	Between said Eudes Jop N and said Thomas Soaper S, abutting formerly Thomas Lemmer E and highway W	22720

so far as any general trend is visible, it was towards a patchwork of fragmented severalties, in which farmers could benefit both from the variety of soil-types offered by a dispersed holding, and from the freedom of choice offered by a compact one.

Conclusion

Later medieval Surrey shared with Kent, and still more closely with East Anglia, agrarian institutions very different from those of the Midlands. Yet where origins are concerned we may accept R A Dodgshon's recent conclusion that 'there was but one type of British field system, articulated into different regional variants, rather than different regional types'.[163] The further back we look, the easier it becomes to view Surrey common-field holdings in the main national stream of development. The basic ingredients are there: regular tenemental shares in the subdivided arable, tenurially-apportioned rights over waste and meadow. What the non-Midland systems lack is additional features: comprehensive rotations, symmetrical distribution of holdings between two or three open fields, the yearly allocation of one fallow field. In other words, it seems likely that subdivided fields which lack regular rotations and symmetrical dispersion, but where land is held in equal shares, merely display absence of the 'second-stage' remodelling. Thus field-systems in Surrey and East Anglia were not fundamentally different from those of the Midlands, but simply preserved a more primitive, once general, type at a stage of arrested development.

Two kinds of factor can be used to explain this: the strength of lordship and the balance of pastoral resources. For B M S Campbell, the individualistic and unsystematic agriculture of Norfolk resulted from light lordship. Free tenure predominated, and lords were unable to introduce the comprehensive systems imposed on peasants elsewhere; thus common fields 'seem to have manifested greatest regularity of layout and management in precisely those areas where manor and vill were most often coincident'.[164] This interpretation seems equally applicable to Surrey, where early signs of agrarian order and control were confined to specific groups of tenants and failed to transcend estate boundaries. Surrey townships never, like their classic Midland counterparts, developed comprehensively into open-field farming communities, but merely came to *contain* such communities. By the 12th or 13th century, no lord here would have found it easy to impose radical rearrangements on the heterogeneous groups of smallholders dominated by freemen.

Recent work tends to place the full development of Midland systems in the 12th and 13th centuries. Fox, however, has argued persuasively that their essential distinctness was already apparent by the Conquest.[165] The central factor in this interpretation is the necessity for fallow grazing: the Midlands were characterised, even in the 10th century, by an exceptional dearth of common waste which led to a close regulation of fallowing superfluous in the 'wood-pasture' regions. Surrey is consistent with this to the extent that wide individual freedom of cropping is accompanied by plentiful rough grazing, though the explicit evidence for communal fallowing is hard to reconcile with Fox's model.

These two factors are not incompatible: the link between free tenure and abundant waste lies at the heart of the basic contrast between 'champion' and 'non-champion' England. Whatever the precise date at which the two types of region diverged on their separate agrarian paths, the Surrey evidence suggests that the contrasts became ever sharper with time. In the Midlands common regulation grew and expanded; in Surrey and East Anglia it atrophied and decayed. We have noted hints that Surrey common fields were more organised in the earlier than in the later Middle Ages; possibly some townships once observed fuller cropping patterns in which only the fallow courses survived late enough to be recorded.

Tightly organised field-systems were not necessarily an unmixed blessing for peasant cultivators. Sometimes they may have become a hindrance, which tenants would gladly have forgone if the constraints of lordship had so allowed.[166] Where soils were so varied, free tenure so dominant and the land-market so active, it is not so surprising that primitive rotations dissolved into heterogeneity rather than evolving into fully-fledged systems on the Midland pattern. Kentish Holmesdale saw a similar development towards a flexible 'multifield' system during the 13th and 14th centuries.[167] In the south-east, smallholders were sufficiently free from corporate and seigneurial controls to progress during the 13th and 14th centuries towards a still wider freedom.

4 The Anglo-Saxon Minster Churches and their Fate

There is now a generally accepted view of the process by which England acquired its rural churches.[1] Kings, and bishops under their patronage, founded churches of a public character in important administrative centres. By the mid 8th century, all or most of the English kingdoms had established a network of minster *parochiae*, typically covering between perhaps five and fifteen modern parishes and served by groups of itinerating priests from the central church.

The main theme of parochial history in the 10th, 11th and 12th centuries is the decline of the minsters as more and more secular lords built manorial churches under their own control. By the time of Domesday Book this process was far advanced, and the late 11th century marks the high point of lay power over churches. The next century saw a redefinition of parochial rights, so that by 1200 the late Saxon and early Norman 'ownership' of churches had been reduced to little more than a *ius presentandi*.[2]

Although valid in general, this framework ignores some important issues. What factors determined the varying fates of mother churches, between the extremes of revitalisation as reformed monasteries on the one hand and total extinction on the other? Were parish churches always the private foundations of laymen, in rivalry with the minster clergy, or were they sometimes established with their consent as out-stations of the mother church? How far did minsters still exercise a restrictive influence on church foundation after 1066? How did the creation of local churches affect habits of worship in rural society?

In his meticulous analysis of provisions in canon law and the English royal codes relating to church ownership, P H Hase shows the vigilance with which, in theory at least, the monopoly of established churches over ecclesiastical revenue was guarded. Canonists strenuously denied the power of a founding lord to divert tithe to his own church or take over existing rights, and the compromises which the Church was in practice forced to accept remained hedged around with restrictions. In a celebrated law of 961 $\times$ 3 (Eadgar II.2, repeated Cnut I.12) a thegn was allowed to divert one-third only of his demesne tithe to an estate church with a graveyard. In a weaker position than his Frankish or German counterpart, the English proprietor was obliged to buy off the rights of the mother church with a lump sum or, more frequently, a recurring pension. Through the innate conservatism of ecclesiastical authority, the memory of such arrangements often survived into a better-recorded age in the form of 'evidence of one parish church receiving income, or performing profitable duties, in the parish of another. No matter how late such evidence is, it is almost invariably the case that one can read back from it to the period when the first parish church was a mother church, and the second a church newly founded within its parochia.'[3]

Thus the retrospective evidence of pensions, mortuaries, tithe-divisions and the relationships of dependence between one church and another reveals the growth of a system of rights. At the same time, the meagre written record can be supplemented by viewing churches in the geographical, economic and tenurial setting in which they developed. This and the two following chapters will adopt these approaches as a means of setting the churches in their social context and inferring facts about their pastoral functions.

Hase's work on Hampshire casts doubt on the accepted view that private, 'encroaching' churches were pre-eminent in transforming the rural Church: in that county, daughter churches were at least sometimes served by visiting minster priests. The comparable cases of Thatcham

(Berkshire) and Berkeley Hernesse (Gloucestershire), where mother churches retained limited and ill-defined rights over a proportion of their former chapelries, had already been examined by B R Kemp; in neither case do any of the dependants bear the stamp of private lay foundations.[4] In its emphasis on the continuing influence of old minsters into the 11th and 12th centuries, this recent work reacts against the view, implicit in earlier studies, that south-eastern England was fully parochialised by 1086.[5]

The overall picture remains confused, and can only be clarified by more local studies. Hase suggests that his conclusions are generally valid for southern England; but there are factors, as he acknowledges, which might make Hampshire atypical.[6] In Surrey, the remoter and humbler archdeaconry of the same diocese, implications drawn from the Hampshire evidence may usefully be reconsidered.

The evidence

'That there were such churches in Surrey is certain; where they were is a matter of conjecture', wrote H E Malden in discussing the Anglo-Saxon minster system.[7] While this now seems over-pessimistic, it remains true that the evidence is isolated, incomplete and mostly late, dating from a time when the minsters had already lost much of their importance. And Surrey is singularly deficient, apart from certain specific cases, in the retrospective evidence of burial rights, tithe-portions and the like, showing in this respect a striking contrast to Hampshire.[8]

The patchiness of the evidence will be only too apparent from the discussion which follows. Four minsters are recorded at a very early date, but institutional continuity from the mid-Saxon period onwards can only be glimpsed in the special case of Chertsey Abbey. The other three (Bermondsey, Farnham and Woking) appear in 7th- and 8th-century sources, but survival through the vicissitudes of the 9th and 10th centuries and identity with the Domesday churches cannot be proved. Tenth-century sources give explicit references to two others (Kingston and Godstone) and mention a priest at another likely minster centre (Croydon). Kingston has part of an 8th-century cross-shaft, and Godalming two 9th-century sculpture fragments. Otherwise we have nothing before the indirect and cryptic evidence of Domesday Book, supplemented by general considerations and hints from later material.

The work of the last twenty years makes it possible to accept Domesday terminology with more confidence as evidence for former minsters. In counties where the commissioners recorded churches at all, any description more elaborate than the ubiquitous *ibi ecclesia* or *ibi presbyter* seems generally a mark of superior status.[9] For Surrey it is encouraging that such descriptions correspond well with other evidence in suggesting likely candidates. In view of their terminological importance, the Domesday entries for all churches where the question of minster status arises are worth quoting in full:

> BERMONDSEY (King): 'Ibi nova et pulchra aecclesia'. (30b (I.4))
> CHERTSEY (Chertsey Abbey): 'Ipsa abbatia iacet in Godelei hundredo . . .' (32d (VIII.18))
> CROYDON (Archbishop of Canterbury): 'Ibi aecclesia'. (30d (II.1))
> FARNHAM (Bishop of Winchester): 'Aecclesiam huius manerii tenet de episcopo Osbernus de Ow. Valet 6 libras, cum una hida quam habet in Hantesira'. (31a (III.1))
> GODALMING (King): 'Rannulfus Flanbard tenet de hoc manerio aecclesiam, cui pertinet 3 hidae. Ulmaerus tenuit de rege E. Nunquam geldum reddidit . . . Ibidem tenet isdem Rannulfus alteram aecclesiam quae reddit 12 solidos per anum'. (30d (I.14))
> GODSTONE (Count Eustace): [No church mentioned.] (34b (XV.2))

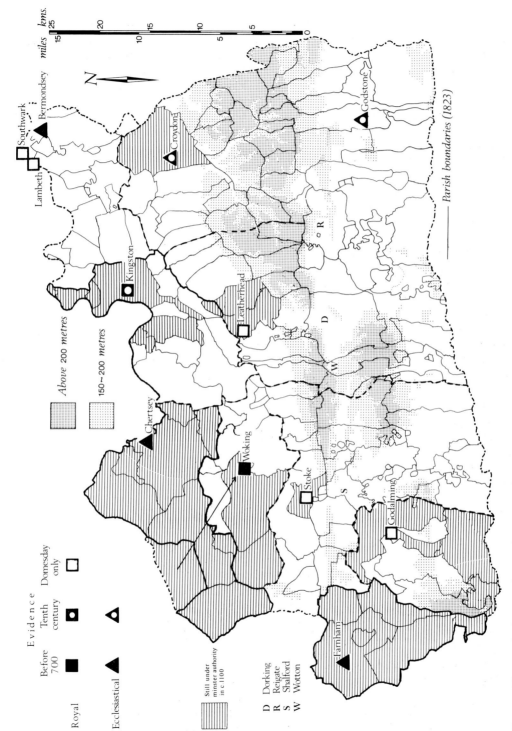

Fig 25   The Anglo-Saxon minster churches and their *parochiae*

KINGSTON (King): 'Ibi aecclesia'. (30c (I.8))

LAMBETH (Lambeth church): 'Terra aecclesiae de Lanchei . . .: Sancta Maria manerium est quod Lanchei vocatur. Goda comitissa tenuit, soror R.E. . . . Ibi aecclesia . . . De isto manerio habet episcopus Baiocensis unam culturam terrae, quae ante et post mortem Godae iacuit in ista aecclesia'. (34a–b (XIV.1))

LEATHERHEAD (King; after entry for the royal manor of Ewell): 'Ad hoc manerium adiacet aecclesia de Leret cum 40 acris terrae. Valet 20 solidos. Osbernus de Ow tenet'. (30c (I.9))

SOUTHWARK (Bishop of Bayeux): 'Ipse episcopus habet in Sudwerche unum monasterium et unum aque fluctum. Rex E. tenebat die qua mortuus fuit. Qui aecclesiam habebat de rege tenebat'. (32a (V.28))

STOKE BY GUILDFORD (King): 'Ibi aecclesia, quam Willelmus tenet de rege cum dimidia hida in elemosina'. (30b (I.3))

WOKING (King): 'Ibi aecclesia. Osbernus tenet'. (30a (I.2))

There is no uniformity about this list. In one entry the word *monasterium* is used, while most of the churches fulfil at least some of the conditions of being 'listed individually, with the names of the successive holders, a description of the holding, and a statement of its liabilities and value'.[10] Others are simpler: the ancient coronation church at Kingston has a plain *ibi aecclesia*, while only the addition of a tenant's name marks Woking as superior. Certainly we cannot argue from silence; Godstone minster, known from one earlier reference, is unmentioned in Domesday Book, and the same may apply to otherwise unknown minsters. Likewise, the distinction between mother church and local church is not quite so clear-cut as most writers have assumed; a few wealthy and long-established estate churches display, on a smaller scale, characteristics otherwise peculiar to old minsters (below, pp113–14). It can only be said that no Surrey churches beyond those listed above are known to have carried into the 11th and 12th centuries the attributes of major early foundations.

The Domesday and pre-Conquest evidence is deficient in one important respect. Since it scarcely ever mentions the bonds between mother and daughter churches, it wholly fails to indicate the original extent of minster *parochiae* or the degree to which they had been eroded by the 11th century. The historian must work backwards, reconstructing the *parochiae* individually and fitting them into an overall pattern, before he can work forwards again to trace their decline.

Chertsey

The earliest recorded Christian enterprise in Surrey was Bishop Eorcenwold's foundation, in or near 666, of sister monasteries at Barking (Essex) and Chertsey.[11] While Ecgbert of Kent was the original patron of Chertsey, the main benefactor was Frithuwold, sub-king of Wulfhere of Mercia.[12] Frithuwold soon afterwards granted a large estate 'ad roborandum idem monasterium quod nuncupatur Cirotesege', and if later forgeries preserve a core of truth the pre-Viking monastery also held more than thirty smaller manors scattered through Surrey (above, pp25, 30–1).[13] A garbled story in the 13th-century Chertsey Cartulary, taken in conjunction with an entry in the Anglo-Saxon Chronicle, suggests that the monastery was sacked by the Vikings in the late 9th century; re-founded in 884, presumably as a secular minster; and finally reformed in 964 when Eadgar expelled the priests and installed monks from Abingdon.[14] In its new guise the monastery maintained that special importance among Thames Valley houses which it had always held thanks to Frithuwold's lavish endowment.[15]

The medieval churches and chapels within the main demesne estate (fig 9A) all belonged to the

Abbey, and there is no hint of alien ecclesiastical rights. Clearly the original *parochia* of Chertsey minster covered at least this area, roughly coterminous with Godley hundred, which the monks still held in 1066 and over which they retained complete control. This estate was carved out of a pre-existing secular *regio* based on Woking (above, p14), and it is not impossible that the first Chertsey priests were intended to have pastoral responsibility for the whole territory, not merely for the portion in their own hands.

Woking

There was a tradition in the 12th century that dependencies of *Medeshamstede* (Peterborough) monastery in *c*690 had included Bermondsey and Woking minsters. This is a late source, but the Peterborough charters include a papal privilege of 708 × 15 addressed to Hædda, abbot of the monasteries founded in the name of St Peter at *Vermundesei* and *Wocchingas*.[16] In *c*775 × 785 King Offa confirmed to Woking church twenty hides 'in loco in quo illud monasterium situm est', at the request of Pusa abbot of Peterborough and the ealdorman Brorda.[17]

There is a reasonable *prima facie* case that this monastery survived, as a secular minster, to be identified with the church on the Domesday royal manor; the present church is in fact dedicated to St Peter. Even in the 13th century its parish was unusually large, including Pirbright as a dependent chapelry (fig 26).[18] More significant, the parochial jurisdiction of Woking church also covered Windlesham, an outlier of Woking manor and hundred cut off by Chertsey land (above, p14). An illuminating verdict given by local jurors in 1233 looks back to events in the reign of Henry II or before for the origin of Windlesham church:[19]

> Aliquando non fuerunt manentes in villa illa [ie Windlesham] nisi tantum tres homines qui fuerunt parochiani pertinentes ad ecclesiam de Wockinges, et aput Wockinges fuerunt corpora sepulti et pueri baptizati; et crevit villa, et quare longe fuerunt de Wokinges venit quidam Honing' qui tenuit in capite de domino rege, et in tantum locutus fuit cum persona qui tunc temporis fuit aput Wockinges quod concessit ei quod faceret ibi quoddam oratorium, in quo aliquando celebravit capellanus de Wockinges et aliquando legit ewangelium.

At the end of the 12th century, the Augustinian priory of Newark was founded in the adjacent parish of Send. Its origins lie in a grant made by a local landowner, Ruald de Calne, in 1191–8:[20]

> Sciant presentes et futuri quod ego Rualdus de Calna et Beatrix uxor mea . . . . dedimus et concessimus deo et beate Marie et beato martiri Thome et canonicis ibidem deo servientibus et servituris . . . terram que dicitur hamma de Pappeworth . . . ad construendam ibidem ecclesiam in honore beate Marie virginis et gloriosi martiris Thome in loco qui dicitur Aldebury . . . Preterea dedimus . . . ecclesiam de Sandes cum oratorio de Ripelia cum omnibus aliis ad eandem ecclesiam pertinentibus.

This document grants the Priory site to an existing body of canons. While this need mean no more than that Ruald had brought the community into existence before providing its home, the name of Newark ('de Novo Loco') which the canons adopted within the next two decades suggests a migration from elsewhere.[21] The 'oratory' of Ripley in Send parish, included in the foundation grant, has been suggested as their earlier home on the strength of its vaulted and lavishly decorated late Norman chancel;[22] but this is identifiable with a small hospital dedicated to St Mary Magdalen.[23] It is tempting to see the regular canons of St Mary and St Thomas the Martyr at Newark as secular canons from Woking, re-established within their old *parochia* under a new guise and dedication; of all religious orders the Augustinian canons were the most

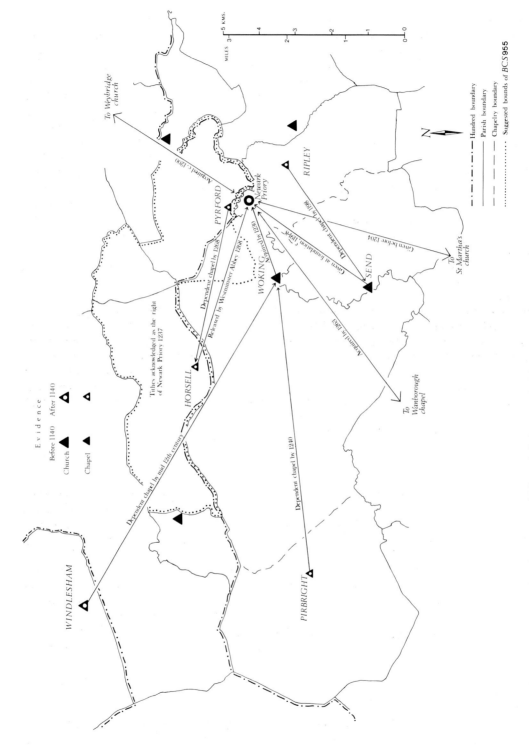

Fig 26   The earlier spiritual endowments of Newark Priory, probably reflecting the remains of Woking minster parish

frequent successors of earlier secular communities (below, pp106–7). Other attributes which passed to the canons of Newark reinforce this idea: Woking church was in their hands by 1230, and parochial rights over Pirbright were recovered shortly afterwards.[24]

The hypothesis of direct continuity from Woking minster to Newark Priory implies that the original *parochia* included not merely Woking, Pirbright and Windlesham parishes but also Send and Ripley; it may be noted that Woking parish church is virtually on the Woking/Send boundary. Other links are suggestive but inconclusive. In 1258 the Priory acquired the chapels on the adjoining Westminster Abbey manor of Pyrford with Horsell – where, significantly, it already held tithe rights.[25] The advowsons of other near though not contiguous parishes were acquired during the 13th century.[26] All in all, there is good circumstantial evidence that Woking minster parish originally comprised the entire Woking *regio* except for the Chertsey estate, and was thus considered to include the detached pasture at Windlesham when this acquired a settled population. Whether Woking or Chertsey minster came first (and the general historical context suggests the latter), the whole territory cannot have been served from a single religious centre for more than three or four decades.

Stoke-by-Guildford

Stoke church stood on a royal manor, and Domesday Book shows it farmed separately with half a hide. This suggests minster status, and the church remained important in the 12th and 13th centuries (below, p106). However, there is no trace of mother-church rights over neighbouring parishes; if Stoke ever had a *parochia* it must have adjoined or crossed the boundary between the 'Woking' and 'Godalming' *regiones*, and it does not fit easily into the general territorial scheme. In the context of reorganisation in this area for military purposes during the 9th and 10th centuries (above, p21), it may be that Stoke-by-Guildford church was a relatively late foundation which had no part in the pre-Viking network of minster parishes.

Farnham

In 685 × 7 the large multiple estate of Farnham was granted by Cædwalla of Wessex to Cedde, Cisi and Criswa 'ad construendum monasterium' (above, p25, fig 9C). It is not explicitly stated that the monastery was itself to be at Farnham; but the Domesday church there, separately farmed and with its large *valet* of £6, bears all the marks of an old minster. Clearly this was an important and well-established mother church.

In 1291 Farnham church with its chapels was taxed on the very high valuation of £94 13s 4d,[27] and as late as 1535 the whole of Farnham hundred was still one parish served by the mother church and three subordinate chapels.[28] It is virtually certain, then, that the original *parochia* included the whole of the Domesday manor and hundred, over which mother-church rights were fully maintained throughout the Middle Ages. If these rights ever extended into other parts of the 'Godalming' *regio* (above, p14), they perished too early to leave any trace in written sources.

Godalming

Two 9th-century sculpture fragments, now loose in Godalming parish church, suggest that by that date there was a church of some importance in the vicinity.[29] Its *parochia* is reasonably well-defined, thanks to the stable estate boundaries and one exceptional source. In 1086 the royal

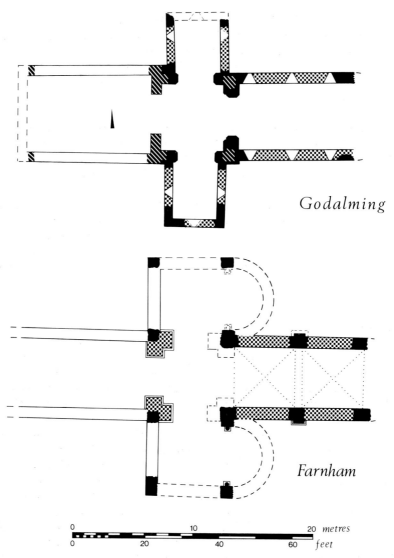

Godalming

Farnham

Fig 27   Godalming and Farnham churches: interpretation of the late Anglo-Saxon and Norman phases
(For key to shading conventions, see px)

'multiple estate' covered the entire hundred except for Gilbert fitz Richer's manor of Witley with
Thursley and the small independent enclaves of Hambledon and Peperharow. Domesday lists
two churches at Godalming, one endowed with three hides and both held by Ranulf Flambard.
Whether Ranulf regained possession on his return from exile is uncertain, but when, in 1109–17,
Henry I granted Godalming church to Salisbury Cathedral as part of a prebend, Ranulf kept a
life-interest as a canon of Salisbury.[30] In 1158 Henry II confirmed 'ecclesiam de Godelming cum
ecclesiis et capellis et terris et decimis ceterisque eidem ecclesie adiacentibus', and a detailed
visitation of the rectory and its appurtenances conducted by the dean of Salisbury in 1220 still
shows the Domesday royal manor as one parochial unit, with no less than five chapels subject in
different ways to the main church (fig 47).[31]

The mother church in 1220 was dedicated to SS Peter and Paul, and should be identified with the present parish church which still bears this dedication. The earliest phase is a little two-cell late Saxon building, greatly extended early in the 12th century (fig 27, upper; cf fig 31).[32] Its exceptionally large glebe, which made Godalming one of the wealthiest churches in Surrey, presumably included Flambard's three hides.[33] But according to the 1220 survey this was not the oldest church on the manor; for

> Item est ibi capella in campo de Godelming, versus Tiwerlei, que est de beata Virgine, ubi primo fuit sita ecclesia de Godelming. Non celebratur in ea nisi ter in anno, scilicet in Purificatione Beate Virginis, in vigilia Assumptionis et in Nativitate Beate Virginis, et hoc fit tantum propter devotionem que habetur ad locum illum; et fuit ibi cymeterium ab antiquo.

Clearly these were the two Domesday churches with their hierarchy reversed. The old mother church, on the hillside at Tuesley a mile or so from the modern town, had declined to a semi-deserted chapel. (In the 1550s it was still known as 'Oldmynster'; it has now vanished, though the site is known and has been excavated after a fashion.)[34] The later and humbler building, more conveniently sited, took on the functions and endowments of its predecessor and was suitably enlarged.[35]

Kingston upon Thames

The holding of an ecclesiastical council at Kingston in 838,[36] the existence in the church of an 8th-century cross-shaft fragment,[37] and the coronations there of several kings between Edward the Elder in 900 and Æthelred in 979,[38] all imply an important church. Domesday Book is unhelpful, but in the 12th century Kingston church emerges with a large parish and dependent chapelries.

The Augustinian priory of Merton was founded by Gilbert the sheriff and established on its final site in 1117 (below, p124). The foundation narrative has little to say of its endowments, but a late list of benefactions preserved by Leland includes 'ecclesia de Kingeston in Surrey cum 4 capellis annexis impropriata', the gift apparently being attributed to Gilbert himself.[39] This is unsatisfactory evidence; but Merton certainly had an interest in Kingston by the 1180s, while in 1231–8 the canons were said to have held the church 'a longis retro temporibus'.[40] In view of this, the absence of Kingston church from a general confirmation of spiritualities made in 1177–88 seems to imply its *presence* in a lost confirmation by Bishop Henry of Blois (1129–72), ratified but not recited in the extant text of the later document.[41] The evidence thus suggests that the church of Kingston royal manor was among Henry I's gifts to Gilbert the sheriff, and that Gilbert gave it to Merton at some date between the Priory's foundation and his death in 1130.

The four chapelries of Petersham, Sheen, Thames Ditton and East Molesey remained dependent on Kingston until 1769.[42] An agreement of 1266 emphasises the subservience of Petersham chapel to the mother church,[43] notwithstanding its appearance in 1086 on the Chertsey Abbey estate. Thus Kingston church had, in addition to its own large parish (above, p20), parochial jurisdicion over the entire Domesday hundred of Kingston except Long Ditton, Malden and their outliers,[44] and even these churches were secured to Merton Priory shortly before 1188. The church of Malden with Chessington chapel was given by Eudes de Malden, and Long Ditton church by Peter de Tolworth, both taking the habit at Merton shortly after.[45] As with the Newark Priory churches, it is unclear if these were free benefactions or prompted by some earlier claim. But the rather cumbersome statement that Long Ditton church was given by Peter de Tolworth 'cuius hereditas terra illa in qua sita est ecclesia fuit' echoes his earlier release

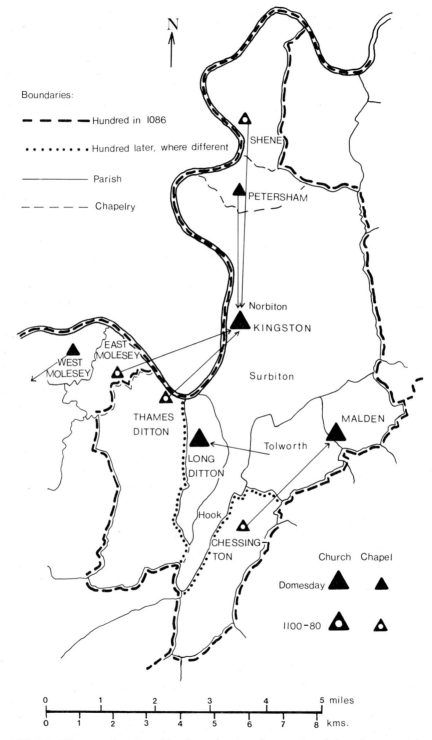

N

Boundaries:

━ ━ ━ Hundred in 1086

• • • • • • Hundred later, where different

──── Parish

─ ─ ─ Chapelry

SHENE

PETERSHAM

Norbiton

KINGSTON

EAST
MOLESEY

WEST
MOLESEY

Surbiton

THAMES
DITTON

MALDEN

LONG
DITTON

Tolworth

Hook

CHESSING-
TON

Church   Chapel

Domesday

1100-80

0   1   2   3   4   5 miles

0 1 2 3 4 5 6 7 8 kms.

Fig 28   Kingston church and its dependencies: the remains of the minster parish

to Lewes Priory of Horne church 'que est in territorio meo' (below, pp153–4); the limiting implication of the phrase (that Peter owned the land only, not the church) suggests that Merton had rights in the church already.

Thus the early minster at Kingston served most and probably all of Kingston hundred as existing in 1086 (fig 28). If the *parochia* was ever larger, it seems most likely that it extended westwards to include Elmbridge hundred; even in 1086 the dependent chapel of East Molesey lay beyond the hundred boundary. In support of this is the likelihood (above, pp14–17) that the two hundreds had formed the northern end of a single primary provincial territory.

Leatherhead

In the central area of the same territory, another major church can be identified. Of all the Surrey minsters, Leatherhead is the most mysterious in its eventual fate.[46] The royal manor appears in King Alfred's will, and later evidence associates official functions with Pachenesham manor on the claylands in the north of the parish (above, p20). The Domesday church and its 40 acres, farmed in 1086 for 20s, has generally been identified with the present parish church and its large glebe. This view, however, involves some problems.

The present church and virtually the whole glebe lie within the territory of Thorncroft manor, a Domesday property of Richard fitz Gilbert. Soon after 1100 Eudes Dapifer gave it to his newly-founded abbey of Colchester. Since Richard fitz Gilbert was Eudes's father-in-law it seems most likely that Eudes had acquired the church from him as his wife's dowry, and the link with Thorncroft manor is emphasised by the phrase of the Colchester charter, 'in Turnecruft ecclesiam ipsius ville et unam hidam terre'.[47] This is hard to reconcile with the Domesday entry, which lists Leatherhead church as a member of the royal manor of Ewell without any Thorncroft connection; while a pre-1086 grant of two-thirds of the tithe from Richard's demesne at Thorncroft may even suggest that, in thus depriving the old minster of its due under Eadgar's laws, he was reserving the remaining third for an estate church there ignored by Domesday (below, pp148–9).

On the other hand, an enclave of land in the north of the parish surrounded by Pachenesham territory was held of Ewell manor from at least the 13th century at 20s rent.[48] This location, near a manorial centre owing services associated with county jurisdiction, is a plausible site for the minster. One explanation best fits the puzzling circumstances: that the Domesday church had disappeared, its 20s *valet* remaining fossilized as a rent from the former glebeland.[49] The residual attributes of the old minster passed to a private estate church more conveniently sited near the river crossing: the former Thorncroft church emerges with parochial jurisdiction over the whole of Leatherhead parish and its adjoining chapelry of Ashtead.[50] These developments, if correctly interpreted, are more surprising than in the parallel case of Godalming, for the two Leatherhead churches were in different hands.

Southwark

The transition from secular to regular community, hinted at in the case of Newark, is quite clear at Southwark: the Domesday *monasterium*, in royal hands TRE, was reformed as St Mary's Augustinian priory. The 'aque fluctum' attached to it in 1086 (above, p94) can only be identified with St Mary Overy (now St Saviour's) Dock, and excavations here in 1980 between the Priory church and the river encountered a large 10th-century culvert which had evidently formed part of a dock.[51] In the 16th century the Priory preserved a garbled tradition that a community of sisters on the site preceded a house of secular canons, themselves finally replaced by Augustinian regulars.[52] The Priory's own Annals, in a manuscript of *c*1206, record under 1106 that 'Hic constitutus est ordo canonicorum in ecclesia Sancte Marie de Suthewerca'.[53] Probably the earliest original authority is a grant to the canons by William de Warenne II which is dated 'primo anno quo in eadem ecclesia canonici regulares effecti sunt'.[54]

The independent use of these elliptical phrases implies that the establishment of Austin canons was more a regularisation than a foundation *de novo*. This accords so well with the general pattern of early Augustinian houses that continuity from the pre-Conquest *monasterium* can scarcely be doubted.[55] As J C Dickinson has pointed out, 'ordo canonicorum' need not necessarily mean Augustinians; regularisation a decade or so after 1106 might better suit the chronology of other Augustinian foundations. The traditions which name William Giffard, bishop of Winchester, as the founder, and which state that he established secular canons at Southwark, may preserve memories of an intermediate phase.[56] The hypothesis that Giffard received this royal minster while the king's chancellor (1094–1101), and re-founded it as a secular college which was regularised shortly afterwards, accords with a wider pattern.[57]

By contrast, there seems to be no real evidence for survival of mother-church status in a jurisdictional sense. The early endowments all result from Norman benefactions (below, pp146–7), and no residual rights over churches in the form of pensions or portions can be identified.

Lambeth

According to Domesday Book (above, p94), Lambeth manor had been in the hands of King Edward's sister Godgifu before her death in 1056; in 1086 St Mary's church of Lambeth held it from the crown except for one field, then in the hands of Odo of Bayeux, which had belonged to the church in Godgifu's time. Soon afterwards the church and the whole vill were apparently given by William Rufus to Bishop Gundulf and his monks at Rochester.[58] Perhaps the best interpretation is that Godgifu had herself founded some kind of collegiate minster, endowing it with the whole manor. The only other Domesday holding of St Mary's church at Lambeth was Aston Subedge (Gloucestershire), and since this too had belonged TRE to Godgifu it supports the hypothesis of a fairly recent endowment.[59] The naming of the dedication by Domesday Book,[60] the language of the Domesday entry and the big endowment all suggest something more than an ordinary manorial church, even though there is no evidence of any special status after its acquisition by Rochester.[61] A note that Rochester removed from Lambeth a gold and silver shrine, gospel-books, rich crucifixes and other ornaments, all of which had belonged to Godgifu,[62] may mark the end of a private college or minster.

Bermondsey

The Peterborough sources which record a minster at Woking at the beginning of the 8th century (above, p95) mention another at *Vermundesei*, almost certainly to be identified with modern Bermondsey.[63] Nothing is known of its later Anglo-Saxon history, though recent excavations have produced a late Anglo-Saxon boundary ditch, and a piece of sculpture for which an 8th-century date has been claimed.[64] Nor is it possible to establish a direct link with the Cluniac priory of St Saviour, Bermondsey. This was traditionally founded in 1082, and although the first monks from La-Charité-sur-Loire did not arrive until 1089, it can scarcely be doubted that Domesday's 'nova et pulchra aecclesia' was the great Romanesque church which was to house them.[65] Bermondsey may therefore be one genuine case of a minster totally destroyed by the Vikings.

Croydon

The easternmost territorial division of Surrey contained a royal 'central place' at Wallington and an archiepiscopal one at Croydon, the latter perhaps the focus of a 'multiple estate' with strong Kentish links (above, pp17–18, 25). Despite the importance of Wallington, no church is recorded there beyond a small medieval chapel built over a pre-Conquest domestic site.[66] Croydon was one of two manors in Surrey which the see of Canterbury is likely to have acquired before c800, and in 1086 it was easily the most populous and valuable property in Reigate and Tandridge hundreds.[67] The ecclesiastical synod held at Croydon in 809[68] suggests a centre of religious importance under the Mercian kings. Ælfsi priest of Croydon appears in a Kentish will of 973 × 87,[69] and Domesday Book mentions a church. In the later Middle Ages, Croydon church was exceptionally valuable and the centre of a rural deanery,[70] though there are no references to mother-church rights extending beyond the medieval parish. The weight of evidence suggests that when the Surrey/Kent border area came to acquire a minster, it was built neither at Wallington westwards nor at Sutton-at-Hone eastwards, but on a new archiepiscopal complex in between.

Godstone

Domesday Book lists Godstone (*Wachelestede*) as the most valuable manor in Tandridge hundred, but mentions no church. There is no sign that the existing late Norman building, first mentioned in 1193, ever had more than ordinary parochial status.[71] Yet in 973 × 87 Brihtric and Ælfswith bequeathed 'ða tyn hyda on Straettune into þæm mynstre to Wolcnesstede'.[72] However loose the usage of 'mynstre', an endowment of ten hides suggests something a good deal more important than an ordinary estate church. As the identification seems certain,[73] the bequest must record an otherwise unknown religious community which disappeared during the next century or so. The will is Kentish, and also mentions a priest at Croydon (above). Perhaps the minster was founded relatively late, in the Wealden hinterland of the original Croydon estate (above, pp17–18), to serve developing communities in the Tandridge and Lingfield area.[74]

The political and territorial context of the minster churches

There are now strong indications that many, perhaps most of the English kingdoms had acquired a coherent system of *parochiae* by the early 8th century.[75] It is therefore perfectly possible that most of the Surrey minsters were as old as this, though specific evidence only exists in the cases of Chertsey, Farnham, Woking and Bermondsey. Farnham, founded in 685 × 7 after Cædwalla had won ascendancy from Mercia, may be the latest of the four. Chertsey, which must be the earliest, was built by a king of Kent, but its main estate came from Frithuwold, a Mercian sub-king; clearly it was brought under Mercian control and patronage within a very few years of its foundation.[76]

There is one further piece of evidence which links the origins of Chertsey, Woking and Bermondsey minsters and sets them in a wider world. Frithuric, the presumed kinsman of Frithuwold who appears as first witness to his Chertsey charter (above, p7), can almost certainly be identified with Friduric, *princeps* of King Æthelred of Mercia, who in 675 × 91 gave land at Breedon-on-the-Hill, Leicestershire, to Peterborough to found a daughter monastery.[77] Hædda, first abbot of Breedon, was also abbot of Woking and Bermondsey by 708 × 15 (above, p95), and the order of entries in a 12th-century Peterborough list suggests some possibility that Woking, Bermondsey and Repton minsters were dependencies of Breedon.[78] In other words, the sister or perhaps mother house of Woking and Bermondsey was founded by a relative or close associate of the main benefactor of Chertsey. Evidently the first Surrey minsters must be seen in the wider context of patronage by a noble dynasty under the successive overlordships of Wulfhere and Æthelred.

Origins in or before the 9th century can be claimed on sculptural evidence for Kingston and Godalming, and *prima facie* seem likely enough for Croydon and Leatherhead. But not all minsters were so early. Southwark and Stoke-by-Guildford, both associated with *burh* towns and both lacking recorded *parochiae*, may belong to the category of 'burghal minsters' originating with the re-conquest under Alfred and his successors.[79] Geographical considerations suggest that Godstone minster was relatively new (or even completely new) when it was endowed so lavishly in 973 × 87; while Lambeth college, if it was such, may have been founded by one of the last Anglo-Saxon aristocrats. These cases emphasise the fact that in the 10th and 11th centuries the college of priests was still acceptable ecclesiastically, even if it was becoming obsolete parochially.

In terms of the early territorial geography, there is a basic difference between minsters set on their own large estates (Chertsey, Farnham, ?Croydon), and the larger number built near centres of royal power. Whether the parochial functions of the former group ever extended outside their own lands is uncertain, though it may be that the earliest *parochiae* were coterminous with the provincial territories and were subdivided during the 8th and early 9th centuries as more minsters were established. The same period saw the breakup of the old provincial framework, progressively overlain by the accretion of manorial rights and fragmented into the smaller districts which were to emerge as hundreds. In this period of flux a wide range of political, territorial and pastoral factors, varying between different parts of England, are likely to have dictated the choice of minster sites.[80]

At all events, minsters and hundreds were closely related in late Saxon Surrey (fig 4). Most minsters stood near the medieval centres of hundred jurisdiction and the settlements bearing the hundred names. Without circularity of argument it is hard to demonstrate in general terms that hundreds and *parochiae* were coterminous, but this is certainly true in the particular cases of Farnham, Chertsey and probably Godalming. No hundred contained more than one minster except Brixton, where Southwark may well have been a post-Danish successor to Bermondsey rather than co-existing with it, and Woking, where Stoke-by-Guildford church may also be relatively late. Nor is there any trace of minster jurisdictions crossing hundred boundaries apart from the dependence of East Molesey on Kingston church, which is explained by the evident relationship between Elmbridge and Kingston hundreds. Further, to regard Elmbridge with Kingston and Copthorne with Effingham as two groups of paired hundreds (above, p17) leaves no hundred without its minster, excepting only the conspicuous gap formed by the Weald and Greensand hundreds of Blackheath, Wotton and Reigate (fig 25).

Surrey, then, displays that close relationship between minsters and hundreds which is a conspicuous feature of some parts of England and as conspicuously absent in others: it applies, for instance, in Hampshire and in parts of Kent and Sussex, but apparently not in Devon.[81] Most of the minsters are probably older than the final crystallisation of the hundreds; indeed, they may themselves have influenced the topography of hundred centres and boundaries. They were fixed points, foci of involvement for widely scattered populations and probably powerful stimuli for the growth of settlements around them.[82] They may have enhanced the status of the *villae* with which they were associated, and helped these to emerge superior to others when old units were re-moulded.

It seems possible that the siting of minsters in Surrey was influenced, partly at least, by a deliberate pastoral scheme. At all events, the distribution of mother churches existing in the century or so before the Conquest (that is, excluding Lambeth and Bermondsey) is logical in practical terms (fig 25). Six-mile radii around the relevant sites include almost the whole county, excepting once again the central Weald. At a time when these minsters were all active, no inhabitant of Surrey was more than half a morning's walk from one of them unless he lived in the remoter parts of Blackheath, Wotton or Reigate hundreds. This geographical coverage suggests a network established with some degree of planning, at a date before the substantial settlement of the Weald.[83] If the nature of the ministry is obscure, we can at least say that an institutional basis existed for it by a relatively early date.

The survival of mother-church attributes and functions

Recent work has greatly modified the old picture of minsters destroyed by the Danes, overshadowed by the Benedictine abbeys, pastorally moribund. It is now clear that hundreds of secular minsters survived well into the 11th and probably into the 12th century, and that official support for the small minority which were reformed failed to divert lay patronage from the unreformed majority.[84] In Surrey, only Chertsey minster became Benedictine and has thus left written evidence of its fortunes. There is no reason why community life should not have continued in the others, but for them the evidence is little more than scattered traces.

No entry in the Surrey Domesday lists a group of clergy; only at Southwark is one perhaps implied in the word *monasterium*, though even this is equivocal. This is not negative evidence, but simply absence of evidence: it is abundantly clear that Domesday does not always or even usually mention such communities when they existed. Such information was less readily included where the habitual formula was *est ibi ecclesia*, as in Surrey, than in counties where *est ibi presbyter* or *est ecclesia cum presbytero* were employed.

For the Domesday commissioners unregularised minsters, like almost everything else, were first and foremost property. Whatever their internal constitution or functions, they share with ordinary estate churches the status of manorial appurtenances; in Surrey only Chertsey Abbey and the recently-endowed church at Lambeth are tenants in their own right. Minsters received fuller treatment than other churches in 1086 largely because most were farmed separately. At Kingston and Croydon we find a simple *ibi ecclesia* since these mother churches, exceptionally, were still in royal and archiepiscopal demesne with the manors themselves: to specify endowments was needless when there was no question of divided tenure.[85]

Both before and immediately after the Conquest, many minsters (especially royal ones) were in the hands of clerical farmers.[86] The king had direct control of Southwark minster in 1066, though the statement that 'qui aecclesiam habebat de rege tenebat' suggests that it had been farmed in the recent past. Wulfmær, who had held Godalming minster geld-free, is the only named pre-Conquest tenant of a Surrey church; probably he was identical with the king's priest of that name, a minor TRE landowner in Buckinghamshire and Bedfordshire.[87] Royal priests were the most frequent recipients of valuable churches, and the unidentified William who held Stoke-by-Guildford church in alms in 1086 may have been another cleric in the Conqueror's household.

The other two TRW tenants of Surrey churches are more significant figures. The great Ranulf Flambard held both royal churches at Godalming. One Osbern 'de Ow', tenant of the royal minsters of Woking and Leatherhead and the episcopal minster of Farnham, must have been another wealthy ecclesiastic. He can probably be identified with the Osbern 'de Auco' who held a St Paul's prebend in *c*1100,[88] and perhaps also with the Osbern son of Hugh de Eu who appears as a Sussex landowner in 1086.[89] Both belonged to the class of great ecclesiastical pluralists and 'collectors' of minsters best typified by the Confessor's clerk Regenbald.[90]

Though generally clerics, such men clearly held their churches *in absentia*. Apparently they were left free to exploit as best they could the incidents of mother-church status in return for a fixed farm based on the value of the glebelands;[91] it was above all the large glebes which encouraged farming of old minsters, and marked them out as 'rectory manors' in the later middle ages.[92] In the half-century or so before 1086 kings and bishops had come to view many of their mother churches as appropriate gifts for faithful servants or useful sources of revenue, neither more nor less.

Yet it need not follow that the pluralists were careless of their churches' spiritual functions, or that proprietorship was incompatible with a flourishing religious life. Our sources are concerned with tenure, and we cannot expect them to throw much light on the motives of the tenants. To the early Norman mentality proprietary monasteries were as acceptable as proprietary churches, and the new owners might very well have taken an active interest in the internal life of old secularised minsters. In fact it is clear that many small religious bodies of uncertain nature existed under Norman patronage, sometimes based on former minster clergy and sometimes newly founded. Whether or not they observed any formal rule (and generally this is impossible to establish), they shared with contemporary estate churches the status of property. Only a brief period elapsed before the percolating ideals of Gregorian reform, and the institutional structure of the new religious orders, made them obsolete. With hindsight it is easy to forget that colleges of secular canons had an entirely natural place in 11th-century society, and that the Conquest may briefly have revitalised them.[93]

Surrey probably contained some of these evanescent re-foundations. Southwark, with its confused legend of a community of sisters and then one of canons preceding the Augustinians, may preserve some memory of the three-stage development outlined above. At Godalming, the extensive enlargement of the later church and its substitution for the old minster may well be Flambard's own work, and it is interesting to compare this with Christchurch Priory (Hampshire), another minster which he held in the 1090s. Here the old secular college was not refounded as an Augustinian priory until 1150, but a narrative source describes how Flambard had destroyed the old church, together with nine smaller ones around the cemetery and the canons' houses, to build the grand Norman church which still survives, financing this from the prebends and gradually reducing the number of canons.[94] Does the cruciform church at Godalming (fig 27, upper) reflect another such reorganisation by Flambard of an unrecorded collegiate body?

Farnham church was rebuilt very sumptuously in the mid 12th century, to a cruciform plan and with a vaulted two-bay chancel (fig 27, lower).[95] It is doubtful if arguments about status can rely much on architectural evidence, but both here and at Godalming the lavish plans (exceptional among Surrey churches), and especially the large chancels, may at least imply a staff of more than an ordinary parish priest. The cruciform plan of Kingston church could also be earlier than its Gothic detail, and beside it lay a detached Norman building.[96] The belief of Tudor townsfolk here 'that wher their toun chirche is now was sumtyme an abbay'[97] hints at memories of a collegiate body surviving until its annexation to Merton Priory, and an oath taken in Kingston churchyard in 1258–63 to conclude a dispute about common of pasture between Thames Ditton and Claygate underlines the continued importance of the church in hundred affairs.[98] Stoke-by-Guildford church emerges as head of a rural deanery, and a charter witness-list of c1160–80 beginning with 'Gileberto decano, Godardo presbitero, Rogero sacerdote de Stoches' may reflect a small residual staff.[99] Direct continuity from Woking minster to Newark Priory (above, p95) would imply a community of some kind surviving through the 12th century, and the fine Norman west door at Woking, with its elaborate contemporary ironwork, suggests a higher-than-average status.

Whether such bodies retained a significant role in the parochial structure is unclear. The strong popular appeal and involvement of the Austin canons made them fitting successors of old minster communities, and there is good evidence that in their early days they sometimes served parish churches in person.[100] With Benedictine monks, where the positive evidence is much less concrete, the position is still equivocal.[101] Monastic or collegiate staffs might have been pastorally active in two ways: by going out to the people like earlier minster-priests, or by encouraging or forcing the inhabitants of the old *parochiae* to attend regular service at their mother churches. This is a different matter from the mere enforcement of financial or jurisdictional rights over resident clergy and their parishioners.[102]

The survival into the Norman period of something resembling the minster system may be indicated by areas conspicuously lacking 11th-century churches. In Surrey the Chertsey Abbey endowments demonstrate this most clearly (fig 38). By 1086 all demesne manors lying more than nine miles from the Abbey had their own churches; but on the main estate in north-west Surrey Domesday lists only three churches, lying at distances of eight, eight and thirteen miles respectively. It is only during the later 12th century that churches or chapels appear at Chertsey itself, Thorpe and Egham, as well as on the detached but reasonably near demesnes of Cobham and East Clandon (below, p129). Since Domesday mentions some of the local churches belonging to Chertsey, the blank can scarcely result from a consistent under-recording of churches on ecclesiastical demesnes.[103] It seems evident that the areas most accessible from the Abbey were only 'parochialised' during the 12th century.

Farnham hundred, served by the mother church and probably only acquiring chapels in the 12th century, is another area where power at the centre may have delayed the foundation of local churches. Likewise, the relative sparseness of Domesday churches in the extreme north-east of Surrey (fig 32) is surprising in a region so densely settled and might reflect the survival of a ministry from Southwark, though the argument here is weaker in that no jurisdictional evidence supports it. Overall, pastoral care in Norman Surrey was already firmly based on local churches; the older system survived in places, but by the beginning of the 12th century it was patchy and residual. Whether the priests still went to the people or the people to the priests is impossible to say, though in the mid 12th century a chaplain still travelled periodically from Woking to serve the 'oratory' of Windlesham (above, p95).

In the 12th century many former minsters had chapels of late foundation. But in this they were not alone; after c1150 bishops were concerned to protect from encroachment the rights of *all* churches, irrespective of their earlier status (below, pp152–3). In Surrey it is hard to trace minster rights over churches which had existed in separate ownership from the 11th century or before. Kingston's chapels seem to have been founded at a relatively early date (above, p99), and one of them, the Chertsey Abbey demesne church at Petersham, is mentioned in Domesday. Apart from this, it cannot be demonstrated that a Surrey minster retained into the 12th century any authority over a church which was not either in the same ownership or founded after c1130; thus Godalming minster, the mother church of the royal manor, had no recorded authority over the few independent estates in the hundred (fig 47). The complex groups of rights and payments which elsewhere seem to reflect the late Saxon enforcement of minster authority are in Surrey completely absent, though there is no real lack of the sources in which they might have appeared.[104]

Conclusion

The relatively poor survival of mother-church authority in Surrey cannot be explained simply. In broad terms it is unsurprising in an area which by 1086 was better provided with local churches than many parts of England.[105] But the contrast with Hampshire, where the *parochiae* appear decidedly more resilient, is remarkable. Perhaps this difference between two halves of one diocese merely reflects Surrey's remoteness from Winchester, and a correspondingly lesser involvement on the part of the bishops. In Hampshire, at the heart of the late Saxon and Norman kingdom, abundant in wealthy monasteries and with many large estates in episcopal hands, centralised ecclesiastical institutions may have been especially well-equipped to preserve their authority against encroachments. It is significant that at Farnham, the one great Surrey manor of the bishopric, the minster preserved its rights so well; in a sense it is more of a piece with the Hampshire than with the Surrey minsters.

The degree of wealth, status and parochial jurisdiction which the minsters still retained in 1066 must have affected their viability in the eyes of new owners and farmers. It is worth contrasting two minsters farmed in 1086 to Osbern de Ow: Farnham, at a *valet* of £6, and Leatherhead, at a *valet* of £1. The former had a dominant and secure position as the church of a single big manor where no alien interests could intrude. The latter was the last remnant of one royal manor now annexed to another, retaining only a fragment of its *parochia*, and with mother-church rights which neighbouring landowners failed to respect.[106] It is symptomatic that Farnham minster survived as a rich, important and architecturally imposing church, while Leatherhead minster disappeared.

Through this discussion it has become increasingly clear that patterns of landholding, not ecclesiastical right, were the prime factor in the ultimate fate of the Surrey minsters. Where economic and demographic under-development favoured the survival of large unitary estates, the mother churches continued to dominate: at Chertsey and Farnham the coterminous estates and *parochiae* continued together. But where small independent manors existed, their late Saxon and Norman owners possessed and founded churches with scant regard for minster authority.[107] Whether a local church had initially been staffed by a resident priest or by a visiting minster-priest seems in this context to be largely immaterial: provided that it was in separate hands by the late 11th century, the mother church was unlikely to retain any hold on it into the later Middle Ages. The minster parish, like the multiple estate, had largely succumbed to the centrifugal tendencies of the age.

5 Local Churches: The Pattern and Chronology of Foundation

By 1066 the estate church was a familiar rural institution. This is clear from the law-codes which, from Eadgar onwards, accord limited tithe rights to thegns' churches with graveyards;[1] from the inclusion of a church among the marks of status by which a ceorl of around the year 1000 could expect to rise to thegnhood;[2] and from the numerous 11th-century Anglo-Saxon and Anglo-Norman church buildings. Above all, it is clear from the regular appearance of churches among manorial assets listed in Domesday Book.[3] Historians have tended to infer parishes from churches, and hence to conclude that the parochial system had already, in essentials, come into being. Thus it has recently been written that 'in most of England, even in 1086, the village church was already a familiar feature of the rural scene; and thereafter, the village and parish communities were identical in many places, making the village an ecclesiastical as well as a secular community'.[4]

Paramount source though Domesday Book is, its very uniqueness encourages an unduly static and homogeneous interpretation. The churches which it lists so tersely and uniformly were in fact extremely varied in status and function, and the process of foundation was far from over in 1086. Only systematic local studies using a wide range of sources can provide the necessary perspective. For the emergence of the parochial system, two questions are central: when and by whom were the churches founded; and how did their status alter over time? This chapter is confined somewhat narrowly to the first question; ch 6 will consider the second in the general context of ecclesiastical reform. It will be argued that while the area was well-supplied with local churches by 1066, the parochial system, as normally understood, was essentially a product of the 12th century.

The evidence

The 1086 data are our basic source, but their value as evidence must be assessed critically in the light of the Survey as a whole. It has long been known that Domesday Book was compiled by commissioners working on seven or perhaps nine circuits, and that between these circuits there are substantial differences in the compilation and presentation of data.[5] The recording of churches varies between the extremes of Circuit 7 (East Anglia), where we are given copious and detailed information, and Circuit 4 (Middlesex, Hertfordshire, Buckinghamshire, Cambridgeshire, Bedfordshire),where churches are only noted occasionally.[6] Standard forms of entry, *est ibi ecclesia*, *est ibi presbyter*, *presbyter habet x carucas* and so forth, also vary according to the circuit groups.

There are also differences *within* circuits. Thus in Circuit 5 Leicestershire, Staffordshire, Warwickshire and Northamptonshire contain numerous recorded churches, but Oxfordshire is a virtual blank; in Circuit 6, churches and priests are listed together in Derbyshire, Nottinghamshire, Rutland, Huntingdonshire and Yorkshire, but not in Lincolnshire. While some genuine regional variations are doubtless reflected, major differences in the quality and completeness of evidence within circuits and between adjoining counties are undeniable.

Surrey, with Kent, Sussex, Berkshire and Hampshire, was covered by Circuit 1. *Est ibi ecclesia* is the normal formula in all these counties, though in Sussex and Hampshire endowments and priests are often mentioned.[7] Kent provides what seems at first sight to be important comparative evidence, for here independent sources show that only about half the churches standing in 1086 were noted by the Domesday commissioners.[8] Certainly there are demonstrable omissions from the Surrey list,[9] and it is easy to argue that a source such as the 'Domesday Monachorum' would probably have revealed more.

Nonetheless, it seems more likely that we have here another case of strong divergence within a circuit; there are good reasons for thinking that the Domesday record of churches is considerably better for Surrey than for Kent. Among a total of 235 separately listed properties in Surrey, 61 (or 26%) are credited with churches. As shown below (tables 12 and 13, p120), however, the incidence of churches is weighted heavily towards the more valuable and populous estates, a large majority of which are stated to have them. If in Surrey, as in Kent, no more than some 50% of existing churches had been recorded, so clear and credible a pattern could scarcely have emerged. The contrast with Kent, where churches are unmentioned on numerous large estates of a kind that would normally have them in the Surrey Domesday, is clear even from a cursory comparison. The later Surrey evidence seems equally incompatible with gross deficiencies in 1086: well over half of the parish churches which existed by c1200 appear in Domesday Book, and many of the remainder are interpretable as post-Domesday foundations. Imperfect though their recording undoubtedly was, it seems a reasonable working assumption that the commissioners listed a large majority of the churches standing in the county when they surveyed it. The equally important issue of whether or not most of these churches had existed twenty years before is best considered in the light of individual local circumstances.

With occasional exceptions the other written evidence is post-1100, and mainly takes the form of charters granting churches to religious houses. Like Domesday Book, these generally only provide a *terminus ante quem* for the foundations, and of course they are heavily biased towards monastic possessions. Some churches in continuous lay ownership escape mention until the late 13th century, even though they retain 11th- or 12th-century structural features. A list of c1270 in Bishop John of Pontoise's register,[10] together with that compiled for the papal taxation of 1291,[11] probably covers all parish churches then existing, though chapels are still only very incompletely recorded.

Discussion of the buildings themselves must now reckon with drastic reappraisals of the latest phase of Anglo-Saxon architecture, to which all Surrey churches with stylistically pre-Conquest features belong. E Fernie has proposed 'a school of minor churches, inhabiting the hundred years from the second quarter of the 11th century to the second quarter of the 12th, which is neither simply "Saxon" nor simply "Norman"', and suggests that 'half, if not the majority, of the surviving buildings commonly grouped under the label "Anglo-Saxon" belong to this category'.[12] It is becoming clear that in the years c1030–1130, new churches were built and old ones rebuilt on such a scale as to justify borrowing from a later period the term 'Great Rebuilding'.[13] The Domesday survey happens to have taken place when this activity was at its height; hence it is virtually impossible to say on architectural grounds that any given church, whether pure late-Saxon, pure Norman or in a mixed style, was or was not standing in 1086.

Nonetheless, patterns may still emerge through studying a substantial group of churches within one region. Among churches of roughly similar status, the less stylistically advanced buildings will in general tend to be older than the more advanced ones. They may also reflect closer links with Anglo-Saxon institutions and personnel, just as up-to-date Norman work may reflect the wealth, power and contacts of a new lord. Archaeology has shown that while some churches of this period replace older (though only slightly older) timber buildings, many do not. So when most churches in a social or tenurial category prove to be architecturally similar, the fact may have some broad chronological significance. The exercise of relating such patterns to the Domesday record of churches, and to the tenurial arrangements of 1066 and 1086, seems worth attempting: a careful over-view may reveal trends which are convincing in their internal consistency, setting a pattern to which obscure areas may be related.

Hence this chapter makes extensive use of physical evidence (whether surviving or, as so often in Surrey, recorded only in watercolours and drawings),[14] and is illustrated with church plans reconstructed to show the earliest visible phases and drawn to a common scale. It is taken as a working hypothesis that such explicitly Anglo-Saxon features as thin, high walls and double-splayed windows, when not associated with any trace of Norman influence, are unlikely to have been built much after 1100; and that features of a rudimentary Norman or Saxo-Norman character, notably single-splayed windows with monolithic or rubble heads, suggest origins no later than *c*1120–40.

Local churches in the pre-Danish period

With churches, as with estate boundaries and field-systems, the evidence for continuity from Romano-British to Anglo-Saxon society is essentially circumstantial. The cult of St Alban at Verulamium could merely be one instance of a wider pattern: it is *prima facie* likely, if hard to prove, that centres of devotion often survived in areas of residual British settlement.[15] The apparent re-use of Roman buildings at Canterbury and Stone-by-Faversham as the nuclei of early Saxon churches has little real weight in the absence of any evidence for continuous use.[16] It is also doubtful how we should interpret such initially impressive evidence as the proximity of so many Essex churches to Roman sites.[17] Upstanding Roman buildings would have offered architecturally imposing settings for new churches at any stage in the Anglo-Saxon period; even demolished ones were sources of rubble. This may account for the two Surrey instances at Stoke D'Abernon and Ashtead (fig 40), and seems especially likely in the latter case: the church is a 12th-century foundation (below, p124), its walls incorporate flue-tiles from a nearby Roman building,[18] and both church and manor-house stand within a convenient levelled and ditched enclosure of Roman origin.

The place-name element *eccles*, a derivative of late Latin *eclesia*, probably implies contact between the early Germanic settlers and native churches with Latin-speaking priests or worshippers. Though commonest in the north-west Midlands, the element also occurs in Kent near rich concentrations of Roman remains.[19] A new and topographically significant example seems worth adding. The Pyrford charter-bounds of 956 pass around the irregular west end of modern Horsell parish (fig 11A). Unfortunately they cannot be plotted exactly, but at some point between *per leage* (Parley Farm) and *mint byrge* (Mimbridge) was an inclosure or meadow called *eceles hamme*.[20] This must have lain near, perhaps almost adjoining, the medieval church of Bisley some fifty yards from the boundary (fig 29).[21] Bisley is an enclave on the edge of the great Chertsey Abbey estate; the nondescript little church need be no older than the 12th century, though it probably appears in Domesday Book as a chapel of Chobham.[22] Although the area is not one of intensive Roman settlement, this seems a significant association between an *eccles* name and a standing church:[23] it is conceivable that some cult had survived around the church site, or around the nearby holy well of St John the Baptist where parishioners were still being baptised within recorded memory.[24]

Other evidence for pre-Danish local churches amounts to very little. Early origins have been claimed for two small hilltop churches: Chilworth because of its unusual dedication (St Martha, suggested as a corruption of a Romano-Celtic dedication to the 'Holy Martyrs'),[25] and Thursley on the hypothesis that it was the direct successor of a pagan Anglo-Saxon shrine (below, p115). Both suggestions are speculative, and neither is supported by any physical remains. Elsewhere in the county, there are no very early references to ordinary churches, and no extant fabric older

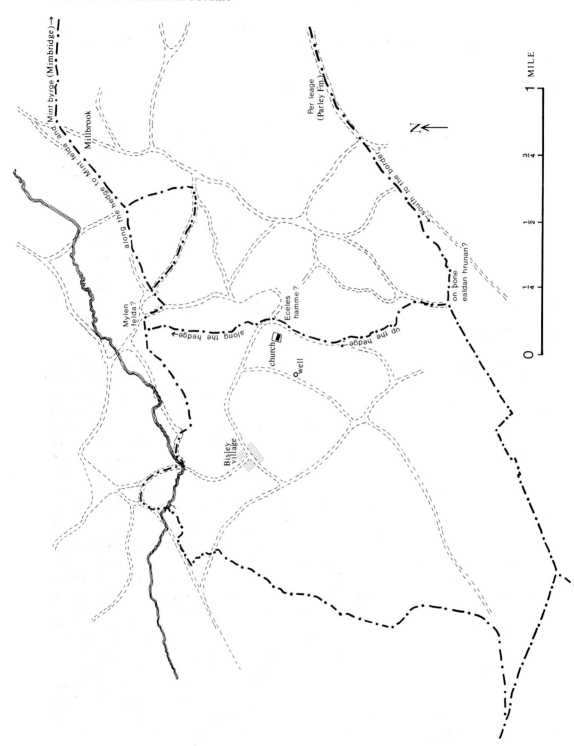

Fig 29   The relationship of Bisley church to *eceles hamme* in the Pyrford charter-bounds (S621)

than Taylor's 'Period C' (950–1100). So Surrey provides no support for those who would claim that private local churches were familiar features in the landscape before the 10th century.

Important pre-Conquest estate churches: the royal demesne

The Domesday churches on former demesne of King Edward have already, with one exception, been identified as old minsters (ch 4). Queen Edith's TRE demesne was a smaller group of manors with further churches which, while less important than the minsters, nonetheless stand out from the main body. With other, mainly Wealden churches they represent an intermediate category, comparable to the 'secondary mother-churches' of Kent recently discussed by Everitt.[26]

Three valuable Wealden estates had belonged to Edith TRE, and all three undoubtedly had churches in 1086. Domesday mentions them at Shere and Dorking, and by the late 12th century both had impressive cruciform buildings which may have reflected an earlier importance.[27] At Reigate, where no church is mentioned by Domesday Book, there survives part of a late Saxon grave-slab or cross-shaft.[28] All three churches originally had parochial jurisdiction over half or more of their respective hundreds. Neighbouring churches, not in royal hands, may have had a similar status. Shalford was the head church of Æthelnoth's great manor of Bramley, already with two subsidiary churches by 1086 at the latest (below, p119). Others in this area, such as Wotton and Betchworth, may once have had wider areas of influence than their definable parishes suggest.

The Queen's ownership of three of these churches suggests a royal origin, and at Reigate, Shalford and Shere the glebes were abnormally large.[29] At Wotton the nave may be pre-Conquest with early Norman additions, and excavation has revealed what appear to be underlying earlier walls.[30] Shalford mother church, with its two daughters (below, p119), can scarcely have been recent in 1086. Just as the old multiple estate economy continued to suit the under-developed Wealden landscape (above, pp25–7), so the churches which served the sprawling Wealden manors resemble, on a small scale, the ancient minsters. A similar response answered a similar need: the primary establishment of the Church in a region of scattered and unstable settlement. As denns gradually gave way to fixed dwellings, the pastoral problem here in the 9th, 10th and 11th centuries must have been similar to that faced by earlier rulers of Surrey on first accepting Christianity. By this time, in the more populous area north of the Downs, the minster *parochiae* were already yielding to a more developed type of ecclesiastical geography.

Extra-Wealden Surrey does, however, contain two churches which fall uncertainly between the categories of minster and local church. One is Wimbledon, the mother church of the archbishop's manor of Mortlake (above, p25), which had chapels at Barnes, Putney and Mortlake; its status as an important late Anglo-Saxon estate church is reflected in the high 1291 valuation of £40[31]. The other case is Walton-on-Thames. It has been suggested (above, p101) that Kingston and Elmbridge hundreds were both served by a minster at Kingston, its *parochia* reduced by 1086 to little more than the hundred in which it stood. Domesday Book only mentions three churches in Elmbridge hundred, of which Walton, with its large parish and valuation of £30 pa in 1291,[32] was always the most important. Of the other two, West Molesey and Stoke D'Abernon, it is significant that the former later emerges as a chapel of Walton.[33] Walton church approaches minster status, dominant in the hundred and with pre-Domesday mother-church rights.[34] But the manor belonged TRE to Earding, a wealthy layman with three other Surrey properties,[35] and it never appears as royal demesne. Possibly the unusual standing of this church reflects the creation of Elmbridge as a 'private' hundred,[36] with minster rights diverted from the old mother church to a new one for the benefit of its owner.[37]

In Surrey the late Anglo-Saxon kings had little need to build churches; their estates were already well-supplied with ancient minsters. Occasionally a supplementary church might be built on a large royal manor. According to a Hyde Abbey chronicle, both Sanderstead and its Wealden denn of Lingfield already had churches when Queen Æthelflaed gave them to the Abbey before 964.[38] The second Domesday church at Godalming (above, pp97–9) may have been built either by the king or by the clerical farmer in Edward the Confessor's reign. But the main initiative in church-building had now passed to landowners with a more immediate local interest.

Late Anglo-Saxon ecclesiastical proprietors

It is entirely predictable that abbots and bishops should have been enthusiastic church-founders. The 10th and 11th centuries, the great age of growth for local churches, were also the age of the reformed monasteries. English bishops following in the footsteps of St Dunstan, often of monastic origin and closely associated with the great Benedictine houses, showed concern for the quality of the rural priesthood, the stabilisation of relationships between churches and pastoral care in general.[39] The religious climate must have favoured the building of new churches on episcopal and monastic estates, even though this activity is not conspicuous in the literary sources. Surrey was a county in which two great ecclesiastical institutions – Chertsey Abbey and the Archbishopric of Canterbury – had major interests, and by 1086 the manors of both were abnormally well-endowed with churches.

The preservation of minster rights made the neighbourhood of Chertsey Abbey a striking blank on the ecclesiastical map (above, p107). Equally striking, however, is the abundance of churches on the Abbey's manors which lay outside a six-mile radius from it (fig 38). They are listed on seven of the eleven scattered manors, in addition to nearby Chobham;[40] of the four churchless manors,[41] two were trivial properties of a kind virtually devoid of churches in the Surrey Domesday, while Cobham may have been considered near enough to Chertsey for the maintenance of direct pastoral contact. Expressed another way, churches are listed on eight of the ten manors which fall within a value range of £2 to £20 pa. Comparison with table 12 shows that this provision is well above the average for the Surrey Domesday as a whole. Among these, furthermore, Chobham had a church and chapel, while Epsom and Sutton each had two churches, almost certainly identifiable with the modern parish churches of Epsom and Ewell on the one hand and Sutton and Horley on the other.[42]

The distribution of these buildings suggests pastoral motives extending beyond a simple policy of planting a church on each administrative unit in the Abbey's estate. Chobham church with its chapel (probably Bisley church) served distant regions of the main estate. The pairing of Sutton and Horley churches, together with that of Sanderstead and Lingfield already mentioned, provides our earliest evidence for the secondary establishment of churches in discrete denns of head manors. The small contiguous manors of Coulsdon and Waddington had separate churches, an arrangement which was rationalised (presumably in response to settlement change) in the late Middle Ages by the abandonment of Waddington church.[43] The remaining three churches served scattered properties: the relatively large manor of Great Bookham and the smaller ones of Petersham and Tooting.

Were these churches built before the Conquest? Structural evidence, confined to a possible late Saxon nave shell at Coulsdon (fig 30),[44] is unhelpful.[45] But Wulfwold, the last pre-Conquest abbot of Chertsey, had retained office until his death in 1084,[46] and Norman influence on his habits of church-building seems unlikely. Except for Tooting (below, p122), the Chertsey Abbey churches are best interpreted as the work of English abbots.

The archiepiscopal estate in Surrey, comprising Mortlake (valued at £32 TRE),[47] Croydon

(£12),[48] Merstham (£8),[49] Cheam (£8),[50] East Horsley (£4),[51] and Walworth (£1 10s),[52] was equally abundant in Domesday churches: only the East Horsley entry fails to include one. Conceivably we see here the hand of Lanfranc. But Cheam provides strong evidence for a foundation shortly before the Conquest: Christ Church Canterbury had acquired the manor from a layman in 1018,[53] the existing building is late Saxon in style, and its dedication is to St Dunstan, whose cult was in eclipse during Lanfranc's pontificate.[54] Only a fragment of this church now remains, but an old plan[55] suggests that it comprised a rectangular nave/chancel with a western annexe longer in the north–south than in the west–east dimension (fig 30). If so, the archiepiscopal church of East Horsley, unmentioned by Domesday Book but Saxo-Norman in style (fig 30), is sufficiently similar to suggest a direct parallel for this relatively unusual plan-form.[56] If this architectural relationship is genuine, it may tend to suggest that Cheam and East Horsley churches were both built by the same patron at around the Conquest period.

The Chertsey and the Canterbury churches alike suggest a continuing process of foundation which the Conquest need neither have stimulated nor interrupted. The secondary character of some of the Chertsey foundations (the Wealden church at Horley and the pair serving Coulsdon and Waddington) suggests a context of relatively recent topographical development, and it seems *prima facie* likely that all or most post-date the Abbey's regularisation in 964. Both groups suggest a programme of church-building spread over perhaps no more than one or two generations: not so much a general tendency for religious bodies to found churches[57] as active and deliberate pastoral care on the part of two great institutions. Tenants were either to have ready access to churches of their own or, in the case of Chertsey, to be served from the Abbey itself.

Late Anglo-Saxon lay proprietors

It is above all to late Saxon thegns that the building of local churches should be ascribed. While the prominence given to private lay churches in the law-codes may partly be due to their tendency to become independent, there can be no doubt that thousands of English parish churches owe their existence to 10th- and 11th-century private landowners. The nature of lay patronage has often been discussed, but there are some central issues which can only be tackled in a local context: what were the motives of church-building thegns; how socially restricted was the practice; and was it normal or exceptional for one man to have multiple churches?

The possessions of the house of Godwine collectively overshadowed all other lay estates in the county. Despite their high value in 1066, the manors of Harold, Swein and Leofwine were not particularly well-endowed with churches.[58] Churches are, however, recorded at Witley and Oxted, two large manors of Godwine and Gytha respectively.[59] Both Witley parish church and its chapel at Thursley are stylistically Anglo-Saxon, but in neither case is a pre-Conquest date likely. Both churches have walls over three feet thick; at Witley it has now been demonstrated that the lavish early 12th-century scheme of wallpaintings is almost certainly contemporary with the building (which must therefore have replaced the church mentioned in 1086).[60] Thursley chapel is not mentioned in Domesday; its hilltop site, its dedication to St Michael and the 'Thor' place-name might suggest the conscious replacement of some pagan cult, but they conform equally well to a group of what seem to be relatively late Kentish churches with this dedication.[61]

Half-a-dozen other landowners, each with an estate valued at more than £20 pa in 1086, make up the leading local aristocracy on the eve of the Conquest. Osweard's three manors all lack recorded churches, though at Godstone, the largest, an omission seems likely.[62] Earding held the important manor and church of Walton-on-Thames (above, p113), but his smaller properties seem somewhat deficient in churches.[63] In the cases of Ælfmær and Azur, the names are common and it is not certain in either case that we are dealing with one man; at all events, only two of the

Fig 29a   The destroyed late Anglo-Saxon church at Hascombe: view from the south-east by H. Hussey, 1845. (Bod. Lib. MS Top Gen f 18 f.35ᵛ. Reproduced by permission of the curators of the Bodleian Library.)

twelve small, scattered estates assigned to Ælfmær have recorded churches.[64] On manors ascribed to Azur the provision seems good: churches are listed at Beddington, Woodmansterne, Albury, Warlingham and Henley,[65] comprising all but one of his properties valued at over £5 pa. The fact that all these manors (except Henley, which Azur gave to Chertsey Abbey after 1066) were held TRW by Richard fitz Gilbert suggests that the estate of one man named Azur was transferred *en bloc*. Adopting this criterion for separating him from possible namesakes, we may say that four of Azur's five former manors, or perhaps five of six, had churches TRW,[66] and of these Albury retains a possible late Saxon building (fig 30).[67]

The implication of the evidence for Godwine and Azur – that a wealthy man might have churches in proportion to his tenants' needs – is reinforced by the cases of Beorhtsige and Æthelnoth. As 'Brixi cild', Beorhtsige appears as a major landowner in the Kent and Surrey sections of Domesday Book, and occurs also in Hampshire and Essex.[68] Of his four Surrey manors, churches are mentioned at Compton (valued at £8 pa TRE)[69] West Horsley (£8)[70] and Stoke D'Abernon (£4),[71] leaving only Hatcham (£2)[72] lacking one. In all three cases there may be surviving pre-Conquest fabric. Stoke D'Abernon church (fig 30) had an aiseless nave, with a west gallery approached through a high-level doorway in the south wall, and an apsidal chancel.[73] Although the great age recently claimed for this church[74] must be discounted, it is certainly a pure late-Saxon building; the interpretation of its gallery as a mark of lay proprietorship, a forerunner of the family pew,[75] may still be valid. The nave and possibly tower at Compton,[76] and the nave at West Horsley,[77] are also early work with no visible sign of Norman influence.

Æthelnoth of Canterbury was one of the most important Kentish thegns of the mid 11th century. He was among William's leading hostages of 1067, and as 'Alnod cild' he is a frequent TRE tenant in Kent and neighbouring counties.[78] In Surrey he appears six times, no churches being listed at Blechingley, which he held jointly with two others (TRE value £13 pa),[79] or at Chivington (£11) which is now in Blechingley parish.[80] Churches occur, however, at Banstead

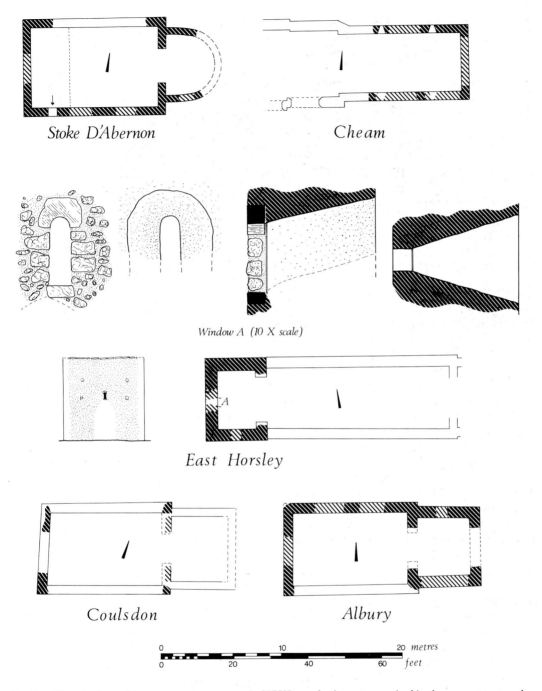

Fig 30   Church plans. (For sources see accounts in *VCHSy*, and other sources cited in the present text under references to the individual churches. The plan and detail of East Horsley church are from a personal survey. For key to shading conventions, see px)

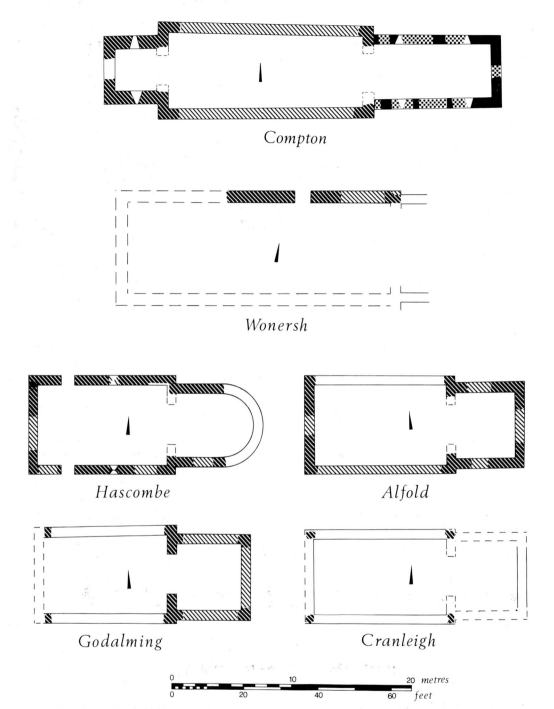

Compton

Wonersh

Hascombe

Alfold

Godalming

Cranleigh

Fig 31   Church plans. (For sources see accounts in *VCHSy*, and other sources cited in the present text under references to the individual churches. The plans of Wonersh (surviving portion) and Alfold churches are from personal surveys. For key to shading conventions, see px)

(£10),[81] Tillingdown (£7),[82] and Buckland (£5),[83] while Bramley (£40)[84] had no less than three. Architectural evidence, inconclusive in the first three cases,[85] is helpful where Bramley is concerned. Not Bramley church itself but Shalford church was the mother church of this great Domesday estate; both Bramley and Wonersh are recorded as its chapelries, the former being still subject to Shalford's burial rights in the late 16th century.[86] Also within the area of Domesday Bramley are the parish churches of Dunsfold and Hascombe (fig 9D). Both its site (on the older-settled northern part of the estate) and the normal implications of ecclesiastical dependence suggest that Shalford was the senior as well as the dominant church.[87] Of the other four, there is no reason to think that churches existed at Bramley and Dunsfold before the existing 12th- and 13th-century buildings.[88] But the churches at both Wonersh and Hascombe formerly retained late Saxon double-splayed windows, in the latter case (figs 29a, 31) in a small, lofty nave of distinctively pre-Conquest proportions.[89] Thus the three Domesday churches of Bramley should almost certainly be identified with the modern parish churches of Shalford, Wonersh and Hascombe, and of these both subsidiary churches were Anglo-Saxon in style. Once again, a pre-Conquest origin is suggested: it seems much more likely that these churches were founded by Æthelnoth or a predecessor than by Odo of Bayeux, the tenant in 1086.

The smaller TRE landowners were much less frequently proprietors of churches. A recurring pattern is for one man to have held a small group of manors, at a total TRE value of some £10 to £20 pa, with a church mentioned at one alone. Thus a church appears only at West Molesey among Tofi's four manors,[90] only at Wisley among Osweald's six,[91] and only at Titsey among Godtovi's three.[92] Only Betchworth, the most valuable of Cola's three manors,[93] had a recorded church, and here a late Anglo-Saxon shaft-capital re-used in the early Norman fabric indicates a pre-Conquest stone building.[94] On estates of the humbler *antecessores*, with a total value of £10 pa or less, churches are distinctly unusual and sometimes occur in circumstances suggesting post-Conquest foundation (below, p122).

Overall, the incidence of churches was markedly higher not only on the more valuable manors, but also on individual manors of proprietors who were generally the most wealthy. The structural evidence tends to suggest that post-Conquest foundations have not distorted this pattern very seriously: it is significant, for instance, that the estates of Beorhtsige, Æthelnoth and the archbishop include between them about half of all Surrey churches known to contain stylistically Anglo-Saxon work. There is, of course, no evidence for how the 1066 pattern had evolved: many of the older churches may have changed hands many times with the estates on which they stood. We can only say that the mid 11th-century evidence suggests a correlation between wealth and certain norms of church possession.

R V Lennard successfully refuted the belief that a late Saxon thegn, no matter how numerous his estates, would normally have a church on one only.[95] Nonetheless, the Surrey evidence suggests that church-founding habits varied somewhat according to the standing of the founder. Such cases as Thursley, Wonersh and Hascombe must have been subsidiary 'out-churches' to serve regions within great lords' estates. A single church, however, often seems to have answered the convenience or status of a lesser thegn, even when his properties were scattered. Even this was only normal among men considerably above the lowest ranks of thegnhood: only a minority of TRE landowners with manors totalling five to ten hides in Surrey (and some of course had them in other counties too) have listed Domesday churches. More so, apparently, than during the Norman period, church ownership was still usually accompanied by considerable wealth and extensive local interests.

The Church in Domesday Surrey (Fig 32)

Tables 12–13 show the incidence of Domesday churches in relation to TRW values and population figures. Clearly this incidence is highest on the more valuable and populous manors, a distribution which would be still more marked if the large churchless properties surrounding Chertsey Abbey were excluded. As we have seen, there is a more subtle weighting, within this pattern, towards individual components of the larger TRE estates: great men were more liable than others to build churches on their manors. But equally, as table 13 shows, the manors most likely to acquire them were those with a large body of tenants: such properties afforded both a pastoral need and a handsome yield of tithes.

The TRW data are consistent with the view that where new foundations are concerned, the Norman contribution had so far been slight. Thus subinfeudated manors and the demesnes of tenants-in-chief had churches in roughly equal proportion within each value group: survivals from the past, the churches fail to reflect the tenurial structure of 1086. And while the new style had certainly begun to influence the continuing process of rebuilding, it seems unlikely that it was yet widespread except on estates of wealthy men.

The new aristocracy was rebuilding favoured churches in a way which gave them permanent distinction, with fine masonry and spacious proportions. Perhaps most characteristic of these

TABLE 12   The incidence of churches in the Surrey Domesday in relation to 1086 values

	Above £20	£11–£20	£6–£10	£1–£5	Below £1	Not Valued	Total
Total of listed holdings*	12	30	41	103	25	24	235
Total with listed churches	8	19	21	13	nil	nil	61
Percentage with listed churches	66.7	63.3	51.2	12.6	nil	nil	26.0

* This excludes Guildford and Southwark.

TABLE 13   The incidence of churches in the Surrey Domesday in relation to 1086 listed population

	Above 60	46–60	31–45	16–30	1–15	Nil	Total
Total of listed holdings*	9	12	24	48	110	32	235
Total with listed churches	7	7	16	17	13	1	61
Percentage with listed churches	77.8	58.3	66.7	35.4	11.9	3.1	26.0

* This excludes Guildford and Southwark.

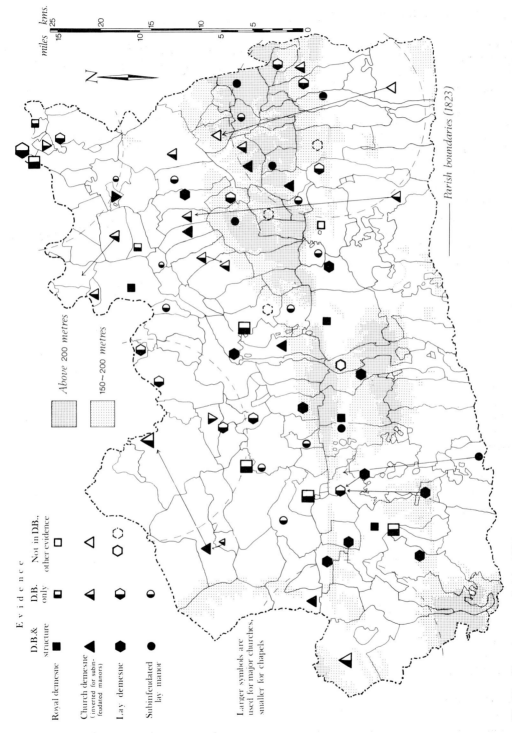

Fig 32   Churches recorded in 1086

greater estate churches is the three-cell axial-tower type, of which Carshalton (fig 33) may provide one of the earliest Surrey examples.[96] The demesne manors of Richard fitz Gilbert still retain more than their share of big early Norman churches (fig 33): at Betchworth, where Cola's stone church was replaced by a fine axial-tower building;[97] at Walton-on-Thames, where there is evidence for a large nave of Norman proportions;[98] at Thorncroft, where the original Norman church (not listed in Domesday) seems to have been very similar in plan to Betchworth;[99] and at Blechingley, where the church with its big west tower (again unmentioned in 1086) was built in or soon after Richard's day to serve the contiguous estates of Blechingley and Chivington.[100] There are suggestions here of a campaign, still uncompleted in 1086, to provide the Clare demesnes with fine new churches and perhaps where necessary to found them *ab initio*.[101]

Although some of the simple early-Norman churches probably replaced Saxon buildings, a handful listed by Domesday Book on small subinfeudated manors may be recent foundations marking the beginnings of a new phase: Chaldon, held by Ralph from the Bishop of Bayeux (valued at £4 pa TRW);[102] West Clandon, held by Hugh from Edward of Salisbury (£3);[103] Chelsham, held by Robert de Wateville from Richard fitz Gilbert (£7);[104] Long Ditton, held by Picot from Richard fitz Gilbert (£2 10s);[105] Gatton, held by Herfrid from Odo of Bayeux (£6);[106] and Tooting, held by Hamo the sheriff from Chertsey Abbey (£3 10s).[107] There is evidence for substantial early-Norman work at Chaldon (fig 34), Gatton and Tooting churches,[108] while the dedication of Chelsham church to St Leonard suggests a post-Conquest foundation.[109] Four of the six manors were exceptionally small and sparsely populated in relation to others with churches in Domesday.[110] These examples conflict with the suggested late Saxon pattern and accord with post-Domesday developments: already by 1086 a new, distinctively Norman element in the pattern of churches had begun to appear.

As we look back over the centuries preceding 1086, chronology remains an intractable problem. Overall, however, Domesday Book and related evidence leave a strong impression that there had been much activity in the recent past. The Wealden 'satellite' churches of Lingfield, Horley, Thursley, Wonersh and Hascombe, founded within larger and older tenurial units, foreshadow the future too closely to be interpreted as anything other than the early stages of an emergent pattern.

Four churches in south-west Surrey provide especially interesting evidence for the intensity of activity during the 'Great Rebuilding'. The primary ground-plans of Hascombe and Godalming churches, daughters respectively of Shalford church and Godalming minster (above, pp119, 99) are identical both with each other[111] and with those of two neighbouring churches, Alfold and Cranleigh (fig 31). At Cranleigh, in the Wealden hinterland of Domesday Shere, the early history of the church is obscure and the structural evidence inconclusive.[112] Alfold church seems to have been yet another pre-Domesday Wealden 'satellite': when first recorded in the mid 13th century it was appurtenant to East Shalford, eight miles northwards, and it is almost certainly identical with the church listed on that manor in 1086.[113] Structural analysis suggests that the fabric is 11th-century, and the font is an early one.[114] So at least three and perhaps four standard two-cell churches, all secondary elements in the ecclesiastical pattern and within a few miles of each other, were built to common dimensions in a late Saxon style. The uniformity of both context and fabric suggests that we are dealing with new foundations; these simple buildings are surely a physical testimony to the rapid expansion of the Weald. The Conquest probably had little direct effect on a process which was of relatively recent origin but had already gathered rapid momentum.

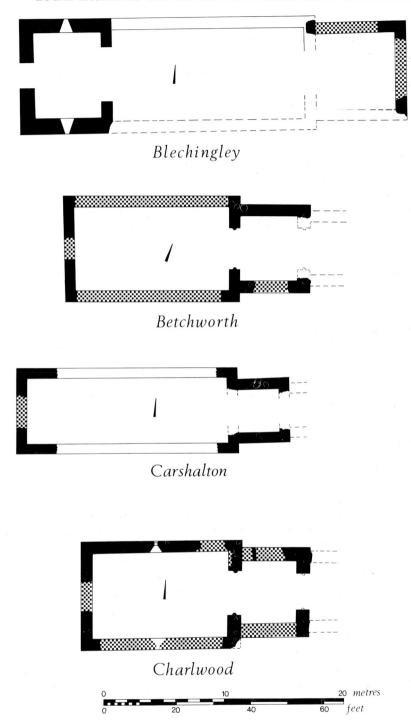

Fig 33   Church plans. (For sources see accounts in *VCHSy*, and other sources cited in the present text under
references to the invidividual churches. The Betchworth and Carshalton plans are based on
personal surveys of the surviving remnants. For key to shading conventions, see px)

The private churches of laymen, 1086–1140

The conquerors brought with them an attitude to local churches which was probably more anarchic and proprietary than that of their English predecessors.[115] Their disregard of ancient minster rights has already been noted (above, pp107–8), and for two generations the promptings of ambition and status in the matter of church-building had free rein. With the rapid progress of subinfeudation in a developing countryside, the incentives for new foundations were bound to increase. Thus in the last decades of the 11th century the social range of church ownership rapidly increased to include a broad class of minor feudal tenants.

Throughout the Anglo-Norman period, lords of manors continued to build churches for their own and their tenants' use.[116] In Surrey it is very striking that nearly all the churches which first appear between 1086 and 1140 were in lay hands. One exception is Barnes church, which stood on land held of the see of Canterbury by the canons of St Paul's and was presumably built either by the canons or by the Archbishop.[117] Another may be the fine axial-tower church at Charlwood (fig 33), though the tenure of this manor by Christ Church Canterbury cannot be traced before the 13th century. Urban expansion is reflected in the appearance of three churches at Southwark (St Olave, St Margaret and St George),[118] in the enlargement of St Mary's Guildford around its mid 11th-century tower,[119] and perhaps in Norman fabric at Holy Trinity Guildford.[120] Merton church may have been built by Gilbert the sheriff for his community of canons and then assigned for ordinary manorial use when they moved to a new site shortly afterwards, though all the visible details date from much later in the 12th century.[121]

However, it is a group of some sixteen churches on minor lay manors, more evidently private in character than those of any later (and perhaps of any earlier) period, which represent the real Anglo-Norman contribution to church-building. The concentration of these on the Downs and dip-slope, where 11th-century manorial fission seems especially prominent (above, pp33–4), emphasises that the proliferation of churches followed naturally the proliferation of small manors.[122]

The strip manors across the dip-slope of the Downs were established by 1066 (above, pp33–4), but it was essentially in the Norman period that the line of churches serving them took shape with no less than five additions. At Cuddington Ilbert de Lacy (Domesday tenant of Odo of Bayeux), or his successor Hugh Laval, built a church which had passed by c1120 to the king's scribe Bernard; excavation has shown that the standard Saxo-Norman building of c1100 (fig 34) was the first to occupy the site.[123] Ashtead is a clear case: a charter of Bishop William Giffard (1107–29) records the dedication of the church as a chapel of Leatherhead with an endowment given by the lord Laurence de Rouen, and the simple original building (fig 34) is still clearly traceable.[124] Similar in plan was the early Norman church of Little Bookham (fig 34), a small manor already subinfeudated by 1086 to one Hansard whose descendants remained immediate lords until c1300.[125] Fetcham church (fig 34), Saxo-Norman in style but unmentioned by Domesday Book, is of unknown origin; it must have served either the Warenne or the Clare third of this manor, or possibly marks the union of both at an early date in the tenure of the d'Abernon family.[126] Finally, Effingham church, granted to Merton Priory by the *dominus fundi* at some unknown date before 1153 (below, p152), served property held by Osweald from Richard fitz Gilbert in 1086 and subinfeudated soon afterwards to the Dammartin family.[127]

Small Downland estates were also rapidly acquiring churches. Addington church (fig 36) is dated to c1120–40, both by the structure[128] and by its initial endowment by the grandfather of Bartholomew de Chesney who gave it to Southwark Priory in c1180.[129] Early Norman churches remain at Farleigh (fig 34) and Tatsfield, respectively subinfeudated by 1086 to Robert de Wateville and Anschetil de Ros whose descendants retained long-term possession in both cases.[130] Caterham had a little early 12th-century apsidal church (fig 36).[131] The tiny Saxo-Norman

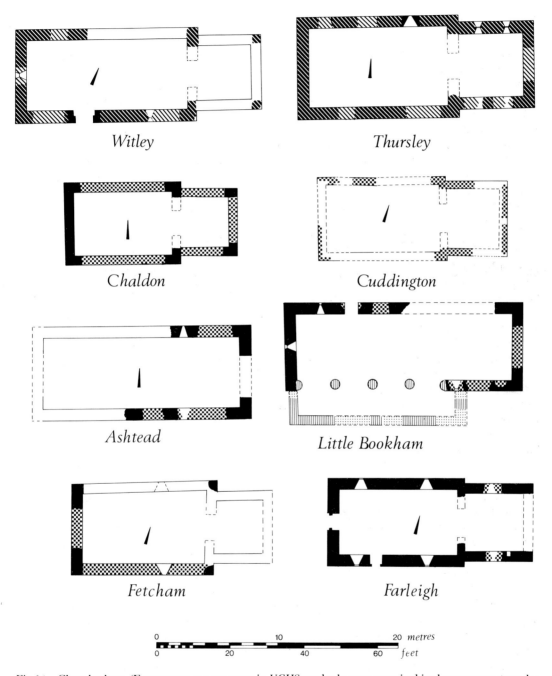

Fig 34   Church plans. (For sources see accounts in *VCHSy* and other sources cited in the present text under references to the individual churches. The footing of the demolished S aisle at Little Bookham is as published by J M G Blair, Excavations at Little Bookham church, 1952–3, *SyAC*, **60** (1963), 83–5). (For key to shading conventions, see px)

church of Headley (fig 36)[132] served a manor which was held by Ralph de Felgeres in 1086 and subsequently passed to the Tilers family.[133] Chilworth church, on a demesne estate of Odo of Bayeux which had been subinfeudated to the local Utworth family by the late 12th century,[134] had a large early-Norman west tower.[135] Walton-on-the-Hill, which may have been held of the Clare honour by the Dammartins during the 12th century, possesses a fine lead font of c1150.[136] Yet another case was perhaps the lost church of Burgh, in modern Banstead parish, given by John de Burgh to Southwark Priory at some date before c1180.[137]

None of these churches appears in Domesday or has pre-Conquest features. The case for a Norman origin seems strong at Cuddington, Ashtead and Addington, while Caterham church bears the characteristically post-Conquest dedication of St Leonard.[138] Fetcham, Headley and Ashtead churches all have (or had) tile-turned single-splayed windows, a feature (otherwise unknown in Surrey) which may reflect local building-practice over a limited period in an area abundant in Roman tile. As a group, these churches should be seen as products of subinfeudation, the work of minor Norman families with some local but little national importance such as the Watevilles,[139] the Dammartins,[140] the Rouens[141] and the Chesneys.[142] The manors, especially those on the Downland, were small: only Ashtead (£12), Cuddington (£9 12s) and Walton (£6) were valued above £5 pa in 1086,[143] and of the remainder only Addington and Headley above £3.[144] As already mentioned (p122), some half-dozen Domesday churches are of a like kind. It seems clear that the incentives created by subinfeudation had given a new impetus to the process of church-building, one which was particularly active among the small estates on the North Downs.

In the Weald these incentives were still stronger, and it is no surprise to find churches appearing in the former denns as they emerged as economic and tenurial entities. Hambledon, where the font (below, p155) shows that a church existed by the early 12th century, was the only one of these manors which had developed sufficiently by 1086 to merit an independent Domesday reference.[145] Leigh church, in Warenne hands before c1135,[146] had presumably been built on outlying Wealden land of either Reigate or Betchworth. At nearby Chivington, the Wealden hinterland which was to become Horne parish was probably already subinfeudated by 1086 (above, p54) and here a chapel, formerly an independent church held by the lay tenant, existed in c1150–60.[147] Another case may be Crowhurst, though its early history is obscure: the nave seems to be early Norman, and the dedication to St George suggests a date of foundation after c1100.[148] The standard two-cell church at Burstow (fig 36),[149] serving an old archiepiscopal denn subinfeudated to a local family by the 1090s (above, pp53–4), existed during St Anselm's reign (below, p147). The dedication of this church to St Bartholomew is interesting in view of the archiepiscopal connection, for his cult grew in England after a relic was brought to Canterbury between 1020 and 1035;[150] this, and the nearby dedications to St Bartholomew at Leigh and Horley, suggest a localised 11th-century cult in the eastern Surrey Weald.

These minor lay foundations constitute a remarkably homogeneous group, which seem characteristic of the fifty or sixty years after the Domesday survey and largely confined to that period. Such rapid proliferation of new fiefs which were independent economic units would never occur again; nor would the men for whom the fiefs were created ever again enjoy such freedom to control the churches on their land. By the years of the Anarchy, we seem to detect a new phase, in which the initiative had passed once more to ecclesiastical landlords.

The 'pastoral' churches of religious houses, 1140–80

There is a striking consistency about the churches which are first mentioned during the third quarter of the century and where the earliest architectural features are of c1140–60. A few are on royal demesne: Bramley chapel,[151] St Nicholas Guildford,[152] Merrow[153] and Puttenham (fig

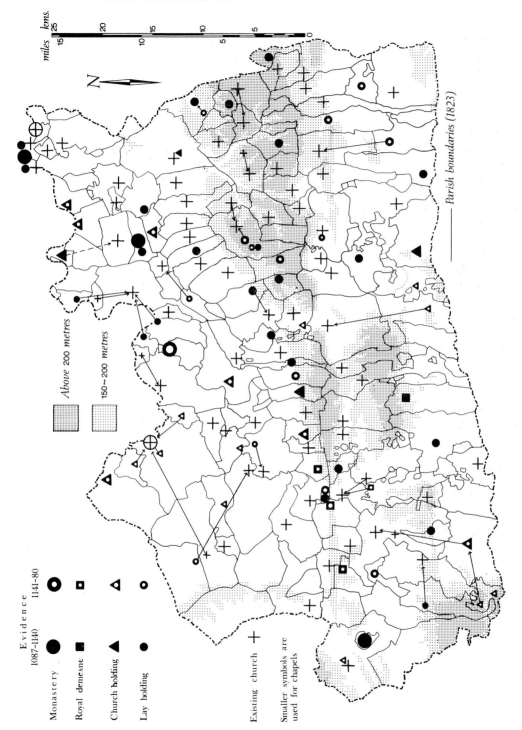

Fig 35 Churches first recorded during 1087–1180

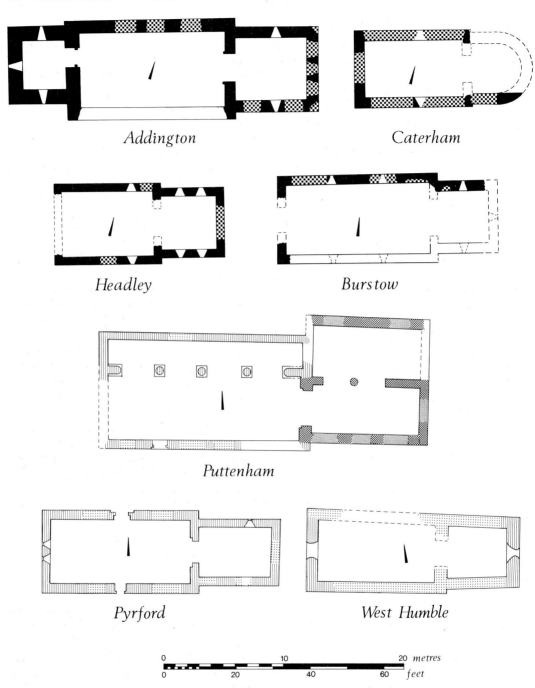

Fig 36   Church plans. (For sources see accounts in *VCHSy*, and other sources cited in the present text under references to the individual churches. The plans of Caterham and Burstow churches are from personal surveys. For key to shading conventions, see px)

36),[154] all dated on structural evidence. The majority, however, provide two points of contrast with previous decades: they were founded by monasteries, and they were usually built as chapels to serve fringe areas of larger units rather than as main estate churches.

Religious houses, in other words, seem to have begun providing for the spiritual needs of their tenants with a renewed vigour. The reasons for this are far from clear, and we should probably not look for a single overriding factor. Perhaps a generally heightened pastoral awareness expressed in episcopal advice or pressure combined with a tendency for laymen, in the new religious climate of these years, to sponsor monastic foundations rather than found churches of their own. The prospect and actuality of civil war may have contributed to this process.[155]

Churches and chapels now appear on the main Chertsey Abbey estate, which had so conspicuously lacked them (fig 37): a papal confirmation of 1176[156] lists them at Chertsey, Egham, Thorpe, Cobham, East Clandon and Weybridge, and in all cases except the last two, where there is no evidence, the earliest recorded features are of the mid to late 12th centuries.[157] Westminster Abbey had likewise built churches on its manors at Pyrford, Horsell, Wandsworth, Battersea and Morden by 1157,[158] though the only physical survival is Pyrford church (fig 36),[159] with its characteristic plan of c1140–60 and contemporary wallpaintings. At Capel, in the Wealden area of Dorking parish, a chapel existed in the hands of Lewes Priory by the 1160s; the place-name (ie *Capella*) suggests that the chapel acted as a focus for the emergent settlement.[160] In 1138–47 William de Warenne III had given Dorking church to Lewes Priory,[161] the builders of at least one new chapel in Sussex during the second quarter of the century,[162] and Lewes may well have also founded the Capel chapel soon after acquiring the mother church.

Foundations of monastic origin may occasionally have resulted, directly or indirectly, from lay patronage. Although the evidence is never explicit, such was perhaps the case with the Southwark Priory chapels which were based on small land-holdings and tithe-portions rather than on whole manors. Thus the Priory's right to a chapel at Addington, on a small freehold appurtenant to the nearby archiepiscopal manor of Croydon, was apparently connected with a grant of tithes made in the second quarter of the century.[163] The undocumented chapel of c1140–60 at West Humble (fig 36),[164] in the Polesden area of Mickleham parish, is perhaps associated with a grant to Southwark Priory at about that date of the tithe of Polesden.[165] Hamelin de Warenne confirmed Newdigate chapel to the canons in 1164–86 as 'elemosinam meam et antecessorum meorum',[166] though it seems likely that they had recently built it themselves in the parish of Leigh church, previously acquired from the second William de Warenne.[167] In some at least of these cases, the donors may have envisaged from the outset that their grants would result in new chapels.

The later 12th and 13th centuries (fig 37)

By Henry II's reign the provision of parish churches was largely complete; later foundations were no more than the minor infilling of an established pattern. The area near London, most affected by economic growth, had a tendency to split into smaller parishes requiring new churches at Clapham,[168] Bermondsey,[169] Rotherhithe[170] and Putney.[171] Occasional independent churches which first appear in the 13th century may have developed from earlier chapels. The Wealden church of Dunsfold is an exceptional case, built on the royal manor of Bramley in a sophisticated style of c1270 and clearly a piece of deliberate royal patronage.[172]

But if there were few churches, the period is marked by a proliferation of satellite chapels, continuing the pattern of the 1140s and 1150s. By 1200 Farnham mother church had at last come to share its pastoral duties with three chapels: Elstead, where excavated footings suggest a predecessor to the present building of c1220;[173] Frensham, moved to a new site in 1239[174] but

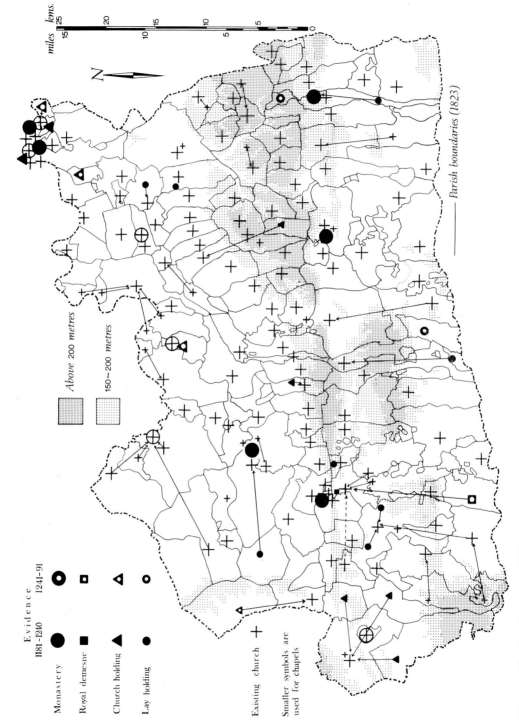

Parish boundaries (1823)

Above 200 metres

150–200 metres

N

Evidence
1181-1240   1241-91

Monastery

Royal demesne

Church holding

Lay holding

Existing church

Smaller symbols are
used for chapels

Fig 37   Churches first recorded during 1181–1291

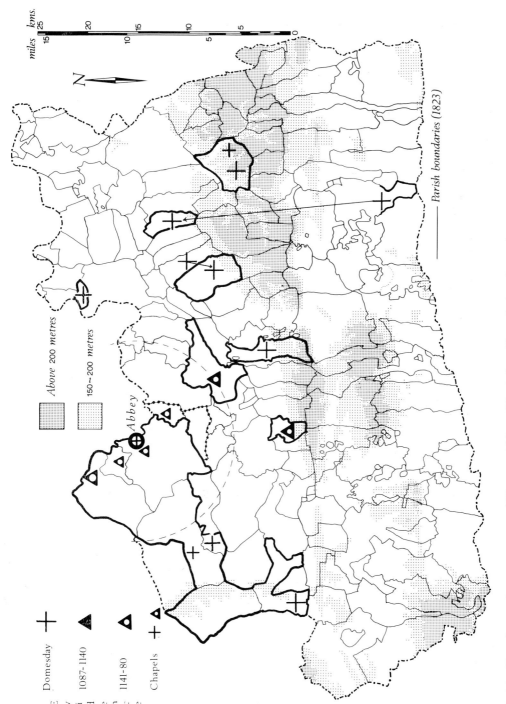

Fig 38   Churches on demesne manors of Chertsey Abbey. (The inferred boundaries of 1086 demesne manors are shown in heavy outline.)

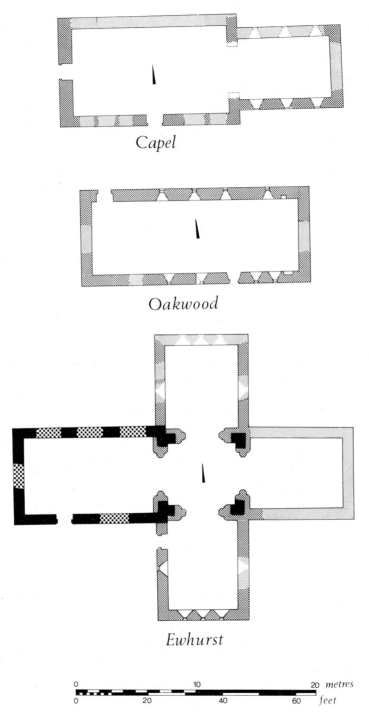

Capel

Oakwood

Ewhurst

0   10   20 *metres*
0   20   40   60 *feet*

Fig 39   Church plans. (For sources see accounts in *VCHSy*, and other sources cited in the present text under
references to the individual churches. For key to shading conventions, see px)

retaining its late 12th-century font; and Seale, a fine little early Gothic axial-tower church.[175] Godalming mother church had a chapel at Chiddingfold by *c*1180,[176] and the foundation of an 'oratory' at Windlesham in response to population growth in the Windsor Forest area is explicitly described (above, p95). Nor was it only ecclesiastical patrons who were active: the lay churches of Malden and Wotton had acquired their chapels at Chessington[177] and Oakwood[178] (fig 39) by *c*1180 and *c*1220 respectively.

How new were these developments? To some extent they merely reflect legal changes: within the broad class of religious buildings a firm line now existed between *ecclesia* and *capella*. But there is also a difference in kind: whereas the early Norman churches were built to serve estates, these chapels of the later 12th and 13th centuries generally served peripheral areas. On the other hand, stray references from the mid 12th century onwards reveal the existence of a whole distinct class of chapels, serving manor-houses and individual farms, ill-documented and often mysterious in their origins. The status and function of these chapels is part of a general problem, the Church's role as a rural institution, which must be discussed in the context of the emerging parochial organisation (below, pp155–7).

The most lasting and conspicuous development of this period was the general enlargement of church buildings. Aisles began to be added from *c*1140 onwards, and Surrey retains numerous late 12th-century nave arcades with their characteristic scalloped capitals. An exceptional work of this period is the magnificent reconstruction, on two tiers, of the chancel at Compton.[179] In the third quarter of the century some aisled churches were built *de novo*, as at Puttenham (fig 36) and perhaps also the destroyed Southwark Priory church of Woodmansterne.[180] Some small two-cell Wealden churches were extended to a cruciform plan by building a tower over the old chancel and throwing out a new choir and transepts, as at Ewhurst (fig 39) and Witley.[181] At the end of the century Lewes Priory rebuilt their little chapel of Capel in an early Gothic style (fig 39).[182] Early in the 13th century some important churches, such as Reigate and Leatherhead,[183] were greatly enlarged, and Southwark Priory must have spent lavishly on extending and beautifying Banstead church.[184] The enlargement of chancels and the addition of western belfries were standard improvements. Some churches in the poorer parishes of the Weald and Downland, as at Hascombe, Tatsfield and Headley, were little affected by this process. Overall, however, the physical presence of the church in the Surrey countryside was transformed between 1150 and 1300, a transformation which reflects not only prosperity but also a fundamental change of status. As the parochial system became firmly established, buildings which had been inconspicuous and private became stately and public.

Conclusion

The chronology which this analysis has suggested can be summarised briefly. By 1086, probably by 1066, some 60 to 70% of the churches which were fully parochial in the later Middle Ages already existed. These mainly stood on manors of two wealthy ecclesiastical proprietors and a handful of leading lay nobility, who not only built churches in areas of established settlement but were also beginning to found them in the Wealden hinterland. Post-Conquest subinfeudation stimulated humbler foundations, notably on the Downs and their northern edge, while the establishment of churches in the Weald continued steadily. The overall impression is that churches were appearing rapidly through the 11th and early 12th centuries, a flood which probably owed much to contemporaneous land clearance and settlement nucleation and which Domesday Book catches in full spate. New foundations continued in the middle years of the century, but these were usually monastic and nearly always of the 'satellite chapel' rather than the 'estate church' type. They represent the last touches to a pattern which was fully established in its essentials by the late Anglo-Saxons and Normans.

6 The Church in Rural Society: Endowment, Ownership and the Concept of the Parish

The last chapter tried to establish a chronology for local churches; this will attempt to set them in the context of contemporary religious attitudes and pastoral organisation. Here the sources are indirect and seldom explicit; such evidence as tithe-portions, grants to religious houses and relationships of dependence between one church and another cannot be understood without some knowledge of local circumstances. Within the confines of one county we can at least hope to view individual transactions in their immediate setting, even if much that we would wish to know about the day-to-day relationships of lords, clergy and peasants remains forever lost.

The aim here is to examine the Church's position in the society of Norman and early Angevin Surrey. Churches were private property in the sense that their 'owners' founded and endowed them, and might give them to religious houses. Also, however, they were public institutions with public functions, and this aspect became ever more marked as the 12th century progressed. Distinct from both ownership and function was the growth of parochial jurisdiction, one of the most dramatic changes in the institutional history of the medieval Church. It is the development from estate church to parish church that gives the two centuries following the Norman Conquest their particular importance for a study of the Church in English society. The central theme is the complex structure of rights and interests which crystallised into the stable parochial system of later medieval England.

The building and its topographical setting

The proprietary nature of late Saxon and Norman churches is reflected in their small scale and frequent proximity to manor-house sites. The structural evidence described above makes it clear that churches in Surrey were usually stone-built by c1100. Before c1150, most were fairly uniform in both size and shape, being two-cell, aisleless and varying little from a norm of some fifty by twenty feet overall. Exceptional features such as the single-cell plans at Ashtead and Little Bookham, and the apsidal chancel at Caterham, are evidently unrelated to status and probably reflect no more than the whims of patrons and the practice of local builders.

The minute size of a few early Norman churches, as at Chaldon and Headley (figs 34 and 36), deserves comment. These little naves, only twenty-six by seventeen feet, were not built to accommodate numerous households, and at Chaldon indeed no Domesday population is recorded.[1] We may suspect that some of the humbler private churches resulting from the Norman settlement (above, pp122, 124–6) were built purely for household use. Architecturally, no clear distinction was made between such essentially private buildings, chapels-of-ease for subsidiary settlements (as at West Humble, fig 36), and the majority which served both pastoral and proprietary functions. Their original appearance was plain and unimpressive, their only advantage over domestic buildings that of durability.

Some distinctions are, however, suggested by the relationship of churches to manor-houses, parsonages and settlements. The quality of the evidence is not satisfactory. Surviving remains of associated secular buildings are uncommon from the 13th and 14th centuries and very rare indeed from the 11th and 12th, while useful written evidence is hard to find. For general purposes we are forced to rely on early editions of the Ordnance Survey maps, and it clearly cannot be claimed that any individual arrangement recorded there necessarily dates back to the 12th century.

Nonetheless, the picture is consistent with other evidence about the origin of churches to an extent which suggests that it is broadly accurate. It seems *prima facie* unlikely that the classic church/manor-house grouping is frequently a late development. At the same time, the interpretation of settlement nucleation proposed in ch 2 would suggest that villages are not necessarily older than the churches serving them: population may have been attracted to an existing nucleus, or settlement and church may have come into existence together.

The largest single group of churches, those near manor-houses (figs 40 & 42), are almost all of lay origin. As well as numerous pre-Domesday foundations (for instance Stoke D'Abernon), they include a majority of those identified above as products of subinfeudation (as at Ashtead, Chaldon, Farleigh and Hambledon). Abinger, with its church and castle mound of *c*1100, is a particularly good illustration.[2] Characteristically these church/manor groups stand apart from both village and parsonage, though in the same general area of the parish. Late medieval desertion is not a factor here, for the churches usually lie within half a mile of an established nucleated settlement (as in the dip-slope parishes, fig 15). Less frequently, as at Buckland (fig 40) and Compton, the village lies at the same nucleus as the church and manor-house. Churches of proprietary origin with adjacent parsonage houses are notably rare; one instance is Burstow, where the rectory moat was occupied from at least the 13th century,[3] though this may owe something to the early donation of this church to Lewes Priory (below, p147).

The other main group comprises churches sited in villages (fig 41), often adjacent to parsonages but only rarely to manorial sites. Some are of lay origin, but it is significant that in almost all such cases other evidence is consistent with foundation by a non-resident lord for the use of his tenants. As pointed out above (pp56–8), the Clare churches of Blechingley and Leatherhead stand on estate boundaries and were evidently foci for settlement formation after the unification of each pair of manors. At Walton-on-the-Hill, where the village divides the manor house and Norman motte from the church and rectory, the church was probably built by the Dammartin family who had several other Surrey manors (above, p126). Other examples include churches built by lay lords on the Wealden denns of their manors, as at Alfold (fig 42), Cranleigh (fig 41), Ewhurst and Leigh.[4] But most striking is the preponderance of ecclesiastical foundations in this category, comprising not only pre-Conquest churches of Chertsey Abbey and Christ Church Canterbury such as Great Bookham (fig 18), Ewell (fig 41), Sutton and Cheam,[5] but also most of the 12th-century chapels-of-ease. The group includes chapels on the Bagshot sands, as at Chobham (fig 18), Weybridge and Horsell, as well as Wealden ones such as Charlwood, Newdigate (fig 41), Capel and Chiddingfold.[6]

The minor Norman (and probably late Saxon) resident landowner would, as a matter of course, build his own church next to his own house. If convenience or the availability of material suggested a new site (cf above, p111), he might build church and house together. His tenants would use the church and give its priest their tithes, but even if they did not already have a nucleated settlement elsewhere, the establishment of one around it was incidental. But in other cases a lord might build a church for different motives, specifically for the benefit of tenants on a manor or outlying portion of a manor. Nor surprisingly, the churches founded on monastic property both before and after the Conquest belong to this second group, for the motives in foundation were the same. The common factor among these churches is that proximity to peasant settlement, not proximity to the founder's dwelling, seems to have dictated the choice of site.

The glebe and parsonage

Priests needed land to support them, and inadequate church endowments by founders was, in theory at least, a matter for episcopal correction. As early as 1102 Anselm's canons forbade the

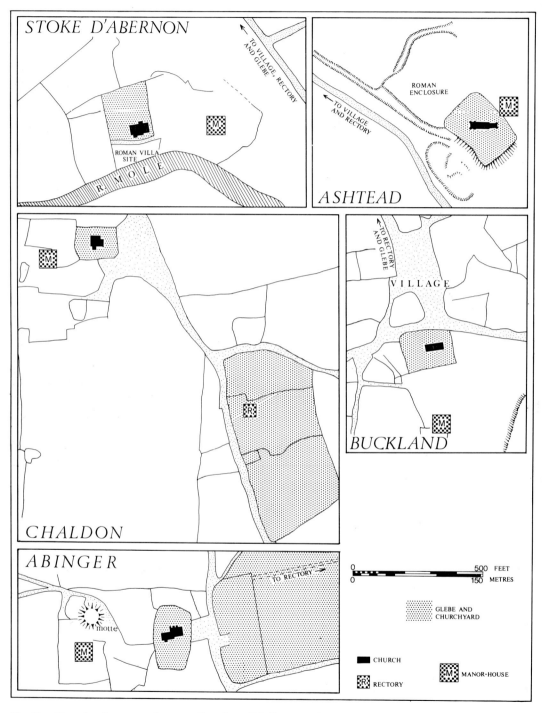

Fig 40   Churches by manor-houses. (Based on OS Surrey 25″ 1 edn sheets)

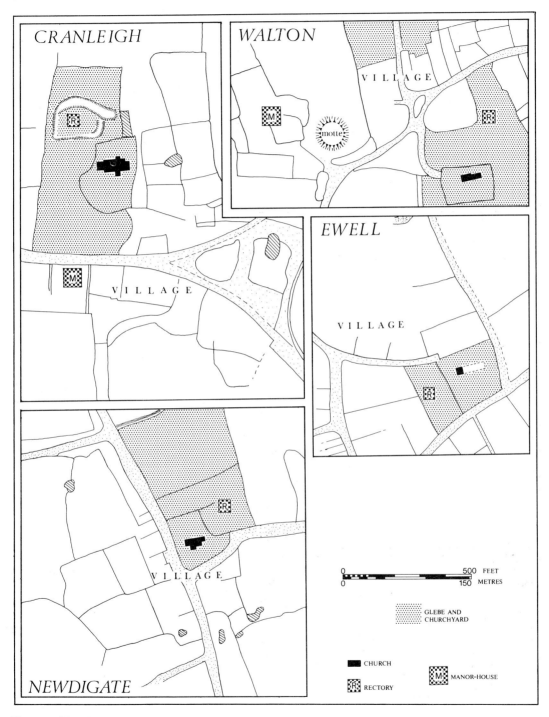

Fig 41 Churches by villages and rectories. (Ewell based on reconstructed map of Ewell in *c*1400 reproduced *Fitznells cartulary*, opp cxxix; the others based on OS Surrey 25″ 1 edn sheets)

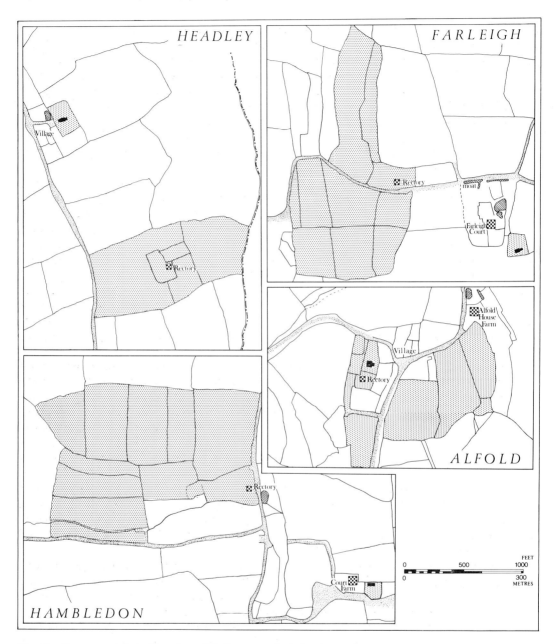

Fig 42   Compact glebes. (Based on OS Surrey 25″ 1 edn sheets, with additional information from the following sources: Headley: terrier, 1616 (GLRO, DW/S/58b), tithe-map, 1840; Farleigh: estate map, 1768 (Merton College Muniments); Alfold: terrier, 1764 (GLRO, DW/S/2), tithe-map, 1839; Hambledon: terrier, 1764 (GLRO, DW/S/56), tithe-map, 1845)

founding of new churches without sufficient glebe endowments, and Bishop Gilbert of Limerick suggested one ploughland as an acceptable minimum.[7] There is no evidence that the original glebe of any Surrey church was provided by anyone other than the lord of the estate, whether monastic or lay, and the two cases with contemporary documentation are clear on this point. Bishop William Giffard dedicated Laurence de Rouen's early 12th-century chapel at Ashtead 'cum una virgata terre quam Laurentius in dedicatione ei dedit, et cum omnibus decimis de dominio et de rusticis'.[8] When Bartholomew de Chesney gave Addington church to Southwark Priory in c1180, it was 'cum 24 acris terre quas avus meus et pater meus ecclesie illi in liberam et perpetuam elemosinam dederunt, quarum 12 assignate sunt ad inveniendum in ea luminare perpetuo singulis noctibus anni'.[9]

In discussing Danelaw churches, Stenton argued that the impression of unitary origin given by most 12th-century charter texts often conceals a corporate endowment.[10] This pattern seems particularly appropriate to eastern England with its communities of independent sokemen; at all events 'the churches which are characteristic of this region, those in which a plurality of lords possessed an interest'[11] (and where this points to a communal origin), fail to appear in Surrey. The odd case of divided rights results from nothing more than a partition of the founding lord's estate. Thus in the 13th century the lords of the neighbouring manors of Abinger and Paddington presented to separate half-shares in Abinger church;[12] yet the two estates had been held by the same man both TRE and in 1086.[13] Similarly, when Reynold de Lucy gave half of Godstone manor as his daughter's dowry in the late 12th century he included half the church, later giving the other half to Lesnes Abbey.[14] To all appearances, manorial churches in Surrey were endowed by lords of manors.

Sometimes, however, an existing glebe might receive small additions. Recorded Surrey cases all concern churches in monastic ownership. In the late 12th century Lewes Priory held both the Domesday church of Dorking, acquired in the 1140s from Isabel countess Warenne, and the 'terra que fuit Aeilaui quam Ysabel comitissa Warenn' donavit prenominate ecclesie Sancte Marie de Dorking'.[15] Sometimes the grant was made to the church and its monastic proprietor jointly, or to the latter on behalf of the former. In c1190 Gilbert de Puttenden gave ten acres in Woodmansterne, adjoining the existing glebe, 'deo et ecclesie Sancte Marie de Sutwerch' et canonicis ibidem deo servientibus et ecclesie eorum de Wudemaresth'.[16] Land at Mitcham was granted to Southwark Priory in the early 12th century for finding candles in St Peter's church there,[17] and at Addington half of the 24-acre glebe was assigned to maintaining a nightly lamp in the church (above). Although the absence of such grants to lay-owned churches may merely reflect the bias of the sources, there is no real evidence for a general practice of granting land piecemeal to local churches.[18]

An overall view of Surrey glebes is not provided by any contemporary source, or indeed by any source before the *Valor Ecclesiasticus* in 1535 and glebe terriers of the 17th and 18th centuries. The *Valor* often seems to under-estimate,[19] and even accurate figures from this period are obviously not reliable evidence for the extent of the glebes when first created. On the other hand, there is no particular reason why glebes of lay-owned churches[20] should have changed greatly in size between the 12th and 17th centuries, and of all kinds of small land-unit these are the most predictably stable. At all events, these late sources are not inconsistent with the fragments of early evidence, and they probably give a broadly accurate picture.

Some exceptionlly large glebes, as at Godalming[21] and Leatherhead,[22] represent the remains of Anglo-Saxon minster endowments and may be regarded as *sui generis*. As mentioned above, (p113), however, late Saxon royal churches in the Weald were also characterised by extensive endowments, and most of the other large glebes were attached to churches on the Weald clay or greensand: Compton with 54½ acres,[23] Blechingley with 60, Ockley with 95,[24] and Cranleigh with 170½.[25] At Godstone, the 30 acres which Reynold de Lucy gave to Lesnes Abbey with half the church in 1193 suggest an entire glebe of 60 acres.[26] It is argued above (p74) that the abnormally big virgates of Wealden peasants reflect abundance of assart land in an under-developed terrain, and it is significant that large glebes also occur in the other main area of colonisation on infertile ground, the Bagshot sands of north-west Surrey. The late sources list endowments of 72 acres at Chobham,[27] and 50 at Egham,[28] approximating in both cases to the position in c1330.[29] Clearly these glebes were either generous from the outset, or augmented by intakes of heathland like the peasant holdings around them during the late 12th and 13th centuries.

Elsewhere in Surrey, glebes generally contained between ten and 50 acres. In and around the dip-slope parishes, acreages often correspond closely to the standard open-field smallholdings of c24–32 and c12–16 acres (above, pp71–2). Ashtead church, originally endowed with one virgate (above, p139), had 30 acres in 1535.[30] The glebes comprised 31 and 37 acres at Fetcham and Sutton,[31] 25 and 26 acres at Beddington and West Clandon.[32] Apparent instances of 'half-size' units are Great Bookham (fourteen acres),[33] Epsom (eighteeen acres),[34] and perhaps Barnes (ten acres in 1181).[35] On the Downland few glebes exceed 30 acres and most were smaller: the fifteen acres at Headley (fig 42),[36] twelve at Tatsfield and fourteen at Mickleham[37] seem to be typical, and in the 12th century Addington church had a basic and probably primary glebe of twelve acres.[38] The glebe of Farleigh church, reckoned as 22 acres in 1290,[39] remained of much the same size when it was mapped in 1768 (fig 42).

The character and size-range of these glebes seems much in accordance with the Suffolk data for 1086: 'in general similar to that of the peasant holdings of Domesday, at least in this respect – that it combined a large range of difference, and a great number of individual irregularities, with a marked tendency for most of the holdings to fall into definite classes'.[40] The Surrey evidence, blurred and distorted though it is by the passage of time, seems to preserve both the general early pattern and the range of geographical variation. Most Surrey glebes can be defined quite simply as typical local peasant holdings corresponding to the virgates and half-virgates of smallholders. This does not of course mean that the economic position of the average Surrey priest was no higher than that of his parishioners, for he received tithe and a range of financial benefits. But often he can only have avoided hardship by exploiting these to the full. The rector of Headley who incurred episcopal anger in 1308 by refusing to bury a parishioner when no mortuary was forthcoming[41] may have been prompted by necessity rather than greed; he and his unrecorded predecessors can scarcely have lived in luxury on their fifteen acres of chalk and clay.

Topographically, too, the glebes seem essentially similar to other smallholdings. Generally they comprised a collection of field strips and small closes, though a recurring pattern (as at Chaldon, fig 34) is for the parsonage house to stand in a compact enclosure of a few acres. At Chobham, where the vicarage moat still remains, the vicar in 1331 had 'unam mansionem honestam bene et honorifice constructam et domibus edificatam, cum una placea clausa adiacente continente sex acras bosci et terre, in qua quidem mansione omnes vicarii . . . dicte ecclesie habitare consueverunt'.[42] At Fetcham the only large enclosure in the post-medieval glebe, nine acres called Clerks Closes, may be identified with the 'croftam persone de Feccham que vocatur Clerekescroft' in a deed of c1230–50.[43] In c1190 the Downland church of Woodmansterne had land in large enclosed blocks.[44]

Although appropriation involved a partition of revenues from monastically-owned glebes to provide a vicar's portion, this need not normally have involved physical rearrangement. Often the old parsonage might continue to house the vicar,[45] though a monastic patron with substantial property in the parish might build a separate grange or curial building, as Southwark Priory did in several cases.[46] Chapels-of-ease such as those on the Chertsey estates may never have had rectories: it was an easy transition of status from chaplain appointed by the founding monastery to vicar of an appropriated living.[47]

Small churches of purely pastoral character, at least in the Weald, may often have originated as

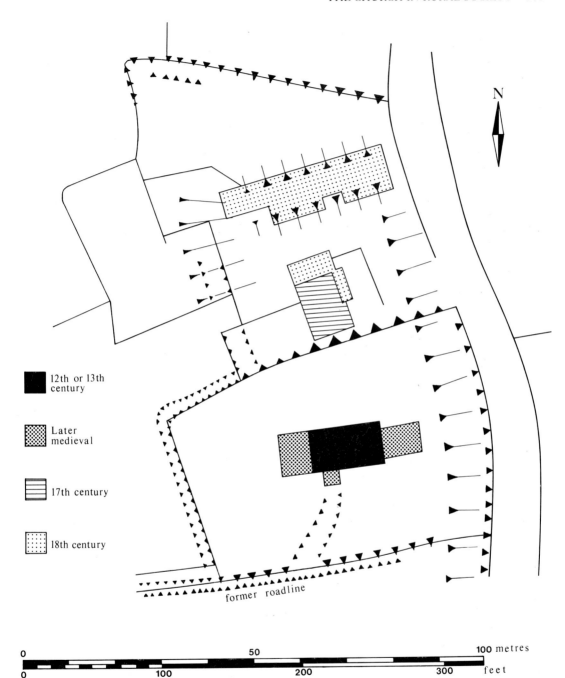

12th or 13th century

Later medieval

17th century

18th century

Fig 43   The church and Church Farm, Horne. (From W J Blair, Surrey endowments of Lewes Priory, fig 10)

simple 'field chapels', with a chaplain's house and some tithe, but little or no glebe. At Newdigate only two acres in addition to the parsonage (which adjoins the churchyard) were noted in 1535,[48] while the land of Horley church seems to have been confined to a 'mansionem . . . cum grangio, curtillagio et quodam crofto terre adiacente sicut fossatis et sepibus decenter includitur' which housed the vicar.[49] Horne church, isolated except for a ditched farmstead on its northern side (fig 43), was granted to Lewes Priory by its owner in c1160 with no more than 'terram de Impaghe que iacet iuxta ecclesiam ad partem aquilonis, et omnes domus in terra illa, et totam decimam totius feni mei'.[50]

Once again, function is reflected in the topographical evidence. Where churches adjoin manor-houses the priests' houses are characteristically set apart, typical farmsteads on typical smallholdings.[51] But with churches founded primarily for the benefit of tenants the most constant relationship is between church and parsonage, whether isolated, in a village or surrounded by a unitary glebe. Fig 42 points this contrast clearly, between Farleigh and Hambledon on the one hand and Alfold on the other. The widely varying circumstances which surrounded church foundation and endowment in 11th- and 12th-century Surrey remain more clearly visible in the countryside than in any written document.

Monastic Patronage, 1086–1200

The 12th century saw fundamental change in the English Church, locally as much as nationally. One process is especially conspicuous; the flood of churches and other possessions from the hands of laymen into those of religious houses.[52] Patterns of endowment vary among the religious orders, a fact less evident from the gifts of noble founders and protectors than from those of humbler men. A baron's relationship with the house which he patronised, whether by adoption or family tradition, was one of mutual temporal advantage, and he would have a natural tendency to endow it in proportion to his means.[53] The generosity of lesser benefactors, operating in an elusive context of personal relationships, is harder to analyse. Churches were one among several sources of revenue, and the problem may usefully be approached by examining all types of monastic patronage within one limited region; the implications of church grants for the formation of the parochial system will be discussed in a later section.

Pious grants of churches, whether individually or as components of manors, were sometimes made to the great Benedictine houses before 1100. Henley (Ash) church presumably accompanied the manor when the Englishman Azur gave it to Chertsey Abbey for his soul in King William's day, and Colchester Abbey acquired the valuable church of Leatherhead from Eudes Dapifer.[54] But during the century after Domesday Book the new orders reaped the main benefits. In the 12th and 13th centuries Chertsey Abbey seems to have made virtually no acquisitions outside the area of its pre-Conquest estate, and scarcely a single Surrey church passed after 1100 to an old Benedictine community.

Even among the new houses there are gaps, either through failure to acquire or through loss of the record. The Cistercian order avoided acquiring churches as a matter of general principle: hence the very restricted endowments of even a house so celebrated as Waverley Abbey.[55] In its early years the Cluniac priory of Bermondsey was endowed mainly from outside the county, and though it did acquire four churches in north-eastern Surrey[56] it was not much patronised by Surrey men. The Austin canons of Merton possessed an abundance of churches and land there by c1200, but it is impossible on the evidence available to recover the background to these acquisitions.[57] However, two well-documented houses, the Cluniac priory of Lewes and the Augustinian priory of Southwark, serve to define similarities and contrasts between the patronage of different orders.

Lewes Priory, founded by William de Warenne in 1077, quickly attained the status of a great house through the support of numerous benefactors. While its endowments lay in several counties, the bulk were in Sussex within convenient range of the Priory.[58] The Surrey properties (fig 44, table 14) lay on the fringe of this main group, a fact which explains their concentration in the south-east of the county. The importance here of aristocratic patronage is obvious: a high proportion of the Surrey endowments, probably the bulk in terms of revenue, stemmed from the generosity of the Warennes and the Clares. In choosing their gifts great landowners could afford to take some account of future convenience, and it seems likely that the valuable churches of Dorking and Blechingley were selected for Lewes specifically because they lay near Burstow church, acquired earlier, and the Sussex border. Lewes's gains in Surrey may be characterised as few but substantial, the minor gifts being in general related to, or stemming from, the large ones.

Very different were Southwark Priory's acquisitions in the county (fig 45, table 15). A numerical comparison would be invalid since these, unlike the Lewes endowments just discussed, formed the main core of an estate which spread out into surrounding counties.[59] But they are also notable for the numerous grants by minor gentry families and for a strong tendency to concentrate in groups. Nearly all lie within three-mile radii of either Southwark, Mitcham, Banstead, Addington or Reigate. In the second of these groups, for instance, the acquisition of Mitcham church (within a few years of the Priory's foundation at the beginning of the 12th century) was followed quickly by two tithe-portions from demesnes of local landowners, at least three handsome grants of land, and a church with further land and tithe in the adjoining vill of Tooting. The aristocratic element is certainly present; but Southwark, much more than Lewes, owed its prosperity to the accretion of modest grants from to a wide range of the land-holding class.

TABLE 14   Lewes Priory acquisitions in Surrey before 1200

Date	Property	Donor
1086–1121	Gatton: church and land	Herfrid
1086–1121	Gatton: half-virgate	Odo de Dammartin
c1090–1121	Southwark: St Olave's church	William de Warenne I or II
c1105–17	Shalford: tithe	Gilbert de Clare
1114–21	Burstow: church	Walter de Burstow
1115–35	Sutton in Woking: tithe	Stephen count of Mortain
1121–36	Blechingley: land called Gruteners	Richard de Clare
1121–45	Godstone: land at Felbridge	William de Dammartin
c1130–45	Blechingley: tithe	Gilbert de Curtuna
1138–47	Dorking: church (with Capel)	Isabel de Warenne
1138–52	Blechingley: church, croft, pannage	Gilbert de Clare
1147	Reigate, Betchworth, Shere, Fetcham: tithe	William de Warenne III
?	'Baldwin's land': tithe	?
1148–59?	Stoke-by-Guildford: church	William de Warenne IV
1148–59	'Burchard's land', for a hospice	William de Warenne IV
c1150–75	Horne: church, land called Impaghe	Peter de Tolworth
c1150–70	Lingfield: land at Chartham	William de Dammartin
	Chipstead: half-virgate	
	Mickleham: tithe	

Sources: See W J Blair, Surrey endowments of Lewes Priory, 115

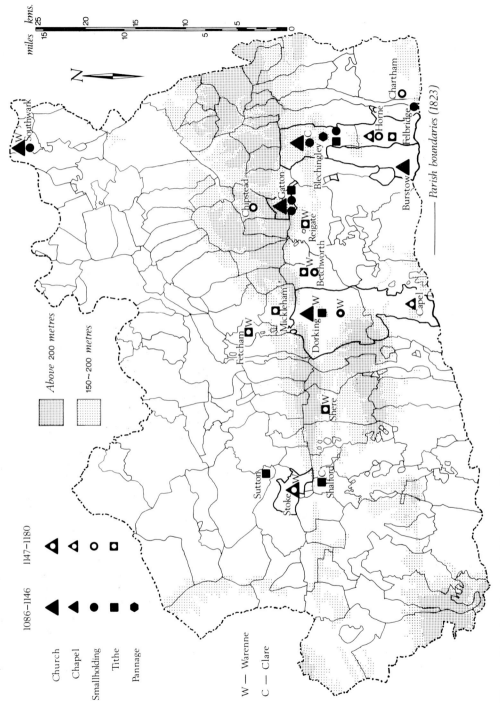

Fig 44   Churches, land and tithe acquired by Lewes Priory

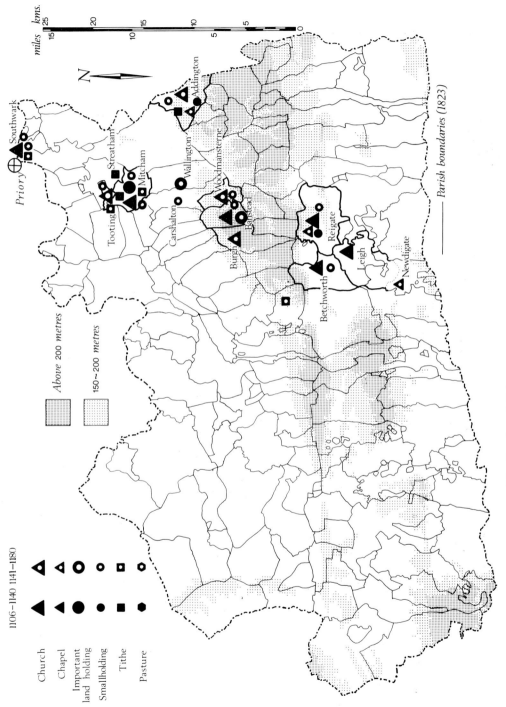

Fig 45   Churches, land and tithe acquired by Southwark Priory

TABLE 15   Southwark Priory acquisitions in Surrey before 1200

Date	Property	Donor	Source (see below)
1106?	Reigate: church	William de Warenne II	Vincent, p113
1107–29	Banstead: church	Tirel de Manières	Vincent, p115
1107–29	Southwark: St Margaret's church	Bishop William Giffard	Inspex (6)
c1110–30	Mitcham: church	?	H; Add 6040(1)
c1110–30	Mitcham: Wihtrichescrofte etc	Richard de Whitford	Add 6040(1)
c1110–40	Streatham and Mitcham: tithe	William de Abinger	Add 6040(17)
1118–35	Betchworth and Leigh: churches	William de Warenne II	Vincent, p114
c1130–50	Addington: tithe	Gervase de Cornhill	H
1139–52	Southwark: tithe of farm	King Stephen	Inspex (1)
1146–55	Southwark: 3s rent	Cristine Gos	BL MS Cotton Nero C. iii f 200b
c1150–70	Mickleham(?): tithe of Polesden	John de Whitford	Add 6040(2)
c1150–70	Mitcham: tithe of Whitford	John de Whitford	Add 6040(2)
c1150–80	Burgh (Banstead): church and land	John de Burgh	R; Vincent, p125
c1150–80	Woodmansterne: church	Geoffrey de Delce	Vincent, p126
c1150–80	Carshalton: 12 acres	Felicia de Cantelowe	SRO, 2609/11/5/22; Vincent, p127
c1150–80?	Mitcham: various parcels	De Rouen family	Vincent, p129
1164–86	Newdigate: chapel	Hamelin de Warenne (confirmation)	BL MS Cotton Nero C. iii f 188
c1164–86	Banstead: orchard and 5 acres	Nigel de Mowbray	Bod Lib MS Eng Hist A II no 38
c1164–90	Banstead: 3 acres	Nigel de Mowbray	Vincent, p117
1164–1202	Reigate: 10 acres	Hamelin de Warenne	Inspex (13)
c1164–80	Tooting: church	Hamo de Gravenel	R
c1164–80	Tooting: tithe	Hamo de Gravenel	Add 6040(9)
c1164–80	Tooting: 1 acre meadow	Hamo de Gravenel	Add 6040(10–11)
By 1171	Mitcham: virgate at 'Bukingrave'	?	H
By 1171	Betchworth: virgate	?	H
By 1171	Reigate: castle chapel	?	H
By 1171	Mitcham: land where their houses are	Whole parish	H
By 1171	Banstead(?): tithe of 'Nutebrake'	?	H
c1170–89	Wallington: all his land	Alexander fitz Gerald	Vincent, p122
1172–90	Banstead: 2 virgates	Ralph Viniton	BL Cotton Ch xvi.41
1173–88	Addington: church and chapel, with glebe and common of pasture	Bartholomew de Chesney	SRO, 2609/11/5/1
1173–1200	Southwark: 12d rent in Westrate	Alwin de Tandridge	BL Harl Ch 46.H.40
c1190–1200	Woodmansterne: 10 acres	Gilbert de Puttenden	BL Harl Ch 55.A.30
1199	Banstead: 2 virgates	Sewal son of Robert	BL MS Cotton Nero C. iii f 197

Sources:

Add 6040   British Library Add MS 6040: leaves from Southwark Priory Cartulary. The transcripts of deeds are cited by number.

H   Confirmation by Henry bishop of Winchester, c1150–71 (Add 6040(16))

Inspex   Inspeximus of Southwark Priory charters on Patent Roll 13 Richard II pt i (PRO C66/328 mm 14–13). Transcripts of deeds are cited by number.

R   Confirmation by Richard bishop of Winchester, *c*1177–88 (printed Dugdale, *Monasticon*, 6, 172–3).

Vincent   Transcripts and notes from lost Southwark Priory Cartulary in College of Arms, MS Vincent 46

Other references are to original deeds

Why did such men patronise one house rather than another? A covert motivating factor is the influence of magnates on their feudal dependents. Thus Lewes was patronised not only by the Clares but also by Odo and William de Dammartin, tenants on Surrey manors which had been held in 1086 by Richard de Clare.[60] The Southwark material provides a clearer case. Early 12th-century grants of land and tithe at Mitcham and Whitford, by Richard de Whitford and William de Abinger, share with Hugh de Stoke's grant of Stoke Poges church (Buckinghamshire) at about the same date the common factor that all three manors had been held in 1086 by William fitz Ansculf. Although neither fitz Ansculf nor his successor Fulk Paynel is recorded as an early benefactor of the Priory, it must be concluded that one or the other of them patronised it vicariously by encouraging his knights to offer donations.[61]

A lord who was also a great ecclesiastic was especially well-placed to augment monastic endowments in this way. Burstow church, founded on a Wealden fief of the great archiepiscopal estate (above, pp53–4), provides an early instance. A writ of Archbishop Ralph (1114–22), addressed to the local tenant Walter de Burstow, recounts how the church had been pledged to Lewes during Anselm's reign:[62]

> Scias quia venerabilis predecessor noster dominus Anselmus archiepiscopus, et ego postea, ecclesiam de Burestou secundum petitionem patris tui cum omnibus ad eam pertinentibus R fratri tuo concessimus. Nunc itaque, quia idem frater tuus deo inspirante apud S Pancratium monacus factus est, eandem ecclesiam eisdem monacis S Pancratii liberam et quietam concedimus, secundum devotionem patris tui et matris, qui eundem filium suum cum predicta ecclesia apud eundem locum Sancti Pancratii quondam devotissime deo voluerunt offerre, sicut ipse bene nosti.

The original motivation here may well have come from Anselm: he apparently expressed his affection for Lewes by encouraging a tenant to offer his infant son as an oblate monk there, with Burstow church for dowry.[63] In ratifying and enforcing the donation, Ralph was able to combine support for monastic life and the freeing of a church from lay control with enhancement of his own prestige, and when he confirmed Lewes's endowments in 1121 he recorded Burstow church as his own gift.[64]

Except where such tenurial links can be demonstrated, the influence of personal contacts on the pattern of benefactions is elusive. But only a few of the numerous small grants to Southwark Priory suggest lord-tenant relationships; other motives must be sought for what must often have been free, genuinely pious offerings made under no duress. Surely we trace here the strong popular appeal of the Augustinian Canons, in close touch with everyday life and attractive objects of spiritual investment for those of limited means. 'The secret of their success was the modesty of their needs, their proximity to a flourishing town, and the services they performed for benefactors who were by no means rich by the standards of ancient feudal greatness'.[65] The benefits of confraternity, or burial within the canons' cloister, were powerful incentives to generosity.[66] Above all, the pastoral interests of the Austin Canons made them especially fitting recipients of parish churches.

The close grouping of their Surrey properties suggests that the canons of Southwark tended to win local support once an initial grant of a church or land had given them a foothold in an area. It is hard to tell how far a deliberate policy of purchase was operating, but virtually all the extant deeds are phrased in the language of free elemosinary grants for the welfare of souls. The most frequent patrons were minor local gentry such as the de Whitfords and the de Gravenels, with an occasional London citizen holding Surrey property like Gervase de Cornhill. One exceptional acquisition, among their Mitcham holdings, was the land 'in qua domus eorum fundate sunt in eadem parochia, quam ex concessione et donatione totius parochie habent et possident'.[67] Though its nature eludes us, we should clearly envisage frequent personal contact between the canons and their humbler patrons.

The alienability of tithe

In the normal course of events (as at Ashtead, p139 above), a manorial church would be dedicated with the whole tithes, both demesne and peasant, of the estate which it was destined to serve. If it then passed to a religious house, its glebe and tithe rights would accompany it automatically. But by the end of the 11th century the practice of granting tithe-portions on their own, widespread on the Continent, was firmly established in England. It is obvious that these grants were detrimental to the interests of local churches, and insofar as they cut across a church's ecclesiastical supremacy over its parish they ran counter to the whole concept of parochialisation. This was certainly a matter over which bishops claimed authority, and the ways in which they permitted, restricted and defined such grants help to illuminate 12th-century conceptions of parochial jurisdiction.[68]

Only demesne tithes, and tithes of seigneurial revenues,[69] were regarded by the Normans as separable: the alienation of peasant tithes from their local destination seems virtually unknown in this period.[70] Even of demesne tithes, it was common practice to divert only two parts out of three from the uses of the local church. Demesne tithe grants were made frequently before c1160, and often form a significant proportion of a monastery's recorded endowment (tables 14 & 15). Freedom to alienate was apparently enjoyed by great and lesser landowners alike. Despite frequent claims to the contrary,[71] tenants-in-chief do not seem to have been barred from alienating the tithe of subinfeudated manors: at Shalford, where Gilbert de Clare granted the demesne tithe to Lewes Priory in c1105–17, his father had enfeoffed Robert de Wateville with the manor by 1086.[72] Perhaps more surprisingly, tithe grants could apparently override existing monastic interests. In 1147 William de Warenne III gave to Lewes Priory the tithe of all his demesnes, and this was applied to Reigate and Betchworth despite the fact that his father had given both churches to Southwark Priory.[73] In such cases a landowner could doubtless accomplish much if the diocesan bishop favoured the object of his generosity.

The two-thirds demesne tithe-portion was a very common type of grant during the first half-century of Norman rule.[74] A great lord might make a series of such donations: in the early 1080s Richard fitz Gilbert gave to Bec Abbey two-thirds of the tithes from all his significant demesnes in Surrey, with a villan (presumably to collect them) at Blechingley.[75] Slightly later, Chertsey Abbey was acquiring two-thirds portions from the demesnes of lesser men: Walter fitz Other at Horsley, Robert Oil de Larrun at Chipstead, and Robert Albus at Fetcham.[76]

The origin of this ubiquitous fraction lies in the law of Eadgar, which had allowed a thegn owning a church with a graveyard to endow it with a third of his demesne tithe.[77] Two-thirds remained due to the old minster, but in the 11th century these portions suffered the general fate of minster rights: as Stenton wrote, 'the Norman lord of a village, unlike the thegn of Edgar's laws, was free to give two-thirds of his demesne tithes to any religious object which pleased him, without regard to the vested interests of any ancient minster'.[78] In a sense the ancient principle had been inverted: the third with which the 10th-century thegn had been allowed to endow his local church was now, by custom, considered that church's due. We cannot be confident that a church existed on every demesne from which a Norman lord alienated only two-thirds of the tithe, though in Surrey this does generally seem to be the case.[79] But it is implicit in these limited grants that they safeguard, either actually or potentially, the interests of an estate church.

Not all grants were of this kind: a monastery might sometimes receive the *whole* tithe from a patron's demesne. Occasionally this happened in disregard of an existing church, as when Walter fitz Other, who had held Compton and its church in 1086, gave to Chertsey Abbey tithes there later defined as 'omnes decimas eiusdem ville'.[80] But after c1100, the Surrey evidence suggests that normally such grants were only made from demesnes with no churches of their own to support. Thus on the Clare manor of Shalford the only church was one serving a Wealden outlier (above, p122) and this was probably supported by the surrounding assart smallholdings, not by the main demesne; in the early 12th century Gilbert de Clare was therefore able to endow Lewes Priory with 'rectam decimam de Escaldeford, scilicet in annona, in porcellis, in agnis, in vitulis, in pasnagio, et decimam de molendino et de lana, et in ceteris rebus unde decima datur'.[81] Similar grants to Lewes were made by the future King Stephen from Sutton near Woking and by Gilbert de Curtuna from land near Blechingley (table 14), for no church had been founded on either property.

The distinction suggested here between full demesne tithe grants and those merely involving two-thirds is supported by Bishop Henry of Blois's confirmation of Lewes Priory's spiritualities in his diocese, issued between 1153 and 1167.[82] This describes two of the three donations just cited as 'decimam de dominio Roberti de Dunest' apud Scaldef'' and 'decimam Roberti de Hech apud Suttonam'. By contrast, portions resulting from a general grant made in 1147 of the full tithe from all Warenne demesnes[83] are described in the same document as 'duas partes decime de Reigata et de Bechew', scilicet de dominio comitis', and 'duas partes decime de Sira de dominio Rogeri de Clera'. The reason for this must be sought in the fact that the Warenne manors of Reigate, Betchworth and Shere all had churches. Thus the confirmation brings out a distinction which the original grants lack. By the mid-century it was evidently unacceptable to alienate from an estate church the share of demesne tithe which custom assigned to it, and the limitation is introduced according to circumstances, regardless of the original wording. Through the confirmation the bishop makes his authority felt: in confirming he defines, and in defining he limits.

The principle thus expressed is less one of respect for parochial authority than of responsibility towards churches which the prospective tithe-donors or their ancestors had built. Just as a founder must endow a new church adequately from the resources of his estate, so he is restricted in later reducing that endowment. This is consistent both with the concern (expressed by bishops from Anselm onwards) that local churches should remain economically viable,[84] and with Henry of Blois's known character as a defender of the Church's status. But it also suggests a governing concept which was still one of property rather than of parish, of a balance of rights between church and *dominus fundi* rather than between church and parishioner. No landowner, apparently, was restrained from alienating the full tithe of his demesne on the grounds that it lay within the parish of a church founded on another man's estate.

The Southwark Priory material includes several full demesne tithe grants from small manors and individual farms, continuing into the second half of the century (table 15). Thus in its early years the Priory acquired from William de Abinger, tenant of the small fitz Ansculf manor at Mitcham, 'omnem decimam terrarum quas teneo apud Stratham et Micham . . . ex omni re unde decima dari debet'.[85] John de Whitford subsequently granted tithe from two holdings of the same barony, 'decimam de Polesdene et omnes decimas meas de Wichford',[86] and of these the former was an outlier, probably identifiable with two hides valued at £1 pa in 1086, now contained within Mickleham parish.[87] Indeed, the four tithe-portions listed when Henry of Blois confirmed

Southwark's endowments in c1150–71, 'decimam de Wichford, et decimam de Polesdene, et decimam de Nutebrake, et decimam de dominio Gervasii de Corenella totam apud Edintune',[88] all derived from what are now mere localities within larger parishes.

This apparent freedom for laymen to tamper with parochial rights is not easily compatible with a fully-fledged parochial system. Henry's encouragement of tithe-grants to religious corporations suggests that the reduction of parochial resources was, in his view, outweighed by the advantages of transferring units of revenue from lay to ecclesiastical hands. The rather sudden cessation of such grants in the third quarter of the century,[89] perhaps associated with the advent of a new bishop in 1173, seems symptomatic of new attitudes and new concepts.

Patrons, bishops and monastic possession

The term 'proprietary church' encourages the view that all founding lords sought, and then jealously guarded, autonomy of control over their churches. This was not inevitably the case: there is no rigid correlation between the jurisdictional status of a church, and its function for the local lord and his tenants. Churches which seem to have been built for the use of founders' tenants rather than the founders themselves (above, p135) include several, such as Alfold and Walton-on-the-Hill, which were jurisdictionally 'free' and 'private'. On the other hand Ashtead church, dedicated as a subordinate chapel with a priest answerable to the priest of Leatherhead (below, p153), is in function a classic proprietary case, situated away from the village and beside the manor-house where its founder Laurence de Rouen probably resided (fig 40).[90] Like the late 11th-century Hampshire lord who built, for his own use, a church to be served by a minster-priest from Christchurch,[91] Laurence's concern was not to create an independent parish, but simply to hear mass in a convenient place. It may be that co-operation between mother church and founding lord was widespread, though it is clear that many 11th-century lords did in fact have a high degree of freedom in the control of their churches.

The foundation of so many monasteries during c1100–60 introduced a new factor. On the one hand, local churches now had more powerful rivals for patronage: the lay lord who would formerly have expressed his pious instincts or concern for his soul by founding a church might now patronise a monastery instead. On the other hand, local churches might themselves be given to monasteries as part of such patronage, and might indeed be founded with this purpose in mind. As the 12th century passed, canon law limited more and more the lay patron's rights. This limitation is seen in the increasingly cautious language of charters: where an early Norman knight would have confidently granted 'his' church, Bartholomew de Chesney gave Addington church to Southwark Priory in c1180 'quantum ad advocatum et dominum fundi pertinet'.[92] Thus by 1150 a lay church transferred to a monastery was useful to its recipient, but cost relatively little to give away.[93]

Monastic acquisition of churches gathered momentum from itself, as what had once been anomalous became normal. By 1180 local churches in religious hands were no longer the minority that they had been a century before. It has been estimated that a quarter of all English churches were in religious hands before 1200.[94] Detailed examination of the Surrey evidence suggests a much higher proportion: of 138 recorded churches and chapels by c1180, 47 had been founded on ecclesiastical manors, 44 had passed from lay to religious hands, and 47 were still in lay patronage (fig 46). Thus the proportion of monastically-owned churches in this county had risen from roughly one-third to roughly two-thirds during the century after Domesday Book. In north-eastern Surrey, the area near London and the major religious houses, scarcely a single lay church remained. Equally important, patronage of the church had now become divorced in a large number of cases from ownership of the land: rural churches could now be regarded as

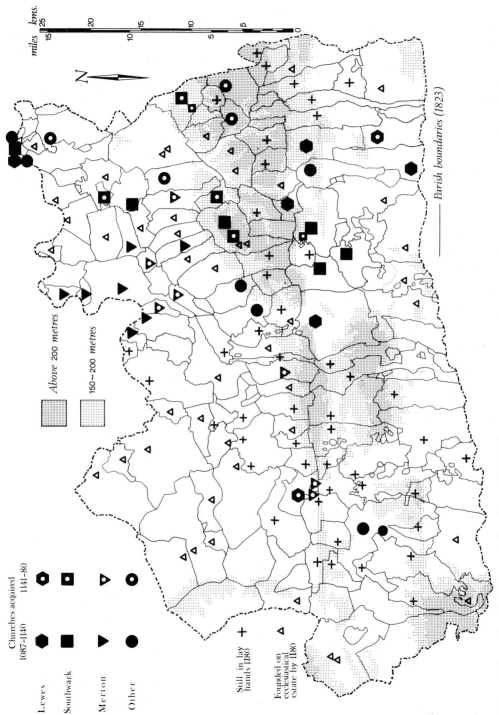

Fig 46 Monastic acquisitions of churches, 1087–1180

independent entities, not merely as pieces of property subject in certain specific ways to outside control.

Thus when the flood of donations subsided towards the end of the 12th century, it left a powerful new church-owning interest and a powerful tool in the cause of reform. And reform was now much in evidence, as the canonists multiplied their definitions. Throughout Christendom, their activities were extending the Church's authority into many new areas, restricting the rights of lay patrons and formalising what had once been fluid: 'the canon law laid its cold hand on the parishes of Europe, and froze the pattern which has in many parts subsisted ever since'.[95] The key figures in putting the new ideas into practice were of course the bishops, in the case of Surrey the two great men who successively ruled Winchester diocese during the formative years: Henry of Blois (1129–71), and Richard of Ilchester (1173–88).

One of the most powerful Englishmen of his day, Henry was known as a papalist, an admirer of Cluny and a strong protector of the Church's interests. As bishop he frequently introduced a new precision into ecclesiastical relationships.[96] On the other hand his *acta*, which reveal him as so careful a definer of individual monastic rights, have little to say on relationships between local churches, and his apparent attitude to tithe-portions (above, p149) seems distinctly old-fashioned. In at least one Surrey advowson dispute, his behaviour would have commended itself little to the reformers. In the 1150s John of Salisbury complained to Adrian IV on behalf of Merton Priory that their church of Effingham, 'quam eis petente domino fundi donavit dominus Wintoniensis, . . . in iniuriam apostolicae maiestatis et confusionem sanctorum canonum contulit memoratus episcopus cuidam publicano fere laico, filio sacerdotis qui in ea ecclesia ministraverat'.[97] Here, as with Archbishop Ralph's intervention for Lewes Priory in the case of Burstow church some forty years earlier (above, p147), the bishop seems motivated less by general principles than by antipathy or affection for a particular house.

Richard of Ilchester stands much more clearly for the new order. Whereas Henry had been a great noble, Richard was a curial with long experience in the royal service. To his high reputation as an administrator can apparently be added a significant role in the development of canon law: several canonical rulings which passed into the permanent corpus were made at his instance, in one case concerning the status of a church which its lay patron had granted to a monastery without episcopal licence.[98] The Church's policy was now to prefer patronage of churches in ecclesiastical hands,[99] and Richard followed it: when in c1180 Bartholomew de Chesney gave Addington church to Southwark Priory, it was 'amore dei et petitione domini Ricardi Wintoniensis episcopi'.[100] In the aftermath of Becket's murder the Church's position was strong, and the climate favourable to a consolidation of gains.[101] At such a time, such a man as Richard might well have taken an active interest in moulding the emergent parochial structure. It seems, at all events, to have been in his episcopate that the Surrey parishes crystallised: territorial units comprising all land-holdings, jurisdictional units comprising all tithes and dues, and pastoral units comprising the whole population.

The consolidation of the parish in 12th-century Surrey

The parish was, of course, a familiar concept to all 11th- and 12th-century ecclesiastics. The territorial structure of the church had developed by a process of subdivision, and the creation of smaller units within minster parishes was a logical sequel to the creation of minster parishes within dioceses. In Europe of the central Middle Ages, it was implicit in both secular and canon law that all churches functioned within a territorial framework of jurisdiction. Explicit statements on the subject invariably place restraints on the independence of new churches and condemn their uncontrolled foundation.[102]

Practice in early Norman England bore little resemblance to this theory. The apparent failure of the Surrey minsters to maintain their control over lesser churches during this period has already been noted (above, p108). But it was not merely a matter of small units replacing large ones: the decay of the minsters left a vacuum which the multitude of estate churches founded by the beginning of the 12th century did not necessarily fill. Writers on the growth of the English parochial system have tended to equate it with the proliferation of local churches. The bias of research towards regions in which vill, parish and manor tend to be coterminous has perhaps obscured the necessity of distinguishing between these two developments. Where parish and lordship are identical, the historian is not forced to an independent definition of the former; where manorial geography is fragmented the problems become more evident.

It is hard to see in what sense we can speak of a parochial system in Domesday Surrey. Most churches belonged to manors smaller than their later parishes; conversely, most parishes include the area of more than one Domesday manor. If a Norman landowner built himself a church, it seems hardly likely that he would thereby establish authority over his neighbours' lands. Neither could he restrain them from building churches of their own, and during the first half-century of Norman rule, foundation seems to have proceeded without reference to neighbouring local churches which already existed.[103] Clear parochial divisions still lay in the future, and when they came they were to be imposed from above.

Perhaps they often stabilised existing arrangements of a private and informal character. It may have been normal for the tenants of two or three manors to worship by mutual agreement in one lord's church, especially if existing economic links gave the 'parish' a unity in terms of farming and settlement. But well into the 12th century the rights of local churches remained linked to territorial lordship; hence the freedom enjoyed by owners of churchless demesnes to apply their resources as they pleased. We should probably imagine a long period of variation and flux, with many gaps left in the unstable balance between declining minster and emergent local church. It would be unrealistic to assume that every peasant had ready access to a functioning church; the abuses attacked so regularly by reformers – an ignorant and servile priesthood, lack of pastoral care, the diversion of tithes to lay uses – can hardly have failed to flourish in such a context. In 1100 the raw materials of a parochial system existed, but they had yet to acquire form and stability.[104]

Early 12th-century bishops did occasionally place restrictions on new foundations, but most if not all of these were for the benefit of former minsters rather than of estate churches.[105] Thus when Bishop William Giffard dedicated Ashtead church 'sicut capellam subiectam, cum omnibus consuetudinibus que ad eam pertinent, ecclesie de Liered', forbidding any priest to sing mass there except by permission of the priest of Leatherhead',[106] he was reaffirming the minster rights which Thorncroft church had inherited from the old mother church of Leatherhead (above, p101). It is thus far from clear that Henry I's bishops would, as a matter of course, recognise and enforce parochial rights of estate churches extending outside the estate boundaries, or indeed have any precise conception of such rights, though it may be wrong to argue too strongly *ex silentio* when so little evidence has survived.[107]

As the 12th century progressed, one sign of change was the sharpening of the distinction between *ecclesia* and *capella*. Domesday references to chapels, confined almost entirely to the south-eastern circuit, occur even there very rarely, often in cases where two churches are listed on one manor.[108] In Surrey a broad class of sub-parochial chapels is slow to appear, and the meaning of the term is somewhat equivocal. The *capellae* listed on several of the Chertsey Abbey demesnes in 1176 are so described not because they were subordinate to parish churches but because they were subordinate to the Abbey itself (above, p129).

An illuminating example is the relationship of Blechingley and Horne, two parishes comprising a broad north-south strip in the Surrey Weald (fig 11G). In the 11th century they had almost certainly formed a single unit, but by c1150 Horne was subinfeudated and possessed an estate church of its own (above, p126). Lewes Priory's acquisition of Blechingley church in the 1140s was followed in c1160 by a release from Peter de Tolworth, tenant of Horne, of 'ecclesiam de Horne que est in territorio meo'.[109] This effectively placed Horne church in subjection to that of Blechingley, and the deed, phrased in the language of a release rather than of a grant, implies recognition of pre-existing rights on the part of Lewes. This transaction, perhaps the result of litigation, suggests an unusual instance of mother-church rights enforced retrospectively, the monks claiming patronage of a layman's church at Horne on the grounds that the would-be mother church of Blechingley was already in their hands. When this relationship came to be stated explicitly, as 'ecclesiam de Blachingelea cum capella sua de Horne',[110] it was in a charter of Bishop Richard of Ilchester. It was also Richard who confirmed to Southwark Priory their separately-acquired churches of Woodmansterne and Burgh as 'ecclesiam de Wudemarestorne et ecclesiam de Berghes, pertinentes ad ecclesiam de Benstede', creating an artificial relationship between a 'mother' church and two 'daughter' churches which was tenurially and topographically convenient but lacked historical justification.[111] At Addington, where the canons of Southwark had previously possessed tithe-rights perhaps associated with a chapel there (above, p129), Richard first secured for them the parish church, and then firmly established its jurisdiction over the chapel in a carefully-worded confirmation which emphasises the lay lord's public subjection.[112]

Whether the initiative in these cases came from the recipients or from the bishop, it is in his *acta* that the new order of things becomes plainly evident. From the end of the 12th century the divisions are clear-cut: an ecclesiastical building must either be a parish church, or a chapel subordinate to such a church. The alienation of tithe ceased, and parishes took on a more cohesive form. Parish boundaries became fixed and remained so until the Victorian changes, preserving in the process many far older features which had survived until the critical years of parochial formation.

Ecclesia and *capella*

By 1200, therefore, the parochial geography of Surrey was well-defined, its network of parish churches largely complete and firmly distinguished from the lower stratum of dependent chapels. But this distinction was essentially a jurisdictional one, based on the priests' status of tenure and the destination of tithes rather than on relative importance in local religious life. *Capella* was not necessarily smaller or less important pastorally than *ecclesia*; it merely occupied an inferior position. This is implicit in the phrase 'dedicavi ecclesiam de Essestede sicut capellam' of William Giffard's charter,[113] while it would be absurd to assume that when Horne church became a chapel of Blechingley, or Waddington church a chapel of Coulsdon, their devotional functions were suddenly diminished.[114]

A chapel could not have a parson in its own right, but was controlled by the rector of the mother church. Generally this merely meant that the rector could farm the chapel at a profit. Thus in the 1180s the Dean and Chapter of Salisbury demised Godalming mother church and its chapel of Chiddingfold to Richard de Chiddingfold, a local cleric, as two separate perpetual vicarages, rendering a total of £6 6s 8d pa and 1 lb wax. In 1220 the same man was in office, but his duties were carried out by a chaplain named Alan who paid him £5 pa for the revenues of the vicarages.[115] In such cases the formal relationship of dependence was probably irrelevant to the nature and quality of the ministry. Nonetheless, chapels were in theory subject to limitations of function, notably in the practice of baptism and burial, which were designed to protect the dignity and fiscal rights of their mother churches. The extent to which these attributes were restricted in practice is a useful measure of the effective differences between churches and chapels-of-ease.

In early medieval Europe, baptismal rights were the clearest mark of mother-church status. English sources of the 10th century and after place more emphasis on the right to take corpses for burial, but baptism still remained important. The frequency with which crude early fonts were preserved when churches were rebuilt around them testifies to the reverence in which they were held throughout the Middle Ages, not only as sacred objects but also, perhaps, as symbols of ancient baptismal status with its connotations of freedom. Tub fonts predictably occur in churches of early Norman lay foundation, as at Hambledon and Little Bookham. At Walton-on-the-Hill the magnificent lead font of c1150 is the only evidence for a church here before the late 13th century.

Other cases fit the expected pattern of baptismal churches less neatly. Eleventh- or early 12th-century fonts remain in the Wealden denn churches of Thursley, Wonersh, Alfold and Ewhurst, and of these the first two were respectively daughter churches of Witley and Shalford (above, pp115, 119). Thames Ditton, one of the chapels of Kingston upon Thames, retains a particularly fine carved font of the same period.[116] Early Norman landowners in Surrey were evidently willing for baptism to be performed in satellite and daughter churches. Nor do restrictions seem to have grown as parochial authority tightened. In the late 12th and early 13th centuries many churches acquired a standard type of font consisting of a square bowl supported on shafts,[117] and examples (or fragments) of these occur at Seale, Frensham, Chessington and Capel, chapels of relatively late appearance. Discounting the unlikely possibility that several fonts have been brought to their present locations from elsewhere, it seems indubitable that 12th-century patrons of churches frequently provided subordinate chapels with baptismal facilities. Practice would probably have varied between owners: it may, for instance, be significant that none of the 12th-century chapels on the main Chertsey Abbey estate is known to have had an early font.

More important, in view of the substantial value of mortuaries, was the right of burial. As far back as Eadgar's reign, possession of a graveyard invested a thegn's church with some degree of public status, and it was this privilege that mother churches guarded most jealously.[118] As late as 1217 Chertsey Abbey disputed with the vicar of Chobham his right to a cemetery, the monks claiming that this might lead to a cessation of their ancient dues from Chobham chapel, 'iam quasi matricem ecclesiam factam', and the vicar complaining of the problems which his flock encountered in transporting corpses along the bad roads to Chertsey. The monks permitted the cemetery in return for an annual pension, but the detailed agreement, defining the chapel's status and guaranteeing to inhabitants of Chobham the free choice of burial at Chertsey, emphasises the delicate and contentious nature of the issue.[119] The frequency of chapel graveyards at this date cannot even be guessed at. The 12th-century burials around a small private chapel at Banstead (below, p156) are an isolated but perhaps revealing piece of archaeological evidence, and in 1220 the Godalming survey mentions a 'cymeterium et baptisterium' at Chiddingfold chapel.[120] At all events, reforming bishops of Henry III's reign were more concerned with the utility of chapels than with the vested interests of mother churches. The Winchester statutes of the 1260s order the preparation of cemeteries for all chapels not already possessing them and lying more than two miles from their mother churches, though a graveyard around Haslemere chapel remained unconsecrated until 1363.[121]

It seems not unlikely that the chapels which played a full pastoral role in the mid 13th century had often done so since their foundation in the 12th, notwithstanding their dependent status. But the problem does not end here, for though the foundation of churches and public chapels-of-ease was slowing to a halt by the end of the 12th century, the number of functioning religious buildings continued to rise in an unobtrusive but not unimportant way.[122]

From the late 12th century there are scattered references to the building of new private chapels, sited within manor-house precincts and unequivocally subject to their parish churches.

Partly at least, they reflect a growing desire to hear mass in more private and convenient places. Thus in *c*1200 Southwark Priory licensed Robert Mauduit to have a chapel in his *curia* at Mitcham, while at about the same date the bishop of Exeter guaranteed to the archbishop of Canterbury, lord of the manor of East Horsley, 'quod ecclesie Beati Petri de Horsleg' nullum fiet preiudicium nullum ve detrimentum in posterum occasione capelle nostre quam ereximus in curia nostra de Horsleg' ad divinorum celebrationem in eadem audiendam'.[123] A deed of *c*1220 records that Gilbert son of William archdeacon of Caux built a chapel of St Katherine in his messuage at Southwark, in which mass could be said either by his own or by another chaplain, saving oblations and 1 lb of incense yearly to St Olave's church.[124] A century later, in 1313, William de Westone received episcopal licence to have chapels or oratories at his manor-houses in Albury and West Clandon parishes, 'cum propter loci distantiam et viarum incomoda prefatas ecclesias sine difficultate et gravamine frequenter adire non valeant, possit . . . per sacerdotem ydoneum divina facere celebrari et ea ibidem audire horis et temporibus oportunis, salvo iure in omnibus ecclesiarum parochialium predictarum'.[125]

For the 13th century the distinction between chapels-of-ease and these newer private chapels might at first seem obvious. The former existed for the benefit of parishioners: in the words of the 1247 Winchester synodal statutes, they were 'capelle, intra parochias nostras contemplatione parochianorum a matrice ecclesia nimis distantium antiquitus erecte, que quandoque bis vel ter in ebdomada sacerdotis gaudebant obsequiis'.[126] The latter have been seen as aristocratic 'status symbols which drew the more affluent parishioners away from regular attendance at the mother church',[127] marks of a lack of concern for corporate parochial life on the part of the wealthy. Yet it is doubtful whether they were so new and exclusive a phenomenon, or so divorced from the mainstream of the Church's work. D M Owen's work in Lincolnshire has shown that the continuing foundation of manorial or demesne chapels was influenced by local settlement conditions, especially the growth of communities in areas of recent and dispersed settlement.[128] There are strong suggestions that the same was true in Surrey.

Manorial chapels of the 13th century belonged to the same tradition as manorial churches of the 11th; what they lacked in relation to their predecessors was the independent capacity to exact obedience from the peasant populace. Considered functionally rather than jurisdictionally, the line drawn between use by the lord's family and use by his dependents and tenants can scarcely be very clear.[129] Even if exclusive family use became increasingly the norm as time passed,[130] the state of affairs in *c*1200 must still have been very fluid. How, for instance, should we classify the chapel excavated in the manorial complex at Preston Hawe, Banstead? A rectangular late 12th-century enclosure contained a succession of halls (the earliest pre-dating the earthwork) with ancillary buildings. The chapel, of the usual small two-cell type, lay alongside the hall, with several burials in an adjacent walled area. The sequence of buildings on the site apparently ended in *c*1300.[131] Here, then, a manorial chapel, sub-parochial and otherwise unknown, was serving a community and receiving its members for burial as late as the second half of the 12th century.

Secondly, we can have virtually no idea of the number of such chapels which once existed, beyond being confident that only a small minority are recorded. In contrast to parish churches, their fiscal subservience rarely made it necessary to record their existence, and their appearance in written sources is rare and incidental. Chapel licences were entered in bishops' registers, but those for Winchester diocese only begin in the late 13th century. Field-names sometimes suggest memories of lost chapels: for instance Church Field on the Wadden estate map (fig 22), or Chapel Plat in South Park, Blechingley, where foundations have been excavated.[132] The buildings themselves rarely remain, for in the later Middle Ages they tended to succumb to social and demographic changes. Parish churches, with enforceable rights over a clearly-defined area, usually survived: throughout England the isolated church is a familiar sight. In Surrey at least, the chapels usually vanished when the houses to which they were attached were rebuilt or abandoned, and as many lost as surviving examples are recorded.

Such evidence as we have does not suggest that chapel ownership was confined to the aristocracy or even to the wealthier gentry. A Wealden yeoman farmer who possessed one was Jordan de Yniggefeld, whose moated homestead is identifiable with Moat Farm in Tandridge parish.[133] In c1230 he granted the chapel there to the Augustinian canons of Tandridge, with the new *curia* around it, a garden with buildings, and a long list of parcels from his own demesne. The gift included a silver chalice, books, vestments and ornaments, and the object of the transaction was a chantry there for Jordan and his family.[134] Did this chapel have wider functions? Moat Farm lies deep in the Weald, four miles south of Tandridge church and village and at the meeting-point of three parishes; for inhabitants of surrounding farms it would have been much easier to travel here than northwards along the often near-impassable clay lanes. A parallel case, the Wealden chapel of Oakwood where a private chantry existed by 1290,[135] does not lie near any manorial site and seems likely to have been founded for pastoral convenience.

Usually this sub-stratum of private chapels is only visible in isolated glimpses, but in the case of Godalming parish the detailed survey compiled in 1220 enables us to view it as a whole (fig 47).[136] Dependent on the mother church were Chiddingfold chapel, with a chapel of its own at Haslemere, and the former old minster at Tuesley. In addition, two of the three private estates within the old royal manor[137] possessed their own chapels. At Hurtmore was a timber chapel dedicated to All Saints, granted two years previously by T de Hurtmore to the summoner of the Guildford chapter who rendered 6s 8d pa for it to the mother church. A chapel of St Nicholas, owing three days' weekly service (presumably of one tenant), stood in the manorial *curia* of Catteshall. But for the survival of this one exceptional source, it would have been impossible to guess at so complex a structure.

Below the parish churches, a large, ill-recorded and now largely vanished class of chapels may be dimly perceived. While they spanned a wide spectrum, some doubtless serving no more than a single family, it seems impossible to draw a firm distinction between the public and private in function, at any rate before the later 13th century. Among the scattered farms of Wealden Surrey, the overall pastoral importance of manorial chapels was probably much greater than among the nucleated villages of open-field country. If Jordan de Yniggefeld's homestead was at all typical, the contribution made by private chapels to the Church's ministry in the countryside may have been far from negligible.

Conclusion

After 1200, changes in the Church's institutional and fiscal structure seem less relevant to its role as a living force in the community. While bishops were taking a greater interest than ever in such matters, the links between churches and the recipients of ecclesiastical revenue were growing ever more distant and formalised. The preoccupations of monastic proprietors lay more and more with tithe and pension rights, less and less with the interests of parishioners.[138]

The Surrey evidence has little to add here to a well-established general picture.[139] The farming of monastic churches at fixed pensions, popular in the years around 1200, was practised systematically by the monks of Lewes, who established pensions of £3 from Blechingley church in 1175–88, £6 from Dorking church in 1191–8, and £1 10s from Gatton church by the 1220s; at St Olave's Southwark a vicarage had briefly been established and the rectory appropriated for the support of guests, but the Priory's interest was quickly commuted here also to a £4 pension.[140]

Twelfth-century pension-paying vicars, such as Richard de Chiddingfold at Godalming (above, p154) and his two contemporaries who held the Merton Priory churches in Guildford for

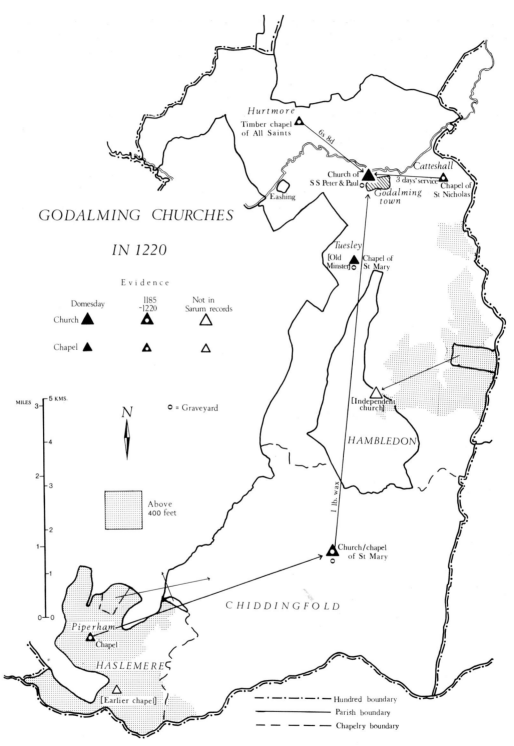

GODALMING CHURCHES

IN 1220

Evidence

	Domesday	1185 -1220	Not in Sarum records
Church	▲	◮	△
Chapel	▲	◭	△

Hurtmore
Timber chapel
of All Saints

6s 8d

Catteshall

Church of
S S Peter & Paul

3 days' service

Chapel of
St Nicholas

Godalming town

Eashing

Tuesley
[Old Minster] Chapel of St Mary

[Independent church]

HAMBLEDON

MILES 5 KMS.

⊙ = Graveyard

N

Above
400 feet

1 lb. wax

Church/chapel
of St Mary

CHIDDINGFOLD

Piperham
Chapel

HASLEMERE

[Earlier chapel]

Hundred boundary
Parish boundary
Chapelry boundary

Fig 47 Godalming parish church and its dependent chapels, according to the Salisbury survey of 1220

3 marks each,[141] must be distinguished from vicars in the normal later medieval sense on account of their higher economic status.[142] Full appropriation, as effected by the monks of Westminster in 1174–88 at Battersea and Wandsworth,[143] was rarer, varying with the success of the proprietor houses in pleading their cases to their bishops. No constant policy can be discerned among the Surrey monasteries; in 1291, for instance, churches in the patronage of Southwark and Merton Priories display a mixture of vicarages, pensions and unappropriated livings.[144] The presence or absence of vicarages in later centuries springs not from the local contexts of churches or the circumstances of their acquisition, but from the means and opportunities of their individual monastic owners in individual cases.

The parochial system of 13th-century Surrey is interesting less for its framework than for its elusive infrastructure of miscellaneous chapels. This suggests something not wholly dissimilar to the groups of chapelries in, for instance, a typical large northern English parish, a similarity obscured by later changes and lost to any superficial examination. The records impose a misleading uniformity on a pattern which, despite the consolidation of its main lines during the 12th century, still had its complexities.

Conclusion

This study has not tried to place Surrey in any distinct cultural region. Some of its institutions appear more clearly (or in a more developed form) in Kent and Sussex, some in the Midlands, and some in East Anglia. Viewed from Surrey, these regions can all be linked to one main course of development during the earlier Middle Ages. Great contrasts there certainly were, but they result more from economic and geographical differences than from different social origins. The idiosyncrasies of Surrey can be seen against a background common to most of lowland England.[1]

The original organisation of Anglo-Saxon Surrey was multi-cellular. Large provincial territories were divisible into local districts or vills, themselves corresponding to regular groups of distinct, individual hides. In later sources the middle-tier units give a strong impression of cohesiveness, often surviving in the form of manors, parishes and townships. When and how did this cohesiveness evolve? The charters show that by the late 7th century many hide-groups were entities to the extent of having their own names, and their long stability suggests internal bonds. Often a hide-group may have had tribal identity as 'a cluster of farms held by agnatic kinsmen', and a form of joint agriculture may have been practised on some of its arable.[2] Possibly, then, the more fertile area within each group was already undergoing a limited subdivision which foreshadowed the common fields of the future. But in Surrey the collections of distinct farms or hamlets never wholly lost their basic primitive character. Their identity is best conceived in terms of their obligations: one group would specialise in different products, and owe the king different renders, from the next. Thus in the early stages they were characterised less by internal organisation than by their relationship with each other and with their commons in the tightly-ordered provincial structure.

The framework of minster parishes makes perfect sense in this context. The obvious way to evangelize a large territory of many constituent parts, all tightly bound to a *villa regia* but lacking internal foci, was by means of priests based on one major church at the centre and itinerating through the dependent vills. Hence the conspicuously 'public' character of the minsters, and the close correspondence of their *parochiae* to hundreds, the direct successors of the early territories. The efficiency, both pastoral and fiscal, of the minster communities must have owed much to their links with centres of royal power.

Manors both complex and simple were also based on the early exploitative system. So long as groups of vills remained linked together in 'extensive' economic systems, it was natural for big manors to perpetuate the old federative structure. But as the pastoral zones developed a significant grain-producing capacity of their own, old links decayed. This was itself a stimulus to further growth, since vills were now driven to develop a self-sufficient agrarian balance within their own bounds.[3] The final stages were working themselves through in the 11th and 12th centuries, when Wealden denns became established farms, and the last dependent wood-pasture tracts were relinquished to develop into new communities; here Surrey was more advanced than parts of Kent, where the denn system still functioned in the 13th century.

Manorial origins have no single course: 'unicellular' manors came into existence from the 7th century onwards by direct royal grant, by the breakup of 'multiple estates', and by the late severance of residual groups attached to royal vills. The archipelagos of denns are different again, since for them no early framework existed; the contrast between hidated tenement groups and pasture zones left its permanent mark in the formless, incoherent manor and parish structure of much of the Surrey Weald.[4] Nonetheless, it seems a fair generalisation that the classic 11th-century manor emerged by a process which went step-by-step with the appearance of a broad, locally-based class of minor aristocracy: the proliferation between 900 and 1066 of the English country gentry. Just as economic and demographic change created conditions more favourable to their existence, so their growing demands for a land-base prompted the fission of existing 'multiple estates', and the ever more rapid alienation of vills which still remained attached to royal centres.

Expansion also stimulated the growth of local foci: by the 11th century settlement was becoming concentrated on nucleated sites. It is symptomatic that two ancient minsters were abandoned because of their distance from the developed pattern, whereas the estate churches of the 10th, 11th and 12th centuries are usually in the general vicinity of their villages, where such exist. Groups of farms which crossed geological strata tended to coalesce, and split into longitudinal townships, as lines of villages developed with pasture links to the north and south and incipient common fields. But settlement nucleation and common fields were largely confined to the fertile zones; the surrounding farms kept their essential primitive character, though sometimes splitting into halves and quarters. Thus the steps towards a coherent village economy were genuine but limited.

The advent of organised, symmetrical arrangements heightened this contrast, for it mainly affected the subdivided core. Regular villages were established, common-field holdings apportioned in equal shares, and obligations defined systematically; but these small versions of the classic Midland townships were islands in a more primitive tenurial sea. Sometimes, indeed, there are incipient signs of a wider integration: references to land held 'in duabus partibus', 'in sud et in nort', in subdivided and compact halves, suggest attempts to create an orderly township structure by forging links between one zone of the manor and another. Identifying the motive force behind such developments is curiously difficult. At least in terms of obligation, it was the demands of lordship which imposed uniformity: on most manors *all* holdings, both compact and subdivided, were assessed in virgates. Beyond this, the contention that systematic organisation was seigneurial and not communal must still rest on inference rather than on clear evidence. It can only be suggested that we see in Surrey the first unfulfilled steps along a road which led elsewhere to integrated townships and fully-fledged two- and three-field systems.

Also with the growth of lordship, between the 10th and 12th centuries came other institutions which have given local communities their identity ever since: the manor-house, the demesne, and the manorial church. Whether staffed by a local priest or by a priest from the minster, whether founded for the lord's household or for his tenants, the last was a manifestation of local identity and rooted in the fabric of manorial life. In the Weald and other pockets of late settlement, churches and manor-houses were probably the earliest foci, providing at least notional centres for communities which otherwise had little to unite them.

The inter-relationship of parishes with manors and townships raises the hardest problems of all, and here there can be no single explanation. Residual minster *parochiae* would have tended to retain everything, however disparate tenurially, which newer churches had not swallowed up; hence the big, sprawling parishes of Woking, Kingston and Croydon. But sometimes the eventual parish of a private church proves to include manors which were independent in 1066 and thereafter. Two explanations are possible: either the sphere of one lord's church was extended beyond his lordship through private agreement or external control, or the parish represents some earlier entity. The first is not inherently unlikely, and may often be correct. The parochial network was imposed from above and embodied broad principles of ecclesiastical government: local anomalies were liable to be submerged. During the 12th century, independent holdings which only acknowledged a tenuous minster authority may have been drawn into subjection to the nearest church. Perhaps some had had their own small churches, which now vanished or sank to the status of chapels. Beneath the 'parochial grid', the dimly perceived sub-stratum of private chapels perpetuates the old, manor-based character of local religion.

But what of the parishes which are made up of separate Domesday manors and which also seem to be economically coherent units? Here the parish is the larger entity, transcending the manor to which the church belonged. Probably in some such cases the whole area had been one manor when the church was founded: unless diverted to a new church, existing patterns of tithe-payment and religious devotion must often have withstood division of lordship. But when the church was of relatively late foundation, its parish boundaries must have been drawn around an area which was now disparate tenurially, but in some other sense unified.

Here we return to arguments for the precedence of village over manor, of township communities maintaining their integrity in vills of divided lordship.[5] But this integrity need not be immemorial: it merely pre-dates the manorial division, and could have evolved only shortly before within a united manor. The splitting of Esher occurred after 1005, while some strip-parishes on the dip-slope which were divided by 1066 seem to have been single manors a century or so earlier (above, pp33–4). In other cases the apparent economic unity of the parish is skin-deep. At Leatherhead, for instance, the lands of the separate manors prove on close inspection to lie in separate blocks, and the series of regular subdivided holdings in the common field was entirely contained within one manor.[6] The lordship-based restriction of common rights (above, pp70–1) heightens the impression that in this parish the manors were self-contained, their organisation not transcending their bounds. Surrey provides nothing to refute the 'view of the farming community as an institution that was manufactured during the medieval period, rather than one that formed an innate part of the organic constitution of society'.[7]

Four general points have recurred in this study. One is the startlingly thorough local organisation of the early to mid Anglo-Saxon period, which left a framework so comprehensive that all future developments, except in regions of very late settlement, were moulded by it. The second is the dramatic effect of growth between the late 9th and mid 12th centuries, when the whole basis of exploitation changed and fragments of the old, 'extensive' structure resolved themselves into the self-contained, internally-focussed entities which we think of as classic manors and classic parishes. The third is the ever-present influence of seigneurial demands from the king's downwards, defining local communities, moulding the expanding economy, and giving an ordered stability to the new patterns of rural life. The fourth point, and the one which explains Surrey's local pecularities, is the distinctness between the 'champion' and the 'wood-pasture' regions of England. It can be stated as a general principle that the shorter the supply of common waste during the 9th to 11th centuries, the more integrated local communities were likely to become, and the more susceptible to the hand of lordship. Surrey retained less waste than Kent, more than the Midlands. Thus in Surrey the underlying early pattern is less obvious than in Kent, less deeply buried than in the classic open-field country. As time passed the contrasts grew, for absence of rigid township control left individual enterprise with a free hand. Hence the 13th-century smallholders of Kent and Surrey could diversify and adapt in ways which were only made available to their Midland counterparts by the solvent forces of the later Middle Ages.

List Of Abbreviations

BCS	*Cartularium Saxonicum*, ed W de G Birch, **1–3** (London, 1883–92)
Bod Lib	Oxford, Bodleian Library, Department of Western MSS
Brit Lib	London, British Library, Department of MSS
Cal Charter R 3	*Calendar of charter rolls*, **3** (London, 1908)
Cal Cur Reg R	*Calendar of curia regis rolls*, **1–** (London, 1922–)
Cal Docs France	*Calendar of documents preserved in France, illustrative of the history of Great Britain and Ireland* (London, 1899)
DB	Domesday Book (see Note on citations below)
ESRO	Lewes, East Sussex Record Office
GLRO	London, Greater London Record Office
MM	Oxford, Merton College muniments
Plac Abbrev	*Placitorum in domo capitulari Westmonasteriensi asservatorum abbrevatio* (Record Commissioners, 1811)
PLDLHS	*Proceedings of the Leatherhead and District Local History Society*
PNSy	J E B Gover, A Mawer and F M Stenton (eds), *The place-names of Surrey*, English Place-Name Soc, **11** (1934)
PRO	London, Public Record Office
S	P H Sawyer, *Anglo-Saxon charters: an annotated list and bibliography* (London, 1968). (See Note on citations of Anglo-Saxon charters below)
SRO	Kingston upon Thames, Surrey Record Office.
SxAC	*Sussex Archaeological Collections*
SyAC	*Surrey Archaeological Collections*
SyAS	Surrey Archaeological Society
SyRS	Surrey Record Society
TPN	*Taxatio ecclesiastica Angliae et Walliae auctoritate P Nicholai IV, circa AD 1291* (Record Commissioners, 1802)
Valor	*Valor ecclesiasticus tempore Henrici VIII auctoritate regia institutus*, **1–2** (Record Commissioners, 1810–14)
VCHSy	H E Malden (ed), *The Victoria history of the county of Surrey*, **1–4** (London, 1902–12)
WAM	London, Westminster Abbey, Dean and Chapter Muniments

Note on citations of Anglo-Saxon charters

Each charter is cited by its number (eg S 1511) in Sawyer, *Anglo-Saxon charters*, which gives references to texts and commentaries. Other sources are only cited if they have a direct bearing on a relevant issue, or have appeared since the publication of Sawyer.

Note on citations of Domesday Book

Each entry is cited from *Domesday Book*, ed A Farley (Record Commissioners, 1783), by reference to folio and column. Since the new Phillimore fascicules provide the only means of exact reference to individual entries, the notation used in *Domesday Book: 3: Surrey*, ed J Morris

(Chichester, 1975) is also cited. For example, the reference for Betchworth, *DB* 35d (XIX.47), means that the entry appears on folio 35 column d of the Farley edition, and is the 47th entry in the 19th section of the Morris edition.

Note on transcripts from original documents

In all transcripts, original spelling is preserved but punctuation and capitalisation are modernised. Roman numerals are converted to Arabic ones.

Bibliography

A MANUSCRIPT SOURCES

Canterbury Cathedral Library

Register containing manorial surveys etc: MS E24
Documents concerning Archbishop Baldwin's college at Lambeth: Cartae Antiquae L 129–38
Newington deeds: Cartae Antiquae W 108–20

Kingston upon Thames, Surrey Record Office

Bramley court rolls: 212/15/1; Acc 580 Box 5
Deeds: 60/11/1; 65/1/1; 2609/11/2/7; 2609/11/5/1; 2609/11/5/22; 2609/11/5/35
Depositions concerning Shalford and Bramley churches: LM 454

London, British Library, Department of Printed Books

Extra-illustrated set of Manning, O & Bray, W, *History and antiquities of the county of Surrey* (4 vols, 1804); shelfmark Crack.1.Tab.1.b.1

London, British Library, Department of Manuscripts

Abingdon Abbey cartulary: MS Cotton Claudius B.vi
Boxgrove Priory cartulary: MS Cotton Claudius A.vi
Chertsey Abbey cartulary: MS Cotton Vitellius A.xiii
Merton Priory cartulary: MS Cotton Cleopatra C.vii
Southwark Priory cartulary fragments: MS Add 6040
Southwark Priory register: MS Cotton Faustina A.viii
Memorandum concerning Hyde Abbey and Sanderstead: MS Cotton Vespasian D.ix, f32
Transcripts of Warenne deeds: MS Cotton Julius C.vii, ff189, 217
Transcript of Alfold deed: MS Add 6167, f370
Drawing of window in Tooting church: MS Add 36389, f57,
Deeds: Add Chs 5528; 5531–2; 5547; 5556; 5564; 5569; 5572; 5934; 7598; 7599; 8139; 8811; 17278; 22712–22739; 22747–22772; 22783; 22795; 22801; 22808–9; 22818; 22821; 22833; 22847; 22851; 22859; 22866; 22873; 22923; 22926–7; 22937; 22938; 22941–3; 22950; 22954; 22958; 22967; 22976; 22978; 22990; 22992; 22996; 22998; 23002; 23005; 23023; 23038; 23040; 23046; 23049; 23050; 23051; 23060; 23080; 23409; 23516; 23662; 23671; 23677–8; 23684–8; 23693; 24165; 24607; 26728
  Campbell Ch vii.1
  Cotton Chs v.11; viii.10; xvi.41
  MS Cotton Nero C.iii, ff 188, 197, 200 (original deeds pasted in)
  Egerton Ch 6132
  Harleian Chs 46.H.40; 55.A.30; 111.D.44

London, College of Arms

Extracts from lost Southwark Priory cartulary: MS Vincent 46, pp 113–130

London, Greater London Record Office

Glebe terriers: DW/S/79a (Albury/Shere); DW/S/2 (Alfold); DW/S/6 (Beddington); DW/S/10 (Great

Bookham); DW/S/37 (Chobham); DW/S/32 (West Clandon); DW/S/28 (Compton); DW/S/33 (Cranleigh); DW/S/46 (Epsom); DW/S/49 (Fetcham); DW/S/56 (Hambledon); DW/S/58b (Headley); DW/S/81 (Sutton)

Plan of Woodmansterne church: DWOP/W/227

London, Guildhall Library

Documents concerning Wimbledon and Barnes churches: MSS 25122/641, 1426, 1428

London, London Borough of Lambeth, Minet Library and Lambeth Borough Archives

Deeds: Surrey Deeds 3605; 3608; 3610; 3615–16

Watercolours etc of Surrey churches: SP49/713 and S4822 Pls 5301–6 (Addington); SP190/713 (Betchworth); K31660/17 (Bramley); K31660/57 (Gatton); LO9541/66 (Hascombe); LP25/713 and SP25/713 (Tooting); LO9541/137 (Woodmansterne)

London, Lambeth Palace Library

Archbishop's cartulary: MS 1212
Account-roll for Surrey manors, 1236/7: ER 1193
Wimbledon customal: LR 2068

London, Public Record Office

Charter rolls: C53/107; C53/131
Patent rolls: C66/149; C66/328
Cartae antiquae roll GG: C52/31
Forest eyre rolls: E32/194; E32/195
Fetcham inquisition: C143/271/20
Fines: CP25(i)/225/2(15); 225/2(9); 225/3(67); 225/3(93); 225/4(3); 225/5(47); 225/6(83); 225/9(198); 226/10(229); 226/12(281); 226/12(314); 226/13(123); 226/16(113); 228/31(78)
Deeds: C146/10365; DL25/105; 106; DL27/46;
    E40/4055; 7275; 14136; 14192;
    E41/330; E210/7208;
    E315/31(65); 41(64); 41(106); 42(125); 44(107);
    E326/1912; 4350; 4352; 4873; 4876; 4879; 4880; 4893; 6219; 6665; 6693; 7802; 7907; 7976; 8082; 8090; 8094; 8239; 8242; 8243; 9784; 9854–6; 9878–80; 9908; 9909; 9913; 9915
Survey of Crown Lands, c 1552: LR2/190

London, Victoria & Albert Museum, Department of Prints and Drawings

Plan of Carshalton church: E1104–1930

London, Westminster Abbey, Dean and Chapter Muniments

Cartulary: the 'Westminster Domesday'
Pyrford accounts: WAM 27392–27428
Pyrford court rolls: WAM 27468–27481
Deeds: WAM 1836; 1891

Maidstone, Kent Archives Office

Leatherhead glebe terriers: CCRC T 213

Oxford, Bodleian Library

John Leland's Collectanea, vol 1: MS Top Gen c. 1
Deeds: MS Ch. Surrey a.2(32); MS Ch. Surrey a.2(61); MS Eng Hist A II no 38

Plan of Addington church: MS Top Gen c. 80, f3
Paintings of Hascombe church: MS Top Gen f18, ff35v–36
Painting of Merrow church: MS Top Gen f13, f70

Oxford, Corpus Christi College

Catalogue of monastic foundations: MS D 256, ff196v–198

Oxford, Merton College Muniments

Farleigh rentals and court rolls: MM 4890; 4894; 4901; 4904
Malden court roll and rental: MM 4706, 4782
Thorncroft survey book, 1629: MM 5.28
Thorncroft rentals and court rolls: MM 5734; 5777c; 5778; 5779; 5779d; 5781; 5786; 5788; 5791
Thorncroft accounts: MM 5724; 5758
Deed: MM 918

Windsor, Dean and Chapter Archives

Cartulary: the 'Arundel White Book'

California, Henry Huntington Library

Battle Abbey Cartulary: B A vol 29 (consulted from microfilm)

B PRINTED SOURCES

The Anglo-Saxon chronicle, trans G N Garmonsway, 2nd edn (London, 1972)
Annales monastici, ed H R Luard, **2 & 3**, Rolls Ser **36**, 2 & 3 (1864–6)
The Beauchamp cartulary, ed E Mason, Pipe Roll Soc, n s **43** (1971–3)
Bede: *Historia ecclesiastica*, ed C Plummer, **1–2** (Oxford, 1896)
Bracton's note book, ed F W Maitland, **1–3** (London, 1887)
Calendar of charter rolls, **3** (HMSO, 1908)
Calendar of curia regis rolls, **1–** (1922–)
Calendar of documents preserved in France, illustrative of the history of Great Britain and Ireland, ed J Horace Round (London, 1899)
The cartae antiquae rolls 11–20, ed J C Davies, Pipe Roll Soc, n s **33** (1957)
Cartularium monasterii Sancti Johannis Baptiste de Colecestria, ed S A Moore, **1** (Roxburghe Club, London, 1897)
Cartularium Saxonicum, ed W de G Birch, **1–3** (London, 1883–92)
The cartulary of Shrewsbury Abbey, ed U Rees, **1–2** (Aberystwyth, 1975)
Chartulary of the Priory of St Pancras of Lewes, ed L F Salzman, **1–2**, SxRS **38**, **40** (1932–4)
Chertsey Abbey court rolls abstract, ed E Toms, SyRS **38 & 48** (1937, 1954)
Chertsey cartularies [eds anon], **1–2**, SyRS **12** (1915–33)
Sir Christopher Hatton's book of seals, eds L C Loyd & D M Stenton (Oxford, 1950)
Corpus iuris canonici, ed E Friedberg (Leipzig, 1881)
Councils and ecclesiastical documents, ed A W Haddan & W Stubbs, **1–3** (Oxford, 1869–71)
Councils and synods, with other documents relating to the English church, **1**, eds D Whitelock, M Brett & C N L Brooke (Oxford, 1981), and **2**, eds F M Powicke & F R Cheney (Oxford, 1964)
Customals of Battle Abbey, ed S R Scargill-Bird, Camden Soc 2nd ser **41** (1887)
Documents illustrative of the social and economic history of the Danelaw, ed F M Stenton (London, 1920)
Domesday Book, ed A Farley (Rec Comm, 1783)
Domesday Book: 3: Surrey, ed J Morris (Phillimore, Chichester, 1975)
The Domesday of St Paul's, ed W H Hale, Camden Soc **69** (1858)
Eadmer: *Historia novorum in Anglia*, ed M Rule, Rolls Ser **81** (1884)
Early Yorkshire charters: 8: the honour of Warenne, ed C T Clay, Yorkshire Archaeol Soc extra ser **6** (1949)

Fitznells cartulary, ed C A F Meekings and P Shearman, SyRS **26** (1968)

Flores historiarum, ed H R Luard, **2**, Rolls Ser **95** 2 (1890)

The itinerary of John Leland, ed L Toulmin Smith, **7–8** (London, 1909)

Johannis Lelandi antiquarii de rebus Britannicis collectanea, ed T Hearne, **1** (Oxford, 1715)

The letters of Abelard and Heloise, trans B Radice (Penguin, 1974)

The letters of John of Salisbury, **1**, eds W J Millor, S J & H E Butler & C N L Brooke (London, 1955)

Manorial records of Cuxham, Oxfordshire, ed P D A Harvey (HMSO, 1976)

Ordnance Survey Maps: Surrey 25″ 1st edn (1870), sheets **XI** 16; **XVII** 4, 8, 12

Papsturkunden in England, ed W Holtzmann, **1** (Berlin, 1930)

Placitorum in domo capitulari Westmonasteriensi asservatorum abbreviatio (Record Commissioners, 1811)

Regesta regum anglo-normannorum, eds H W C Davis *et al*, **1–3** (Oxford, 1913–68)

Register or memorial of Ewell, Surrey, ed C Deedes (London, 1913)

The register of St Osmund, ed W R Jones, **1**, Rolls Ser **78** (1883)

Registrum Henrici de Woodlock, ed A W Goodman, **1–2**, Canterbury & York Soc **43–4** (1940–1)

Registrum Johannis de Pontissara, ed C Deedes, **1–2**, Canterbury & York Soc **19** (1915) and **30** (1924)

The rolls and register of Bishop Oliver Sutton, ed R M T Hill, **3** (Lincolnshire Rec Soc **48**, 1954)

Rotuli litterarum clausarum, **1–2** (Record Commissioners, 1833–44)

Rotuli litterarum patentium, **1** (Record Commissioners, 1835)

Sarum charters and documents, ed W R Jones & W D Macray, Rolls Ser **97** (1891)

The 1235 Surrey eyre, ed C A F Meekings, **1**, SyRS **31** (1979)

Taxatio ecclesiastica Angliae et Walliae auctoritate P Nicholai IV, circa A D 1291 (Record Commissioners, 1802)

Valor ecclesiasticus tempore Henrici VIII, **1–2** (Record Commissioners, 1810–14)

C   SECONDARY WORKS

[Anon], General notes and documents: Blechingley, *SyAC*, **36** (1925), 111–12

[Anon], SyAS, Report of the Council for the year ended Dec 31, 1950: Excavations – Saxon hut at Ham near Kingston, *SyAC*, **52** (1952), 101–2

[Anon], The search for the 'lost' village of Watendone, *Bourne Soc Local Hist Rec*, **6** (1967), 3–6

ADAMS, N, The judicial conflict over tithes, *Engl Hist Rev*, **52** (1937), 1–22

ADDLESHAW, G W O, *The development of the parochial system from Charlemagne to Urban II*, St Anthony's Hall Publ, **6**, 2 edn (York, 1970)

ALDSWORTH, F & HILL, D, The Burghal Hidage – Eashing, *SyAC*, **68** (1971), 198–201

ARNOLD-FOSTER, F, *Studies in church dedications*, **1–3** (London, 1899)

ASTON, T H, The origins of the manor, *Trans Roy Hist Soc*, 5 ser **8** (1958), 59–83

AULT, W O, *Open-field farming in medieval England* (London, 1972)

BAILEY, K A, Medieval Putney: a planned village?, *Wandsworth Historian*, **51** (1968), 1–8

———, The Middle Saxons, in S Bassett (ed), *The origins of Anglo-Saxon kingdoms* (Leicester, 1989), 108–22

———, & GALBRAITH, I G, Field systems in Surrey: an introductory survey, *SyAC*, **69** (1973), 73–87

BAKER, A R H, Open fields and partible inheritance on a Kent manor, *Econ Hist Rev*, 2nd ser **17** (1964–5), 1–23

———, Some fields and farms in medieval Kent, *Archaeol Cantiana*, **80** (1965), 152–74

———, Field systems in the Vale of Holmesdale, *Agric Hist Rev*, **14** (1966), 1–24

———, & BUTLIN, R A (eds), *Studies of field systems in the British Isles* (Cambridge, 1973)

BARFOOT, J F & WILLIAMS, D P, The Saxon barrow at Gally Hills, Banstead Down, Surrey, *SyAS Res Vol*, **3** (1976), 59–76

BARLOW, F, *The English church 1000–1066* (London, 1963)

BARROW, G W S, *The kingdom of the Scots* (London, 1973)

BASSETT, S, Beyond the edge of excavation, in H Mayr-Harting & R I Moore (eds), *Studies in medieval history presented to R H C Davis* (London, 1985), 21–39

———, (ed), *The origins of Anglo-Saxon kingdoms* (Leicester, 1989)

BASTIAN, F, Rogers of the rectory, *PLDLHS*, **2**. 4 (1960), 103–12

BEDWIN, O, The excavation of the church of St Nicholas, Angmering, 1974, *SxAC*, **113** (1975), 16–34

BERESFORD, M, *New towns of the Middle Ages* (London, 1967)

BETHELL, D, The lives of St Osyth, *Analecta Bollandiana*, **88** (1970), 75–127

BIDDLE, M, Nonsuch Palace 1959–60: an interim report, *SyAC*, **58** (1961), 4–7

——, & HILL, D, Late Saxon planned towns, *Antiq J*, **51** (1971), 70–85

——, HUDSON, D & HEIGHWAY, C, *The future of London's past* (Worcester, 1973)

BIGMORE, P, Villages and towns, in L Cantor (ed), *The English medieval landscape* (London, 1982), 154–92

BIRD, J & BIRD, D G (eds), *The archaeology of Surrey to 1540* (SyAS, 1987)

BIRD, D G, CROCKER, A G, CROCKER, G & McCRACKEN, S, Archaeology in Surrey 1976–8, *SyAC*, **72** (1980) 231–53

——, Archaeology in Surrey 1985–6, *SyAC* **78**, (1987) 133–48

BIRD, D G, The Romano-British period in Surrey, in J & D G Bird (eds), *The archaeology of Surrey to 1540* (SyAS, 1987), 165–96

BISHOP, T A M, Assarting and the growth of open fields, *Econ Hist Rev*, **6** (1935–6), 13–29

BLAIR, J M G, Excavations at Little Bookham church, 1952–3, *SyAC*, **60** (1963), 83–5

BLAIR, W J, The early manorial records of Leatherhead, Part 1, *PLDLHS*, **3**. 8 (1974), 218–43, and Part 3, *PLDLHS*, **3**. 9 (1975), 290–7

——, The origins of Leatherhead parish church, *PLDLHS*, **3**. 10 (1976), 323–9

——, A military holding in 12th-century Leatherhead: Bockett Farm and the origins of Pachenesham Parva, *PLDLHS*, **4**. 1 (1977), 3–12

——, Churches, in A A Jackson (ed), *Ashtead: a village transformed* (Leatherhead, 1977), 117–31

——, A late 13th-century survey of buildings on estates of Southwark Priory, *Antiq J*, **58** (1978), 353–4

——, The destroyed medieval church at Headley, *PLDLHS*, **4**. 2 (1978), 39–44

——, Medieval deeds of the Leatherhead district, Parts 1 to 5, *PLDLHS*, **4**. 2 (1978) to **4**. 10 (1986)

——, The Surrey endowments of Lewes Priory before 1200, *SyAC*, **72** (1980), 97–126

——, William fitz Ansculf and the Abinger motte, *Archaeol J*, **138** (1981), 146–8

——, The early history of Horne: an addendum, *SyAC*, **73** (1982), 179–80

——, Secular minster churches in Domesday Book, in P H Sawyer (ed), *Domesday Book: a reassessment* (London, 1985), 104–42

——, Local churches in Domesday Book and before, in J C Holt (ed), *Domesday studies* (Woodbridge, 1987), 265–78

——, (ed), *Minsters and parish churches: the local church in transition 950–1200* (Oxford Committee for Archaeology, 1988)

——, Minster churches in the landscape, in D Hooke (ed), *Anglo-Saxon settlements* (Oxford, 1988), 35–58

——, The early middle ages; the late middle ages, in E Vardey (ed), *History of Leatherhead* (Leatherhead, 1988)

——, Frithuwold's kingdom and the origins of Surrey, in S Bassett (ed), *The origins of Anglo-Saxon kingdoms* (1989), 97–107, 231–6

——, *Introduction to the Surrey Domesday* (Alecto Historical Ed, 1990)

BLOXAM, R N, The dedication of Ripley Chapel, *SyAC*, **50** (1949), 166–7

——, A Surrey charter of King John, *SyAC*, **54** (1955), 58–65

BONNEY, D J, Pagan Saxon burials and boundaries in Wiltshire, *Wiltshire Archaeol & Natur Hist Mag*, **61** (1966), 25–30

——, Early boundaries in Wessex, in P J Fowler (ed), *Archaeology and the landscape: essays for L V Grinsell* (London, 1972), 168–86

——, Early boundaries and estates in southern England, in P H Sawyer (ed), *Medieval settlement* (London, 1976), 72–82

BONY, J, *The English Decorated style* (Oxford, 1979)

BRANDON, P F, The common lands and wastes of Sussex, London Univ Ph D thesis (1963)

——, Medieval clearances in the East Sussex Weald, *Trans Inst Brit Geogr*, **48** (1969), 135–53

——, *A history of Surrey* (London, 1977)

BRETT, M, *The English church under Henry I* (Oxford, 1975)

BROOKE, C N L, The missionary at home: the church in the towns 1000–1250, in G J Cuming (ed), *Studies in church history*, **6** (1970), 59–83

BROOKS, N P, The pre-Conquest charters of Christ Church Canterbury, Oxford Univ D Phil thesis (1968)

————, *The early history of the church of Canterbury* (Leicester, 1984)

————, The creation and early structure of the kingdom of Kent, in S Bassett (ed), *The origins of Anglo-Saxon kingdoms* (1989), 55–83

BROWN, A, London and north-west Kent in the later Middle Ages: the development of a land-market, *Archaeol Cantiana*, **92** (1977), 145–55

BROWNE, A L, The early archdeacons of Derby, *Derbyshire Archaeol J*, n s **13** (1939),

BURROW, I, *Hillfort and hill-top settlement in Somerset in the 1st to 8th centuries AD*, Brit Archaeol Rep British Ser, **91** (1981)

CAM, H M, Manerium cum hundredo, *Engl Hist Rev*, **47** (1932), 353–76

————, Early groups of hundreds, in J G Edwards, V H Galbraith & E F Jacob (eds), *Historical essays in honour of James Tait* (Manchester, 1933), 13–26

————, The 'private' hundred in England before the Norman Conquest, in her *Law-finders and law-makers* (London, 1962), 59–70

CAMERON, K, Eccles in English place-names, in M W Barley & R P C Hanson (eds.), *Christianity in Britain 300–700* (Leicester, 1968), 87–92

CAMPBELL, B M S, Population change and the genesis of commonfields in a Norfolk manor, *Econ Hist Rev*, 2nd ser **33** (1980), 174–91

CAMPBELL, J (ed), *The Anglo-Saxons* (Oxford, 1982)

————, *Essays in Anglo-Saxon history* (London, 1986)

CHARLES-EDWARDS, T M, Kinship, status and the origins of the hide, *Past & Present*, **56** (1972), 3–33

————, Boundaries in Irish law, in P H Sawyer (ed), *Medieval settlement* (London, 1976), 83–7

CHENEY, C R, *From Becket to Langton* (Manchester, 1956)

CHERRY, B, Ecclesiastical architecture, in D M Wilson (ed), *The archaeology of Anglo-Saxon England* (London, 1976), 151–200

CHIBNALL, M, Monks and pastoral work: a problem in Anglo-Norman history, *J Eccles Hist*, **18** (1967), 165–72

CLARK, A, A cross-valley dyke on the Surrey/Kent border, *SyAC*, **57** (1960), 72–4

CLARKE, D K, The Saxon hundreds of Sussex, *SxAC*, **74** (1933), 214–25

CLEERE, H & CROSSLEY, D, *The iron industry of the Weald* (Leicester, 1985)

COATES, R, Methodological reflections on Leatherhead, *J Engl Place-Name Soc*, **12** (1979–80), 70–4

COLKER, M L, Latin texts concerning Gilbert, founder of Merton Priory, *Studia Monastica*, **12** (1970), 241–70

COLVIN, H M (ed), *The history of the king's works*, **2** (London, 1963)

CONSTABLE, G, *Monastic tithes* (Cambridge, 1964)

————, Monasteries, rural churches and the *cura animarum* in the early Middle Ages, in *Settimane de Studio del Centro Italiano di Studi sull'Alto Medioevo*, **38**.1 (Spoleto, 1982), 349–89

COPLEY, G J, Stane Street in the Dark Ages, *SxAC*, **89** (1950), 98–204

COX, J C, *The little guide to Surrey*, revised P M Johnston, 5th edn (London, 1926)

CRACKLOW, C T, *Views of the churches and chapels-of-ease in the county of Surrey* (London, 1827)

CUNLIFFE, B, Saxon and medieval settlement pattern in the region of Chalton, Hampshire, *Medieval Archaeol*, **16** (1972), 1–12

DARBY, H C, Place-names and the geography of the past, in A Brown & P Foote (eds), *Early English and Norse studies presented to Hugh Smith* (London, 1963)

————, *Domesday England* (Cambridge, 1977)

————, & CAMPBELL, E M J (eds), *The Domesday geography of south-east England* (Cambridge, 1962)

DAVIES, W & VIERCK, H, The contexts of the Tribal Hidage: social aggregates and settlement patterns, *Frühmittelalterliche Studien*, **8** (1974), 223–93

DAVIS, R H C, The college of St Martin le Grand and the Anarchy, 1135–54, *London Topogr Rec*, **23** (1972), 9–26

DEANESLY, M, The late Old English church: bishops and pastoral care, in her *Sidelights on the Anglo-Saxon church* (London, 1962), 104–36

DENHOLM-YOUNG, N, The Winchester-Hyde chronicle, *Engl Hist Rev*, **49** (1934), 85–93

DENNIS, G, Southwark, Hibernia Warf, *SyAS Bull*, **168** (1980), 5–6

DICKINSON, J C, *The origins of the Austin canons and their introduction into England* (London, 1950)

DICKINSON, T M, On the origin and chronology of the early Anglo-Saxon disc brooch, in S C Hawkes, D Brown & J Campbell (eds), *Anglo-Saxon studies in archaeology and history*, **1**, Brit Archaeol Rep British Ser, **72** (1979), 39–80

DODGSHON, R A, *The origin of British field systems: an interpretation* (London, 1980)

DODGSON, J McN, The place-name Burstow, *SyAC*, **63** (1966), 65

———, Place-names from -*hām*, distinguished from -*hamm* names, in relation to the settlement of Kent, Surrey and Sussex, *Anglo-Saxon England*, **2** (1973), 1–50

DODWELL, B, Holdings and inheritance in medieval East Anglia, *Econ Hist Rev*, 2nd ser **20** (1967), 53–66

DORNIER, A, The Anglo-Saxon monastery at Breedon-on-the-Hill, Leicestershire, in A Dornier (ed), *Mercian studies* (Leicester, 1977), 155–68

DREWETT, P, RUDLING, D & GARDINER, M, *The South-East to AD 1000* (London 1988)

DRUCE, G L, The symbolism of the goat on the Norman font at Thames Ditton, *SyAC*, **21** (1908), 109–12

DRURY, P J, & RODWELL, W J, Investigations at Asheldham, Essex, *Antiq J*, **58** (1978), 134–7

du BOULAY, F R H, Denns, droving and danger, *Archaeol Cantiana*, **76** (1961), 75–87

———, *The lordship of Canterbury* (London, 1966)

DUFTY, A R, The parish church of St Andrew, Farnham, *SyAC*, **61** (1964), 86–98

DUGDALE, W, *Monasticon anglicanum*, enlarged edn, **1–6** (London, 1817–30)

DUGGAN, C, Richard of Ilchester, *Trans Roy Hist Soc*, 5 ser **16** (1966), 1–21

DUMVILLE, D N, Essex, Middle Anglia and the expansion of Mercia in the South-East Midlands in S Basset (ed) *The origins of Anglo-Saxon kingdoms* (1989), 123–40

DUNNING, R W, The minster at Crewkerne, *Somerset Archaeol & Natur Hist*, **120** (1976), 63–7

DYSON, T, London and Southwark in the 7th century and later: a neglected reference, *Trans London & Middlesex Archaeol Soc*, **30** (1980), 83–95

EDWARDS, H, *The charters of the early West Saxon kingdom*, Brit Archaeol Rep British Ser, **198** (1988)

EKWALL, E, Old English *forræpe*, *Studia Neophilologica*, **16** (1943/4), 38–48

EVERITT, A, River and wold, *J Hist Geogr*, **3**.1 (1977), 1–19

———, *Continuity and colonisation: the evolution of Kentish settlement* (Leicester, 1986)

FAITH, R J, Peasant families and inheritance customs in medieval England, *Agric Hist Rev*, **14** (1966), 77–95

FARMER, D H, *The Oxford dictionary of saints* (Oxford, 1978)

FERNIE, E, *The architecture of the Anglo-Saxons* (London, 1983)

FINNY, W E St L, The Saxon church at Kingston, *SyAC*, **37** (1927), 211–19

FLEMING, A, Coaxial field systems: some questions of time and space, *Antiquity*, **61** (1987), 188–202

FLEMING, R, Monastic lands and England's defence in the Viking age, *Engl Hist Rev*, **100** (1985), 257–61

FORGE, J W L, The church of St Mary, Walton-on-Thames, *SyAc*, **66** (1969), 99–105

FOURNIER, G, Rural churches and rural communities in early medieval Auvergne, in F L Cheyette (ed), *Lordship and community in medieval Europe* (New York, 1968), 314–40

FOWLER, D J, Wotton: excavations at St John's Church, *SyAS Bull*, **127** (1976)

FOWLER, P J, Agriculture and rural settlement, in D M Wilson (ed), *The archaeology of Anglo-Saxon England* (London, 1976), 23–48

FOX, H S A, The chronology of enclosure and economic development in medieval Devon, *Econ Hist Rev*, 2nd ser **28** (1975), 181–202

———, Approaches to the adoption of the Midland system, in T Rowley (ed), *The origins of open-field agriculture* (London, 1981), 64–111

FREEMAN, E A, *The reign of William Rufus*, **2** (Oxford, 1882)

GALBRAITH, V H, *The making of Domesday Book* (Oxford, 1961)

GELLING, M, Place names and Anglo-Saxon paganism, *Univ Birmingham Hist J*, **8**.1 (1961), 7–25

———, *The place-names of Berkshire*, **3**, Engl Place-Name Soc, **51** (1976)

———, Latin loan-words in Old English Place-Names, *Anglo-Saxon England*, **6** (1977), 1–13

———, *Signposts to the past* (London, 1978)

———, *The early charters of the Thames valley* (Leicester, 1979)

GEM, R D H, The English parish church in the 11th and 12th centuries: a great rebuilding?, in W J Blair (ed), *Minsters and parish churches* (1988), 21–30

————, The Romanesque architecture of old St Paul's Cathedral and its late 11th-century context, *Brit Archaeol Assoc Conf Trans*, **10**: *London* (forthcoming)

GIBSON, J H, Compton church: the oratory, *SyAC*, **51** (1950), 154–5

GIFFORD, D H, The parish in Domesday Book, London Univ PhD thesis (1952)

GLASSCOCK, R F, *The lay subsidy of 1334* (London, 1975)

GOLLIN, G J, The medieval manor house of Ashtead, *PLDLHS*, **4**.2 (1978), 46–51

GOODIER, A, The formation of boundaries in Anglo-Saxon England, *Medieval Archaeol*, **28** (1984), 1–21

GOVER, J E B, MAWER, A & STENTON, F M (eds), *The place-names of Surrey*, Engl Place-Name Soc, **11** (1934)

GOWANS, H M, WILKS, M, & BRAY, J (eds), *Courts of the manors of Bandon and Beddington 1498–1552* (London Borough of Sutton, 1983)

GRAHAM, R, *English ecclesiastical studies* (London, 1929)

GRAY, H L, *The English field systems* (Cambridge, 1915)

GREENWOOD, J, A suggested model for the settlement development of the Reigate hundred, with special reference to Horley (forthcoming)

GREGSON, N, The multiple estate model: some critical questions, *J Hist Geogr*, **11**.4 (1985), 339–51

GRINSELL, L V, An analysis and list of Surrey barrows, *SyAC*, **42** (1934), 26–60

————, Surrey barrows 1934–1986: a reappraisal, *SyAC*, **78** (1987), 1–42

GULLEY, J L M, The Wealden landscape in the early 17th century and its antecedents, London Univ. Ph D (1960)

HALL, D, The origins of open-field agriculture – the archaeological fieldwork evidence, in T Rowley (ed), *The origins of open-field agriculture* (London, 1981), 22–38

HALLAM, H E, *Rural England 1066–1348* (Glasgow, 1981)

HANWORTH, R, The Iron Age in Surrey, in J & D G Bird (eds), *The archaeology of Surrey to 1540* (SyAS, 1987), 139–64

————, & TOMALIN, D J, *Brooklands, Weybridge: the excavation of an Iron Age and medieval site*, SyAS Res Vol, **4** (1977)

HART, C R, *The early charters of eastern England* (Leicester, 1966)

————, The Tribal Hidage, *Trans Roy Hist Soc*, 5th ser. **21** (1971), 133–57

————, Shoelands, *J Engl Place-Name Soc*, **4** (1971–2), 6–11

HART, E & BRAUN, H, West Humble chapel, *SyAC*, **47** (1941), 1–11

HARVEY, B F, The population trend in England between 1300 and 1348, *Trans Roy Hist Soc*, 5th ser **16** (1966), 23–42

————, *Westminster Abbey and its estates in the Middle Ages* (Oxford, 1977)

HARVEY, J H, 'The Mounts', Pachenesham: an historical note, *PLDLHS*, **1**.1 (1947), 9–11

————, The hundred of Copthorne and Effingham, *SyAC*, **50** (1946–7), 157–61

————, Polesden: the name and the place, *SyAC*, **50** (1946–7), 161–4

————, A short history of Bookham, *PLDLHS*, **1**.8 (1954), 10–14

————, A cartographical survey of the area: **6**: the Middle Ages, *PLDLHS*, **2**.4 (1960), 101–3

HARVEY, P D A, *A medieval Oxfordshire village* (Oxford, 1965)

HARVEY, S P J, Domesday Book and Anglo-Norman governance, *Trans Roy Hist Soc*, 5th ser **25** (1975), 186–93

————, Evidence for settlement study: Domesday Book, in P H Sawyer (ed), *Medieval settlement* (London, 1976), 195–9

HASE, P H, The development of the parish in Hampshire, Cambridge Univ Ph D thesis (1975)

————, The mother churches of Hampshire, in W J Blair (ed.), *Minsters and parish churches* (1988), 45–66

HASLAM, J, Parishes, churches, wards and gates in eastern London, in W J Blair (ed) *Ministers and parish churches* (1988), 35–43

HAWKES, S C, The Early Saxon period, in G Briggs, J Cook & T Rowley (eds), *The archaeology of the Oxford region* (Oxford, 1986), 64–108

HEALES, A & HUMBERT, L M, Chiddingfold church (with an appendix), *SyAC*, **5** (1871), 157–76

HEWLETT, G, Stages in the settlement of a Downland parish: a study of the hedges of Chelsham, *SyAC*, **72** (1980), 91–6

HILL, B D, *English Cistercian monasteries and their patrons in the 12th century* (Urbana, 1968)

HILL, D, The Burghal Hidage: the establishment of a text, *Medieval Archaeol*, **13** (1969), 84–92

HOHLER, C, St Osyth and Aylesbury, *Recs of Buckinghamshire*, **18** (1966–70), 61–72

HOLLING, F W, The early foundations of St Mary's church, Guildford, *SyAC*, **64** (1967), 165–8

HONEYBOURNE, M B, The pre-Norman bridge of London, in A E J Hollaender & W Kellaway (eds), *Studies in London history presented to P E Jones* (London, 1969), 17–39

HOOKE, D, *Anglo-Saxon landscapes of the west Midlands: the charter evidence*, Brit Archaeol Rep British Ser, **95** (1981)

——, *The Anglo-Saxon landscape: the kingdom of the Hwicce* (Manchester, 1985)

——, (ed), *Anglo-Saxon settlements* (Oxford, 1988)

HOOPER, W, Bondmen at Reigate under the Tudors, *SyAC*, **38** (1930), 149–55

HOPE-TAYLOR, B, Celtic agriculture in Surrey, *SyAC*, **50** (1946–7), 47–72

——, Excavation on Farthing Down, *Archaeol News Letter*, **2**.10 (March 1950), 170

HUDSON, W, The ancient deaneries of the diocese of Chichester, *SxAC*, **55** (1912), 108–22

HYAMS, P R, The origin of a peasant land-market in England, *Econ Hist Rev*, 2nd ser **23** (1970), 18–31

JOHNSON, D J, *Southwark and the City* (Oxford, 1969)

JOHNSTON, P M, Send church and the chapel of Ripley, *SyAC*, **16** (1901), 168–89

——, The church of Witley and Thursley chapel-of-ease, *SyAC*, **18** (1903), 80–95

——, Stoke D'Abernon church, *SyAC*, **20** (1907), 1–61

——, West Horsley church, *SyAC*, **22** (1909), 168–83

——, Notes on the history and architecture of Farley church, *SyAC*, **23** (1910), 83–90

——, Stoke D'Abernon church: some recent discoveries, *SyAC*, **26** (1913), 121–33

——, Great Bookham church, *SyAC*, **27** (1914), 103–22

——, Discovery at Rotherhithe church, *SyAC*, **27** (1914), 141–3

——, An early window and wall paintings in Witley church, *SyAC*, **31** (1918), 28–44

——, Albury old church, *SyAC*, **34** (1921), 52–94

——, Witley and Thursley churches: recent discoveries, *SyAC*, **39** (1931), 104–11

——, Ewhurst church: recent discoveries, *SyAC*, **42** (1934), 100–8

JOLLIFFE, J E A, The Domesday hidation of Sussex and the Rapes, *Engl Hist Rev*, **45** (1930), 427–35

——, *Pre-feudal England: the Jutes* (Oxford, 1933)

——, The 'Era of the Folk' in English History, in F M Powicke (ed), *Oxford studies in medieval history presented to H E Salter* (Oxford, 1934), 1–32

JONES, G R J, Multiple estates and early settlement, in P H Sawyer (ed), *Medieval settlement* (London, 1976), 11–40

——, Multiple estates perceived, *J Hist Geogr*, **11**.4 (1985), 352–63

KEMP, B R, The mother church of Thatcham, *Berkshire Archaeol J*, **63** (1967–8), 15–22

——, The churches of Berkeley Hernesse, *Trans Bristol & Gloucestershire Archaeol Soc*, **87** (1968), 96–110

——, Monastic possession of parish churches in England in the 12th Century, *J Eccles Hist*, **31** (1980), 133–60

KENNETT, W, *Parochial antiquities*, **1** (Oxford, 1818)

KENYON, G H, *The glass industry of the Weald* (Leicester, 1967)

KERSHAW, I, The great famine and agrarian crisis in England, 1315–1322, *Past & Present*, **59** (1973), 3–50

KETTERINGHAM, L L, *Alsted: excavation of a 13th–14th century sub-manor house with its ironworks in Netherne Wood, Merstham, Surrey*, SyAS Res Vol, **2** (1976)

——, Excavations at the church of St John the Evangelist, Coulsdon, *SyAC*, **71** (1977), 101–10

KEULEMANS, M, Old St Nicholas's church, Tooting Graveney, *SyAC*, **57** (1960), 93–9

KING, C R B, St Mary's church Blechingley, *SyAC*, **19** (1906), 203–4

——, The tower of St Mary's church, Blechingley, *SyAC*, **24** (1911), 169–72

KING, E, *Peterborough Abbey 1086–1310* (Cambridge, 1973)

KNOWLES, D, *The monastic order in England*, 2nd edn (Cambridge, 1950)

——, & HADCOCK, R N, *Medieval religious houses: England and Wales* (London, 1971)

LAMBERT, H, *History of Banstead in Surrey* (Oxford, 1912)

——, The Banstead court rolls in the reigns of Richard II and Henry IV, *SyAC*, **37**, (1927) 164–79

——, *Woodmansterne: a brief historical account* (Sutton, 1931)

————, Some account of the Surrey manors held by Merton College and Corpus Christi College, Oxford, in the 17th century, *SyAC*, **41** (1933), 34–49

LAMBERT, U, *Blechingley: a parish history* (London, 1921)

————, *Godstone: a parish history* (1929)

LE NEVE, J, *Fasti ecclesie anglicanae 1066–1300: I: St Paul's Cathedral; II: monastic cathedrals*, (ed D E Greenway) (London, 1968, 1971)

LENNARD, R V, *Rural England 1086–1135* (Oxford, 1959)

LEWIN, S, The Pyrford fresco, *SyAS Bull*, **161** (1979)

LILLIE, H W R, The North Downs trackway in Surrey, *SyAC*, **61** (1964), 18–28

LIVETT, G M, Whitfield alias Beuesfeld, *Archaeol Cantiana*, **40** (1928), 150

LOWTHER, A W G, Ashtead and its history, part **9**, *PLDLHS*, **2**.3 (1959), 88–93

————, RENN, D & RUBY, A T, Pachenesham, Leatherhead: the excavation of the medieval moated site known as 'The Mounts', *SyAC*, **74** (1983), 1–45

McPHAIL, R I & SCAIFE, R G, The geographical and environmental background, in J & D G Bird (eds) *The archaeology of Surrey to 1540* (SyAS, 1987), 31–51

MAITLAND, F W, *Domesday Book and beyond* (Cambridge, 1897)

————, The surnames of English villages, in H A L Fisher (ed), *The collected papers of Frederic William Maitland*, **2** (Cambridge, 1911), 84–95

MALDEN, H E, The Domesday survey of Surrey, in P E Dove (ed), *Domesday studies*, **2** (London, 1891)

————, *A history of Surrey* (London, 1900)

————, *The Victoria history of the county of Surrey*, **1–4**, index (London, 1902–1912)

————, Holmbury Hill and the neighbourhood, *SyAC*, **17** (1902), 72–6

————, Villeinage in the Weald of Surrey, *SyAC*, **20** (1907), 143–52

————, The three field system of farming in Surrey, *SyAC*, **37** (1927), 251–4

————, Kingsland in Newdigate and Newdigate in Copthorne Hundred, *SyAC*, **39** (1931), 147–9

MANNING, E, *Saxon Farnham* (Chichester, 1970)

MANNING, O, & BRAY, W, *The history and antiquities of the County of Surrey*, **1–3** (London, 1804–14)

MARGARY, I D, The North Downs main trackways, *SyAC*, **52** (1952), 29–31

————, The North Downs trackway in Surrey, *SyAC*, **62** (1965), 80–2

MARSHALL, C J, *A history of the old villages of Cheam and Sutton* (Cheam, 1936)

MASON, E, The role of the English parishioner 1100–1500, *J Eccles Hist*, **27** (1976), 17–29

————, Timeo barones et donas ferentes, in D Baker (ed), *Religious motivation: studies in church history*, **15** (1978), 61–75

————, A truth universally acknowledged, in D. Baker (ed), *The church in town and countryside: studies in church history* **16** (1979), 171–86

MASON, J F A, The rapes of Sussex and the Norman Conquest, *SxAC*, **102** (1964), 68–93

MEEKINGS, C A F, The early history of Sandon Hospital, *SyAC*, **57** (1960), 75–84

————, Notes on the de Abernon family before 1236, *SyAC*, **77** (1980), 157–73

MILLER, E, La société rurale en Angleterre (X^e–XIIIe Siècles), in *Agricoltura e Mondo Rurale in Occidente nell' Alto Medioevo: Settimane di Studio del Centro Italiano di Studi sull' Alto Medioevo* **13** (Spoleto, 1966), 111–34

————, & HATCHER, J, *Medieval England: rural society and economic change 1066–1348* (London, 1978)

MOORE, J S The Domesday teamland: a reconsideration, *Trans Roy Hist Soc*, 5 ser **14** (1964), 109–30

MORRIS, J, A gazetteer of Anglo-Saxon Surrey, *SyAC*, **56** (1959), 132–58

MORRIS, R, *The church in British archaeology*, Counc Brit Archaeol Res Rep **47** (1983)

MORTIMER, R, The beginnings of the honour of Clare, *Proc Battle Abbey Conf*, **3** (1980)

MUCKELROY, K W, Woodcote, or Woodcote Warren, once a city, according to tradition, *SyAC*, **69** (1973), 37–45

MUMFORD, W F, The manor of Oxted 1360–1420, *SyAC*, **63** (1966), 66–94

MYRES, J N L, The Angles, the Saxons and the Jutes, *Proc. Brit Acad*, **56** (1970), 145–74

————, *The English settlements* (Oxford, 1986)

NAIL, D, The meeting-place of Copthorne hundred, *SyAC*, **62** (1965), 44–53

NORRIS, N E S, & HOCKINGS, E F, Excavations at Balsdean chapel, Rottingdean, *SxAC*, **91** (1953), 53–68

O'CONNELL, M, *Historic towns in Surrey:* SyAS Res Vol, **5** (1977)

———, and POULTON, R, The towns of Surrey, in J Haslam (ed), *Anglo-Saxon towns in southern England* (Chichester, 1984), 37–51

OLLARD, S L, Dunsfold and its rectors, *SyAC,* **31** (1918), 45–84

ORTON, C, Excavations at 32 Burleigh Avenue, Wallington, 1921 and 1976, *SyAC,* **72** (1980), 77–82

OWEN, D M, Chapelries and rural settlement: an examination of some of the Kesteven evidence, in P H Sawyer (ed), *Medieval settlement* (London, 1976), 66–71

———, *Church and society in medieval Lincolnshire* (Lincoln, 1981)

PAGE, W, Some remarks on the churches of the Domesday Survey, *Archaeologia,* **66** (1914–15), 61–102

PARK, D, The Romanesque wall paintings of All Saints church, Witley, Surrey, *SyAC,* **74** (1983), 157–67

PARKER, J H, The church of St Mary, Guildford, *Archaeol J,* **29** (1872), 170–80

PEARCE, C M H, An account of the buildings of Newark priory, *SyAC,* **40** (1932), 1–40

PERCY, K, Limpsfield: interpretation of the Domesday Book entry, *SyAS Bull,* **156** (1979)

PHYTHIAN-ADAMS, C, Rutland reconsidered, in A Dornier (ed), *Mercian studies* (Leicester, 1977), 63–84

PIGGOTT, S (ed), *The agrarian history of England and Wales: I.1: Prehistory* (Cambridge, 1981)

POULTON, R, Cherchefelle and the origins of Reigate, *London Archaeologist,* **3**.16 (1980), 433–8

———, Excavations on the site of the Old Vicarage, Church street, Reigate, 1977–82, Part 1 Saxo-Norman and earlier discoveries, *SyAC,* **77** (1986), 17–94

———, Saxon Surrey, in J & D G Bird (eds) *The archaeology of Surrey to 1540* (SyAS, Guildford, 1987), 197–222

RACKHAM, O, *Trees and woodland in the British landscape* (London, 1976)

RADFORD, C A R, The church of St Mary, Stoke D'Abernon, Surrey, *Archaeol J,* **118** (1961), 165–74

RAFTIS, J A, *Assart data and land values* (Toronto, 1974)

RAHTZ, P, Buildings and rural settlement, in D M Wilson (ed), *The archaeology of Anglo-Saxon England* (London, 1976), 49–98

REICHEL, O J, The church and the hundreds of Devon, *Trans. Devonshire Assoc,* **71** (1939), 331–42

RENN, D F, The early church at Great Bookham, *PLDLIIS,* **3**.1 (1967), 19–24

———, The early church at Fetcham, *PLDLHS,* **3**.2 (1968), 56–7

———, *Norman castles,* 2nd edn (London, 1973)

ROBERTS, B K, Moated sites in midland England, *Trans Birmingham Archaeol Soc,* **80** (1965), 26–37

———, A study of medieval colonisation in the Forest of Arden, Warwickshire, *Agric Hist Rev,* **16** (1968), 101–13

———, Village plans in County Durham, *Medieval Archaeol,* **16** (1972), 33–56

———, *Rural settlement in Britain* (Folkestone, 1977)

ROBINSON, D M, *The geography of Augustinian settlement in England and Wales,* Brit Archaeol Rep British Ser **80** (1980)

ROBO, E, *Medieval Farnham* (Farnham, 1939)

RODWELL, W, & RODWELL, K, *Historic churches: a wasting asset,* Counc Brit Archaeol Res Rep, **19** (1977)

ROUND, J H, Some early grants to Lewes Priory, *SxAC,* **40** (1896), 58–78

———, Bernard, the king's scribe, *Engl Hist Rev,* **14** (1899), 417–30

RUDLING, D R, Downland settlement in East Sussex, in B L Burnham & H B Johnson (eds), *Invasion and response: the case of Roman Britain,* Brit Archaeol Rep British Ser **73** (1979), 339–56

RUMBLE, A R, The Merstham (Surrey) charter bounds, AD 947, *J Engl Place-Name Soc,* **3** (1970/1), 6–31

———, Place-names and their context, with special regard to the Croydon survey region, *Proc Croydon Natur Hist & Sci Soc,* **15**.8, 161–84

RUSSELL J C, The Tribal Hidage, *Traditio,* **5** (1947), 192–209

SALTER, H E, Cogges Priory, *Oxon Architect Soc Rep & Papers* **75** (1930), 322–3

SALWAY, P, *Roman Britain* (Oxford, 1981)

SALZMAN, L F, Sussex Domesday tenants; 4: the family of Chesney or Cheyney, *SxAC,* **65** (1924), 20–53

———, The rapes of Sussex, *SxAC,* **72** (1931), 20–9

SAUNDERS, P R, Saxon barrows excavated by General Pitt-Rivers on Merrow Down, Guildford, *SyAC,* **72** (1980), 69–75

SAWYER, P H, *Anglo-Saxon charters: an annotated list and bibliography* (London, 1968)

———, (ed), *Medieval settlement* (London, 1976)

———, *From Roman Britain to Norman England* (London, 1978)

SCHÄRER, A, *Die angelsächsische Königsurkunde im 7 und 8 Jahrhundert* (Vienna etc, 1982)

SEARLE, E, Hides, virgates and tenant settlement at Battle Abbey, *Econ Hist Rev*, 2nd ser **16** (1963–4), 290–300

———, *Lordship and community* (Toronto, 1974)

SEWILL, R, & LANE, E, *The free men of Charlwood* (London, 1951)

SHEARMAN, P, Ewell in 1577, *SyAC*, **54** (1955), 102–23

———, The topography of medieval Ewell and Cuddington, *SyAC*, **71** (1977), 139–44

SHERLOCK, R J, Sir Stephen Glynne's notes on churches in Surrey, *SyAC*, **55** (1958), 65–117

SMITH, A H, *English place-name elements*. **1–2**, Engl Place-Name Soc, **25–6** (1956)

SMITH, J T, The pre-Conquest minster at Southwark, *Trans. London and Middlesex Archaeol Soc*, **19** (1958), 174–9

SOUTHERN, R W, *Western society and the church in the Middle Ages* (London, 1970)

STAFFORD, P, The king's wife in Wessex, *Past & Present*, **91** (1981), 3–27

STENTON, F M, Medeshamstede and its colonies, in *Preparatory to Anglo-Saxon England* (ed D M Stenton), (Oxford, 1970), 179–92

———, The English occupation of southern Britain, in *ibid*, 266–80

———, The thriving of the Anglo-Saxon ceorl, in *ibid*, 383–93

———, *Anglo-Saxon England*, 3rd edn (Oxford, 1971)

STRAKER, E, The intrenchment on Riddlesdown, *SyAC*, **42** (1934), 120–1

STOW, J, *A survey of London*, ed C L Kingsford, **1–2** (Oxford, repr 1971)

TAYLOR, C C, *Dorset* (London, 1970)

———, The Anglo-Saxon countryside, in R T Rowley (ed), *Anglo-Saxon settlement and landscape*, Brit Archaeol Rep British Ser, **6** (1974), 5–15

———, Polyfocal settlement and the English village, *Medieval Archaeol*, **21** (1977), 189–93

———, Aspects of village mobility in medieval and later times, in S Limbrey & J G Evans (eds), *The effect of man on the landscape: the lowland zone*, Counc Brit Archaeol Res Rep **21** (1978), 126–38

———, *Village and farmstead* (London, 1983)

TAYLOR, H M & TAYLOR, J, *Anglo-Saxon architecture*, **1–3** (Cambridge, 1965–78)

TAYLOR, J G, *Our Lady of Batersey* (London, 1925)

THACKER, A T, Some terms for noblemen in Anglo-Saxon England, in D Brown, J Campbell & S C Hawkes (eds), *Anglo-Saxon studies in archaeology and history*, **2**, Brit Archaeol Rep British Ser, **92** (1981), 201–36

THIRSK, J, The common fields, *Past & Present*, **29** (1964), 3–25

THOMAS, J B (ed), *St John's Wotton* (Wotton PCC, 1978).

THOMPSON, F H, Three Surrey hillforts: excavation at Anstiebury, Holmbury and Hascombe, 1972–77, *Antiq J*, **59** (1979), 245–318

THORNHILL, L, *A Croydon backcloth: some little-known estate maps in Lambeth Palace Library* (Croydon Natur Hist & Sci Soc, 1975)

———, Report on field work at Addington, Surrey, 1970–72, *Proc Croydon Natur Hist & Sci Soc*, **14** (1975), 500–9

———, Croydon: a summary of work by the CNHSS on medieval Croydon, *SyAS Bull*, **160** (1979)

THORPE, J, *Registrum Roffense* (London, 1769)

TITFORD, C F, Medieval Ewell and Cuddington, *SyAC*, **69** (1973), 27–35

TITOW, J Z, Medieval England and the open field system, *Past & Present*, **32** (1965), 86–102

TURNER, D J, A moated site near Burstow Rectory, *SyAC*, **63** (1966), 51–65

———, Medieval pottery from Watendone, Kenley, *SyAC*, **69** (1973), 214–18

———, Moated site near Moat Farm, Hookwood, Charlwood, *SyAC*, **71** (1977), 57–87

———, Moated sites in Surrey: a provisional list, *SyAC*, **71** (1977), 89–94

———, The North Downs trackway, *SyAC*, **72** (1980), 1–13

———, Nutfield and the settlement of the Weald, *Surrey History*, **2**.2 (1980/1), 62–5

——, Archaeology of Surrey, 1066 to 1540, in J & D G Bird (eds) *The archaeology of Surrey to 1540* (SyAS, Guildford, 1987), 223–61

——, Thunderfield, Harrowsley and Thunderfield castle, *SyAC* (forthcoming)

——, & BLAIR, W J, Manors and churches in Blackheath hundred, *SyAC* (forthcoming)

TURNER, F, *Egham, Surrey* (Egham, 1926)

TWEDDLE, D, Anglo-Saxon sculpture in south-east England before *c* 950, in F H Thompson (ed), *Studies in medieval sculpture*, Soc Antiq Occas Paper, **11** (London, 1983), 35–6

VINOGRADOFF, P, *The growth of the manor* (London, 1905)

VOSS, L, *Heinrich von Blois, Bischof von Winchester (1129–71)* (Berlin, 1932)

WADE-MARTINS, P, The origins of rural settlement in East Anglia, in P J Fowler (ed), *Recent work in rural archaeology* (Bradford-on-Avon, 1975), 135–57

WALKER, T E C, Esher: the Fullinga Dic, *SyAC*, **69** (1973), 193

WELMAN, S, *The parish and church of Godalming* (London, 1900)

WHITELOCK, D, *Some Anglo-Saxon Bishops of London* (The Chambers Memorial Lecture, 1974)

WITNEY, K P, *The Jutish forest: a study of the Weald of Kent from 450 to 1380 AD* (London, 1976)

WOOD, E S, A medieval glasshouse at Blunden's Wood, Hambledon, Surrey, *SyAC*, **62** (1965), 54–79

WOODS, H, Excavations in Reigate 1974, *SyAC*, **70** (1974), 70–94

WOODS, P, The parsonage or rectory manor of Godalming, and a 14th-century custumal thereof, *SyAC*, **22** (1909), 115–36

——, On a 14th-century rental of the principal manor of Godalming, with some remarks on cotholders, *SyAC*, **23** (1910), 91–107

WORMALD, P, Bede, *Bretwaldas* and the origins of the *Gens anglorum*, in P Wormald (ed), *Ideal and reality in Frankish and Anglo-Saxon society* (Oxford, 1983), 99–129

——, *Bede and the conversion of England: the charter evidence* (The Jarrow Lecture, 1984)

YATES, E M, A Study of settlement patterns, *Field Studies*, **1**.3 (1961), 65–84

YOUNG, C R, *The royal forests of medieval England* (Leicester, 1979)

Notes

Introduction

1   P Vinogradoff, *The growth of the manor*, 235. For this interpretation, see also F W Maitland, *Domesday Book and beyond*, 318–40
2   T H Aston, The origins of the manor, 73
3   E Miller & J Hatcher, *Medieval England: rural society and economic change 1066–1348*, 20
4   See P Salway, *Roman Britain*, 544–5
5   P F Brandon, *A History of Surrey*, 15. A very useful survey of the geographical and ecological background by R I MacPhail & R G Scaife has now appeared in J Bird & D G Bird (eds), *The archaeology of Surrey to 1540*, 31–51
6   Brandon, *History of Surrey*, 18
7   These tracks have been much discussed: I D Margary, The North Downs main trackways; H W R Lillie, The North Downs trackway in Surrey; Margary, The North Downs trackway in Surrey; D J Turner, The North Downs trackway. Cf comments by R Poulton in Saxon Surrey, 211, and by D G Bird in The Romano-British period in Surrey, 168
8   For the closely analogous pattern of Kentish lanes and droveways see A Everitt, *Continuity and colonisation: the evolution of Kentish settlement*, 36–9, 267–70
9   For a new assessment of Roman Surrey see D G Bird, The Romano-British period in Surrey
10 *The Anglo-Saxon chronicle*, 18–19
11 See for instance J N L Myres, The Angles, the Saxons and the Jutes; P Drewett, D Rudling & M Gardiner, *The South-East to AD 1000*, 256; Poulton, Saxon Surrey, 216
12 Myres, *The English settlements*, 137–9
13 G J Copley, Stane Street in the Dark Ages
14 For the 'Wandle Saxons', see J Morris, A gazetteer of Anglo-Saxon Surrey, 148–58. See also the works cited in n 11 above
15 *PNSy*, xiv–xv. cf also Myres, *The English settlements*, 106 n, and the remarks on the hunting rights of the citizens of London in F M Stenton, *Anglo-Saxon England*, 58
16 M Gelling, *The place-names of Berkshire*, 3, 813–14, 820–2. However, her view that the main area of Berkshire was settled from East and Middle Anglia, in contrast to the eastern arm which was settled from the south, is at variance with some current archaeological opinion: see F M Stenton, The English occupation of Southern Britain, 273; S C Hawkes, The early Saxon period, 85; T M Dickinson, On the origin and chronology of the early Anglo-Saxon disc brooch, 54
17 Gelling, *Place-names of Berkshire*, 3, 840–1, 925–39
18 *ibid* 3, 841
19 S 1165. The authenticity of this charter has been much debated, but despite obvious modifications the core of the text stands up to criticism. The main point in its favour is that it shares a preamble with Hodilred's charter for the sister foundation at Barking, and belongs to a distinctive group of early charters linked by the activities of Bishop Eorcenwold: see P Wormald, Bede and the conversion of England: the charter evidence, 9–11. The charter is also vindicated by H Edwards, *The charters of the Early West Saxon Kingdom*, 132–7. The strictures of A Scharer, *Die angelsächsische Königsurkunde im 7 und 8 Jahrhundert*, 129–41, are therefore over-severe. See also D Whitelock, *Some Anglo-Saxon bishops of London*, 5–10, and below, p14. I am grateful to Roger Bacon for allowing me to read the detailed discussion of the same problems in his undergraduate dissertation.
20 cf J Campbell, *Essays in Anglo-Saxon history*, 88
21 As first suggested by Wormald, Bede, *Bretwaldas* and the origins of the *Gens Anglorum*, 112. cf below, pp103–4
22 See C Hohler, St Osyth and Aylesbury, 63–4, 66; D Bethell, The lives of St Osyth

23   This argument is developed more fully in W J Blair, Frithuwold's kingdom and the origins of Surrey, 97–107, 231–6.

24   cf the papers of Bailey, Blair and Dumville in Bassett, *The origins of Anglo-Saxon kingdoms*

25   Bede, *Historia ecclesiastica*, 218. cf Campbell, *Essays*, 86–7, 113

26   For fuller discussion of these possibilities, see the papers by Bailey and Blair in Bassett, *The origins of Anglo-Saxon kingdoms*.

27   Drewett, Rudling & Gardiner, *South-East to 1000*, 288–90; A Clark, A cross-valley dyke on the Surrey–Kent border. cf also below, p181 n 23.

28   J C Russell, The Tribal Hidage, 197. This suggestion is not considered by W Davies & H Vierck, The contexts of the Tribal Hidage: social aggregates and settlement patterns, 232, 240, who prefer to locate 'Noxgaga' (5,000 hides) and 'Ohtgaga' (2,000 hides) in the Surrey region; however, Russell op cit, 203, suggests reasons for placing these tribes in South Wales. The suggestion of C R Hart (The Tribal Hidage, 147–8) that 'Noxgaga' = 'Woxgaga' = 'Woxinga' = 'Woccingas' (ie the inhabitants of the Woking region) seems over-speculative.

29   *VCHSy*, **1**, 276–7. This misquotes the Burghal Hidage figures, for which a preferred version (1,800 hides to Southwark, 600 hides to Eashing) is given by D Hill, The Burghal Hidage: the establishment of a text, 86–7.

30   S 235; cf Stenton, *Anglo-Saxon England*, 69–71, and *PNSy*, xiii

31   cf Stenton, *Anglo-Saxon England*, 72–3; Hart, *The early charters of eastern England*, 120–2

32   BCS no 133

33   *Anglo Saxon chronicle*, 60–1

34   cf Gelling, *Place-names of Berkshire*, **3**, 844, who suggests that it may not have been until after 825 that the south-east boundary of the Sonning province was selected as the shire boundary.

35   cf Stenton, *Anglo-Saxon England*, 439. Surrey had probably long been part of Winchester diocese, perhaps since the days of Cædwalla and Ine. It is possible, though not certain, that it had previously belonged to Eorcenwold's East Saxon diocese: cf *ibid*, 73.

36   H C Darby, *Domesday England*, 243

37   See R Mortimer, The beginnings of the honour of Clare

38   V Gibbs (ed), *The Complete Peerage by G E C* (London, 1910), **12**.1, 494

39   See Mortimer, Beginnings of honour of Clare, 124

40   See W J Blair, The Surrey endowments of Lewes Priory before 1200, 110–12

41   DB 34c (XIX. 1–2). Recent excavations have defined the late 11th-century masonry building at Blechingley Castle as a double-pile, two-storey house resembling the first phase at Castle Acre: see D J Turner in Archaeology of Surrey, 1066–1540, 253–4, and Bird, Crocker & McCracken, Archaeology in Surrey, 1985–6, 139

42   See W J Blair, Surrey endowments of Lewes Priory, 104–9

43   For which see J F A Mason, The rapes of Sussex and the Norman Conquest

44   See D F Renn, *Norman castles*, 197–9, 187–9, 111, 291

45   See W J Blair, William fitz Ansculf and the Abinger motte

46   *VCHSy*, **1**, 349–50

47   *VCHSy*, **2**, 64ff, 77ff, 94ff, 107ff

48   For a fuller account of the Forest, see *VCHSy*, **1**, 356–9

49   *DB* 32b (VI.5) and 30b (I.3)

50   *Rotuli litterarum clausarum*, **2**, 56

51   *Rot litt claus*, **2**, 56; *VCHSy*, **1**, 358. For the 1226 disafforestation see H E Malden, *A History of Surrey*, 121

52   Brandon, *History of Surrey*, pl 18

53   Darby, *Domesday England*, 90–4, 127–32

54   R F Glasscock, *The lay subsidy of 1334*, map p xxvii

55   H E Hallam, *Rural England 1066–1348*, 81

56   Brandon, *History of Surrey*, 42–3

57   *ibid*, 43. A late 13th-century Addington man called himself 'Robert Timbermongre', and depicted a tree on his seal (SRO 2609/11/2/7)

58   *VCHSy*, **2**, 263, 295–6; H Cleere & D Crossley, *The iron industry of the Weald*, 87–110; E S Wood, A

medieval glasshouse at Blunden's Wood, Hambledon, Surrey, 54–79; G H Kenyon, *The glass industry of the Weald*

59 *VCHSy*, **4**, 424
60 PRO, DL27/46, 25/105–6; Brit Lib, Cotton Ch.xvi.41
61 S 1165; S 235
62 S 1508; S 1511
63 S 528
64 See especially Malden, The Domesday survey of Surrey; J H Round in *VCHSy*, **1**, 275–93; H C Darby & E M J Campbell, *The Domesday geography of south-east England*, 364–405; W J Blair, *Introduction to the Surrey Domesday*
65 *VCHSy*, **1**, 275

Chapter 1

1 J E A Jolliffe, *Pre-feudal England: the Jutes*. K P Witney, *The Jutish forest: a study of the Weald of Kent from 450 to 1380 AD* develops Jolliffe's analysis of Kent, though unfortunately clinging to the ethnic preoccupations of *Pre-feudal England*. For some problems with Jolliffe's hypothesis see N P Brooks, The creation and early structure of the kingdom of Kent, 69–83
2 Jolliffe, *Pre-feudal England*, viii
3 Jolliffe, The 'Era of the Folk' in English history
4 For a convenient over-view see G W S Barrow, *The kingdom of the Scots*, 7–68
5 S Bassett (ed), *The origins of Anglo-Saxon kingdoms*
6 Campbell, *Essays*, 95–6; cf *ibid*, 110–16
7 cf H M Cam, Manerium cum hundredo; *idem*, Early groups of hundreds
8 Cam, Manerium cum hundredo
9 Witney, *Jutish forest*, 35–8, 66–77; A Everitt, River and wold; D Hooke, *Anglo-Saxon landscapes of the West Midlands: the charter evidence*, 48–50; Everitt, *Continuity and colonisation, passim*
10 The evidence for mother church/daughter church relationships will be found in Chs 4–6 and the accompanying maps; that for parish outliers surviving into the 19th century on the first editions of the OS six-inch maps. All pre-Conquest tenurial links, and all significant post-Conquest ones, are cited in Ch 2 below, or in *VCHSy*. Two previous attempts have been made to compile this map. G P Moss's map in D J Turner, Moated site near Moat Farm, Hookwood, Charlwood, 65 is accurate but less complete. Brandon, *History of Surrey*, 32 gives various Wealden dependencies of Ewell (omitted from the present map) on the dubious assumption that a group of Merton Priory holdings (listed in Brit Lib, MS Cotton Cleop C.vii, f103) all belonged to this manor.
11 S 1165
12 *Huneuualdesham* of the 672 × 4 charter, identifiable with a lost location in Weybridge (*PNSy*, 98), was presumably the easternmost part of the estate, though there is no independent evidence that it lay west of *Fullingadic*. T E C Walker, Esher: the Fullinga Dic, tries to identify the boundary with an 'old ditch' crossed by Esher charter-bounds of 1005. This seems much too far to the east.
13 OS Surrey 25″ 1st ed (1870), sheets XI.16; XVII.4,8,12. I am grateful to Shirley Corke for drawing my attention to the bank between Shere and Abinger.
14 Jolliffe, *Pre-feudal England*, 91, identifies the early boundary with Beverley Brook, on the east side of Kingston parish. However, Keith Bailey makes the following comment, based on his detailed local research: 'The western boundary of Brixton hundred did not, apparently, follow parish boundaries in the Mortlake/Wimbledon area, but ran along a line marked in part by the NE wall of Richmond Park, so that, although the Park included part of Putney and Mortlake parishes, these lands, which were open fields and uninhabited, lay in Kingston hundred. The boundary then ran roughly N-S across Wimbledon Common, passing near or through Bensbury. Most of the evidence for this comes from much later, but would seem to preserve the original boundary between the two early units.' (pers comm)
15 This was the Domesday hundred boundary, pre-dating the union of Banstead and Burgh as a single parish wholly in Copthorne hundred (below, p154).

16   J H Harvey, The hundred of Copthorne and Effingham, 157–61; *idem*, Polesden: the name and the place, 161–4. Harvey has shown that the hundreds were 'paired' at least by the late 13th century; evidence for an older focal point in Copthorne hundred (below, p21), does nothing to show that they were ever separate.

17   W J Blair, Surrey endowments of Lewes Priory, 100 and n 23. In the 1230s Burstow was still regarded as part of Wimbledon for accounting purposes (Lambeth Palace Library, Estate Record 1193).

18   J Greenwood, A suggested model for the settlement development of the Reigate hundred, with special reference to Horley, (forthcoming). I am most grateful to Mr Greenwood for generously giving me a copy of his paper, written partly in response to an earlier draft of the present chapter, before publication; it has rescued me from several errors.

19   Jolliffe, *Pre-feudal England*, 91; Witney, *Jutish forest*, 40, 217–22; K Percy, Limpsfield: interpretation of the Domesday Book entry

20   S 1202

21   S 1508. Sanderstead and Lingfield were reputedly still linked in the late 10th century (Brit Lib, MS Cotton Vesp D. ix, f32)

22   S 1511

23   The Beddington/Croydon parish boundary is a straight ridge called Mere Bank. It continues south as a roadline around the west side of Sanderstead, passes through Caterham village and then joins the Roman road. Between Warlingham, Coulsdon and Caterham the line is marked by a substantial ditch (E Straker, The intrenchment on Riddlesdown).

24   For the Westerham estate immediately to the east, which runs down the Kent side of the boundary, see Everitt, *Continuity and colonisation*, 79

25   As argued by D J Bonney, Pagan Saxon burials and boundaries in Wiltshire; *idem*, Early boundaries in Wessex; *idem*, Early boundaries and estates in southern England; A Goodier, The formation of boundaries in Anglo-Saxon England. The statistical basis of Goodier's paper has not been widely accepted. T M Charles-Edwards, Boundaries in Irish law, gives Celtic evidence for the legal and magical significance of burials on boundaries.

26   J Morris, Anglo-Saxon Surrey, 145; L V Grinsell, An analysis and list of Surrey barrows, 38; *idem*, Surrey barrows 1934–1986: a reappraisal, 22

27   Grinsell, Analysis and list, 29–30, 34–6; it has not been proved that these are Anglo-Saxon.

28   Grinsell, Analysis and list, 43–5; *idem*, Surrey barrows 1934–1986, 28–30; J F Barfoot & D P Williams, The Saxon barrow at Gally Hills, Banstead Down, Surrey

29   Grinsell, Analysis and list, 50; *idem*, Surrey barrows 1934–1986, 24; P R Saunders, Saxon barrows excavated by General Pitt-Rivers on Merrow Down, Guildford

30   Grinsell, Analysis and list, 45–7; Morris, Anglo-Saxon Surrey, 136–7; B Hope-Taylor, Excavation on Farthing Down

31   cf Poulton, Saxon Surrey, 200–1

32   cf A T Thacker, Some terms for noblemen in Anglo-Saxon England, 210–13

33   S 1507

34   cf I Burrow, *Hillfort and hill-top settlement in Somerset in the 1st to 8th centuries AD*, which shows that at least 25% of Somerset hilltop sites were re-occupied during AD 0–700. For hillforts in Berkshire and the West Midlands identifiable as post-Roman foci, see Hooke, *Anglo-Saxon landscapes*, 57–66, and Gelling, *Place-names of Berkshire*, **3**, 812, 823–4, 830–1

35   For the latest survey of Surrey hillforts see R Hanworth, The Iron Age in Surrey

36   Malden, Holmbury Hill and the neighbourhood

37   *Councils and synods, with other documents relating to the English Church*, **1**, 49, 54–7

38   *PNSy*, 295

39   Brit Lib, Add Ch 23516 (land between Wedreshulle and Thondrefeld)

40   J McN Dodgson, The place-name Burstow

41   However, D J Turner, Thunderfield, Harrowsley and Thunderfield castle, (forthcoming), will suggest evidence for a Romano-Celtic religious site at Horleylands Farm not far away.

42   These names are discussed by Gelling, Place-names and Anglo-Saxon paganism; *idem*, *Early charters of the Thames Valley*, 150–1. See also *PNSy*, xii

43   cf Gelling, *Signposts to the past*, 125, 184–5

44 S 144 (757 × 96); S 280 (838)

45 BCS 421. I owe this suggestion to Patrick Wormald. See also Edwards, *Charters of early W. Saxon kingdom*, 286

46 *PNSy*, 63. Recent excavations suggest that Kingston may have been an island site in the earlier Anglo-Saxon period, cut off by a silting-up branch of the Thames (pers comm from excavators).

47 R Coates, Methodological reflections on Leatherhead

48 J H Harvey, 'The Mounts', Pachenesham: an historical note; cf below, p 101, for the site of the church

49 C Orton, Excavations at 32 Burleigh Avenue, Wallington, 1921 and 1976

50 S 1165

51 D Nail, The meeting-place of Copthorne hundred. Mrs Nail demonstrates the importance of 'Nutshambles', but fails to show any evidence that it was ever the meeting-place of the hundred.

52 Jolliffe, *Pre-feudal England*, 43–7

53 Witney, *Jutish forest*, ch 2; cf the strictures of Brooks, Creation and early structure, 69–83

54 Jolliffe, The Domesday hidation of Sussex and the rapes; L F Salzman, The rapes of Sussex; D K Clarke, The Saxon hundreds of Sussex, and comment by Mason, Rapes of Sussex and Norman Conquest, 89n. Mark Gardiner comments (pers comm): 'I do not find Clarke's reconstruction credible; it seems to be an exercise in numerology. At least it is clear that Hastings of Domesday Book is a post-Conquest formation . . . The primary units may be correct with the exception of Hastings, but the secondary units I do not find very meaningful.'

55 S 235, 1165

56 S 1248; *DB* 32b (VI.1)

57 S 144; no Domesday hidation

58 Merstham (S 528), Merton (S 551, 747) and Send (S 1447) were each of 20 hides in the charters and TRE. Esher (20 hides in S 911) was in fragments totalling 18½ hides by 1066. In the spurious Chertsey Abbey list (S 1181), which may have some pre-Conquest basis, eight of the 26 manors are of 20 hides and six others of 10.

59 The evidence is not, of course, inconsistent with the more familiar arguments for five-hide units (cf Darby & Campbell, *Domesday geography of south-east England*, 373); it merely suggests that symmetry was on a larger scale than this.

60 This applies to Beddington (70 hides in S 1444, 815); Pyrford (16 hides in S 621); Thames Ditton (9 hides in S 847); and various manors in Ealdorman Alfred's will (S 1508). The 10 hides of Stratton (S 1511) were presumably absorbed into the TRE 40 hides of Walkhampstead.

61 Jolliffe, *Pre-feudal England*, 83–4; cf *idem*, 'Era of Folk', 9–14. On the meaning of *forræpe*, see, however, E Ekwall, Old English *forræpe*, which interprets it as 'land from which roots etc have been torn up', ie assart land. I am grateful to Mark Gardiner for the following Sussex references, which seem, rather, to support the translation 'land outside the rape': (a) grants to Lewes Priory, *c*1100 and *c*1160, describing land as *forsrap*; two holdings are said to 'owe no hidage nor any other service because they are of *forsrap*' (*The chartulary of the Priory of St Pancras of Lewes*, 73, 118, 137); (b) Bosham, 1616/18, distinction between free land, customary land and *forrep* land (ESRO, Sussex Archaeol Soc Box 19).

62 S 528: 'pedan hrycg and æt lace þæt forræpe on þunres feld norþan an hid'. A R Rumble, The Merstham (Surrey) charter bounds, AD 947, 8, translates this as 'Peda's ridge and at the watercourse which detaches one hide to the north in Punor's field'. But *þaet* can scarcely be a relative pronoun and *forræpe* can scarcely be a verb. Ekwall, Old English *forræpe*', 34–5, says that 'the *forræpe* is located *on þunresfeld norþan*' and that '*ān hīd* must refer to the *forræpe*'. However, a more convincing version would be 'Petridge and at Lake the *forræpe*; in the north part of Thunderfield a hide'. I am grateful to Brian Miller for advice on the grammar of this passage.

63 The main problems are the vagueness of the primary boundary through Reigate, Horley and Charlwood; the uncertain status of Mortlake and Wimbledon; and the vagueness of the border with Kent. On the last point cf Witney, *Jutish forest*, 40

64 Jolliffe, *Pre-feudal England*, 91

65 Woking 148, Godley 100, total 248 hides; Farnham 60, Godalming 97½, Blackheath 83½, total 241 hides

66 Witney, *Jutish forest*, fig 5; but cf the rather more cautious map in Brooks, Creation and early structure, fig 4.2

67 See Gelling, *Place-names of Berkshire*, **3**, 815, 842

68 See *ibid*, **3**, 810, 842–3, 932–3. For the area north of the Thames generally, important advances are made by K Bailey, The Middle Saxons.

69 cf for instance the caveats expressed by Everitt, *Continuity and colonisation*, 8–11

70 For the capacity of prehistoric communities to divide up territory on a large scale, see A Fleming, Coaxial field systems: some questions of time and space

71 See for instance several essays in S Bassett (ed), *The origins of Anglo-Saxon kingdoms*, and D Hooke (ed), *Anglo-Saxon settlements*; Hooke, *Anglo-Saxon landscapes*, 51–66; Gelling, *Place-names of Berkshire*, **3**, 810, 842–3

72 See notably Everitt, *Continuity and colonisation, passim*

73 Poulton, Saxon Surrey, 216

74 For instance, Cuthwulf's capture of the *tūnas* of Limbury, Aylesbury, Benson and Eynsham in '571' (*The Anglo-Saxon chronicle*, 18–19; cf Stenton, *Anglo-Saxon England*, 27–8, and Campbell, *Essays*, 115) may have been considered important less because these places were significant in a military sense than because they controlled four contiguous *regiones*.

75 E Miller, La société rurale en Angleterre (Xe-XIIIe siècles)

76 G R J Jones, Multiple estates and early settlement, 26–35

77 See especially the recent criticisms by N Gregson, The multiple estate model: some critical questions. This and the accompanying rejoinder (Jones, Multiple estates perceived) provide a convenient survey of the literature to date. Cf Steven Bassett in Bassett (ed), *The origins of Anglo-Saxon kingdoms*, 20, for the view that 'the concept of the multiple estate should be rejected as unhistorical'.

78 *DB* 32d (VIII.18–22)

79 S 1165; for its authenticity see above, p178 n 19. For its contents see also Gelling, *Early charters of Thames Valley*, 148–9, and for the Chertsey forgeries (especially S 1181 and 1035) see *ibid*, 151–2, 163–4. The text of Frithuwold's charter may contain corruptions; however, the consecutive statements that the main estate contained 200 hides plus 5 at Thorpe, and that it contained 300 hides in all, can be made intelligible by supposing that the monastery was given 95 hides when first founded *c*666, which Frithuwold increased to 300 hides.

80 The boundaries of the Chertsey property in fig 9A are based on the assumptions (a) that Frimley, originally as later, was part of Chobham; (b) that Byfleet was included in Chertsey; (c) that Windlesham, as later, was a Woking dependency and never associated with Chertsey. This reconstruction departs from the Domesday hundred boundaries only in excluding Horsell and Pyrford. Henley (ie Ash), in Woking hundred, was only acquired by Chertsey in the 11th century (*DB* 34a (VIII.30)).

81 S 1248; see discussion in Hart, *Early charters of eastern England*, 135–41, 144. For the authenticity of the Chertsey and Barking charters see above, p178 n 19, and Edwards, *Charters of early W Saxon kingdom*, 306–8

82 The outline plot of these bounds in fig 9B, which differs from the solutions offered in J G Taylor, *Our Lady of Batersey*, ch 1, and *PNSy*, 12–13n, has been amended in the light of comments by Keith Bailey.

83 S 235; see comments in Gelling, *Early charters of Thames Valley*, 150–1, and Edwards, *Charters of early W Saxon kingdom*, 132–7

84 S 1263: *DB* 31a (III.1)

85 S 382. Although the charter is a forgery these are probably genuine late 10th-century bounds. They are mapped in E Manning, *Saxon Farnham*.

86 N P Brooks, *The early history of the church of Canterbury*, 106–7

87 *VCHSy*, **4**, 69, 83

88 S 1444. (The Archbishop here leases Beddington to Edward the elder, but refers to 'when my lord [ie Edward] first let it to me'.) cf comments of R Fleming, Monastic lands and England's defence in the Viking age

89 East Shalford, Chilworth and Tyting were already independent by the Conquest, while the Wealden parish of Alfold was also alienated from the main estate as a detached pasture of East Shalford. See manorial descents in *VCHSy*, **3**, 72–127; D J Turner & W J Blair, Manors and churches in Blackheath

hundred (forthcoming). cf below p31, for the breakup of the manor and p119 for the identity of the Domesday churches of Bramley and Shalford

90   *VCHSy*, **3**, 10–16, 24–42, 45–9; *ibid* 111–21. Gomshall was in Shere parish, and parochial outliers (terrier, GLRO, DW/S/79a) suggest an early relationship between Shere and Albury.

91   U Lambert, *Godstone: a parish history*, 6

92   Three in Selhurst and nine in East Bramley (court rolls of 1485 and 1570, SRO, 212/15/1 and Acc 580 Box 5)

93   *VCHSy*, **3**, 141

94   *DB* 30b–c (I.7,13,12). Edith's only other Surrey property was the relatively insignificant manor of Fetcham (*DB* 30c (I.10)).

95   Cf P Stafford, The king's wife in Wessex, 22–3; C Phythian-Adams, Rutland reconsidered

96   Hooke, *Anglo-Saxon landscapes*, 68–73

97   Hooke, *Anglo-Saxon landscapes*, 34–8, 97–106

98   J McN Dodgson, Place-names from *-hām*, distinguished from *hamm* names, in relation to the settlement of Kent, Surrey and Sussex, 31–3; for other types of name see *PNSy*

99   eg 'Isdem Haimo tenet in Totinges unam hidam de abbate de Certesy. Osuuardus tenuit de rege E et potuit ire quo voluit. Ibi est unus villanus cum dimidia caruca et una acra prati. TRE 15 sol, modo 10 sol' (*DB* 33a-b (VIII.26))

100   *DB* 33a-b (VIII.24); other cases are 30b (I.5), 32c (VIII.4), 34b (XVIII.1), 36d (XXXVI.4)

101   eg 'Ipse episcopus tenet Codintone. Leuuinus comes tenuit. Tunc se defendebat pro 30 hidis, de quibus tenebat comes 20 hidas, et 10 hidas tenebant alodiarii villae . . . Modo de his 10 tenet episcopus 6 cum aliis 20' (*DB* 31d (V.19))

102   For a review of this problem, which suggests that Domesday 'ploughlands' record the number of actual arable hides existing in 1086, see J S Moore, The Domesday teamland: a reconsideration. But for a different view see S P J Harvey, Domesday Book and Anglo-Norman governance, 186–93

103   *DB* 36d (XXXVI.10)

104   *DB* 36a (XXI.5)

105   *DB* 30d (I.15)

106   *DB* 31b (IV.2)

107   *DB* 30d (I.13); cf *VCHSy*, **3**, 146–7

108   *DB* 32c (VIII.7); cf *VCHSy*, **1**,307, **3**, 444

109   Brit Lib, MS Cotton Julius C. vii, f217

110   SRO, 2609/11/5/35; cf C R Hart, Shoelands

111   C Taylor, *Dorset*, 49–75

112   Gelling, *Place-names of Berkshire*, **3**, 808–9; Hooke, *Anglo-Saxon landscapes*, 87–100

113   For which see P J Fowler, Agriculture and rural settlement

114   Survey of Thorncroft manor in 1629 (MM 5.28); these fields were already Thorncroft demesne in the 13th and probably the late 11th century (*PLDLHS*, **3.**10 (1976), 324).

115   *VCHSy*, **3**, 249–50; *PLDLHS*, **1.**7 (1953), 18–19; map reproduced *PLDLHS*, **1.**10 (1956), opp 21

116   See for instance P J Drury & W J Rodwell, Investigations at Asheldham, Essex; S R Bassett, Beyond the edge of excavation (and other works by the same author cited there). For comments on the present hypothesis regarding Ashtead see Drewett, Rudling & Gardiner, *South-East to AD 1000*, 272, and D G Bird, The Romano-British period in Surrey, 179–80

117   See Rumble, Place-names and their context, 173–5, who argues that these manors illustrate the imposition of bookland on the economic organisation of folk-territories. It is interesting that most of them appear in the list preserved in Chertsey forgeries S 420 and S 1181.

118   cf parallels from Kentish lathe organisation in Jolliffe, *Pre-feudal England*, 54–5. See also Rumble, Place-names and their context, 173, who argues for the confluence of parish boundaries around Banstead and Coulsdon that 'the logic behind this arrangement was . . . to allow the sharing of two areas of upland pasturage, the *dunland* of Banstead Downs and of Coulsdon (*Cuðraedesdun*) between neighbouring *bocland* estates'.

119   Some such arrangements would explain the celebrated reference to common meadow in Ine's laws: cf the comment in R A Dodgshon, *The origin of British field systems: an interpretation*, 76.

120   Aston, Origins of manor

121 S 1165; cf above, p25. *Getinges* is Eaton Farm in Cobham (*PNSy*, 88). For the 'ten hides by the port of London where the ships come to land' see T Dyson, London and Southwark in the 7th century and later: a neglected reference. However, the subsequent archaeological discovery of the mid-Saxon *wic* of London along the Strand now suggests that the Chertsey land lay opposite it on the south bank.

122 Brooks, The pre-Conquest charters of Christ Church Canterbury, 248–50

123 Gelling, *Early charters of Thames Valley*, 156–62

124 Miller, La société rurale; Hooke, *Anglo-Saxon landscapes*, 68–9

125 Notably S 1181. See discussions of authenticity in Gelling, *Early charters of Thames Valley*, 151–2; Rumble, Place-names and their context, 168–9; R Fleming, Monastic lands and England's defence, 257–61

126 Brooks, Pre-Conquest charters of Christ Church, 280–312

127 *DB* 30d-31a (II.1–6)

128 Mickleham, Fetcham, Effingham and Wisley (*DB* 32d (VIII.20); 35a (XIX.19); 36d (XXXVI.1,3,5))

129 cf Miller, La société rurale, 121–2

130 *DB* 35a (XIX.23); W J Blair, A military holding in 12th-century Leatherhead

131 Byfleet, 8 hides (*DB* 34a (VIII.28)); Chertsey, 2½ hides (32d (VIII.18))

132 Egham, 3 hides; Chobham, 6 hides (*DB* 32d (VIII.21–2))

133 *DB* 31a (III.1)

134 *DB* 31b (V.1); C A F Meekings, The early history of Sandon Hospital, 81–2

135 Hooke, *Anglo-Saxon landscapes*, 34–8

136 Aston, Origins of manor, 65–8

137 Jones, Multiple estates and early settlement, 15

138 cf Everitt, *Continuity and colonisation*, 175–9, 280–1, for conclusions which were arrived at independently of my own in these paragraphs, but point in much the same direction.

139 S 815; *DB* 34d–35a (XIX.15); 36c (XXIX.1)

140 S 1181. For 'paired' place-names see also Darby & Campbell, *Domesday geography of south-east England*, 366–7

141 Brit Lib , MS Cotton Julius C.vii, f189

142 Dodgshon, *Origin of British field systems*, 130

143 S 911; *DB* 32a (V.25); 32c (VIII.7–8); 32d (VIII.16); 34a (X.1); 36d (XXXV.1). The holding listed 32c (VIII.7) was apparently Norwood Farm (above, p28), so the Esher bounds evidently extended into later Cobham.

144 cf Dodgshon, *Origin of British field systems*, chs 5–6, and the present Ch 3

145 Dodgshon, *Origin of British field systems*, 115–19; F W Maitland, The surnames of English villages

Chapter 2

1 P H Sawyer (ed), *Medieval settlement*, 2

2 *PNSy*, 341–9; it should be noted that these lists exclude fieldnames.

3 Poulton, Saxon Surrey, 198–201; Drewett, Rudling & Gardiner, *South-East to AD 1000*, 256

4 S 847; Gelling, *Early charters of the Thames Valley*, 162; *PNSy*, 90n. Cf the forged writ of 1058 × 66 (S 1137) referring to trees in 'Kingswood', Ditton

5 S 645; Gelling, *Early charters of the Thames Valley*, 167; *PNSy*, 14–15

6 Brit Lib, Add Ch 8139, Harl Ch 111.D.44; WAM, 1891. However, more than half of Penge was still common land at the time of its inclosure in 1827.

7 *PNSy*, 95–6; Brit Lib, Add Chs 5528, 5531–2

8 Fine, PRO, CP25(1)/226/12(281)

9 *PLDLHS*, **4**.2 (1978), 31 and 37 no 25

10 Dodgson, Place-names from -*hām*, 15; Drewett, Rudling & Gardiner, *The South-East to AD 1000*, 294–6. For one extensively excavated site, which produced a small quantity of 8th-century material and a 12th-century farmhouse, see R Hanworth & D J Tomalin, *Brooklands, Weybridge: the excavation of an Iron Age and medieval site*.

11   *Bracton's note book*, **2** 125–6

12   cf C R Young, *The royal forests of medieval England*, 87, 109

13   *Bracton's note book*, **3**, 148–9 (case 1129)

14   PRO, E32/195 and E32/194

15   A H Smith, *English place-name elements*, **2**, 102–3

16   PRO, E40/4055

17   See J A Raftis, *Assart data and land values*, 101

18   *ibid*, loc cit

19   WAM, 27392–27428; WAM, 27468–27481; *Chertsey Abbey court rolls abstract*. I am very grateful to Miss Barbara Harvey for the use of her transcripts of the Westminster rolls.

20   WAM, 27397, 27398

21   *Chertsey court roll abstract*, nos 256, 258; WAM, 27477, m1

22   The Pyrford evidence is cited by B F Harvey, The population trend in England between 1300 and 1348, 40–1

23   Everitt, *Continuity and colonisation*, 124–64

24   *ibid*, 175–80

25   Dodgson, Place-names from *-hām*, 15

26   J Morris, Anglo-Saxon Surrey, 140–1. Note also the cemetery at the Goblin Works, Leatherhead: Poulton, Saxon Surrey, 214

27   S Piggott (ed), *The agrarian history of England and Wales: I.i: Prehistory*, 96–129

28   B Hope-Taylor, Celtic agriculture in Surrey. There is no inherent geographical reason inhibiting Downland agriculture: see MacPhail & Scaife, Geographical and environmental background, 47–8.

29   Rudling, Downland settlement in East Sussex

30   F H Thompson, Three Surrey hillforts, 296

31   J Morris, Anglo-Saxon Surrey; Dodgson, Place-names from *-hām*, 13–15

32   S 1508

33   S 528. See Rumble, The Merstham (Surrey) charter bounds, AD 971, and *idem* Place-names and their context, 165–6

34   See Gelling, Latin loan-words in old English place-names, 5–8

35   Rumble, Merstham (Surrey) charter bounds, boundary – points 12–16

36   *ibid*, boundary-points 2, 4, 6

37   S 753. Uncertainty surrounds this text, which evidently does not, as has been claimed (*Place-names of Essex*, 58–9), refer to Kelveden in Essex. The form *Cealvadune* is consistent with early spellings of Chaldon (*PNSy*, 42)

38   cf comments in Dodgson, Place-names from *-hām*, 13

39   *PNSy*, 43

40   Ex inf D J Turner

41   Rumble, Merstham (Surrey) charter bounds, 12–13

42   *PLDLHS*, **4**.1 (1977), 9–11

43   G Hewlett, Stages in the settlement of a Downland parish: a study of the hedges of Chelsham

44   On principles of hedge dating, see O Rackham, *Trees and woodland in the British landscape*, 166–8

45   Excavation of a lynchet in field near Addington village and church dated the first ploughing to the early 12th century: L Thornhill, Report on field work at Addington, Surrey, 1970–1972.

46   eg at Punesherst in Leatherhead as late as 1316: a croft called Pynchonesgrove 'ubi grava prius fuit assarta' (*PLDLHS*, **4**.8 (1984), 205 no 271)

47   *The cartae antiquae rolls 11–20*, no 620

48   Brit Lib, MS Cotton Cleop C.vii, f69

49   *ibid*, ff63ᵛ–64

50   *ibid*, ff80ᵛ–81, 143, 93

51   PRO, C52/31 (Cartae antiquae roll GG), no 18

52   For the later medieval topography, including a discussion of the bounds of Bandon, see H M Gowans, M Wilks & J Bray (eds), *Courts of the manors of Bandon and Beddington 1498–1552*

53   S 1444

54 *Calendar of curia regis rolls*, **2**, 107, 248; **5**, 111. Cf K W Muckelroy, 'Woodcote, or Woodcote Warren, Once a City, According to Tradition'

55 The phrase occurs in the Chertsey forgeries, which evidently use genuine pre-Conquest descriptions (above, p30–1)

56 Brit Lib, Egerton Ch 6132. I am grateful to Elizabeth Gardner for bringing this deed to my attention.

57 Brit Lib, MS Cotton Nero C.iii. f197c

58 Quoted in Sawyer (ed), *Medieval settlement*, 1

59 *ibid*, 2–4

60 A R H Baker & R A Butlin (eds), *Studies of field systems in the British Isles*, 380

61 Witney, *Jutish forest*; Everitt, *Continuity and colonisation*

62 See for instance P H Sawyer, *From Roman Britain to Norman England*, 136–8

63 Maitland, *Domesday Book and beyond*, 13–14

64 *Anglo-Saxon Chronicle*, 84–5

65 J Morris, Anglo-Saxon Surrey

66 Dodgson, Place-names from *-hām*; J Morris, Anglo-Saxon Surrey, map, p149

67 Sawyer (ed), *Medieval settlement*, 4, 5–7; *idem*, *Roman Britain to Norman England*, 143–5

68 A H Smith, *English place-name elements*, **1**, 90–1; Darby, Place-names and the geography of the past, 8–9; Witney, *Jutish forest*, 104–10; Everitt, *Continuity and colonisation*, 49–52.

69 This problem is discussed for the Weald in general by Darby, Place-names and the geography of the past, 14–18.

70 However, Mark Gardiner (pers comm) comments that in Sussex *'denn* occurs more commonly than *The place-names of Sussex* would lead one to expect. In some areas, such as the north-western section of Hastings rape, it is the most common placename element in parish-, farm- and field-names.'

71 Darby, Place-names and the geography of the past, 17

72 *ibid*, 17–18; Smith, *Place-name elements*, **1**, 276–7, 157–8

73 Smith, *Place-name elements*, **2**, 18–22

74 S 1508

75 Brit Lib, MS Cotton Vesp D.ix, f32

76 S 1511

77 In this context it is worth noting the current excavations at Cranleigh Rectory, some 50m from Cranleigh parish church, where the pottery indicates initial occupation in the mid to late 11th century (ex inf J English).

78 cf Hooke, *Anglo-Saxon landscapes*, 111: 'It is in previously densely wooded areas that charter bounds become most often difficult to solve and quite obviously do not always follow modern boundary lines.'

79 Witney, *Jutish forest*, passim; J L M Gulley, The Wealden landscape in the early 17th century and its antecedents, 458 and map facing

80 *VCHSy*, **3**, 201; below, p114

81 S 420, 752

82 S 528

83 S 815

84 Brit Lib, Add Roll 23023

85 S 1181

86 Canterbury Cathedral Library, MS E24, f154

87 For which see court roll evidence cited in H Lambert, The Banstead court rolls in the reigns of Richard II and Henry IV

88 Greenwood, Model for settlement development of Reigate hundred (forthcoming)

89 See *VCHSy*, **3**, 310. When Hamelin de Warenne confirmed Newdigate chapel to Southwark Priory as 'elemosinam . . . antecessorum meorum' (below, p129) he was almost certainly regarding it as a member of Reigate, Betchworth or Leigh church, all of which his ancestors had given to the Priory.

90 *VCHSy*, **3**, 246

91 MM, 5777c, 5778, 5788, 5791 etc

92 MM, 5.28, f39

93 W J Blair, Medieval deeds of the Leatherhead district, Part IV, *PLDLHS*, **4**.5 (1981), nos 112, 146–9

94 A W G Lowther, Ashtead and its history, part 9, 88

95 Malden, Kingsland in Newdigate and Newdigate in Copthorne hundred

96 Research in progress by Mr P J Gray (pers comm)

97 Above, p51. Lingfield fails to appear in Domesday Book, presumably being included in the Sanderstead entry.

98 D J Turner, Nutfield and the settlement of the Weald

99 *DB* 30d (I.14). In the Surrey Domesday the terms 'bordar' and 'cottar' seem generally to be near-synonymous alternatives; see Malden, Domesday survey of Surrey, 469–70.

100 *DB* 36b (XXIV.1)

101 The proportion of serfs is the same in both cases (16%).

102 cf, for Kent, Witney, *Jutish forest*, 116–18

103 W J Blair, Surrey endowments of Lewes Priory, 100

104 *DB* 34c (XIX.1)

105 W J Blair, Surrey endowments of Lewes Priory, 109–10; *idem*, The early history of Horne: an addendum

106 cf S P J Harvey, Evidence for settlement study: Domesday Book

107 Heather Warne (pers comm) notes that Keymer and Ditchling, Sussex, shared a wood called Frekeburgh which was apparently kept as such until the Conquest, but subsequently broken up into assart plots by the Warennes.

108 Brit Lib, Add Ch 24607

109 Canterbury Cathedral Library, MS E24, f154^v

110 Battle Abbey Cartulary, Henry Huntingdon Library, California, BA vol 29, ff185–196^v

111 Analysis of Winchester pipe rolls for Farnham by Philip Brooks, in progress

112 E Searle, Hides, virgates and tenant settlement at Battle Abbey; *idem, Lordship and community* 44–68; Brandon, Medieval clearances in the East Sussex Weald. An explicit Sussex example of 1121 is cited by Round, Some early grants to Lewes Priory, 67–8. Heather Warne (pers comm) notes a contrast between the large-scale clearances around Battle Abbey and the much more piecemeal, small-scale assarting of the central Sussex Weald.

113 Witney, *Jutish forest*, 154–61; F R H du Boulay, Denns, droving and danger

114 See Gulley, Wealden landscape, 411–12. A good mid 12th-century example, granting pannage in the wood of Blechingley to Lewes Priory, is printed in W J Blair, Surrey endowments of Lewes Priory, 117.

115 Brit Lib, MS Cotton Cleop C.vii, ff135^v–136. For a thorough discussion of residual droving and grazing rights in the Weald as a whole, see Gulley, Wealden landscape, 405–11

116 Gulley, Wealden landscape, 307–19, 392–7

117 E M Yates, A study of settlement patterns, 65–84

118 For a summary of recent work on these problems see P Bigmore, Villages and towns, 157–69

119 P Rahtz, Buildings and rural settlement, 58–63

120 B Cunliffe, Saxon and medieval settlement-pattern in the region of Chalton, Hampshire; Fowler, Agriculture and rural settlement, 43

121 C C Taylor, Polyfocal settlement and the English village; *idem*, Aspects of village mobility in medieval and later times. A synthesis of Taylor's work is now available in his *Village and farmstead*.

122 P Wade-Martins, The origins of rural settlement in East Anglia

123 J Morris, Anglo-Saxon Surrey, 140; Anon, Saxon hut at Ham, 101; Orton, Excavations at 32 Burleigh Avenue, Wallington; Bird *et al*, Archaeology in Surrey 1976–8, 250. For an up-to-date map and discussion, with further references, see Poulton, Saxon Surrey, 198, 207.

124 For an outline survey see also M O'Connell & R Poulton, The towns of Surrey, 37–51. See also Poulton, Saxon Surrey, 208–11

125 Hill, Burghal Hidage, 86–7

126 F Aldsworth & D Hill, The Burghal Hidage – Eashing, 198–201

127 M Biddle & D Hill, Late Saxon planned towns, 84

128 O'Connell, *Historic towns in Surrey*, 29–32; O'Connell & Poulton, Towns of Surrey

129 Dyson, London and Southwark in the 7th century and later, argues that the *burh* was founded in conjunction with a rebuilding of London Bridge in *c*900

130 See D J Johnson, *Southwark and the city*, chs 1–2; *VCHSy* **4**, 125–6. M Biddle, D Hudson & C Heighway, *The future of London's past*, fig 9, shows the possible perimeter of the *burh*.

131 This is discussed more fully, and the evidence summarised, in Darby & Campbell, *Domesday geography of south-east England*, 397–400.

132 For some archaeological evidence see Drewett, Rudling & Gardiner, *South-East to AD 1000*, 307

133 O'Connell, *Historic towns in Surrey*

134 On the rather complex town plan of Godalming, see O'Connell, *Historic towns in Surrey*, 25–8

135 O'Connell, *Historic towns in Surrey*, 19–23, 45–8. For Reigate see also M Beresford, *New towns of the Middle Ages*, 491; the first clear evidence for urban status is a reference to a burgage in a charter of Earl Hamelin de Warenne (royal inspeximus, PRO, C66/328 m13). Excavations on the south side of Reigate High Street have produced 12th- to 13th-century pottery (H Woods, Excavations in Reigate, 1974). See also Poulton, Cherchefelle and the origins of Reigate. For evidence of a Saxo-Norman, pre-town nucleus around the church, see Poulton, Saxon Surrey, 211

136 *Regesta regum anglo-normannorum*, **2**, no 1768

137 Bird *et al*, Archaeology in Surrey, 1976–8, 238–9. See also O'Connell, *Historic towns in Surrey*, 11–14

138 O'Connell, *Historic towns in Surrey*, 35–9; Beresford, New towns, 490–1

139 *Cal Cur Reg Rolls* **16**, 322; see also O'Connell, *Historic towns in Surrey*, 15–18

140 *VCHSy*, **4**, 217–18; Lambeth Palace Library, MS 1212, ff64ᵛ–65 (deeds of 1286); see also L Thornhill, Croydon: a summary of work by the CLHSS on medieval Croydon

141 W J Blair, *The early town of Leatherhead*, 3–5

142 W J Blair, Surrey endowments of Lewes Priory, 106–9

143 See especially B K Roberts, *Rural settlement in Britain*, ch 5

144 *ibid*, 124–7

145 See K Bailey, Medieval Putney: a planned village?, 1–8

146 Brit Lib, Add Chs 17278, 5572, 8811

147 SRO, 2609/11/5/35

148 Witney, *Jutish forest*, 139–48

149 Ewell: *Fitznells cartulary*, cxxiv–cxl; P Shearman, Ewell in 1577; C F Titford, Medieval Ewell and Cuddington; Shearman, The topography of medieval Ewell and Cuddington. Great Bookham, 1273 (Brit Lib, Add Ch 5569); Walton-on-Thames, 1316 and 1324 (PRO, E326/7976, 7802); *Chertsey cartularies, passim*

150 Brit Lib, Add MS 6040, nos 2 and 1

151 Brit Lib, MS Cotton Cleop C.vii, f78

152 B K Roberts, Village plans in County Durham

153 *The letters of Abelard and Heloise*, 195

154 Brit Lib, MS Cotton Cleop C.vii, f123ᵛ

155 For the purprestures and diversion of roadways see J H Harvey in *PLDLHS*, **1**.2 (1948), 8–10, and W J Blair in *ibid*, **4**.2 (1978), 31–2, 37. For the manor-house excavations see below, p190 n 163. Curiously, but probably coincidentally, the planned settlement must have been very near the site of the ancient minster church and *villa regia* of Leatherhead (above, p20).

156 Inquisition and survey printed *PLDLHS*, **3**.9 (1975), 292–7

157 *PNSy, passim*; almost every parish contains at least one or two isolated habitation sites recorded by, or not long after, *c*1280–1320.

158 *PNSy*, 349

159 cf Smith, *Place-name elements*, **2**, 273–4, which notes the large number of compounds with personal names and comments that *-weorþ*, 'would not . . . seem necessarily to denote an enclosure for agricultural purposes, but it may have been one enclosing a dwelling . . .; it may well be that the *worð* was something like a *topt*, the small enclosure in which a single dwelling stood in the settlement'. Rumble, Place-names and their context, 175–6, suggests that in this part of Surrey *worþ*, reflects (mostly lost) habitation sites. cf Hooke, *Anglo-Saxon landscape: the kingdom of the Hwicce*, 47–50, who notes that in the West Midlands *worþ*, occurs 'in the more wooded areas of secondary development where relatively minor settlements were able to become parish nuclei'.

160 Dodgson, Place-names from -*hām*, 22–4

161 *PNSy*, 342–3

162 *PNSy*, 100, 239
163 A W G Lowther, A T Ruby & D Renn, Pachenesham, Leatherhead: the excavation of the medieval moated site known as 'The Mounts'; L L Ketteringham, *Alsted: excavation of a 13th–14th century sub-manor house with its ironworks in Netherne Wood, Merstham, Surrey*; H M Colvin (ed), *The history of the king's works*, **2**, 950–2, and Bird *et al*, Archaeology in Surrey, 1976–8, 232–3
164 D J Turner, Moated site near Moat Farm, Hookwood, Charlwood, 57–87; Bird *et al*, Archaeology in Surrey, 1976–8, 240, 242
165 Bird *et al*, Archaeology in Surrey, 1976–8, 240–1
166 Brit Lib, MS Cotton Cleop C.vii, f93. For the moat (national grid TQ 295 440) see Turner, Moated sites in Surrey: a provisional list, 93
167 B K Roberts, A study of medieval colonisation in the Forest of Arden, Warwickshire, 109–12; *idem*, Moated sites in midland England
168 D J Turner, Moated site near Moat Farm, 66. Since this section was drafted, an important general discussion of Surrey moats by D J Turner has appeared in Bird & Bird (eds), *Archaeology of Surrey to 1540*, 230–46.
169 See C C Taylor, The Anglo-Saxon countryside. The desertion of very small nucleations in response to the 'balling' process is possibly suggested by the units of one or two hides which supported small groups of peasants in 1086 but emerge as single farms in the 13th and 14th centuries (above, p28).
170 D Hall, The origins of open-field agriculture – the archaeological fieldwork evidence, 35
171 Wade-Martins, Origins of rural settlement in East Anglia

Chapter 3

1 H L Gray, *The English field systems*, 356–69; A R H Baker & R A Butlin (eds), *Studies of field systems in the British Isles*, 419–29.
2 K A Bailey & I G Galbraith, Field systems in Surrey: an introductory survey
3 For a fuller discussion see Baker & Butlin, *Studies of field systems*, 379–81
4 It would be impracticable to list all references individually. The main sources are: for the 13th and 14th centuries, PRO fines and deeds (CP25(i) and Ancient Deeds classes), Brit Lib and SRO deeds; for the 15th, 16th and 17th centuries, surveys quoted by Gray, *Field systems*, 356–69; and for the 18th and 19th centuries, SRO inclosure awards and tithe maps and references in *VCHSy*. For an earlier discussion of this question see *VCHSy*, **4**, 408–10.
5 For similar evidence for Kent, see Baker & Butlin, *Studies of field systems*, 402–5. It has been asserted that the Surrey Wealden townships of Charlwood, Burstow and Horley had common fields (D J Turner, Moated site near Moat Farm, Hookwood, Charlwood, 84, and sources cited there), but the first case is based on a misunderstanding of a document and in the others the evidence is late and equivocal.
6 W F Mumford, The manor of Oxted 1360–1420, 70–5
7 cf evidence for Kent and Sussex discussed by du Boulay, *The lordship of Canterbury* 131–3
8 Well shown on map in J H Harvey, A cartographical survey of the area: **6** the Middle Ages, opposite p103
9 eg Brit Lib, Add Chs 22795, 22723, 22747, 22866, 22851, 22764
10 eg Brit Lib, Add Chs 22758, 23046, 22847, 23060, 22859, 22873, 23040, 22733, 22833
11 eg Leatherhead deeds calendared *PLDLHS*, **4.2** (1978), 37–8; **4.4** (1980), 95–6; and a reference to the 'common field of [East] Clandon called le Southefeld' (*Chertsey cartularies*, **2**, no 868)
12 1629 Thorncroft survey, MM, 5.28; *VCHSy*, **4**, 109; Gray, *Field systems*, 361. Keith Bailey comments (pers comm) that 'there is some evidence of one larger field at Wandsworth (South Field) and Putney (Sixth or Thames Field), and only one common field at Battersea'.
13 *VCHSy*, **4**, 409; for Hurtmore fields see also PRO, E315/41(106), 31(65), 42(125), 44(107)
14 Including 'Teynturefeld' (PRO, E326/9878, 9879, 9880, 9915), the 'small field' (E326/6665, 9913), and the Marsh (E326/6693, 9784, 9908)

15   PRO, E326/4352, 4876, 4879, 4880

16   PRO, E315/41(64), E326/4350, 9854–6, 9909

17   Gray, *Field systems*, 366–8

18   Malden, The three field system of farming in Surrey, 251–4. (I am grateful to Shirley Corke for pointing out that the inquisition which Malden ascribed to Abinger actually relates to Paddington.)

19   Bailey & Galbraith, Field systems in Surrey, 76, 79–80

20   R Sewill & E Lane, *The free men of Charlwood*, 8–9

21   E Robo, *Medieval Farnham*, 33, 123. In the 14th century there were also three-course shifts on the demesnes of Thorncroft (a lease of 1303 stipulating that after three years all fields are to have the fruits now in them: MM, 632, printed *PLDLHS* **4.4** (1980), 93–4 no 88) and Oxted (Mumford, Manor of Oxted, 75).

22   Brandon, *History of Surrey*, 41–2. cf the case of Westcott in 1392 (cited by Yates, Settlement patterns), where the demesne lay in numerous named fields but was subject to a three-course rotation.

23   Brit Lib, MS Cotton Faust A.viii, f157

24   Fox, Approaches to the adoption of the Midland system, 67–8

25   Brit Lib, Add Ch 22808

26   Bailey & Galbraith, Field systems in Surrey, 76–7

27   MM, 4706. I am grateful to Ralph Evans for this reference.

28   Bailey & Galbraith, Field systems in Surrey, 77

29   Thus at Thorncroft in 1629 the tenants of the manor had depasturing *in the manor's lands* in the common field (MM, 5.28 f40); there is no suggestion of comprehensive grazing rights there enjoyed by the whole township of Leatherhead. On the other hand, Keith Bailey (pers comm) notes that 'grazing arrangements at Wandsworth were later organised on a parochial basis, ignoring the division of the common fields between four manors'. More work is needed here on the later sources.

30   MM, 918

31   *Fitznells cartulary*, xxx

32   cf Baker, Some fields and farms in medieval Kent, 168–9

33   Brandon, Common lands and wastes of Sussex, 39–43; Gulley, Wealden landscape, 102–4, 319–22

34   This is clear from its survival to a much later date. Gulley, Wealden landscape, 364–6, points out that the individualistic nature of Wealden tenure did not preclude intercommoning on a large scale.

35   *Bracton's note book*, 3, 293–5 (no 1284); Brit Lib, MS Cotton Cleop C.vii, f105. cf the similar dispute between Claygate and Thames Ditton in WAM, Westminster Domesday, f468ᵛ.

36   H Lambert, Some account of the Surrey manors held by Merton College and Corpus Christi College, Oxford in the 17th century, 44

37   By *c*1300 the lord of Pachenesham Parva had several pasture here in la Hoke, la Upcrofte and le Brewer (*PLDLHS*, **3.8** (1974), 232), and in 1288 the lord of Pachenesham Magna was enclosing his common pasture of 'bruera' in the same area (*PLDLHS*, **4.2** (1978), 37). For a detailed perambulation of Thorncroft common in 1450/1 see MM, 5734

38   *PLDLHS*, **3.8** (1974), 228

39   Meekings, Notes on the de Abernon family before 1236, 173, n77; *PLDLHS*, **4.2** (1978), 34, no 9

40   eg common of half a virgate in Surbiton in the early 13th century (PRO, E326/4893)

41   Charter of Ingram d'Abernon, inspeximus in Pat R 11 Edw II pt ii (PRO, C66/149), m36; Brit Lib, Add Ch 5531–2

42   Charter of Gilbert d'Aquila, inspeximus in Pat R 11 Edw II pt ii (PRO, C66/149), m36

43   Goats are most commonly mentioned, as at Cobham in 1271/2 (Brit Lib, Add Ch 5547).

44   Brit Lib, MS Cotton Faust A.viii, f155ᵛ

45   eg at Tolworth, 'unam dol prati in Pukemed sicut loth condonat . . . quantum pertinet ad unam dimidiam virgatam terre (PRO, E40/7275); and at Surbiton, common pertaining to a half-virgate (E326/4893). cf early 14th-century conveyances of meadowland apportioned by lot, eg *Chertsey abstract*, no 1085

46   eg *PLDLHS*, **4.2** (1978), 34, no 7

47   Bailey & Galbraith, Field systems in Surrey, 77–8, discussing the customal printed in *Register or memorial of Ewell, Surrey*, 135–8

48   PRO C143/271(20); Brit Lib, MS Cotton Cleop C.vii, f125

49   W J Blair, A military holding in 12th-century Leatherhead

50   *Chertsey abstract*, no 139

51   *Manorial records of Cuxham, Oxfordshire*, 78

52   Listed in Thorncroft court roll 1307 (MM, 5781, m23ᵛ) as of the tenement of Giles atte Boxe; presumably half of one of Giles's two virgates of 1279 (MM, 5786)

53   Listed in Thorncroft rental 1332 (MM, 5779d) as 'tenementum que fuit Johannis de Chereborgh' que est dimidiam virgatam terre': presumably John's half-virgate of 1279 (MM, 5786)

54   Listed in Pachenesham Parva rental *c*1300 (*PLDLHS*, **3**.8 (1974), 228–9); one of William le Malevile's two virgates, the other comprising 13 acres in Catebardene

55   Gray was much struck by these irregular virgates and gives a large collection of examples (*Field systems*, 360ff).

56   H Lambert, *History of Banstead in Surrey*, 69–87

57   The key is MM, 5.28, a detailed survey with maps compiled in 1629. See Lambert, Some account of the Surrey manors, 41–6. The fields can be traced back from this to 13th- and 14th-century rentals; the most important earlier documents are MM, 5777c, MM, 5779d.

58   Heather Warne (pers comm) notes a similar contrast in Ditchling and Keymer, Sussex, between (a) subdivided 16-acre virgates in open fields near the Greensand villages, and (b) compact virgates of 40 to 200 acres in the Weald.

59   For which see B Harvey, *Westminster Abbey and its estates in the Middle Ages*, 218–19

60   Scutage at Thorncroft and Farleigh (MM, 5777c, MM, 4904) and tallage at Pyrford (WAM, 27469) were assessed on the virgate; at Merrow rents were imposed at a standard 1s per virgate (Brit Lib, MS Cotton Claud A.vi, f13).

61   Wealden outliers described in Banstead customal printed Lambert, *History of Banstead*, 65–9. However, Mark Gardiner suggests to me that ferlings in the Sussex Weald (eg Brandon, Medieval clearances, 135–53) are 'in all respects identical to the virgates (or wists) elsewhere in the Weald; there is no evidence that they were fragments of larger virgates'.

62   Searle, Hides, virgates and tenant settlement. I am grateful to Heather Warne for the information that Balcombe, Sussex, contained compact virgates, held of Keymer manor, of up to 200 acres per virgate.

63   This is clear from a Hambledon deed of *c*1220, granting a recently-assembled holding, which is endorsed 'Ista carta tenetur pro dimidia virgata terre' (PRO, E326/8090).

64   O Manning & W Bray, *The history and antiquities of the county of Surrey*, **2**, 70; Malden, Villeinage in the Weald of Surrey

65   Brandon, Common lands and wastes of Sussex, 50–2

66   Dodgshon, *Origin of British field systems*, ch 3, esp 71

67   Canterbury Cath Lib, MS E24, ff153–6 for Cheam and Croydon; Lambeth Palace, LR 2068 (cited here from notes kindly provided by Keith Bailey) for Wimbledon

68   P Woods, The parsonage or rectory manor of Godalming, and a 14th-century customal thereof

69   Woods, On a 14th-century rental of the principal manor of Godalming with some remarks on cotholders; note especially a tenant who died in 1357 holding a toft and 12 acres of land called *cotlond*. An interesting parallel for the house-plots is provided by Toddenham (Gloucestershire), where five *cotmanni* dwelt side-by-side in a croft apart from the other tenants (B F Harvey, *Westminster Abbey*, 262n).

70   Jones, Multiple estates and early settlement, 31

71   *Register or memorial of Ewell*, 137ff

72   W Hooper, Bondmen at Reigate under the Tudors

73   This is best seen at Ewell; compare the names of tenants in the list of *iugera* with the 1411 survey and the reconstructed map of the village plots (*Register or memorial of Ewell*, 135ff, 169ff; *Fitznells cartulary*, opp cxxix). Two Leatherhead virgates are stated to have messuages adjoining those of other tenants (above, p73, and *PLDLHS*, **3**.8 (1974), 226).

74   See especially the recent re-formulation of this view by Dodgshon, *Origin of British field systems*, ch 2

75   For which see Baker & Butlin, *Studies of field systems*, 393–408

76   Baker & Butlin, *Studies of field systems*, 311, argue for a compact origin, but B M S Campbell, Population change and the genesis of commonfields in a Norfolk manor, 177–8, concludes that the *eriung* was generally fragmented.

77 Note, for instance, the frequency with which the same furlong names recur in the Thorncroft-Pachenesham Parva rentals, MM 5779d and *PLDLHS*, **3**.8 (1974), 224–33

78 B M S Campbell, Population change and the genesis of commonfields, 178

79 B Dodwell, Holdings and inheritance in medieval East Anglia

80 R V Lennard, *Rural England 1086–1135*, 346–7

81 *PLDLHS*, **3**.8 (1974), 228–9

82 Fine, PRO, CP25(i)/225/3(93). (The plots had, however, been held by several tenants.)

83 Brit Lib, MS Cotton Cleop C.vii, ff 113ᵛ–114

84 Brit Lib, Add Chs 24165, 23662

85 For exactly this process in relation to compact holdings cf below, p84; see also Dodgshon, *Origin of British field systems*, ch 4

86 Dodwell, Holdings and inheritance for East Anglia; below, Ch 6, for Surrey glebes

87 Dodwell, Holdings and inheritance, 58

88 *Documents illustrative of the social and economic history of the Danelaw*, xxviii–xxxi (though in these cases it appears that both halves normally consisted of dispersed strips)

89 Fox, Approaches to adoption of Midland system, 86–8; cf Dodgshon, *Origin of British field systems*, ch 2

90 Brit Lib, Add Ch 5556

91 *PLDLHS*, **3**.8 (1974), 228

92 MM, 5779

93 *PLDLHS*, **4**.4 (1980), 94 no 91

94 *PLDLHS*, **3**.8 (1974), 224–8

95 *PLDLHS*, **4**.7 (1983), 173–4, no 215

96 *PLDLHS*, **3**.8 (1974), 228

97 *PLDLHS*, **4**.7 (1983), 177–8, no 242

98 Bailey, Medieval Putney, 1–8

99 Canterbury Cath Lib, MS E24, ff147–8

100 MM, 5786; the present summary uses related evidence from the court rolls to distinguish free from unfree holdings and eliminate outliers in Mickleham and Newdigate.

101 MM, 5779d

102 *PLDLHS*, **3**.8 (1974), 226

103 cf the case of Aldenham, Hertfordshire, where 'the insistence of the monks of Westminster of that period upon bringing to the surface all inter-tenant sales of land' produced an illusion that the number of tenants had suddenly doubled (Harvey, *Westminster Abbey*, 211n). The passing in 1290 of the *Quia Emptores* statute, which replaced subinfeudation with substitution, may have affected manorial policy. However, see also I Kershaw, The great famine and agrarian crisis in England 1315–1322, 40, who notes the fragmentation, under market pressures, of assessed holdings on St Albans manors during *c*1315–25, and points out that 'by the 1330s tenants were willing to pay fines to have the rents and services of their disintegrated tenements properly apportioned'

104 *PLDLHS*, **4**.4 (1980), 95 no 93

105 eg MM, 5781, m3, court of 1283: list of holdings seized for unlicensed alienation

106 Brit Lib, MS Cotton Claud A.vi, f13

107 *ibid*, f100 ff

108 At a court of 1291 (MM, 4904) the homage stated that half a virgate contained 16 acres, and that an aid to marry the lord's daughter should be levied at a rate of 2s per virgate.

109 Rental, MM, 4890

110 Rental printed *Customals of Battle Abbey*, 137–63 (excluding outliers in Broadham and Prinkham)

111 For this process in Kent see Baker, Open fields and partible inheritance on a Kent manor; Baker & Butlin, *Studies of field systems*, 407–8. cf also Bailey & Galbraith, Field systems in Surrey, 77–9, on Ewell

112 eg Brit Lib, Add MS 6040(1–2) (Mitcham); *Fitznells cartulary* no 53 (Ewell)

113 PRO, CP25(i)/225/1–226/17

114 For which see Harvey, *Westminster Abbey*, 107–15

115 *ibid*, 207

116 *ibid*, 212

117 For which see *ibid*, 214-5. cf the case of Pyrford (*ibid*, 301-2), where alienations of customary land were permitted, but subjected to increments of rent which caused the land in question to appear twice in the same customal.

118 For the same process in Kent, see A Brown, London and north-west Kent in the later Middle Ages: the development of a land market

119 Brit Lib, Add Chs 22727, 22728, 22730, 22783, 22801, 22809, 22967, 22990

120 Brit Lib, Add Chs 22976, 22978, 23002, 23050, 23677, 23678, 23684, 23685, 23687, 23688

121 Brit Lib, Add Chs 22723, 22724, 22763, 22771, 22772, 22821, 22927, 22942

122 *Fitznells cartulary*, l-lxxxviii

123 See *PLDLHS* **4**.8 (1974), 203-19; W J Blair, Later middle ages (*Hist. of Leatherhead*), 49-51

124 For instance, he acquired property in Epsom by a fine of 1311 (CP25(i) 228/31(78)).

125 There is virtually no evidence for smallholders' flocks. But they certainly existed: the Thorncroft manorial accounts sometimes note the hire of sheep for manuring the demesne, including 120 sheep from John le Heyward and 420 from Gilbert Burgeys in 1343/4 (MM, 5758), and 160 from Gilbert Burgeys and 90 from William le Baker in 1344/5 (MM, 5724). I owe these references to Ralph Evans.

126 P D A Harvey, *A medieval Oxfordshire village*, 115-7; E King, *Peterborough Abbey, 1086-1310*, 116-17

127 This is very consistent with Paul Hyams's conclusion, drawn mainly from legal and manorial sources, that a villein land-market had developed in 'non-champion' areas by the 1240s and elsewhere by *c*1300 (P R Hyams, The origin of a peasant land-market in England). The market in free land would naturally have developed more precociously than that in villein land.

128 eg 'terra de Gretenerse' in Blechingley in the 1140s (W J Blair, Surrey endowments of Lewes Priory, 117); half a hide called la Berne in Charlwood in 1199 (fine, PRO, CP25(i)/225/2(9)). A Titsey deed of *c*1148 defines an earlier holding as '10 solidatas terre apud Bradested' (PRO, C146/10365).

129 As at Oxted (Mumford, Manor of Oxted, 70-5)

130 Brit Lib, Add Ch 26728; fine, PRO, CP25(i)/225/5(47). Cf below, p195 n151

131 Fine, PRO, CP25(i)/225/6(83)

132 For instance: 8 acres land in le Slefhurst (Ewhurst, late 13th cent, Brit Lib, Add Ch 5564); 6 acres in my field called Rude as they are enclosed (Hambledon, late 13th cent, PRO, E326/8242); a piece of land in a croft called le Longeham delimited by metes and bounds (Wonersh, 1315, PRO, E326/6219)

133 Brit Lib, Add Chs 22941, 22943, 23005, 22926, 22942; his land scattered elsewhere in the parish is disposed of in Add Chs 22992, 22713, 22736, 22739, 22737, 22712.

134 Brit Lib, Add Chs 22958, 22950, 23038, 23049, 23051, 23693

135 Brit Lib, Add Ch 7598

136 Inspeximus, Chart R 14 Edw II (PRO, C53/107), m8

137 Fine, PRO, CP25(i)/225/2(15); Brit Lib, Cotton Ch xvi. 41

138 PRO, E326/8094, 8090

139 Two good examples in deeds of *c*1230-50 are PRO, E210/7208 (Shere) and E326/8082 (Hambledon)

140 Gray, *Field systems*, 368; fine, PRO, CP25(i)/226/12(314)

141 Abuttals of 13th-century Wealden deeds often mention lanes leading to other tenants' 'doors' or 'houses'; eg Brit Lib, Add Ch 5934; PRO, E326/8082.

142 Gulley, Wealden landscape, 342-56, 364-6

143 T A M Bishop, Assarting and the growth of open fields, 13-29; see also general discussion in Baker & Butlin, *Studies of field systems*, 368-9

144 B M S Campbell, Population change and the genesis of commonfields

145 Baker, Some fields and farms in medieval Kent

146 R J Faith, Peasant families and inheritance customs in medieval England, 82-4, 95. The Borough English principle is formulated in a late 13th-century Beddington deed in which Thomas Colswein grants a curtilage to his son Hugh, with reversion to Hugh's brother Alan; if Alan dies without issue, 'volo . . . quod totum tenementum . . . descendet ad proximum juniorem filium meum vel filiam meam post ipsum' (Brit Lib, Add Ch 22958).

147 cf discussion of this in Dodgshon, *Origin of British field systems*, 38-43

148 Fine, PRO, CP25(i)/225/9(198)

149 As in a Wisley fine of 1206 which defines components of a half-hide and half-virgate, scattered through a long series of fields, as the northern, western or southern halves (PRO, CP25(i)/225/3(67));

and a Headley fine of 1218 which states that half a holding 'iacet versus partes boreales' of its component fields (PRO, CP25(i)/225/4(3))

150   As in a Wimbledon fine of 1248 where each of the five open-field strips lies next land of William fitz Peter (PRO, CP25(i)/226/13(323))

151   PRO, E326/8239; the depth of the new ditch was to be 'ad mensuram consued' patrie', the ditch itself to be on the grantor's land but the bank on the grantee's. cf E326/8243

152   Brit Lib, Add Ch 7599

153   *Chertsey cartularies*, **2**, nos 702, 721, 820, 824

154   *Chertsey cartularies*, **1**, no 359; WAM, 27473. For a third case see *Chertsey cartularies*, **2**, no 676.

155   *Chertsey cartularies*, **1**, nos 169–240, especially 173, 176–7, 195, 207–8, and 230. For a comparable group of assarts in Egham see *ibid*, **2**, no 687

156   This distinction occurs at Egham as late as 1484 (*Chertsey cartularies*, **2**, no 738), and is suggested in a survey of the Chobham glebeland made in 1331 (*ibid*, **1**, no 77).

157   For the same process in the champion country see P D A Harvey, *Medieval Oxfordshire village*, 20–1

158   Brandon, *History of Surrey*, 42

159   Canterbury Cath Lib, Cartae Antiquae W 108–20

160   *Chertsey abstract*, **1**, xxxiv and **2**, no 1150

161   Brit Lib, Add Chs 23080, 22714

162   Fox, The chronology of enclosure and economic development in medieval Devon

163   Dodgshon, *Origin of British field systems*, 155

164   B M S Campbell, Population change and the genesis of commonfields, 174–7, 191–2

165   Fox, Approaches to the adoption of the Midland system, especially his critique of the chronology first proposed by J Thirsk, The common fields. The same problems are discussed by J Z Titow, Medieval England and the open field system; Baker & Butlin, *Studies of field systems*, 650–3; Dodgshon, *Origin of British field systems*, 17–21.

166   For the general line of argument in this paragraph, cf B M S Campbell, Population change and the genesis of commonfields

167   Baker, Field systems in the Vale of Holmesdale, 15; cf Baker & Butlin, *Studies of field systems*, 416–19

Chapter 4

1   Until recently, the standard modern account has been G W O Addleshaw, *The development of the parochial system from Charlemagne to Urban II*, 4–11. The last ten years have produced a flood of new research on the minster system and its collapse. The most recent general survey is W J Blair, Secular minster churches in Domesday Book, which lists other work on 104 n1. There are other relevant papers in W J Blair (ed), *Minsters and parish churches: the local church in transition 950–1200*.

2   M Brett, *The English church under Henry I*, 141–6

3   P H Hase, The development of the parish in Hampshire, 16–34. See also his article based on his thesis: *idem*, The mother churches of Hampshire

4   B R Kemp, The mother church of Thatcham; *idem*, The churches of Berkeley Hernesse

5   See for instance D H Gifford, The parish in Domesday Book. But a different emphasis, which the recent work tends to support, was expressed long ago by W Page, Some remarks on the churches of the Domesday Survey

6   Hase, Parish in Hampshire, 9–10

7   *VCHSy*, **2**, 4

8   cf Hase, Parish in Hampshire

9   W J Blair, Secular minster churches in Domesday Book, 105–6

10   F Barlow, *The English church 1000–1066*, 188; cf W J Blair, Secular minster churches in Domesday Book

11   For the authenticity of the early Chertsey and Barking charters, and their relationship to each other, see above, p178 n19.

12 Bede, *Historia ecclesiastica*, iv.6 (**1**, 218–19); Brit Lib, MS Cotton Vitell A.xiii, f20. See discussions of the foundations in Hart, *Early charters of eastern England*, 117–22, and W J Blair, Frithuwold's kingdom

13 S 1165. Both R Fleming, Monastic lands and England's defence, and Rumble, Place-names and their context, argue for a genuine basis to the Chertsey forgeries.

14 Brit Lib, MS Cotton Vitell A.xiii, ff33–5; *Anglo-Saxon chronicle*, 116. The evidence is printed and discussed by W J Blair, Frithuwold's kingdom, 231–6.

15 For a general account see *VCHSy*, **2**, 55–6

16 BCS no 133; F M Stenton, Medeshamstede and its colonies, in *Preparatory to Anglo-Saxon England*, 186–7

17 S 144. The Chronicle entry under 779 (*Anglo-Saxon chronicle*, 53) is derived from this charter.

18 Fine of 1240, PRO, CP25(i)/226/10(229)

19 *Bracton's note book*, **2**, 586–8. See also *Cal Cur Reg R*, **12**, 310–11

20 Royal inspeximus, charter roll 14 Edward II (PRO, C53/107), m8; printed incompletely in W Dugdale, *Monasticon anglicanum*, **6**, 382. Date: the witnesses include Amicius archdeacon of Surrey, appointed after *c*1190 (J le Neve, *Fasti ecclesiae anglicanae 1066–1300: II: monastic cathedrals*, 94), and Ives, archdeacon of Derby, in office *c*1189–98 (A L Browne, The early archdeacons of Derby, 52–4). The presence of seven witnesses who regularly attest for Godfrey bishop of Winchester (cf for instance Blair, 'Surrey endowments', p120) may suggest that this charter was executed under episcopal advice or pressure; Godfrey's confirmation of it appears in the same inspeximus. For Ruald de Calne and his family see C M H Pearce, An account of the buildings of Newark Priory, 24–32; *The 1235 Surrey eyre*, **1**, 238–40

21 Compare Gilbert Basset's 'foundation charter' of 1182–5 for the Augustinian priory which superseded the old minster of Bicester (Oxfordshire), printed W Kennett, *Parochial antiquities*, **1**, 186: 'Notum sit universitati vestre quod ego dedi et concessi Johanni priori de Bernecestre et canonicis ibidem deo servientibus . . . ecclesiam de Bernecestre cum omnibus pertinentiis suis . . .' In both the Newark and Bicester charters, the other endowments listed are odd collections of small pieces of land which might be interpreted as residual minster glebes.

22 P M Johnston, Send church and the chapel of Ripley

23 R N Bloxam, The dedication of Ripley chapel

24 The fine of 1240 by which Peter de Pirbright acknowledges the Prior of Newark's right to Pirbright chapel as an appurtenance of his church of Woking (n18 above) mentions an earlier grant of his church of Woking. But the royal manor of Woking was never in Peter's hands (*VCHSy*, **3**, 382; cf *The 1235 Surrey eyre*, **1**, 227); the 1240 fine had followed genuine litigation (a plea of last presentation), and it seems very likely that he had only 'granted' Woking church to the canons after failing to establish claims against them. However, a mysterious reference to an early 12th-century grant of Woking church by Ingram d'Abernon to Stoke-by-Clare Priory (Meekings, Notes on the d'Abernon family, 158) may hint at an earlier connection with Pirbright: d'Abernon was elsewhere a Clare tenant, and Pirbright first appears as a member of the honour of Clare.

25 Fine of 1258, PRO, CP25(i)/226/16(113); *Chertsey cartularies*, **1**, no 92

26 Weybridge, *c*1200 (*Chertsey cartularies*, **1**, no 87); St Martha's Chilworth, by 1204 (*Cal Cur Reg R*, **11**, no 2753); and Wanborough, by 1262 (*VCHSy*, **2**, 103; cf *Valor*, **2**, 34)

27 *TPN*, 208 (values of rectory and vicarage combined); the text actually reads 'ecclesia de Farham cum capella', but there is evidence for chapels at both Elstead and Frensham before this date (below, p129), and 'ecclesia de Farnham . . . et capellis adiacentibus eidem' occurs in 1300 (*Registrum Johannis de Pontissara*, **1**, 105).

28 *Valor*, **2**, 32; a fourth chapel, at Bentley, lay over the county boundary (cf n89 below).

29 Illustrated *VCHSy*, **3**, 39. A 9th-century date is claimed for both pieces by D Tweddle, Anglo-Saxon sculpture in south-east England before *c*950, 35–6; this cites artistic parallels and illustrates the major piece.

30 Sarum charters and documents, 3

31 *The register of St Osmund*, **1**, 203, 296–8

32 For the building see S Welman, *The parish and church of Godalming*; *VCHSy*, **3**, 37–40; H M & J Taylor, *Anglo Saxon architecture*, **1**, 258–61

33 *The register of St Osmund*, **1**, 297–8; P Woods, The parsonage or rectory manor of Godalming. In 1291 the rectory and vicarage were taxed at a combined value of £50 (*TPN*, 208).

34   A survey of crown lands in *c*1552 (PRO, LR2/190 f237) notes that 'Laurencius Eliot tenet ad voluntatem unam capellam in Godalmyng vocatam Oldmynster cum cimiterio circumiacente' for 12d p a (I am grateful to Christopher Whittick for this reference). Excavations at Tuesley revealed the footings of a small three-cell church (Welman, *Parish and church of Godalming*, 6; Poulton, *Saxon Surrey*, 204–5), marked on OS Surrey 25" 1 edn. The site is now marked by a modern statue of the Virgin Mary.

35   The later church, on the present interpretation, bears what would normally be considered the earlier dedication. Early dedications to the Virgin do, however, occur, especially for subsidiary churches, and her cult became increasingly popular from the late 8th century; see F Arnold-Foster, *Studies in church dedications*, **1**, 41–2, and A Dornier, The Anglo-Saxon monastery at Breedon-on-the-Hill, 160. Alternatively, it is possible that the dedication of the minster was transferred together with its attributes.

36   *Councils and ecclesiastical documents*, **3**, 617–20. See also Brooks, *Early history of church at Canterbury*, 197–203

37   Illustrated W E St L Finny, The Saxon church at Kingston, pl opp 212

38   *VCHSy*, **3**, 487; *Anglo-Saxon chronicle*, 105, 122–3

39   John Leland's 'Collectanea', **1** (Bod Lib, MS Top Gen c.1), p67; printed *Johannis Lelandi antiquarii de rebus Britannicis collectanea*, **1**, 70

40   Brit Lib, MS Cotton Cleop C.vii, ff59ᵛ, 60, 66ᵛ, 67; f99ᵛ. The source for Leland's statement that Henry II appropriated Kingston church to Merton Priory (*The itinerary of John Leland*, **7–8**, 85) has not been traced.

41   Brit Lib, MS Cotton Cleop C.vii, ff61ᵛ–62. Richard bishop of Winchester confirms the early endowments 'sicut pie recordationis H quondam Winton' episcopus decessor noster ea vobis episcopali auctoritate confirmavit, in quibis h' propriis duximus exprimendi vocabulis: villam ipsam de Meriton etc.' The original presumably recited Henry's confirmation *in toto*.

42   Private Act, 9 Geo III cap 5; cf *Valor*, **2**, 36. Kew parish was formed out of Sheen (modern Richmond) at the same date.

43   Brit Lib, MS Cotton Cleop C.vii, ff124–5; the men of Petersham are described as 'parochianos ecclesie de Kyng'', and the chaplain of Petersham is to operate 'iure dicte matris ecclesie de Kyngestone integro remanente'.

44   Thames Ditton, now in Elmbridge hundred, was in Kingston hundred in 1086, but this fact is probably of little importance given the close administrative links between the two hundreds.

45   Both appear in the episcopal confirmation (n 41 above); see also *Plac Abbrev*, 50 (Malden), and *Bracton's note book*, **3**, 467 (Long Ditton).

46   These paragraphs summarise an argument set out in full in W J Blair, The origins of Leatherhead parish church.

47   *Cartularium monasterii Sancti Johannis Baptiste de Colecestria*, **1**, 1–4. This charter is heavily inflated, but the phrase recurs in genuine royal confirmations and agrees too well with the other evidence to be dismissed as a forger's invention.

48   Brit Lib, MS Cotton Cleop C.vii, f103. Merton Priory had acquired Ewell manor from the crown in 1158 (above, p48).

49   Gifford, Parish in Domesday Book, 252–8, concludes that *valet* applied to a Domesday church generally refers to the value of the glebe, excluding other ecclesiastical revenues. If Leatherhead church was farmed on the terms which she proposes as normal, a fixed annual sum need not necessarily have been affected by the disappearance of the building.

50   W J Blair, Origins of Leatherhead parish church.

51   G Dennis, Southwark, Hibernia Wharf; Bird *et al*, Archaeology in Surrey, 1979–80, 154. M B Honeybourne, The pre-Norman bridge of London, 28–9, points out the connection, though she unaccountably tries to identify the *monasterium* with St Olave's church.

52   J Stow, *A survey of London*, **2**, 56

53   Brit Lib, MS Cotton Faust A.viii, f133ʳ; a late medieval hand has written against the entry 'per W Gifford'.

54   College of Arms, MS Vincent 46 (notes from lost Southwark cartulary), p113

55   It has been argued, very unconvincingly, that the Priory church incorporates the shell of a late Saxon minster with a westwork (J T Smith, The pre-Conquest minster at Southwark).

56   See J C Dickinson, *The origins of the Austin canons and their introduction into England*, 119–20; but cf criticisms in D Knowles & R N Hadcock, *Medieval religious houses: England and Wales*, 174. The narrative sources associating the foundation with Bishop William Giffard and William de Pont de l'Arche are late though to some extent supported by charter evidence; the statement that Giffard instituted secular canons at Southwark (Dugdale, *Monasticon*, **6**, 171, derived from late medieval notes transcribed in Oxford, Corpus Christi College, MS D256, f197r) has no known early authority. References in the Bermondsey and Worcester Annals and by Matthew Paris to the foundation of the Priory in 1106 all derive from the Southwark Annals (not from Florence of Worcester as Dickinson states in the second case); see N Denholm-Young, The Winchester-Hyde chronicle.

57   See W J Blair, Secular minster churches in Domesday Book, 138 and n173

58   *Regesta regum anglo-normannorum*, **1**, nos 301–2; Brit Lib, Campb Ch vii.1 and Cotton Ch. viii.10. These two 'originals', however, are forgeries: see M Brett, Forgery at Rochester, in *Fälschungen im mittelalter* (MGH 33, iv, Hannover, 1988), 403, 405. Rochester's later claim that Godgifu had given them the manor before the Conquest (J Thorpe, *Registrum Roffense*, 2) was presumably baseless.

59   *DB* 66a

60   cf Gifford, Parish in Domesday Book, 162

61   It is curious, but perhaps merely coincidental, that Archbishop Baldwin chose Lambeth as the site of his proposed college of secular canons in 1188; see *VCHSy*, **2**, 127, and Canterbury Cathedral Library, Cartae Antiquae L 129–38.

62   Thorpe, *Registrum Roffense*, 119

63   The tentative identification with Warmington (Northamptonshire) proposed by Knowles & Hadcock, *Medieval religious houses*, 485, is etymologically impossible.

64   Information from John Schofield. I am grateful to Jeffrey West for the view that in its abraded state the fragment is almost impossible to date, and may well be much later.

65   For the problems of the 1082 and 1089 dates see R Graham, *English ecclesiastical studies*, 92–7. For the architectural implications see R D H Gem, The Romanesque architecture of Old St Paul's Cathedral and its late 11th-century context (forthcoming)

66   This was ruinous and used as a barn in the 18th century (*VCHSy*, **4**, 169). It is mentioned in a deed of 1295 and a lease of 1502 (Brit Lib, Add Chs 23671, 23409). The site has been excavated and the simple plan recovered; burials associated with it were found in 1976, overlying probable mid-Saxon occupation and ovens (Orton, Excavations at 32 Burleigh Avenue, Wallington). K W Muckleroy, Woodcote, or Woodcote Warren, 42–4, is surely wrong in locating the chapel at Woodcote.

67   Brooks, *Early history of church of Canterbury*, 106–7; *DB* 30d (II.1)

68   BCS, no 328

69   S 1511

70   In 1291 the rectory and vicarage were taxed at a combined value of £50 (*TPN*, 208); cf *Valor*, **2**, 59. All churches in Croydon deanery were peculiars of the see of Canterbury.

71   *VCHSy*, **4**, 288–90; notes about the manor and advowson in PRO, E41/330 (late medieval collection of deed transcripts)

72   S 1511

73   'Wolcensted' is the usual late medieval spelling, and 'Strættune' is probably Stratton in Godstone parish: *PNSy*, 319–20.

74   It is an odd coincidence, but probably no more, that yet another Augustinian house, Tandridge Priory, was founded nearby in the late 12th century (*VCHSy*, **2**, 112).

75   For such an argument applied to one county see Hase, Parish in Hampshire, 13; for the ways in which patronage of minsters may have utilised existing systems of secular obligation, see J Campbell (ed), *The Anglo-Saxons*, 61

76   cf C R Hart, *Early charters of eastern England*, 117–22

77   F M Stenton, Medeshamstede and its colonies, 182; Dornier, The Anglo-Saxon monastery at Breedon-on-the-Hill, 157–8; W J Blair, Frithuwold's kingdom, 105–6

78   Dornier, Anglo-Saxon monastery at Breedon, 159–60

79   See the various papers by J Haslam, especially his Parishes, churches, wards and gates in eastern London, 35–43

80   Thus the striking concentration of minsters in East Kent (Gifford, Parish in Domesday Book, 145–54;

Barlow, *English church 1000–1066*, 181) is clearly due to the ecclesiastical importance of Canterbury. It is worth stressing the abnormality of this much-quoted example.

81 Hase, Parish in Hampshire, 1–3, 38–40; Page, Remarks on churches of Domesday Survey, 79–83 (and for Sussex see also W Hudson, The ancient deaneries of the Diocese of Chichester); O J Reichel, The church and the hundreds of Devon. See also W J Blair, Secular minster churches in Domesday Book, 118–19 and n56

82 See comments in J Campbell (ed), *Essays in Anglo-Saxon history*, 140–2, and the evidence for settlement growth within monastic precincts discussed by W J Blair, Minster churches in the landscape, 47–50.

83 This is close to the position in Hampshire, where Hase (Parish in Hampshire, 1) concludes that even in the 8th century nowhere was more than six miles from a church.

84 See W J Blair, Secular minster churches in Domesday Book

85 *ibid*, 113–14

86 *ibid*, 124–6

87 *VCHBucks*, **1**, 266b; *VCHBeds*, **1**, 227b, 264a

88 J le Neve, *Fasti ecclesiae anglicanae 1066–1300: I: St Paul's Cathedral*, 69; this Osbern was succeeded in the prebend by his son Robert de Auco, who first appears as a canon in 1111/2.

89 *VCHSussex*, **1**, 393a, 395b, 406a; this last entry relates to a royal charter of 1070/1, falsified in its present form, which confirms a gift to Battle Abbey by Osbern son of Hugh de Eu, with the consent of his lord the count of Eu (*Regesta regum anglo-normannorum*, **2**, addenda, 391, no 59a). Land at Bentley held of the bishop of Winchester by Osbern in 1086 (*VCHHants*, **1**, 463b) was probably the half-hide in Hampshire mentioned in the Domesday entry for Farnham church (cf. note 28 above).

90 On Regenbald, and this kind of ecclesiastical pluralist generally, see J Campbell, *Essays in Anglo-Saxon history*, 149–50; W J Blair, Secular minster churches in Domesday Book

91 This interpretation of Domesday *valet* proposed by Gifford, Parish in Domesday Book, 254–8, seems convincing, though it need not be confined, as she implies, to episcopal churches.

92 Cf Gifford, Parish in Domesday Book, 187–8. Even in so late a source as the 1291 taxation, the former minsters are notable for their high valuations. For mother church glebes see Gifford, Parish in Domesday Book, 159–62; Hase, Parish in Hampshire 37–8

93 For the central argument of this section see W J Blair, Secular minster churches in Domesday Book, 131–7

94 Hase, Parish in Hampshire, 181ff; *idem*, The mother churches of Hampshire

95 See A R Dufty, The parish church of St Andrew, Farnham

96 Plan in *VCHSy*, **3**, 509; see also Finny, Saxon church at Kingston. Taylor & Taylor, *Anglo-Saxon architecture*, **2**, 353, are surely wrong in calling the chapel Anglo-Saxon.

97 *Itinerary of John Leland*, **7–8**, 85

98 WAM, 1836

99 PRO, E40/14192, a Lewes Priory deed calendared L F Salzman, *Chartulary of the Priory of St Pancras of Lewes*, **2**, 99–100. Lewes probably acquired Stoke church during 1148 × 59 (W J Blair, Surrey endowments of Lewes Priory). Was 'Gilebertus decanus' the rural dean or dean of a college? Brett, *Church under Henry I*, 213, sees no antecedents to English rural deaneries, but the possibility of some institutional continuity in cases where old minsters became the head churches of deaneries would be worth pursuing.

100 See D M Robinson, *The geography of Augustinian settlement in England and Wales*, 174–7

101 M Chibnall, Monks and pastoral work: a problem in Anglo-Norman history, minimises the pastoral involvement of monks. But for a vigorous statement of the alternative view see G Constable, Monasteries, rural churches and the *cura animarum* in the early Middle Ages, 349–89

102 Which might, for instance, include compulsory visits to the mother church on certain feast-days

103 Such as suggested by Gifford, Parish in Domesday Book, 274–5

104 Thus there is no likelihood of a pre-Conquest origin for any of the pensions or portions in the Surrey sections of *TPN* or *Valor*. Enforcement of burial in the mother-church cemetery is only recorded in cases of chapelries of late foundation (Windlesham to Woking, p95 above) or within the same estate (Chobham to Chertsey, p155 below). Contrast Hase, Parish in Hampshire, passim; Kemp, Mother church of Thatcham; and Churches of Berkeley Hernesse; several papers in W J Blair (ed), *Minsters and parish churches*.

105 Contrast the west-country evidence in Gifford, Parish in Domesday Book, 97–100, and R W Dunning, The minster at Crewkerne, 63–7

106 Richard fitz Gilbert's grant of two-thirds demesne tithe-portions (below, p148), must have harmed it considerably.

107 cf the examples of minster authority linked with tenurial unity cited Brett, *Church under Henry I*, 223

Chapter 5

1 Eadgar II.2; see Hase, Parish in Hampshire, 25–7

2 FM Stenton, The thriving of the Anglo-Saxon ceorl, 383–93

3 The best general account remains that of Lennard, *Rural England*, ch 10. Gifford, Parish in Domesday Book, provides a meticulous analysis of all the Domesday data for churches. See also W J Blair, Local churches in Domesday Book and before

4 Miller & Hatcher, *Medieval England*, 107

5 V H Galbraith, *The making of Domesday Book*

6 For the rest of this paragraph and the next two, see Gifford, Parish in Domesday Book, 91–117, and W J Blair, Local churches in Domesday Book and before

7 Gifford, Parish in Domesday Book, 91–6

8 Lennard, *Rural England*, 293–4, and evidence cited there

9 Lingfield and Sanderstead; probably Wotton, Thursley and Godstone; and perhaps Thorncroft and Blechingley

10 *Reg Pontissara*, 606–9

11 *TPN*, 206–9

12 E Fernie, *The architecture of the Anglo-Saxons*, 171

13 R Gem, The English parish church in the 11th and 12th centuries: a great rebuilding?, 21–30

14 Poverty and decay in the early modern period, followed by Victorian prosperity and suburban growth, resulted in the rebuilding or savage restoration of many Surrey churches, often those which had retained their early form most completely and were hence small and inconvenient. The main collections of drawings used here are those in the Minet Library (Petrie, Porden and Hassell), Bodleian Library (Hussey), and British Library (extra-illustrated Manning & Bray, *History of Surrey*, shelfmark Crack.1.Tab.1.b.1).

15 cf Sawyer, *From Roman Britain to Norman England*, 91–3; R Morris, *The church in British archaeology*, 19–48

16 B Cherry, Ecclesiastical architecture, 156–8. On Canterbury cf, however, Brooks, *Early history of church of Canterbury*, 16–22

17 W Rodwell & K Rodwell, *Historic churches: a wasting asset*

18 W J Blair, Churches, in A A Jackson (ed), *Ashtead: a village transformed*, 117–18

19 K Cameron, Eccles in English place-names; Gelling, Latin loan-words

20 This is the correct reading of the MS (a 13th-century cartulary copy, Brit Lib MS Cotton Claud B. vi, f55), misspelt in the *PNSy* analysis.

21 An alternative interpretation, but one which spaces the boundary-points less evenly, would be to place *mylen felda* near modern Millbrook; this would leave *eceles hamme* at the north-west corner of Horsell parish, further but still not very far from Bisley church. This site, nearer the river, would suggest a rendering of *hamme* as 'meadow' rather than 'enclosure' (but cf above, p46).

22 *DB* 32d (VIII.22). No early details remain in the simple aisleless nave, but a watercolour (Brit Lib Crack.1.Tab.1.b.1, vol xviii, before p 190) shows a round-headed north door.

23 In a compound minor name such as this the derivation from *eclesia* is not conclusive, though the most likely. cf *eceles beorh*, in an area of Iron Age occupation on the Berkshire Downs, in charter bounds which also include a *halige stowe* (Gelling, *Place-names of Berkshire*, 3, 682–3, 686)

24 *VCHSy*, 3, 398. cf now the discussion of holy wells in Everitt, *Continuity and colonisation*, 296–300.

25   Arnold-Foster, *Studies in dedications*, **2**, 509–11, 559–60; *PNSy*, 244–5

26   Everitt, *Continuity and colonisation*, 196–8

27   *DB* 30c (I. 12–13). For Shere see *VCHSy*, **2**, 434; **3**, 117–21; for Dorking see W J Blair, Surrey endowments of Lewes Priory, 104–5

28   *VCHSy*, **3**, 240. The early name of Reigate, *Cherchefelle*, might mean 'church field', though variant spellings make this etymologically unlikely (see *PNSy*, 281–2). The earliest written reference to the church is in 1106 or soon after (below, p146). For excavated evidence for 11th- and 12th-century occupation near Reigate church, see Poulton, Excavations on the site of the Old Vicarage, Church Street, Reigate, 1977–82, Part 1, Saxo-Norman and earlier discoveries, 25–36. (This publishes an orientated burial, some 300 m north-west of the church, which could be a remnant of a Christian Anglo-Saxon cemetery.)

29   Reigate church was later appropriated to Southwark Priory, which had 87 acres in demesne and numerous tenant holdings there in *c*1300 (Brit Lib, MS Cotton Faust A.viii, ff155–7). For Shalford rectory manor see *VCHSy*, **3**, 110. The glebe of Shere church was 80 acres in 1535 (*Valor*, **2**, 29), and would have been much bigger if the glebes of Cranleigh (below, p139) and Ewhurst (32 acres, *Valor*, **2**, 30) were partitioned from it. The 1291 values were: Dorking £66 13s 4d, Reigate £18 16s 8d, Shalford £36 13s 4d, Shere £23 6s 8d (*TPN*, 208).

30   For excavations at Wotton see D J Fowler, Wotton: excavations at St John's church; J B Thomas (ed), *St John's Wotton*. The excavator interprets the present west tower as the axial tower of an early Norman church, later extended eastwards and with the original nave demolished. However, inspection of the standing fabric suggests that the tower is built up against the west end of an earlier nave, the west wall of which, pierced by a Norman arch, survives as the east wall of the tower. On this hypothesis, all four nave walls (including the chancel-arch wall) are 70–72cm thick and may therefore be pre-Conquest.

31   *TPN*, 208. For Barnes as a chapel of Wimbledon see below, p204 n117; Putney and Mortlake chapels are both late medieval.

32   *TPN*, 208

33   *VCHSy*, **3**, 456

34   Inexplicably, it was established in 1279 that tithes at Ottershaw, deep in Chertsey Abbey territory, were due to the rector of Walton-on-Thames in the right of his church (*Chertsey cartularies*, **1**, 95)

35   *DB* 35b (XIX.26), 34d (XIX.11), 35a (XIX.23), 35a-b (XIX.24)

36   cf H Cam, The 'private' hundred in England before the Norman Conquest

37   For parallel cases in Hampshire, linked with the appearance of ecclesiastical franchise hundreds, see Hase, Parish in Hampshire, 293–308

38   Brit Lib, MS Cotton Vesp D.ix, f32

39   See M Deanesly, The late Old English church: bishops and pastoral care

40   Great Bookham, *DB* 32d (VIII.17); Chobham, *DB* 32d (VIII.22); Coulsdon, *DB* 32c (VIII.2); Epsom, *DB* 32c (VIII.9); Petersham, *DB* 32d (VIII.14); Sutton, *DB* 32c (VIII.3); Tooting, *DB* 33a-b (VIII.25); Waddington, *DB* 32c (VIII.1)

41   East Clandon, *DB* 34a (VIII.29); Cobham, *DB* 32c (VIII.6); Malden, *DB* 32d (VIII.13); East Molesey, *DB* 35b (XIX.30)

42   In neither case is there any other candidate for the second church. For Ewell, see *VCHSy*, **3**, 283. The first subsequent reference is in each case in 1176 (*Papsturkunden in England*, 406).

43   Waddington church was a chapel of Coulsdon in 1291 (*TPN*, 207), disused by the 16th century and destroyed in *c*1780 (*VCHSy*, **4**, 205). It is probably identifiable with a building excavated in 1966, associated with burials and with pottery spanning the 12th to mid 14th centuries. ([Anon], The search for the 'lost' village of Watendone; D J Turner, Medieval pottery from Watendone, Kenley)

44   See Ketteringham, Excavations at the church of St John the Evangelist, Coulsdon. The original walls were only 76cm thick.

45   The nave of Great Bookham church, which has plain single-splayed windows in walls only 76cm thick, might also be pre-Conquest; see Johnston, Great Bookham church, and Renn, The early church at Great Bookham, which suggests that the shell of the chancel is contemporary with the nave, possibly with an axial tower. Except at Tooting, there is no evidence in churches of this group of

substantial Norman work which would suggest a post-Conquest but pre-Domesday building.

46   *Anglo-Saxon chronicle*, 215.

47   *DB* 30d–31a (II.3)

48   *DB* 30d (II.1)

49   *DB* 31a (II.5)

50   *DB* 30d (II.2)

51   *DB* 31a (II.6)

52   *DB* 31a (II.4)

53   S 1641

54   Taylor & Taylor, *Anglo-Saxon architecture*, **1**, 153–4; D H Farmer, *The Oxford dictionary of saints*, 113

55   Made 1746, reproduced C J Marshall, *A history of the old villages of Cheam and Sutton*, 23

56   The tower is built of small flint rubble, with a capping-course of dressed blocks, surmounted by later heightening. One standard single-splayed window (illustrated fig 30) remains in the west wall. A high early arch is said to have existed between tower and nave (*VCHSy*, **3**, 351–2). For an excavated Sussex parallel for this unusual plan see O Bedwin, The excavation of the church of St Nicholas, Angmering, 1974.

57   On other monastic and episcopal properties in the county, even relatively valuable ones, churches are conspicuously lacking. cf the manors of Westminster Abbey (*DB* 32b (VI.2–3)); Barking Abbey (*DB* 34a (XII.1–2); the bishop of Exeter (*DB* 31a-b (IV.1)); St Paul's Cathedral (*DB* 34a (XIII.1), 30d (II.3)); Hyde Abbey (*DB* 32b–c (VII.1)); and the bishop of Winchester (*DB* 31a (III.1)). At Farnham the minster had of course existed from an earlier period (above, p97), while the Hyde Abbey churches of Sanderstead and Lingfield (neither mentioned by Domesday Book) had apparently existed before Hyde acquired the manors (above, p114).

58   Churches are mentioned on Harold's manors at Merton, Limpsfield and Bermondsey (*DB* 30b (I.5); 34a (XI.1); 30b (I.4); but see above, p102 for Bermondsey). At Wotton, Domesday probably omits a church (above, p113). The only churches listed on former manors of Swein and Leofwine were at Gatton (but cf below, p122) and Wanborough (*DB* 31c-d (V.11); 36b (XXV.3)).

59   *DB* 36b (XXIV.1); 34b (XV.1)

60   For Witley, see Johnston, An early window and wall paintings in Witley church, and the same author's articles on Thursley; Taylor & Taylor, *Anglo-Saxon architecture*, **2**, 676–8. The wall paintings are discussed by D Park, The Romanesque wall paintings of All Saints' church, Witley, Surrey, the critical evidence being presented on 158 and 164–5. For Thursley see Johnston, The church of Witley and Thursley chapel-of-ease, and *idem*, Witley and Thursley churches: recent discoveries; Taylor & Taylor, *Anglo-Saxon architecture*, **2**, 916–18

61   Everitt, *Continuity and colonisation*, 252

62   Godstone, Addington and Tooting (*DB* 34b (XV.2); 36d (XXXIV.1); 33a-b (VIII.26)). See above, p103 for Godstone minster; Addington and Tooting churches were probably Norman foundations (below, pp124, 122).

63   Malden and Streatham (*DB* 35a (XIX.23); 34d (XIX.11)) had chapels, but the latter case was probably a post-Conquest foundation by the monks of Bec who held the manor of Richard fitz Gilbert.

64   Long Ditton and Ockham (*DB* 35a (XIX.21); 35d (XIX.45))

65   *DB* 34d–35a (XIX.15–16); 35c (XIX.36); 34d (XIX.6, not named but identified from later descent); 34a (VIII.30))

66   The manors ascribed to Azur which lack churches are at Walton-on-Thames, Effingham and Hambledon (*DB* 36b (XXVII.1); 35d (XIX.44); 36b (XXVII.2)).

67   See Johnston, Albury old church; Taylor & Taylor, *Anglo-Saxon architecture*, **1**, 19–20

68   He is discussed by C A R Radford, The church of St Mary, Stoke D'Abernon, Surrey, 171.

69   *DB* 36a (XXII.1)

70   *DB* 36b (XXII.5)

71   *DB* 35b (XIX.32)

72   *DB* 31c (V.10)

73   Johnston, Stoke D'Abernon church; *idem*, Stoke D'Abernon church: some recent discoveries; Taylor & Taylor, *Anglo-Saxon architecture*, **2**, 573–4

74   Radford, Church of St Mary, Stoke D'Abernon. The comparisons made here with early Kentish apses have little weight; whereas the long-and-short quoins which formerly existed on the west corners of the nave are a specifically 10th- or 11th-century feature (Fernie, *Architecture of the Anglo-Saxons*, 144–5).

75   Radford, Church of Stoke D'Abernon

76   See photograph in *VCHSy*, **3**, opp 22. Taylor & Taylor, *Anglo-Saxon architecture*, **1**, 172, are unaccountably sceptical; the tower, with rubble quoins and windows with non-radial rubble voussoirs, adjoins (possibly as a later addition) a high, thin-walled nave.

77   The early Norman tower is butted up against an earlier nave with walls only 80cm thick; see Johnston, West Horsley church.

78   *VCHSy*, **1**, 282–3. Mortimer, Beginnings of honour of Clare, 125, seems unnecessarily cautious about the identity of 'Alnod': the suffix 'cild' suggests that the Surrey man was of notable importance.

79   *DB* 34c (XIX.2)

80   *DB* 34c (XIX.1)

81   *DB* 31c (V.8)

82   *DB* 34d (XIX.5)

83   *DB* 34d (XIX.14)

84   *DB* 31b (V.1a)

85   The nave shells at Banstead and Tillingdown (Tandridge) suggest pre-Conquest building methods, but the evidence is far from conclusive. *VCHSy*, **3**, 260–2 (Banstead, commenting on the high, thin walls of the nave, which pre-dates enlargements of *c*1200); *VCHSy*, **4**, 324–6 (Tandridge, with plan showing that the early Norman chancel deviates from the axis of a probably earlier nave)

86   *VCHSy*, **3**, 86, 127; *Reg Pontissara*, 26–7; *Cal Charter R*, **3**, 52. cf *Cal Cur Reg R*, **1**, 61, 88, and *Bracton's note book*, **2**, no 913. A late 16th-century set of depositions (SRO, LM 454) complains that Shalford is the mother church even though Bramley has more households, which 'have had alleweyes service in the church of Bramley tyme out of mynde': 'the township of Bramley hathe byn ever severed from Shalford by the holywater weke, . . . and hath had allso all the sacramentes mynistred in the church of Bramlye, onlye buryall excepted for the wich we pay unto Shaulford onlye vj d a yere'. I am very grateful to Elizabeth Stazicker for this reference.

87   It was wholly rebuilt in the late 18th century.

88   *VCHSy*, **3**, 85–6

89   Wonersh; *VCHSy*, **3**, 124–6; J C Cox, *The little guide to Surrey*, 209. Manning & Bray, *History of Surrey*, **2**, 112, give the dimensions of the early nave before shortening. Hascombe: painting and notes by R C Hussey, 1845, Bodl Lib MS Top Gen f18, ff35ᵛ–36; painting by H Petrie, 1808, Minet Library, LO9541/66; dimensions given by Manning & Bray, *History of Surrey*, **2**, 66

90   West Molesey (£5), *DB* 36d (XXXV.2); Esher (£5), *DB* 34a, 36d (X.1, XXXV.1; TRW valuation only); Farleigh (£3), *DB* 34d (XIX.8); Rodsell (£2), *DB* 31b (V.2)

91   Mickleham (£5), *DB* 35a (XIX.19); Fetcham (£4), *DB* 36d (XXXVI.3); Effingham (£2), *DB* 32d (VIII.20); *Pechingeorde* (£2), *DB* 36d (XXXVI.1); Wisley (£2), *DB* 36d (XXXVI.5); Worth (£1 10s), *DB* 34d (XIX.13)

92   Titsey (£10), *DB* 36c (XXX.1); Tadworth (£5), *DB* 35d (XX.1); Little Bookham (£2 10s), *DB* 35d (XX.2)

93   Betchworth (£9), *DB* 35d (XIX.47); Thorncroft (£5), *DB* 35c (XIX.39); Coombe (£3), *DB* 36d (XXXVI.8; TRW valuation only)

94   This capital, of multi-stepped profile, is now incorporated in a window in the Victorian north aisle; this was built immediately after the demolition of the Norman central tower and incorporates fragments from it, so it seems likely that the capital had been re-used there.

95   Lennard, *Rural England*, 290–1

96   *DB* 36b (XXV.2); *VCHSy*, **4**, 185–8. This church can be reconstructed from the existing building in conjunction with a pre-restoration plan (Victoria & Albert Museum, Dept of Prints and Drawings, E1104–1930). Cf also Drury & Rodwell, Investigations at Asheldham

97   The Norman church can be reconstructed from watercolours in the Minet Library (SP 190/713 etc), the block-plan in C T Cracklow, *Views of the churches and chapels-of-ease in the county of Surrey*, and the existing building (which retains the tower arch capitals re-set).

98   *VCHSy*, **3**, 474–5; J W L Forge, The church of St Mary, Walton-on-Thames. The nave is featureless but pre-dates a mid 12th-century aisle.

99   W J Blair, Origins of Leatherhead parish church; idem in Vardey (ed.), *Hist. of Leatherhead*, 273–5

100 U Lambert, *Blechingley: a parish history*, **2**, 334–48; C R B King, St Mary's church, Blechingley, and *idem*, The tower of St Mary's church, Blechingley

101 Of Richard's other demesne manors in 1086, Stoke D'Abernon retained its Anglo-Saxon church, while the structural evidence for Woodmansterne and Ockham has been lost.

102 *DB* 31c (V.9)

103 *DB* 36b (XXVII.3)

104 *DB* 34d (XIX.7)

105 *DB* 35a (XIX.21)

106 *DB* 31c–d (V.11)

107 *DB* 33a–b (VIII.25)

108 Chaldon: *VCHSy*, **4**, 191–4. Gatton: no early detail now remains, but a watercolour (Minet Library, K31660/57) shows a small round tower on the north side, apparently with a Norman window. Tooting: the demolished old church had a round tower with Norman windows (drawings etc in Brit Lib, Crack 1.Tab.1.b.1, xxiii, before and after 375; Brit Lib, MS Add 36389, f57; Minet Library, LP25/713, SP25/713; see also M Keulemans, Old St Nicholas' church, Tooting-Graveney).

109 Arnold-Foster, *Studies in dedications*, **2**, 111–13; Farmer, *Oxford dictionary of saints*, 244

110 Of all Surrey manors with TRW listed populations of less than nine, only Tooting (five) and Chaldon (nil) have churches.

111 If, as seems likely from parallel cases, the Hascombe apse was a Norman addition.

112 The church is first mentioned *c*1270 (*Reg Pontissara*, 608). Only the remodelled shell of the early building remains.

113 *DB* 35c (XIX.37); Brit Lib, Add MS 6167, f370^v

114 See *VCHSy*, **3**, 79–80. Although no early features remain, the late 12th-century south arcade pierces an earlier nave wall only 69cm thick.

115 See for instance Lennard, *Rural England*, 319ff

116 cf Lennard, *Rural England*, 296–8

117 The earliest building seems to have been of one cell: its south doorway of *c*1100 was discovered in 1980, and the early plan has been elucidated (see D J Turner, Archaeology of Surrey, 1066 to 1540, 235–6). The first known reference is in 1181 (*The Domesday of St Paul's*, 151). Documents from a late 12th-century presentation dispute (Guildhall Library, MSS 25122/641, 1426, 1428) show that Barnes church was considered a chapel of Wimbledon.

118 St Olave's was given to Lewes Priory by the Warennes before 1121 (W J Blair, Surrey endowments of Lewes Priory, 99–100); St Margaret's to Southwark Priory by Bishop Giffard between 1107 and 1129 (inspeximus, PRO, C53/131, m3) and St George's to Bermondsey Abbey by Thomas de Ardern in 1122 (*Annales monastici*, **3**, 433).

119 J H Parker, The church of St Mary, Guildford; *VCHSy*, **3**, 563–7; Taylor & Taylor, *Anglo-Saxon architecture*, **1**, 266–8; F W Holling, The early foundations of St Mary's church, Guildford

120 *VCHSy*, **3**, 567–8

121 M L Colker, Latin texts concerning Gilbert, founder of Merton Priory; *VCHSy*, **4**, 67–8. I am grateful to Freda Anderson for pointing out to me the relatively late date of the architectural features.

122 cf Everitt, *Continuity and colonisation*, 198–205. Although Everitt's chronology for Kent is rather earlier than my own for Surrey, his model of church-building in a context of manorial proliferation is very apposite.

123 *DB* 31d (V.19); Round, Bernard, the king's scribe. Hugh Laval succeeded Ilbert in other TRW manors of Odo. For the building see M Biddle, Nonsuch Palace 1959–60: an interim report. The date of *c*1100 is that proposed by the excavator; the wall-thicknesses suggest that the builders were working in the pre-Conquest tradition.

124 *Cartularium Monasterii de Colecestria*, **1**, 78; W J Blair in Jackson (ed), *Ashtead: a village transformed*, 116–19

125 *DB* 35d (XX.2); *VCHSy*, **3**, 337–8; J H Harvey, A short history of Bookham, 12–13

126 *VCHSy*, **3**, 288–90, **2**, 446; Taylor & Taylor, *Anglo-Saxon architecture*, **1**, 40; Renn, The early church at Fetcham. For origins cf *VCHSy*, **3**, 285–7; the other Domesday third, later held by Merton Priory, is probably ruled out by the absence of any claim to Fetcham church on the part of Merton. Fetcham church occurs *c*1270, and the d'Abernons presented to it in 1284 (*Reg Pontissara*, 607, 16–17).

127 *VCHSy*, **3**, 321–5. The statement that William Dammartin gave the church to Merton apparently cannot be substantiated.

128 *VCHSy*, **4**, 166–8. The destroyed west tower, chancel arch and north nave wall appear in a plan in Bodl Lib, MS Top Gen c.80, f3; see also plan and views in Minet Library, SP49/713, S4822 pls 5301–6.

129 Bartholomew's original charter (SRO, 2609/11/5/1) grants the church with 24 acres 'quas avus meus et pater meus ecclesie illi in liberam et perpetuam elemosinam dederunt'.

130 *VCHSy*, **4**, 282–3, 326–30. For Farleigh see also Johnston, Notes on the history and architecture of Farley church.

131 *VCHSy*, **4**, 268–9 (where the apse evidence is overlooked); noted by G M Livett, Whitfield alias Beuesfeld. The origins of this church are obscure.

132 W J Blair, The destroyed medieval church at Headley

133 *VCHSy*, **3**, 291

134 *VCHSy*, **3**, 88–9, 104–6

135 *VCHSy*, **3**, 105–6. The church is now largely rebuilt, but several drawings and engravings (eg Brit Lib, Crack. 1.Tab. 1.b.1, ix, 118–20) show the ruins of the west tower.

136 *VCHSy*, **3**, 316, 318–19

137 College of Arms, MS Vincent 46, p125; Dugdale, *Monasticon*, **6**, 172–3

138 Arnold-Foster, *Studies in dedications*, **2**, 111–13; Farmer, *Oxford dictionary of saints*, 244

139 cf *1235 Eyre*, **1**, 252–5

140 cf R N Bloxam, A Surrey charter of King John

141 cf *Sir Christopher Hatton's book of seals*, 72

142 cf L F Salzman, Sussex Domesday tenants: 4: the family of Chesney or Cheyney, 45–6

143 *DB* 31d (V.20, 19), 35a (XIX.17)

144 *DB* 36d (XXXVI.7), 36c (XXXII.1)

145 *DB* 36b (XXVII.2)

146 College of Arms, MS Vincent 46, p114

147 W J Blair, Surrey endowments of Lewes Priory, 109–11, 117–18

148 *VCHSy*, **4**, 279–81; Arnold-Foster, *Studies in dedications*, **2**, 471–3; Farmer, *Oxford dictionary of saints*, 166. The church is first mentioned in *c*1270 (*Reg Pontissara*, 606).

149 *VCHSy*, **3**, 180–2; W J Blair, Surrey endowments of Lewes Priory, 100, 102

150 Eadmer, *Historia novorum in Anglia*, 108–10

151 *VCHSy*, **3**, 85–6; pre-restoration external view, Minet Library, K31660/17. First specifically mentioned 1305 (*Cal Charter R*, **3**, 52)

152 This church served Artington, a member of Godalming royal manor; it was in the hands of Salisbury Cathedral by 1324 (*VCHSy*, **3**, 570), but it does not appear in the 1220 Godalming survey (below, pp157–8) and was probably acquired after that date. Rebuilt 1836 and 1875–6, but earlier notes say that 'the lower part [of the west tower] opens by 3 plain arches, one of which is semicircular and has Norman shafts . . . The South aisle has at the west end a Norman window' (R J Sherlock, Sir Stephen Glynne's notes on churches in Surrey, 90–1).

153 First mentioned 1208 (*Rotuli litterarum patentium*, **1**, 78b). Rebuilt 1881; fragments remain of a mid 12th-century door and south arcade, and a painting of 1839 (Bodl Lib, MS Top Gen f13, f70) shows a plain Norman west tower.

154 *VCHSy*, **3**, 57–8; first mentioned *c*1270 (*Reg Pontissara*, 608)

155 cf the consecration of cemeteries *ad refugium* noted by B R Kemp in W J Blair (ed), *Minsters and parish churches*, 86–9

156 *Papsturkunden*, **1**, no 137; cf *Chertsey cartularies*, **1**, no 46

157 Chertsey: nothing now Romanesque, but in 1808 '12th cent. arcades and other interesting features were swept away' (Cox, *Little guide to Surrey*, 78). Egham: the old church had a mid 12th-century north door and south arcade (F Turner, *Egham, Surrey*, 77; print in Brit Lib, Crack 1 Tab 1.b.1, xix, after 258). Thorpe: remains of 12th-century chancel arch (*VCHSy*, **3**, 439; pre-restoration drawing in Brit Lib, Crack. 1 Tab. 1.b.1, xix, 234–5). Cobham: mid 12th-century nave and west tower (*VCHSy*, **3**, 445–6). East Clandon church, with its dedication to St Thomas of Canterbury, was probably very new in 1176.

158 *Papsturkunden*, **1**, no 69

159 *VCHSy*, **3**, 434–6; S Lewin, The Pyrford fresco

160 W J Blair, Surrey endowments of Lewes Priory, 106. For place-names of this type see Everitt, *Continuity and colonisation*, 184

161 W J Blair, Surrey endowments of Lewes Priory, 104

162 Balsdean chapel, firmly dated to between 1121 and 1147 on written and archaeological evidence (N E S Norris & E F Hockings, Excavations at Balsdean chapel, Rottingdean)

163 Henry of Blois's confirmation (Brit Lib, Add MS 6040 no 16) includes a grant of Gervase de Cornhill's tithes in Addington, presumably from the property which Gervase held of the archiepiscopal fee (cf deed, PRO, DL25/106). Subsequently, Bartholomew de Chesney's grant of Addington church in c1180 (SRO, 2609/11/5/1) also included a chapel, which another local landowner, Reynold de Addington, then released to the Priory in the presence of the archdeacon of the Canterbury peculiar (below, p210 n111). These facts suggest that the chapel was on Gervase's land and that the Priory's rights stemmed in some way from the original tithe grant.

164 E Hart & H Braun, West Humble Chapel

165 Brit Lib, Add MS 6040 no 16 (copy of episcopal confirmation)

166 *Early Yorkshire charters, 8: the honour of Warenne*, no 80

167 College of Arms, MS Vincent 46, p114. It is significant that a slightly earlier episcopal confirmation (Brit Lib, Add MS 6040 no 16) fails to mention the chapel.

168 First mentioned 1231–8: Brit Lib, MS Cotton Cleop C.vii, f97

169 First mentioned c1270: *Reg Pontissara*, 608

170 First mentioned c1270: *Reg Pontissara*, 608; see also Johnston, Discovery at Rotherhithe church, 141–3

171 First mentioned 1291: *The rolls and register of Bishop Oliver Sutton*, 145. Keith Bailey informs me that recent excavations, which I have been unable to take into account here, may show that Putney church was considerably earlier.

172 *VCHSy*, **3**, 94–7; S L Ollard, Dunsfold and its rectors. The first reference is in c1270 (*Reg Pontissara*, 608). See also J Bony, *The English Decorated style*, 13 and pl 79

173 *VCHSy*, **2**, 606–7

174 *Annales monastici*, **2**, 323

175 *VCHSy*, **2**, 619–20; largely rebuilt 1861–73, but watercolours (Brit Lib Crack. 1.Tab. 1.b.1, xviii, after 178) show the early Gothic detail.

176 *Register of St Osmund*, **1**, 268

177 Brit Lib, MS Cotton Cleop C.vii, ff61^v–2 (copy of episcopal confirmation)

178 *VCHSy*, **3**, 162–3

179 J H Gibson, Compton church: the oratory, suggests that this was for the use of an anchorite.

180 Now demolished: see plan (GLRO, DWOP W227) and two illustrations of the blocked Norman arcade (Minet Library, LO9541/137, and reproduced H Lambert, *Woodmansterne: a brief historical account*, opp 10)

181 Johnston, Ewhurst church: recent discoveries; *VCHSy*, **3**, 67–9. These may copy the earlier enlargement of Godalming church (fig 27).

182 *VCHSy*, **3**, 137–40; W J Blair, Surrey endowments of Lewes Priory, 106

183 *VCHSy*, **3**, 239–44, 297–300

184 *VCHSy*, **3**, 260–2

Chapter 6

1   *DB* 31c (V.9)
2   Apparently the Abinger motte was built, and the church perhaps rebuilt, soon after William fitz Ansculf established a tenant here. See W J Blair, William fitz Ansculf and the Abinger motte
3   D J Turner, A moated site near Burstow rectory
4   Above, p122; *VCHSy*, **3**, 97–101; above p126
5   Above, pp114–15
6   Above, pp114, 124, 129. Maps show a moat on the rectory site next Charlwood church (Turner, Moated sites in Surrey: a provisional list, 90).
7   Brett, *Church under Henry I*, 127–8, 131
8   *Cartularium monasterii de Colecestria*, **1**, 78
9   SRO, 2609/11/5/1
10 *Documents illustrative of the social and economic history of the Danelaw*, lxx–lxxi. cf the endowment of a Warwickshire church by a group of 'probi homines' (Brett, *Church under Henry I*, 130)
11 *Documents of the Danelaw*, lxxvii
12 *VCHSy*, **3**, 134; *Reg Pontissara*, 22–3 (admission in 1286 to 'portionem que vocatur Patingdenne in ecclesia de Abbingeworth'), 212
13 *DB* 36a (XXI.6–7)
14 *VCHSy*, **4**, 285, 290; Lucy's grant to Lesnes is noted PRO, E41/330(2).
15 W J Blair, Surrey endowments of Lewes Priory, 120
16 Brit Lib, Harl Ch 55.A.30
17 Brit Lib, Add MS 6040 no 2 (cartulary copy of confirmation of earlier grant)
18 As argued for the Danelaw by F M Stenton (*Documents of the Danelaw*, lxxi–lxxii)
19 This is usually apparent where independent evidence is available. The explanation is probably that the *Valor* figures exclude parsonage houses and contiguous glebe.
20 The evidence of ex-monastic glebes is very unreliable, both because of the likelihood of piecemeal amalgamation and because they were frequently divided up to create vicars' portions or at the Dissolution.
21 Above, pp75, 98–9
22 Kent Archives Office, CCRC T 213 (terriers 1599–1730)
23 GLRO, DW/S/28 (17th century terrier)
24 *Valor*, **2**, 45, 30
25 GLRO, DW/S/33 (1618 terrier)
26 Noted PRO, E41/330 (summary of manorial deeds)
27 GLRO, DW/S/37 (early 17th-century terrier)
28 *Valor*, **2**, 29, 31
29 The vicars' portions at Chobham and Egham, which may not have comprised the entire glebes, amounted to something over 58 and 40 acres respectively in 1331 and 1333 and had apparently done so for some time (*Chertsey cartularies*, **1**, nos 70, 77).
30 *Valor*, **2**, 40–1
31 GLRO, DW/S/49 and DW/S/81 (1764 and 1616 terriers)
32 GLRO, DW/S/6 and DW/S/32 (1616 and late 17th-century terriers)
33 GLRO, DW/S/10 (1616 terrier)
34 GLRO, DW/S/46 (1616 terrier). Both a survey of 1331 (*Chertsey cartularies*, **1**, no 80) and *Valor* (**2**, 37) estimate the *vicarage* portion as 15 acres.
35 *The Domesday of St Paul's*, 151
36 GLRO, DW/S/58b (1616 terrier)
37 *Valor*, **2**, 44, 40
38 Above, p139. In the late 13th century the canons of Southwark distinguished the 12 acres which were of the church's dower from 12 acres which maintained a lamp (Brit Lib, MS Cotton Faust A.viii, f 158).
39 MM 4901 (schedule of holdings attached to court roll)
40 Lennard, *Rural England*, 307; cf *ibid*, 314–15

41 *Registrum Henrici de Woodlock*, 232

42 *Chertsey cartularies*, **1**, no 77; D J Turner, Moated sites in Surrey: a provisional list, 90

43 GLRO, DW/S/49 (1764 terrier); SRO, 65/1/1 (deed)

44 Brit Lib, Harl Ch 55 A.30

45 One exception is Leatherhead, which had both rectory and vicarage houses in the Middle Ages (F Bastian, Rogers of the rectory, 103).

46 W J Blair, A late 13th-century survey of buildings on estates of Southwark Priory. Recent excavations on the site of the old vicarage at Reigate have revealed 11th- and 12th-century occupation followed, after a gap, by the building of a hall-house in the 13th century (Poulton, Old Vicarage, Reigate, 23). The canons' 'rectory manor' house (for which see W J Blair, Late 13th-century survey) was evidently on a different site. The first written reference to a vicar of Reigate is not until 1243 (Bodl Lib, MS Ch Surrey a.2 (61)).

47 A series of early 14th-century documents (*Chertsey cartularies*, **1**, nos 68–81) record a systematic attempt to regularise the status and endowments of the Abbey's vicarages.

48 *Valor*, **2**, 32

49 *Chertsey cartularies*, **1**, no 79 (1331 survey); *Valor*, **2**, 44 lists the mansion and 1 acre of land.

50 W J Blair, Surrey endowments of Lewes Priory, 109–11, 118

51 cf Winchester synodal statutes of 1224: 'Precipimus etiam ut omnis persona ecclesie domum habeat in fundo ecclesie positam in qua honeste possit manere' (Winchester i.22, *Councils and synods*, **2**, 129)

52 For this section cf B R Kemp, Monastic possession of parish churches in England in the 12th century, which covers much of the same ground with a wider range of examples. For Augustinian acquisitions see also Robinson, *Geography of Augustinian settlement*, 172–88, 276–84

53 cf E Mason, Timeo barones et donas ferentes

54 *DB* 34a (VIII.30); above, p101

55 *VCHSy*, **2**, 77–8; cf the charters in a royal inspeximus, Patent Roll 11 Edward II pt 1 (PRO, C66/149) mm 36–5. Churches find virtually no place in B D Hill's study of Cistercian patronage (*English Cistercian monasteries and their patrons in the 12th century*. cf Kemp, Monastic possession, 144

56 *VCHSy*, **2**, 64–6. The churches were: St George's Southwark, given by Thomas de Ardern in 1122; Camberwell, by William earl of Gloucester in 1154; and Chelsham and Warlingham, by William de Wateville in 1158 (*Annales monastici*, **3**, 433, 439, 440).

57 The Merton Cartulary (Brit Lib, MS Cotton Cleop C.vii) contains few documents before the late 12th century. An episcopal confirmation of 1177 × 88 (*ibid*, ff61ᵛ–62) lists grants of the churches at Ditton (Peter de Tolworth), Malden with Chessington chapel (Eudes de Malden), Compton(?) (William fitz Ascelin), Carshalton (Faramus de Boulogne), and St Mary and Holy Trinity Guildford. The lost confirmation by Henry of Blois (above, p197 n41) may have mentioned earlier acquisitions: Kingston with its chapels, Cuddington and Effingham (above, pp99, 124, and below p152). Portions and temporalities (including members of Ewell manor, above, p180 n10) are listed *ibid*, f10²ʳ⁻ᵛ.

58 *VCH Sussex*, **2**, 64–6, and map opp 8; W J Blair, Surrey endowments of Lewes Priory

59 The Southwark Priory charters are being reassembled from numerous different sources for an edition to be published by the Surrey Record Society.

60 For association of Odo and William with the Clares see *Regesta regum anglo-normannorum*, **2**, no 1015a; Blair, Surrey endowments, 117; *Cal docs France*, 291. For the Dammartin lands see Bloxam, A Surrey charter of King John

61 See W J Blair, William fitz Ansculf and the Abinger motte

62 W J Blair, Surrey endowments of Lewes Priory, 100, 119

63 For child oblation see D Knowles, *The monastic order in England*, 417–22. Under Lanfranc's scheme (unlike the original Benedictine Rule), the oblate brought up in the cloister made his final profession at adolescence – a likely occasion for the archiepiscopal confirmation of the church. While dowries of land and money were still usual, a church seems exceptional. The *arenga* of Archbishop Ralph's 1121 confirmation (W J Blair, Surrey endowments of Lewes Priory, n 4) expresses the affection of both Anselm and himself towards Lewes.

64 W J Blair, Surrey endowments of Lewes Priory, 100

65 R W Southern, *Western society and the church in the Middle Ages*, 247

66 Thus a grant to the canons of Southwark by Hugh de Fraxineto and his wife in *c*1200 was made on the

occasion of receiving confraternity (Brit Lib, Add MS 6040 no 21), while Hamo de Gravenel gave them an acre of meadow in Tooting in c1170 to maintain a light over his wife's tomb in the cloister (*ibid* no 10).

67 Brit Lib, Add MS 6040 no 16 (cartulary copy of episcopal confirmation)

68 G Constable, *Monastic tithes*, gives a broad survey of monastic tithe-owning and attitudes to it in medieval Europe, without, however, discussing very specifically the development of the custom in England and the ways in which the tithe rights of local churches were safeguarded there. Kemp, Monastic possession, 141–3, distinguishes between 'two-thirds' and 'unrestricted' tithe grants but does not relate this to possession or non-possession of churches by the respective donors.

69 The latter is much less common; one instance, concerning Bramley manor, is Ralph de Fay's confirmation to Lyre Abbey in c1200 of 'decimam denariorum de toto gabulo meo de manerio meo de Bromleya quam consueverunt antiquitus habere de antecessoribus meis' (PRO, E40/14136).

70 The clearest and most recent general discussion of this is Brett, *Church under Henry I*, 225–7.

71 eg H E Salter, Cogges Priory, 322–3

72 W J Blair, Surrey endowments of Lewes Priory, 103–4

73 *ibid*, 110–12

74 cf instances cited Lennard, *Rural England*, 316

75 Windsor Dean and Chapter Archives, Arundel White Book, f127^v

76 *Chertsey cartularies*, **1**, nos 45, 54

77 Above, p200 n1; Barlow, *English church 1000–1066*, 195; Addleshaw, *Development of parochial system*, 14

78 F M Stenton, *Anglo-Saxon England*, 155–6. cf W J Blair, Secular minster churches, 125, and W J Blair (ed), *Minsters and parish churches*, 10–13

79 Discussed further by W J Blair, Origins of Leatherhead parish church

80 *DB* 36a (XXII.1); *Chertsey cartularies*, **1**, nos 45–6, 55, 56

81 W J Blair, Surrey endowments of Lewes Priory, 121

82 *ibid*, 116–17

83 *ibid*, 110–12

84 Brett, *Church under Henry I*, 127–8

85 *DB* 35d (XXI.2); Brit Lib, Add MS 6040 no 17

86 Brit Lib, Add MS 6040, no 2

87 *DB* 36a (XXI.4) and 35c (XIX.43); 32a (V.23)

88 Brit Lib, Add Ms 6040 no 16

89 Some of the Southwark examples (table 15) can scarcely be pushed back before c1150. The grant of demesne tithe in Mickleham by William de Dammartin (ob c1170) to Lewes Priory post-dates Henry of Blois's confirmation, itself no earlier than 1153 (W J Blair, Surrey endowments of Lewes Priory, 120–1, 116–17). But no later cases have been identified. For the proposed change of ideas as to what constituted acceptable practice, cf B R Kemp in W J Blair (ed), *Minsters and parish churches*, 94 n41.

90 G J Gollin, The medieval manor house of Ashtead. Laurence's daughter Mary is described as 'Maria de Estede' in a charter endorsement (Brit Lib, Cotton Ch v.11) and in notes from the lost Southwark Cartulary (College of Arms, MS Vincent 46, p129).

91 Hase, The mother churches of Hampshire, 54–7

92 SRO, 2609/11/5/1. Kemp, Monastic possession, 135–8, discusses this terminological change.

93 cf Brett, *Church under Henry I*, 230–1; Kemp, Monastic possession, 134–5

94 Knowles, *Monastic order*, 597

95 C N L Brooke, The missionary at home: the church in the towns 1000–1250, 72. cf W J Blair (ed), *Minsters and parish churches*, 13–15

96 For Henry as bishop see L Voss, *Heinrich von Blois, Bischof von Winchester (1129–71)*, 77–100, especially the Christchurch *acta* printed *ibid*, 159–64 which mark a new stage in the development of perpetual vicarages. These are discussed by Hase, The mother churches of Hampshire. R H C Davis, The college of St Martin le Grand and the Anarchy, 1135–54, is also relevant to this aspect of Henry.

97 *The letters of John of Salisbury*, **1**, 87

98 C Duggan, Richard of Ilchester; *Corpus iuris canonici*, 3.38.8

99 cf C R Cheney, *From Becket to Langton*, 124–5

100 SRO, 2609/11/5/1 (deed)

101   cf for instance N Adams, The judicial conflict over tithes

102   For a detailed analysis of the concept of the parish in canon law and the Anglo-Saxon law codes see Hase, *Parish in Hampshire*, 16–30; *idem*, The mother churches of Hampshire, 64, n40 and n41

103   For instance: in 1086 Banstead parish as defined by the end of the Middle Ages included the manors of Banstead, Burgh, Tadworth, South Tadworth and an additional nine hides (*DB* 31c, 32a, 35d, 31d, 32c (V.8, V.24, XX.1, V.21, V.8)). Banstead was the largest holding and had the Domesday church, but this did not prevent the later foundation of an independent church at Burgh; the amalgamation of its parish with Banstead resulted purely from a later rearrangement (below, p154).

104   C N L Brooke has summed up the issue succinctly: 'Burial rights, baptismal rights, and tithe . . . were all essential to the making of a parish church; and that is why strict parochial boundaries of the kind familiar to us today can never have existed before the 12th century; and much of the controversy that has raged from time to time about parochial origins has turned on these definitions' (Brooke, Missionary at home, 68).

105   This is certainly true in the cases of Bampton, Ashtead, Astley and Wingerworth (Brett, *Church under Henry I*, 129, 130, 131, 224). However, there is a clear need here for a review of all the early charter evidence, relating it to its ecclesiastical and tenurial background.

106   *Cartularium monasterii de Colecestria*, **1**, 78

107   For the line of argument in this paragraph see also W J Blair (ed), *Minsters and parish churches*, 10

108   Gifford, Parish in Domesday Book, 170–3; cf the 'aecclesia et alia capella' at Chobham (above, p114)

109   W J Blair, Surrey endowments of Lewes Priory, 106–11, 117–18

110   *ibid*, 118–19

111   Episcopal confirmation printed (from lost original) Dugdale, *Monasticon*, **6**, 172–3. Woodmansterne later emerged as an independent parish; Burgh church disappeared and its parish was absorbed into Banstead.

112   *ibid*

113   *Cartularium monasterii de Colecestria*, **1**, 78

114   For other cases of this lack of definition between ecclesia and *capella* see Lennard, *Rural England*, pp298–9, 302–3

115   *Register of St. Osmund*, **1**, 297–303. For this type of perpetual vicarage see Kemp, 'Monastic possession', 148–53

116   See G L Druce, The symbolism of the goat on the Norman font at Thames Ditton

117   Some of these must be near-contemporary with, and perhaps a consequence of, the 1213/14 Canterbury Statutes which stipulate that 'baptisterium habeatur in qualibet ecclesia baptismali lapideum, vel aliud competens, quod decenter operiatur et reverenter conservetur, ita quod in alios usus non convertatur' (Canterbury i.31, *Councils and synods*, 31). So numerous are they that in many cases they must have replaced older fonts, perhaps of a crudity which outweighed their sentimental value.

118   cf several papers in W J Blair (ed), *Minsters and parish churches*

119   *Chertsey cartularies*, **1**, no 74. cf the similar case of Bisley in 1283 (*ibid*, no 83)

120   *Register of St. Osmund*, **1**, 297

121   Winchester iii. 38 (*Councils and synods*, **2**, 709), following a provision which apparently first appears in the Wells statutes a few years before (Wells i. 21, *Councils and synods*, **2**, 602); for a transcript of the licence to consecrate, see A Heales & L M Humbert, Cluddingfold church (appendix), 176

122   The following section was written before the appearance of Everitt, *Continuity and colonisation*, with its strikingly similar analysis of Kentish chapels, 205–21. This especially emphasises the pastoral significance of chapels in regions of late, sparse and scattered settlement.

123   *The Beauchamp cartulary*, no 205; Lambeth Palace Library, MS 1212 (archiepiscopal cartulary), f58.

124   Battle Abbey Cartulary, Henry Huntingdon Library, California, B A vol 29, f112ᵛ: 'Gilbertus filius Willelmi archid' de Chauz, de voluntate Magistri Sampsonis rectoris ecclesie Sancti Olavi de Suthwerk, capellam in honore Sancte Katerine apud mesuagium suum iuxta calceam versus Beremond' construxit, in qua per proprium sive alienum sicut placuerit capellanum divina celebrabuntur, salvis predicte ecclesie oblationibus que in dicta capella pervenerint, et annuatim j librum

thur' (This Battle Abbey deed refers to an agreement with Stephen, prior of Lewes, who resigned in 1220.)

125 *Reg Henrici de Woodlock*, 607

126 Winchester ii. 40 (*Councils and synods*, **2**, 408–9)

127 E Mason, The role of the English parishioner 1100–1500; cf her 'A truth universally acknowledged', 179

128 D M Owen, Chapelries and rural settlement: an examination of some of the Kesteven evidence; *idem, Church and society in medieval Lincolnshire*, 5–19. On the problem of lost chapels see also W J Blair, *Minsters and parish churches*, 15–16; and cf n122 above.

129 Bishops were primarily concerned to protect the financial rights of parish churches, not necessarily to restrain people from worshipping in chapels. The 1268 Legatine Council's statute on this point is concerned entirely with avoiding prejudice to existing rights and ensuring that chaplains made oblations and other dues without difficulty (*Councils and synods*, **2**, 766).

130 The Exeter Statutes of 1287, which severely restrict the taking of the sacrament in chapels lacking their own parishioners, may point to a campaign to tighten control (Exeter ii.9, *Councils and synods*, **2**, 1002–3).

131 This important site unfortunately remains unpublished. The present summary is based on details kindly assembled by D J Turner from the *Surrey Archaeological Society Annual Reports* for 1952, 1953 and 1954, and the *Croydon Advertiser* for 22 August 1952.

132 [Anon], General notes and documents: Blechingley

133 *PNSy*, 336

134 Minet Library, Surrey Deed 3615–6

135 *Reg Pontissara*, 40

136 *Register of St Osmund*, **1**, 296–8

137 Catteshall, Farncombe and Hurtmore (*VCHSy*, **3**, 32–5). The independent parish of Hambledon had its own church by c1100 (above, p126).

138 See Mason, Role of the English parishioner, 19–21

139 For which see Cheney, *Becket to Langton*, 123–34, and the recent fuller summary in Kemp, Monastic possession, 148–59

140 Evidence for all these cited in W J Blair, Surrey endowments of Lewes Priory

141 Brit Lib, MS Cotton Cleop C.vii, ff 74, 75

142 cf Kemp, Monastic possession, 151–3

143 B F Harvey, *Westminster Abbey*, 48

144 *TPN*, 206–9

Conclusion

1 cf Everitt, *Continuity and colonisation*, 336: 'There are a number of ways in which, as we move backward in time, the parallels in other areas tend to increase rather than diminish'

2 T M Charles-Edwards, Kinship, status and the origins of the hide, for one view of the social foundations of hide groups

3 Fox, Approaches to adoption of midland system, 98–102, sees the severance of linked vills as a major impetus for Midland townships to develop their highly organised field-systems.

4 Again, cf Everitt, *Continuity and colonisation*, 262, for the disorganised, 'meaningless' character of Wealden arrangements

5 For this aspect of township assemblies see W O Ault, *Open-field farming in medieval England*, 75–7

6 See W J Blair, The early middle ages; The late middle ages, in Vardey (ed.), *Hist. of Leatherhead*, 32–8, 41–8.

7 Dodgshon, *The origin of British field systems*, 66

Index

NOTE: Places are in Surrey except where otherwise stated. Minor place-names are grouped under their respective parishes, which are as defined by Gover, Mawer and Stenton, *The Place-Names of Surrey*.